Intonation and Its Parts

INTONATION
AND ITS PARTS

MELODY IN SPOKEN ENGLISH

Le Merton

Dwight Bolinger

STANFORD UNIVERSITY PRESS
Stanford, California   1986

Stanford University Press, Stanford, California
© 1986 by the Board of Trustees of the
Leland Stanford Junior University

Printed in the United States of America

Library of Congress Cataloging in Publication Data

Bolinger, Dwight Le Merton, 1907–
    Intonation and its parts.

    Bibliography: p.
    Includes index.
    1. English language—Intonation.   2. English language
—Spoken English.   I. Title.
PE1139.5.B65   1986   421'.6   83-40698
ISBN 0-8047-1241-7

To Fred W. Householder, Jr.

*This dedication acknowledges the debt,
but does not discharge it.*

Preface

This book is by a linguist who believes that intonation is too important a subject to be left just to linguists. It concerns psychologists, since intonation, the least self-conscious and least commented-on side of vocal communication, allows observers to catch communicators off guard and watch certain of their inner workings. It concerns musicians who are interested in the genesis of song, or merely in practical ways of fitting song to lyric. It concerns jurists who, with their background in written law, may be inclined to take too seriously the words of a message when its tune is contradictory. It concerns anthropologists who must look at all communicative behavior as a whole and will find in intonation the spoken counterpart of facial expression and physical gesture. It concerns writers who, for lack of tone marks more subtle than period, quotation marks, and comma, must translate the nuances of intonation into descriptive words. And it concerns all those in the language arts, for whom the coloring of a phrase is as important as the phrase itself, and the mastery of a lilt is a key to sounding like a native.

To make the going easier for so large a family of readers, the first three chapters of the book discuss the field in a broad, leisurely, and informal way. And later chapters are as nontechnical as they could be made, partly for the readers' convenience and partly on principle: the description of intonation has not reached such a state of analytical precision that the language of its description needs to deviate far from ordinary language. This is to some degree because of the nature of the material. On the one hand, a speaker who organizes the words of a sentence faces a truly exacting task: first there is the choice of the words themselves, from more or less arbitrary sets of words; then there are the fairly exact rules of grammar that govern the combinations; and finally everything has to be coded using a precise and limited set of sounds that combine not freely but in ways differently determined for each language. It is largely a *computational* skill. On the other hand, a speaker who composes an intonation is more artist than computer. He faces a canvas on which he must draw freehand. There are rules, but they respond to *feeling* more directly than does any other well-systematized part of spoken language. Emotion is always present, and "ideas" are communicated metaphorically through the feelings that express them: the idea of uttering an aside (such as a paren-thetical remark), for example, is that it is not part of the main business and can therefore be pronounced in a relatively low and hushed voice.

That intonation is different from most of the other channels of com-munication studied by linguists is indicated by the wide divergence of views on how to go about the study of it. The tradition of grammar and phonology is both an aid and a handicap: an aid because it de-mands rigor and consistency, a handicap in that it tempts one to see outlines that are sharper than life. In phonology we take our divi-sions, largely, where we find them: the language itself defines con-trasts of voicing that distinguish *tip* from *dip* and *pan* from *ban*—a high level of agreement on the distinctions is attainable. Nothing so ready to hand is found in intonation. More than elsewhere, structure has to be *imposed*. We try our best to follow natural fault lines, but they are fluid and the way is easily lost. Fortunately a certain consen-sus seems to be emerging among linguists that one can look at such simple values as high and low or up and down, and that melodic shapes can be grouped around certain forms associated with the prominent syllables of an utterance, rather generally termed pitch ac-cents. That is the approach followed here, and it differs from others mainly in its insistence on the independence of intonation from gram-mar. Intonation has more in common with gesture than with gram-mar (see Chapter 9), though both gesture and intonation are tremen-dously important *to* grammar, as their lines intersect.

A more trivial point of difference, one of form rather than sub-stance, is the heavily ostensive nature of this book, its richness of ex-emplification. The reason is the same as the one offered for the com-paratively nontechnical approach: it is more convenient for the reader to be given examples at every point. In part the reason stems from the extremely complex nature of language. If I want to illustrate the pro-nunciation of the diphthong in the word *ride* I can give you just that one word, *ride*. But the spelling is a distraction: it contains a "silent" vowel letter *e* and a couple of consonants that clutter the picture. Can I be sure that you will pick on the sound represented by the letter *i*—can I even be sure that you have understood what is meant by *diphthong* and that you will not be confused by having to associate the notion with just one letter? By offering more examples, *ply, aisle, guy, nigh,* I may be able to ensure that a pattern will emerge from what they all have in common. Such "samenesses" are especially difficult to illustrate in intonation, and may require even more material to round out a pattern.

A second reason for the abundance of examples is the *variable* nature of language. People differ in their modes of expression and interpretation, not enough as a rule to create major problems in communication so long as all use the "same language," but often quite enough to create obstacles to communicating *about* language, particularly since the points of most interest to communicate about are so often the very ones where people differ. By giving a variety of examples it is usually possible to hit at least one that will resonate in the reader's consciousness. The linguist-reader may be uncomfortable with the resulting exuberance; but that discomfort is slight by comparison with what the average reader is apt to feel about theoretical discussions that seem to be all cutting and no meat.

Intonation and Its Parts is not a survey of past and present approaches to intonation. It reckons with others' views but its orientation is the author's. (In a second volume, specific claims of the "grammatical" school of intonology will be examined, but such matters are incidental here.) The list of references is extensive enough to guide the reader to the major works in the field. For a thorough bibliography of earlier materials, Crystal (1969) is a valuable source.

On two issues this book will strike some as controversial. The first is one that has been more ignored than challenged, though it is contrary to much received wisdom: how the English vowel system should be analyzed, as a prelude to understanding how syllables are timed. It mainly concerns Chapters 4 and 5, and the principal discussions of speech melody will be little affected if it is rejected. Appendix A gives supporting arguments.

The second issue is more formidable and involves the emotional and metaphorical approach described above. How far can such an explanatory principle be carried, and does it not signify an oversimplification, a form of "reductionism"? Pleading guilty to such a charge does not preclude a strong defense. If intonation springs from innate dispositions and capacities, shaped by societies into varying forms that may conceal their native source but do not contravene it, then we are obliged to see how well the forms can be explained by forcing them to confront the source at every step. Emotion and attitude do not account for everything, but they must be tested first. As Derek Bickerton writes (1981: 312), "until we know where the innate component stops, we cannot know where any other devices start." Bickerton goes on to speak of general innate capacities, but his words ring truer of intonation than of language in any other of its aspects: "biological language remained right where it was, while cultural language rode off in all directions. However, it was always there, under the surface, waiting to emerge whenever cultural language hit a bad patch, so to speak . . . cultural language could not expand away from the biological base indefinitely" (p. 296). With intonation (and with gesture as a whole) it has traveled the least distance of all.

The reductionism in this book, if the charge is fair, is a matter of first things first.

To recognize by name all those who have promoted my enlightenment would mean an impossible search of forty years of recollections. I thank them all, and hope that if some encounter their ideas without receiving explicit credit, they will treat my oversight as the sincerest flattery.

But two people must be mentioned. The first is D. Robert Ladd, whose meticulous reading of the manuscript exposed many confusions and weak arguments. I have done my best to rectify them, on the theory that if Bob Ladd couldn't understand what I was driving at, nobody could. The second is Karen Brown Davison of Stanford University Press, who guided the manuscript through the various production stages with exquisite care and patience.

D.B.

Contents

PART I. INTRODUCTION

PART II. ACCENTUAL PROSODY

PART III. MELODIC PROSODY

Part I

INTRODUCTION

1. Pitch

"I don't mind what she said, but I don't like the way she said it" is a complaint we have all heard some time or other, and probably have uttered ourselves. What does it mean?

The stream of sound that issues from the human voice box can be cut up into many different kinds of segments, some of which everyone knows or thinks he knows. There are sentences—those lengths of speech that in written form are terminated by periods, or sometimes by question marks or exclamation points. There are clauses and phrases, which in writing are set off by commas, or by semicolons when they might almost as well be regarded as sentences. There are words and parts of words called affixes, like the -er of *speaker* or the *anti-* of *antibody*, and there are distinctive sounds that enable us to tell one word from another, like the [b] of *boy* and the [t] of *toy*. But running through this fabric of organized sound there is a master thread that holds it all together and by its weavings up and down and in and out shows the design of the whole—the motifs from phrase and sentence to paragraph and discourse, the highlights and shadows, and the relevance to the speaker's intent. These points of emphasis that are made so naturally by the human voice can only be suggested in writing, though we all have been taught to believe that everything in the message can be committed to writing with comparative ease. Indeed, we even forget that the master sound is there, for all that we may unconsciously hum it to ourselves; and when someone calls attention to it, we dismiss it as a mere manner of saying, an accompaniment to the message rather than an inseparable part of it.

This Cinderella of the communication complex is called INTONATION. She is only one of several stepsisters who at one time or other have slept beside the hearth; word order is another. Is *That I won't do* just another way of saying *I won't do that*? The words are the same—it is only the way of putting them together that differs. Yet nowadays we regard changes of syntax as a substantial part of the "what": surely it is more than mere "way" that distinguishes *Mary saw John* from *John saw Mary*.

Part of the confusion is due to our ambivalence in deciding what is central to our message: is it the vehicle or is it the intent? From the first standpoint, any alteration in the words is a change in the "what": *John left* is not the same as *My brother left*, even if John is my brother. From the second, *I'm sorry you left* is "the same" as *I regret that you left*; the only difference is in the "way" of paraphrasing the idea.

So it comes down to the part or parts of a message that engage our attention, or that have come to our attention over the course of time. The more we know about how intelligence is communicated from one head to another, the less inclined we are to dismiss any part of it as secondary, as "merely icing on the fully baked cake," to quote A. A. Hill (1982: 16). The study of intonation has come later than that of words, but it has finally made the grade. The study of gesture is only now coming into its own (see Chapter 9).

Of course, mere manner still distinguishes idiosyncrasies that reveal to us the personality of the speaker rather than the intent of what the speaker says. Aileen Sinclair (1944: 40) calls them the "left-over of the voice": thus the querulous person who habitually uses a high pitch "even when not indulging in a tirade," or the grouch whose voice is set in a permanent growl. But personal idiosyncrasies are not of interest here. Rather, we are interested in the "what" of intonation—in how it is systematically used to express meaning.

Tuning the Ear

One cannot easily objectify something that has traditionally been thought of as only a part of the "way" of speaking, and a little ear training may be in order for those who have not been accustomed to thinking of intonation as something that can be analyzed. Many people have difficulty abstracting the ups and downs of pitch from the flow of speech. In fact, informal tests show that when groups of listeners are given a sentence like

```
Does she   ways act that way?
      al
```

practically everyone can tell that the syllable *al-* "stands out," but many will say the pitch goes up instead of down. (There are other ways besides pitch—extra "loudness" for example—to make a syllable stand out. They will be discussed in Chapter 2.)

To train one's ear, the best place to start is with expressions that carry with them a set intonation. There is only one "way" to say them—or maybe two, or a very few—if they are to have the meaning we intend. Take the expression *all right* tagged at the end of a sentence to signify 'It's true, there's no doubt of it.' *All* is at a low pitch, and *right* goes up:

> He didn't say a word; I thought you said he was smart. — Oh, he's smart all right. But he's also cautious.

The pitch curve goes something like this:

```
                 he's smart
        Oh,

                all rig
ht·
```

The exclamation *Hell's bells!* has a tune that seldom varies:

```
        Hell's

            be
ll
s!
```

The pitch is relatively high on *Hell's*, drops abruptly to the start of *bells*, and then glides down. As we shall see later, the tune accords with the meaning: it indicates an objection to something that is already being discussed or acted upon. We do not normally say

```
                be
        Hell's
              ll
s!
```

with a jump up, though that intonation would be perfectly good with *Look out!* for a newly presented danger. The exclamation *A fine thing!* when used ironically generally has the same tune as *Hell's bells!*:

```
            fine
        A
            thi
               n
g!
```

It too objects to something we already know about.

The two words *what ever* (not *whatever*) are commonly used at the beginning of a question that one asks out of the blue (one may easily preface it with *by the way*) concerning something or someone long out of mind. The verbs that usually go with this expression are *come*, *become*, and *happen*. The intonation starts high and descends steadily and gradually to the accented word, which manifests a downward jump; any remaining syllables then continue the gradual descent.

What ever came of that con
                    test you were in?

What ever became of Wendy Ja
                    cobs?

What ever happened with that h
                    o
                     u
                      s
                       e
                    you were planning to build?

The phrase *for a change* is generally tagged at the end of a sentence, as *all right* is, but instead of having a rise on the last word the whole phrase remains at a low pitch:

```
            this
      Try

          tie, for a change.
```

We often use the expression *in no time* to mean 'very quickly.' We then say it with *no* at the highest pitch:

```
            no
      in
            time
```

When the word *rather* is used to signify strong agreement, it carries the same intonation as *Yes, sir!*, *You bet!*, *Right on!*, and other expressions of agreement. The second syllable, which is normally weak (as in *It's rather good*), thus becomes as prominent as the first:

```
      Ra the
        a   r!
```

To convey the idea of innocent ignorance, someone who is asked for information may reply *Search me!*, with a glide up on *search* and a slight drop from the highest pitch on *me*:

```
            me
                e!
      search
```

When someone pushes ahead too fast or takes too much for granted, the expression *(Now) wait a minute!* makes an effective protest when said like this:

```
Wa-a-a-it    min

      a    ute!
```

Here timing is a factor: *wait* is drawled, and *min-* is uttered forcefully following a slight dramatic pause after *a*.

Here are some other expressions to try out. All are stereotyped to some degree in one or more senses (but not necessarily in all dialects of English—the examples listed are typically American):

all too (as in *She is all too careless*)
and then some
Beats me! ('I don't know')
Big deal!
Ho-hum.
Fancy meeting you here!
For crying out loud!
He's a good egg.
Gee whillikers!
How about that! (as comment on something surprising)
No kidding! (surprise plus willingness to believe)
Who wants to know! ('It's none of your business')
I beg your pardon! (as indignant protest)
I should say not! (as emphatic and short-tempered denial)
I could care less!
I'll show him a thing or two!
Is that so! (sneering rejection of an idea)
Not a single, solitary thing.
Now you've done it! (to someone who has blundered)
Oh, I don't know. (expressing skepticism)
Tell you what. (to introduce a proposition)
That's the ticket! (approval)
Naughty-naughty! (same tune as used with *ah-ah-ahh* as a warning)
Can you beat that! (for something unusual, generally said dis-
    approvingly)

In the last example, try saying *Can YOU beat THAT?* and notice how it destroys the stereotype.

In these examples the words are more or less arbitrarily fitted to a conversational purpose, often through some figure of speech (*Big deal!* is ironic, *How about that!* is a rhetorical question), but the intonation answers directly to the meaning. The two together cement the expression as a stereotype: without the particular intonation, *Oh, I don't know* might be a simple statement of ignorance rather than a polite way of showing skepticism.

There is another form of stereotyping, in which the intonation itself is stereotyped and varying combinations of words may range rather freely over it. The most familiar instance is the CHANT, in which the speech tune is actually a musical tune, which we sometimes hum or whistle or sometimes chant with nonsense syllables:

This tune is also used in taunts:

Another example is a chant that American television buffs may remember from the Dick Van Dyke show. When sexual hanky-panky was afoot, one character put on a knowing look and commented with the "words" *Doodle-ee-oodle-ee-oo-doo-doo* set to the following tune in minor mode:

One does not need to be familiar with the program to appreciate the tolerantly amused imputation of naughtiness.

A speech tune that is fairly widespread among the languages of the world is the "calling tune." Its musical intervals are less exact, but it uses steady pitches, partly for the sake of their carrying power:

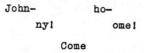

Some tunes are more speechlike, and were probably derived from the intonation of ordinary speech. An example is the intonation that occurs generally with expressions of intense emotion or strong affirmation such as

Whoo-ee!   Yes, sir!
Good God!   You bet!
Oh, boy!   Hell, yes!

This tune is reproduced as the wolf whistle, used mostly by males to show appreciation for a comely female. Another example already noted in connection with the words *Search me!* ('I don't know') can be hummed wordlessly to convey the same meaning:

```
                    m-
          m-m-   m
     m-m-
m-m-
```

As we might expect, the same tune can be used with other synonymous expressions, including the literal *I don't know*:

> Don't look at me.
> Can't prove it by me.
> Don't ask me.

Accent and Intonation

In music, the listener is conscious of pitch in two dimensions: melody and harmony. The melody is the "tune" and the harmony accompanies it. Written music shows the melody (or sometimes two or more melodies interwoven) from left to right, and the harmony as vertical chords. The two are usually fairly easy to tell apart, though sometimes a harmony is spread out like a quick melodic succession (and then is called an arpeggio), and quite often chords are the incidental result of simultaneous melodies.

Speech, too, makes use of pitch in more than one dimension simultaneously, though strictly speaking there is no harmony. The overall tune or melody helps to show the difference between a statement such as

```
Nobody
      saw
          them.
```

and a question such as

```
          them?
      saw
Nobody
```

and in general creates impressions of mood or emotion. Within the melody, certain characteristically abrupt movements are used to make individual syllables stand out. These movements, or ACCENTS, will be our main concern in the early chapters of this book.

There are various ways of giving prominence to an individual syllable, i.e., of accenting it: extra loudness or extra length may be used as well as abrupt movements in pitch—and these will be explained in Chapter 2. For the moment we are concerned only with how prominence is achieved by the use of PITCH.

A syllable that is made to stand out is said to be ACCENTED. (Or STRESSED—but the term STRESS will be assigned a different meaning in this book; see the next chapter.) We can also say that the WORD containing the prominent syllable is accented. Thus in uttering the following sentence,

```
                                  ol
        She  on ly ate a couple of

                                      ives.
```

we accent the syllables *on-* and *ol-*, and we accent the words *only* and *olives*. There is a sort of level established by the syllables in *She -ly ate a couple of*, and the words *only* and *olives* are made prominent each by having one of its syllables stand out above that level. Those two words carry the main information. It would be equally possible to say

```
                                  ol
                     ate
        She  on ly        a  cou ple of

                                      ives.
```

with *ate* and *couple*, but especially *ate*, made to stand out also. It simply depends on how important those words are to the message the speaker wants to convey. In the first case, eating was probably already the topic of conversation (a previous speaker may have said *She ate too much*) and there was no need to emphasize it further. In the second case there may be a distinction between eating and drinking (the previous speaker may have said *She ate and drank too much*, and the reply suggests 'As far as *eating* goes . . . '). For whatever reason, the words that are accented in pitch tend to be the ones that are the most important to the meaning.

In the melody of the sentence, the pitch changes whenever one of these accents occurs. But accents are rather like bumps on a landscape that may otherwise be simply level or inclined. In the preceding example the landscape was roughly level. In other sentences the landscape is not level:

```
                                       like
                    nev  seemed   real    ly
        She    er             to

                                             us.
```

This does not affect the detectability of the accents (on *nev-*, *seemed*, *real-*, and *like*), which stand out on the landscape as a whole. But the landscape itself, first rising and then falling, creates its own impression. This is the second of the two manifestations of pitch that most concern us. It conveys the moods, emotions, and attitudes that are a necessary part of discourse. The baseline (*she -er to -ly us* in the example) contributes to it by slanting up or down, and the accents contribute by taking wider jumps. So an "upness" can be created either by a rising baseline or by a wider upward jump on an accent or both. In the last example the baseline was inclined upward and the accents were also successively higher. It would have been possible to keep the baseline level and still have the overall "up" impression by retaining the successively higher accents:

```
                                        like
                          seemed    real
                 nev
       She       er            to   ly
                                         us.
```

Besides the general keyed-up sensation we get here from the overall rise, we detect a sharper delineation of the accents and infer that the speaker is very emphatic, perhaps indignant.

Though strictly speaking the term INTONATION includes the mere fact of there *being* one or more accents, it is generally used to refer to the overall landscape, the wider ups and downs that show greater or lesser degrees of excitement, boredom, curiosity, positiveness, etc.

Sometimes we speak in a rising melody that has no accents at all except at the end:

```
                                   like
       She never seemed to really
                                     us.
```

The only jumps here are up to and down from the word *like*, and that is the only word that now stands out in importance. *Like* is, of course, the word that stands out most in all three of these examples, but in the last one it is as if the speaker were making a casual remark in which it was not necessary to emphasize anything else.

These are not the only shapes that sentences have, and shapes vary with length and complexity. But always we find an overall melody or intonation, with jumps, narrow or wide, to mark the accents. Questions, for example, normally fail to drop at the end, but the accents still stand out by virtue of the jumps:

```
                       al          rude?
                        ways so
            Are they
```

Here the words *always* and *rude* stand out, *al-* by the up-down jumps and *rude* by the upward jump. For a downward-moving intonation take the example

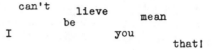

Here, after the beginning relatively low pitch, the line of the accented syllables *can't -lieve mean*, as well as the baseline *be- you that*, goes down.

Tone Languages

In a language such as English, the two functions of pitch just described, accent and intonation, are the ones that we are most aware of and make use of. But in many of the world's languages there is a third way of using pitch that is just as important, though it serves a quite different purpose. These languages are known as TONE LANGUAGES, and they use changes in pitch to indicate differences in the meanings of words. English as most people know it does not do that, but in areas where English has been influenced by tone languages it may pick up distinctions of this sort. In Guyana (and in the Caribbean in general) two levels of pitch may be used to distinguish different meanings of the "same" word. Richard Allsopp (1972: 15) lists the following, among others:

swer	'result in an arith-	an	verb, as in *to answer*
an	metical problem'	swer	
cher	a children's game	cat	'person or thing that
cat		cher	catches' (e.g. dog-catcher)
mas	family name	Christ	the season
Christ		mas	
stant	a non-free-wheeling	con	'continuous, steady'
con	bicycle	stant	

These examples show a two-level contrast, which affects the meaning of words in the same way that changing a vowel or a consonant can change meaning: a change of tone in Guyanese English *turkey* makes the difference between the fowl (low-high) and the country (high-low), just as changing the initial [t] sound of *turkey* to the sound [m] makes the difference between *turkey* and *murky*. There are languages that distinguish more than just two tones: China's official language, for example, has four. Using pitch in this way does not exclude intonation, though it complicates it considerably.

The three uses of pitch just described—accent, intonation, and tone—are all potentially CONTROLLED. Accent and tone in particular

demand more or less conscious attention: accent because it differentiates the important from the unimportant parts of the message, tone
(in tone languages) because it differentiates the meanings of words.
But sometimes pitch goes more or less out of control; the sweep of the
melody as a whole and the size of the jumps that mark the accents
exceed what one expects in ordinary discourse. This is the effect of
EMOTION. With excitement there are greater extremes of pitch; with
depression the range is narrowed. Of course one can always pretend,
and then the uncontrolled becomes controlled. Anger faked uses the
same wide range as anger genuine. One can simulate great surprise
by asking a question with an extremely high pitch at the end: the
pattern remains the same, but it is stretched. Since no human utterance can be totally without emotion, one can never be certain where
the "grammar" of an utterance ends and its "emotion" begins. Intonation lies on the last frontier between primitive and civilized
communication.

2. Accent

When you look up a word in a dictionary, you will generally find—if the word has more than one syllable—that it is divided into syllables and one of the syllables is marked in a special way to show that it is STRESSED. The Merriam Webster *Third New International Dictionary* divides the word *correct* as *cor-rect* and puts a small vertical tick before the phonetic spelling [kə'rekt] to show that the second syllable is the stressed one.

Stress Versus Accent

What does "to be stressed" mean? Ordinarily, when we speak of stressing something, we refer to giving it special emphasis. But it is misleading to think of the stressed syllable of a word as something that is regularly more emphatic than the other syllables. Rather, that syllable is the one that will get the special emphasis whenever the word is emphasized. If we read a passage written like this,

> She said she would NEVER put up with anything like that.

we realize that the writer has intended the word *never* to stand out, but when we read the sentence aloud, respecting the writer's intention, we do not make the whole word stand out phonetically but only the first syllable:

> She said she would NEVer put up with anything like that.

The dictionary tells us which syllable to give the special treatment to, but it does not say that it will actually get it in any particular sample of speech. For instance, in answer to *Would you put up with something like that?* one might say

I

would never put up with it.

emphasizing *I* but nothing else. So although the first syllable of *never* is still stressed (because the dictionary says so), it is not emphasized, or ACCENTED. The stressed syllable is the one that carries the potential for accent.

Accent as Figure and Ground

To understand the nature of accent we must look a little more closely at a notion introduced in the last chapter, that of FOREGROUND-ING, which in turn implies backgrounding. This is to say that there is a continuum or more or less steady state that is interrupted. The interruption in the example just cited occurs along the line of pitch (*I* is higher than its neighboring syllables), though psychologically it does not matter what form the interruption takes, except that it has to be appropriate to the nature of the background: in a visual field the interruption must be visible, and in an auditory one it must be audible, although if communication is proceeding in two or more channels simultaneously, the interruption may occur in any one of them and be attributed to the others. If a speaker wiggled his ears every time he wanted to emphasize a word, he could make the word stand out by the interruption in the visual field. Watching a speaker from a distance—and not understanding a word—one can often tell when an accent is being applied by observing the shifts in bodily movement that take place.

Thus no one signal need be fixed upon as *the* manifestation of figure against ground. Imagine a page of print in which it is desired to have the important words stand out. The printer can use various typographical means to show emphasis. He may use italic, boldface, or small caps; he may use different sizes of type, or a combination of different typefaces; he may print some words in a different color. All these means are legitimate. We do not insist that one of them be set up as somehow more real than the rest. Those who have described speech within the tradition of phonemic analysis have been less flexible. The custom has usually been to identify a single carrier as the essential manifestation of accent. This has led to fruitless debate about which of the several audible ways of interrupting a pitch continuum was most truly the one that bore the accent.

Besides pitch, two other ways are usually mentioned, LENGTH and LOUDNESS. If we pronounce the first example in this chapter according to the following diagram,

```
                 ne-e-e-ev
She  said  she would
                        er put up with anything like tha
                                                        t.
```

we make the syllable *nev-* stand out by lengthening it as well as by putting it on a jump of pitch—that is to say, besides the pitch continuum established by the syllables *She, she would, -er* etc., there is also a continuum of normal syllable length on those same elements within which *nev-* is made to stand out by giving it extra length. Length may be the only cue that tells us what is meant to stand out. (We can refer to any device that serves this purpose as a CUE to the accentual prominence; thus far we have noted pitch, length, and loudness as cues.) In an utterance like the following,

I was so-o-o-o unhappy! (level pitch)

there is no pitch prominence at all, and the cue to the accent on *so* is length alone. The speaker has chosen to express his unhappiness by speaking in a dispirited monotone; it would not suit his purpose to enliven the utterance by any change in pitch, and he falls back on length to make the degree word *so* stand out. (In Japanese, lengthening is reported as the favored means of achieving emphasis; see Aizawa 1981; Onishi 1957.)

Loudness (intensity, volume) is another important cue. It is hard for the casual listener to tell the difference between loudness and pitch prominence, partly because the two so often occur together, and partly because when prominence is achieved by *upward* movement it becomes easier to perceive a given increase in loudness as the pitch rises, and we accordingly "feel" that a higher pitch is louder. Again using an earlier example, we could say:

NE-E-E-EV

She ^{said} she would

er put up with anything like tha
                                                                      t.

Here the syllable *nev-* carries three indicators of accent—pitch obtrusion, extra length, and extra intensity—and the extra intensity is enhanced by the high pitch. But loudness also goes its separate way. We might hear an utterance like this:

I tell you I will NEVer do that!

—a monotone, but without added length on *nev-*. Instead, the syllable stands out by reason of its extra intensity. The speaker is using a monotone for its menacing effect (the threat of emotion repressed), and that rules out the use of pitch. And he snaps his syllables short to suggest tension, thus ruling out the use of length. But even though intensity functions pretty much alone, *nev-* is heard as accented.

Sometimes we find stretches of monotone containing accents that are marked by length or loudness or both, which form parts of intonation patterns that are not altogether monotone. A terminal level is common after a pitch-marked accent. In the following example, the word *that* is pitch-accented:

```
                        that
            What does

                        have to do with it?
```

The speaker can also show restrained irritation by accenting the word *do*, delaying the release of the consonant and increasing the volume— that is, "biting off" the word. Similarly, if someone has been over-insistent on *how* something is done, one may say

```
                    ca
              don't
          I

                    re HOW I do it!
```

with similar emphasis—strong aspiration of the [h] and extra loudness. A downward jab of the head often accompanies such low-pitched accents.

RHYTHM is a further cue. In an utterance like

```
                    nev                      hi
      She said she would   er be happy with   m.
```

we have, in addition to the pitch obtrusion on *said, nev-, hap-,* and *him,* a rhythmic organization that divides the central part of the sentence into three equal measures—in this case, dactylic measures. (A dactyl consists of an accented syllable followed by two unaccented ones.) We could write it this way:

She / said she would / never be / happy with / him.

Once again, the speaker might utter all this in a monotone—as a sort of musing question, at a fairly high pitch level but with little or no variation in pitch. Since we are so accustomed to imposing a rhythmic organization on what we say and hear, we would in this case mentally reconstruct the dactyls and react as if the initial syllable of each dactyl were accented. (The dactyl is not the only rhythmic pattern where this occurs, of course.) In fact, in the total absence of all phonological and visual cues, the psychological tendency to impose an accent is so strong that it will be done as a "best guess" from the syntax. (This is of course what we do when we interpret a written text.) If the follow-

ing is pronounced in a slow monotone with equal length and emphasis on each word,

Do you know how to get there?

a listener will impose a mental prominence on *get* because that is
where a real physical prominence is most apt to go, even though contexts could be devised to sway a choice toward any one of the remaining words. As André Classe pointed out (1939: 18), "It is quite likely
that I shall feel a stress [= accent] in the very place at which I would
have put one myself, even if my interlocutor has spoken in a perfectly
even manner."

Vowel Quality

A cue related to rhythm, which will be dealt with in Chapters 4
and 5, is that of VOWEL QUALITY. It is essentially a negative cue in
that it marks certain syllables—those containing "reduced" vowels—
as unaccentable. For example, the first syllable of the verb *condúct*
[kṇ'dʌkt], unlike that of the noun *cónduct* ['kandʌkt], cannot be accented; this guarantees that in an intonation such as

> Con
>
>   duct, you say?

the pitch cues will be interpreted as follows:

1. For the verb, the syllable *-duct* is accented by being obtruded
downward from the baseline *con-* . . . *you say*, since *con-* cannot carry
the accent.

2. For the noun, the syllable *con-* is accepted as being obtruded upward from the baseline *-duct, you say*, since with its full vowel it *can* be
accented and is configurationally the likeliest candidate for an accent.
(With a shape such as

> Nev
>
>   er conduct like that!

neither *con-* nor *-duct* is intonationally accented, though we have no
trouble telling whether the word is a noun or a verb.) This feature of
reduced vowels is useful because it enables a greater variety of intonational shapes to mark accents unambiguously. A syllable with a reduced vowel is always part of the ground. (Some minor exceptions
will be introduced in Chapter 6.)

Though vowel reduction is mostly a negative cue, it can also be a
positive one with certain words when they occur within a monotone
sentence. These words—mostly pronouns—have competing forms

("allomorphs"), one with a full vowel and the other with a reduced one, and the full-vowel form is usually heard as accented. Thus *me* in *He likes me* takes its reduced form [mɨ] (as in the last syllable of *limey*), and we expect the same to happen in a sentence like

John
isn't going to hurt me!

But if the full form [mi] is used (as in *meter*), the reference will be to John's *selective* intentions: John might hurt other people, but he won't hurt me. No cue other than the full vowel is needed to mark the accent on the pronoun.

Other Cues of Accent

The five cues mentioned thus far—pitch, length, loudness, rhythm, and vowel quality—probably carry the heaviest load as manifestations of accent; but there are other means at speakers' disposal, which seem rather like vocalized gestures. Two of them are DELAYED RELEASE and BREATHINESS. The first is actually a form of extra length, but it is placed on the initial consonant rather than on the vowel, which as often as not is cut short (although the two can be lengthened together). To use an expression noted earlier, we say that the speaker is "biting off his words." For example, in

I'd like to   wring your   n-n-n-neck!

the accent on *neck* is enhanced by delaying the release of the consonant. The lips and jaw tend to be clenched, which adds a visual gesture. Other examples: *I was a f-f-f-fool to do that!*; *It's so wr-r-r-rong!*; *I l-l-l-like it!* If the accented word begins with a vowel, the speaker can put a lengthened glottal stop before it, like a high-pitched creak: *You ʔ-ʔ-ʔ-ʔass!*

Breathiness is one of those curious devices that we use to achieve a desired effect by doing the opposite. Instead of giving more intensity to the accented word, we give it less. The speaker apparently affects the kind of astonishment that strikes him dumb and reduces the accented word almost to a whisper:

Look at
t-h-a-t!

Again there is a visible gesture: eyes wide open and jaw slack and sagging.

So many of the cues of accent—gestural as well as audible—are associated with power that it is tempting to regard ARTICULATORY EFFORT as the basic physiological correlate (cf. Fónagy and Léon 1979: 128–29), and that is no doubt true in a historical sense. But there are many instances, some already mentioned, in which our experience with where accents normally go is so extensive that we assign accents at those points even when no extra effort is expended—where, in fact, there may sometimes be less effort, as in the last example cited above. As we saw, the rhythmic organization may induce an impression of accent at particular places, and the same is true of grammatical organization. Various types of inversion may achieve the desired accentual effect. Instead of the normal order *They were looking for you* we can say *It was you they were looking for*. The pronoun *you* is heard as accented even without special emphasis because of its special grammatical position.

Accent as Pitch Jumps

Accenting a syllable by means of pitch calls for setting it off from its background by a relatively abrupt jump. The abruptness is more important than the extent. Because the human ear is extremely sensitive to frequency changes, a very small shift can be detected without effort. This leaves the overall range of pitch free to be used for other, emotion-laden, purposes, without interfering with the distinctiveness of the accent. The entire following question may be spoken near the top of the speaker's range, and the word *this* will still be heard as accented:

<pre>
Isn't it easier to do your work ^{this way?}
</pre>

By locating the shift on *work* or *your* or *eas-*, each of these elements can be made to stand out as the carrier of accent.

As we saw in the last chapter, accents cued by pitch are like bumps on a relatively smooth plane:

<pre>
                                              al
                              an
                  pare
          got
You've   to pre   for   y eventu it
                                                y.
</pre>

<pre>
                                      al
                              an
                  pare for   y eventu i
          got to pre   t
You've   y.
</pre>

```
                got
                     to pre pare
                                    for  an
                                           y eventu al
      You've                                              it
                                                            y.
```

In these examples the baseline, established by the unaccented syllables, is level, rising, and falling, respectively (the initial and final
pitches, on *you've* and *-ity*, have a special intonational status that is
irrelevant here), and the accented syllables all stand out from that
line. If we imagine a line drawn through the highest pitches, that is,
the accented syllables themselves, we see that they relate to one another in terms of relative height: the line rises in the first two examples and falls in the second, and, as will be illustrated in later chapters, this accentual line may be subject to wide breaks. But for the
moment we are concerned only with the figure-and-ground association of accent and baseline. (All three of these last examples are normal utterances, differing in subtle ways that will be considered in due
course.)

But accent can be marked by a jump down as well as by a jump up.
For instance, to answer the question *Why do you despise him so?* one
might hear either of the following:

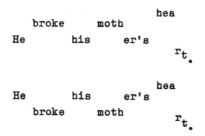

The baseline is the same in both cases—*He his -er's*—but in the first
example the first and second accents jump up whereas in the second
they jump down. (There is a subtle difference: the second is more apt
to be heard from a speaker trying to restrain a degree of impatience at
having to explain the matter at all. Here again, as with breathiness, we
have "force of utterance" reversed; the accent is "held down.") So the
use of pitch to signal an accent is not a matter of which way the jump
goes but simply of jumping. It is pitch OBTRUSION in either direction.

Importance of Pitch

Though it is wrong to identify accent with any one of its various
cues, there are reasons for believing that pitch is the one most heavily

relied on. When conditions are arranged artificially to pit one cue against another, pitch usually carries the day against length and loudness.[1] It is probably the most efficient cue. Length and loudness can be varied in only one dimension, more vs. less; pitch can in addition adopt a variety of shapes, including skips, glides, arrests, and combinations of these. Loudness may be distorted by wind currents, interfering objects, distance, and direction of transmission; pitch patterns are almost immune to such distortion. Length is affected by breathing, fatigue, and the phonetic influence of individual speech sounds to a greater degree than pitch. The ear is more sensitive to minute changes in pitch than to minute changes in length or loudness. And all auditory cues are more efficient than gestural ones because they do not require the receiver to be looking in a particular direction—which is why language is more speech than gesture in the first place. For these reasons, ACCENT as used in this book will normally refer to accent cued by pitch.

Correspondence of Accents and Syllables

The discussion in this chapter has taken for granted what appears to be an obvious fact, namely, that figure and ground are reckoned in terms of syllables. Syllables A, B, and D, say, constitute the ground of a configuration, and C constitutes the figure:

$$\text{C}$$
$$\text{A \quad B \qquad D}$$

While this is true by and large, there are times when the syllables fail us—because of their shape or because they are too few—and then we must improvise. One way is to extend a syllable so as to make it part of both figure and ground:

```
                    kno
              Do you
                       w?
```

Here, *know* is divided between the figure, obtruded upward, and the last portion of the ground, which is the low end pitch. If there were an additional syllable, say the pronoun *it*, the one-syllable *know* would not need to be divided in this fashion:

```
                    know
              Do you
                         it?
```

The shape of syllables is also important, and it may lead to our preferring one word over another that has a syllable less easy to work with. We are more apt to say *I saw a tired soldier* than to say *I saw a fatigued soldier* partly because *tired*, though (like *-tigued*) it is just one syllable, is easier to divide between figure and ground than *-tigued* is with its abrupt stop at the end:

```
          saw    ti    sol
      I      a   red
                         dier.
```

Tired is almost as good as the two-syllable *weary* would be:

```
          saw   wear  sol
      I      a     y
                         dier.
```

More will be said about these manipulations in the chapter on profiles.

Though a visual inspection of the figures should make the location of the pitch accents fairly obvious, in the following chapters the accented syllables will for the most part be provided with an accent mark. This will not necessarily be done if for whatever reason a given accent is irrelevant to the discussion.

3. Intonation

When a syllable is accented by means of pitch, the pitch does two things at once. First, it signals an accent on that syllable. Second, its direction—up, down, or level—contributes to the melody. Since the accent can be marked by a pitch difference either up or down from the reference line, and nothing in language is wasted, the *particular* pitch movement, which makes no difference to the location of the accent, does make a difference to the melody, or intonation in the broader sense.

High and Low Pitch

Here are two utterances differing only in the direction of the pitch accent; they are mirror images of each other:

```
She    ly           to
    ón      wánts
                      hélp.


    ón      wánts      hé

She    ly           to
                         l
                          p.
```

The reference line is the same in both: *She -ly to.* But the contrast in "mood" between the low-pitched accents and the high-pitched ones is striking. The first might be used to soothe someone who has misunderstood the woman's motives. The second, especially if accompanied by any trace of gruffness, is more like a reprimand or at least is "telling" rather than "persuading." Since this difference comes through the melody, it is INTONATIONAL.

The pitch of an accent also affects the overall melody by the way one pitch accent relates to another. The contrast established by having one pitch accent higher or lower than its neighbor influences the meaning. Suppose someone gives you a box of candies and then, after you have tasted a couple, asks how you like them. You might say, smacking your lips,

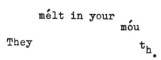

```
      mélt in your   ́
                    móu
  They                  t
                        h.
```

Here *melt* is jumped up to and the first part of *mouth* is both jumped down to and then down from; so these two words stand out. But the important thing is that *melt* is higher in pitch than *mouth*. Now imagine that someone who has been holding the candies objects that they melt in your hands. You thereupon defend the candies by saying

```
                  móu

      mélt in your
  They               t
                     h.
```

This time *mouth* reaches the higher pitch. As we shall see later, this rising pattern is often used in explanations and arguments.

Intonation and Grammar

For the GRAMMAR of a sentence, the most important part of the intonational melody comes at TERMINALS—the end points of phrases, clauses, and sentences. We have already seen how intonation helps in distinguishing between questions and statements. This is especially true when the intonation is the only clue to the difference. If someone asks *When would you like to go?* and you reply

```
      mór

  To    r
        o
        w.
```

you are, in effect, making the statement *I would like to go tomorrow.* But if you reply

```
              w
        mórr o
  To
```

(this could be punctuated with a question mark, but that would prejudge the case), you are probably asking the question *Is it all right with you if I (we) go tomorrow?* *Tomorrow* alone needs the intonation more than does the full question, which might be said with either a terminal rise or a terminal fall:

Is it áĺl right with yóu if I gó to mórroͬoͭw?

Is it áĺl right with yóu if I gó to mór
row?

(The speaker is in a different mood when saying the latter, but the important thing is that both are normal questions and adequate as responses to what the other person has said.)

Terminal intonations also help in marking the internal organization of a sentence, serving, for example, as one kind of link between the more or less independent parts:

him,
sée   téll him I'm lóoking for him.
When you

In this sentence there are two terminals, one at the end, the other just before the comma. The end terminal is typical of points where the speaker stops because he is finished; at such points there is a tendency in all languages for the pitch to slide down. For the opposite reason it goes up on *him*: this is the end of a clause, and it calls for a break of some sort; but the clause is linked to what follows, and the rise cues the hearer to that fact. It can be a very slight rise—indeed, it can be a rise immediately following a fall, as in

sée
téll him I'm lóoking for him.
When you
him,

Here the pitch falls to the first *him* and then rises slightly on that same word. The intonation does not usually work alone in cases like this; there tends to be a slight pause as well. The wider the pause, the greater the break, as a rule; and something similar happens with the intonation terminal—the wider it goes, the greater the break. So, even without the aid of pause, we can tell the difference between two such sentences as the following (an experimenter is giving instructions to a subject taking a psychological test, and has just warned, *Watch it, now!*):

stóp
If you don't   as soon as I   signal   you'll receive a shó
ck.

```
                          sí       signal
                            gnal
                    stóp                              shó
If you don't              as soon as I     you'll receive a
                                                            ck.
```

In writing we would probably punctuate these *If you don't stop, as soon as I signal you'll receive a shock* and *If you don't stop as soon as I signal, you'll receive a shock*. In the first the wider rise at *stop* signals the greater break at that point; in the second, the wider rise—hence the comma—is at *signal*. But both terminals, being rises, show the interdependence of the clauses, as well as—by their extent—the degree of independence.

Even much shorter elements may be split off with rising terminals if their independence is relative. Take the pair

```
                    knów   líkes
You          he          me.

            knów,  líkes
You        he        me.
```

In the first, *know* is accented but does not carry a terminal. The sentence means the same as *You know that he likes me*. In the second, *know* carries both an accent and a terminal. The phrase *you know* is relatively independent; it is a set expression that means, roughly, 'I'm telling you something interesting.' (The break in the second is shown not only by the terminal on *know* but also by the fact that *he* tends to be pronounced with its *h*, not just as *'e*.)

Nevertheless, though intonation is indispensable to grammar, the grammatical functions of intonation are secondary to the emotional ones; speakers *feel* differently about what they say, and the feelings manifest themselves in pitch changes that serve as clues. One proof of the emotional rather than logical nature of intonation—its symptomatic more than symbolic character—is the fact that speakers rarely if ever objectify the choice of an intonation pattern; they do not stop and ask themselves "Which form would be best here for my purpose?" as they frequently do in selecting a word or a grammatical construction. Instead, they identify the feeling they wish to convey, and the intonation is triggered by it. They may make mistakes and have to correct themselves—even automatic choices may occasionally be off target—but the correction will be just as unreflecting as the original choice.

Intonation and Music

Since intonation is synonymous with speech melody, and melody is a term borrowed from music, it is natural to wonder what connection there may be between music and intonation. One can speculate about a common origin and common themes, and many inherently plausible claims can be made. The most obvious connection is that both song and intonation depend on the fundamental pitch of the voice—the pitch that represents the melodic line, excluding the harmonics, or overtones. But there are other resemblances. In both song and intonation the voice tends to go up at the beginning and down to a point of rest at the end. Further, the REGISTERS of the voice (falsetto for the highest, modal for the middle, and creak for the lowest—see Chapter 10, pp. 216–21) have importance for intonation as well as for singing.

The comparison runs into problems when we consider tones that move and tones that are sustained. The concept of "note" (and its materialization in musical notation as a pitch held at a point on the staff) suggests that sustention is very important in music. In a world without absolutes, we know that in any realization of a composer's intent there is bound to be some wavering, but in music, most of the time, the wavering is not intended. What of a *speaker's* intent?

The most casual look at a spectrogram of speech will show that steady pitches are the exception, not the rule. For those who would like to see a close analogy between speech and music, the way to deal with this is through a rather sweeping idealization of certain critical points on a pitch curve as targets. The speaker, if he were more careful, or if he slowed down, would manifest those targets more recognizably as steady tones. This claim of course implies that what comes between the target pitches is accidental and merely part of what you do on the way to the pitch or LEVEL you are aiming at. If we can show that there are differences in meaning between, say, two successive pitches at 120 and 180 hertz and a slide from 120 to 180, then we have refuted this claim.[1]

The notion of target pitches is inviting not only to the music-analogists but to anyone who would like to make the moving scene stand still long enough to take its measure, and above all to linguists who want to digitize the elements of language. It would be simpler to analyze a stream of melody if what we needed to account for were not a continuously varying curve but just an array of x number of pitch levels. (Four has been the favorite through the years; Gage 1958: 125 adds a fifth. See Ladd 1983*b* for discussion.) The gain for notation would be tremendous; instead of the typographical swoops used in the examples of this book, it would suffice to mark the numbers of the pitches in the proper places. Even those who oppose the notion of levels admit the pedagogical advantages of a numbered system—for example, in the rough approximations required in a textbook for teaching a foreign language.

Levels and Glides

Despite the advantages, the target-level approach is rejected here. The reasons will become apparent as we proceed. Still, there *are* levels, if by levels we mean sustained pitches. In Chapter 10, where this point is discussed more fully, these sustained pitches will be referred to as MONOTONES. A number of stereotypes in Chapter 1 use them. It is easy to find instances that consist of two or more successive levels—for example, sayings like

```
It's
     néver too láte to
                        ménd.
```

and particularly monotones where the speaker seems to be displaying no interest (because he is bored, or is holding back, or whatever):

That old story again!
Do you really expect me to believe that!

Levels in this sense—monotones—are found in both speech and music. And in both speech and music they differ from GLIDES. The effect of a glide replacing a succession of levels can be as dramatic in speech as the contrast between the sliding pitch of a trombone and a jump from one pitch to another on the piano. An easy way to hear the difference between glide and jump is in one-syllable questions. If someone calls you and you respond with

```
          es?
      Ye-
```

using two level tones with a skip between, you will seem routinely attentive. But if you answer with a glide,

```
            es?
      Ye-ee
```

you may seem impatient. (A glide needs to be drawled at least slightly, and this adds to the effect; but even when levels and glide are equally drawled, one can still hear the difference.) Similarly if you respond to someone else's remark with *Oh?*, the levels will suggest controlled surprise and the glide something stronger, perhaps disbelief. If you say you have done something and I respond with *You?* the levels will show a kind of affected surprise, the glide something more like in-credulity. For a slightly more complex example, if you are about to be taken in by someone's scheme and I say *It's a come-on*, the levels in

```
            cóme

   It's a

            on.
```

will inform you of what I think about the matter, whereas if I utter *on* with a downglide ending well above the bottom of my speaking range,

```
            cóme

   It's a        o
                  n!
```

I leave something in suspense, perhaps implying that you ought to know better. The glide appears to add "more of" whatever the skip implies—which of course may be enhanced with a drawl, but that is not necessary. Contrasts among movements of this sort will be looked at again later, but for now it is enough to have shown that glides and jumps between levels are separately significant and that there is more to the story than movement between target pitches.

Intervals

Assuming that there are levels in intonation just as there are (more abundantly) in music, is there the further analogy of fixed intervals? All musical scales bear some relationship to the overtone series of which the basic interval is the octave. Up from that comes the perfect fifth, then the perfect fourth, then the major third, and so on, each succeeding note being an even multiple of the fundamental frequency. The ear's appreciation of the basic intervals is no mere mathematical accident. There is a definite physical impression associated with syn-chronized pulsations of sound: a frequency of 200 hertz does not clash with one of 100 since each pulse at 100 coincides with a pulse at 200.

Given that our entire musical tradition is based on our sensitivity to these intervals and that music and language already share so much else, one might expect language also to make use of them. Communi-cation in general is a voracious user of just about anything that can conveniently serve to convey meaning, from snorting to crossing one's legs. Some recent studies of intonation have indeed claimed that the octave, fifth, fourth, third, etc. are individually contrastive in much the same way as other distinctive sounds (see Gardiner 1980; Hirst 1980, esp. p. 4).

The difficulty of proving this thesis is that even if it were not so, it might still seem to be. Intonational contrasts are one-dimensional, and in the hurried pace of conversation there is only so much one can do with that one dimension. If we want, say, to make an audible difference between one interval we have used and the next, we do not as a rule make the second interval only a semitone over or under the one before it. For a robust distinction we are more apt to contrast an octave with something in the neighborhood of a fifth, and a fifth with something in the neighborhood of a third. By the time the space has been parceled out in this manner, even a person who had no motive other than to make A, B, C, and D appreciably different from one another might appear to have been aiming at some precise musical note. The catch is that nobody pretends that the levels used in speech are separated by *exact* musical intervals. The analysts are always willing to accept a semitone or two this side or that, and with a little imagination (not usually lacking in people with a musical ear) the intervals become idealized. But to counter the objections to ideal intervals by pointing out that speech in general hinges on uncertain targets and intonation is no worse in this regard is not a valid argument, because where those other targets have really been demonstrated to exist— as in the case of phonemes, for example—they are known to have several parameters: if one is blurred the hearer still has the others to fall back on. For instance, an /n/, normally dental in articulation, is blurred to palatal in a word such as *inch*, but its nasalization remains intact. Pitch has only one parameter. Change it and no anchor remains.

This is not to say that exact intervals are irrelevant to intonation, only that proof of relevance must come from an abundant empirical demonstration of contrasts that depend on them.

Relational Differences

A more plausible thesis is that the main business of intonation is carried out by differences that are purely relational and not basically musical in the harmonic sense. Take an exclamation that depends for its effect on a relatively narrow interval that seems to hit close to a major third: *Oh, yeah!* said as a jeering response to another person's remark. The intonation is obviously allied to that of *She did?*, *It is?*, *Really?* or any other such expression that comes as an indication of interest and of paying attention. Any of these can be used with the same interval without causing offense, but they are also open to wider intervals, which suggest greater interest, hence more politeness. So it suits the *Oh, yeah?* speaker to restrict the range of the rise, and what is needed for this is to keep it less than some true feeling of interest would lead to, but still sufficient to suggest an ironic pseudo-interest (a major second would seem too much like mere indifference, unless the intervals of the entire conversation had been pretty narrow to begin with). Hence the approximation of the third, which could easily be a fourth or a fifth or more if overall jumps were fairly wide.

The analysis of the whole—or the greater part—of intonation in terms of levels still has its advocates. Liberman (1979: 132–50), for example, grants that some aspects of intonation are not captured by a four-tone analysis; but he puts these down as "ideophonic," borrowing a comparison from lexical studies in which some relatively few words are shown to have a meaning that transcends the literal one: *teeny* and *tiny* both "mean the same," but there is an enhanced smallness in *teeny*. Because these ideophonic distinctions are generally recognized as marginal, a way is thus found to put some intonational facts into an inferior category, outside the pale of intonational grammar.

Thesis of This Book

The thesis of this book is that (1) in intonation there is no distinction between the grammatical and the ideophonic except as they represent extremes of a scale, (2) levels and glides are in contrast, and (3) differences in pitch too slight to be assigned to different levels (without increasing the number of levels unconscionably) are as apt to be "grammatical" as they are to be "ideophonic." Examples of point 2 have already been given, supporting the claim that the glide enhances whatever it is that the skip conveys. Here is another:

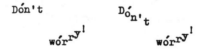

Both utterances use a low-pitched accent to play something down, in this case to play down worry, that is, to reassure; but the downglide shows more concern on the speaker's part, adding to the reassurance.

A good example of point 3 is what tends to happen intonationally when "source" is balanced against "goal." This is a grammatical distinction of some importance, and the intonation reflects the distinction. When one person gives a gift and another receives it, we have a choice between *From John to Henry* and *To Henry from John*. Suppose you ask me what the card accompanying the gift says, and I reply with the first phrase; I would probably say

Hén

Jóhn

From   to

ry.

But if I reply with the second phrase, my intonation will probably be

```
          Hénry
                      Jó
      To          from
                      hn.
```

Both orders tend to preserve the higher pitch for the goal and the lower one for the source. There are circumstances that can alter this, and one almost automatically suggests itself when we reverse the height with the second phrase:

```
                      Jó
          Hénry
      To          from
                      hn.
```

This suggests that the speaker was surprised that the giver was John. It is too precise an interpretation of the intonational meaning to say 'goal' and 'source' here, as will be brought out in later discussion; but at this point all we need is to demonstrate a grammatical use of relative height. And the height in this case is indeed relative: all that is necessary is that one of the peaks be *appreciably* higher than the other, by whatever interval.

A similar example of what happens when a grammatical order is reversed is provided by personal names when, for such purposes as enlistments and enrollments, they are given backwards. In answer to *What is your name?* one may hear either of the following,

```
            Fór                  Fór
    lín                                  lín
  Me   da De    est.        De    est, Me    d
                                             a.
```

but most unlikely

```
                        lín
            Fór
    De      est, Me    d
                       a.
```

unless to correct some misunderstanding of the given name.

A further complication for the notion of exact intervals is what happens with parentheses. This will be discussed in a later chapter, but an example can be given here. Take a sentence like

```
                  tér
        spóke                    xi
  She          with    ri           e
                       ble    an   ty.
```

The word *terrible* is highlighted because of its emotional impact, and if there is a "highest" level that word commands it. But when this sort of sentence is turned into an ascription, that is, a formula that attributes a quotation to someone, it becomes a sort of parenthesis at the end:

$$dó$$

What are you

$$tér$$

ing, she said, with rible anxíety.

Now whatever contrasts need to be shown in the end portion have to be compressed within the narrow range of the parenthesis. It is the *relative* height of the syllable *ter-* that carries the emotional impact that was allowed to reach skyward in the first example.

The affective, attitudinal, emotive side of intonation is inextricably intertwined with the grammatical side. There is no way to set aside what is "ideophonic" just to make the grammarian's task easier.

Part II

ACCENTUAL PROSODY

4. Vowels and Syllables

The term PROSODY is applied to patterns of sound that range more or less freely and independently over individual sounds and individual words. One can beat out a rhythm or hum a tune without drawing upon any of the particular smaller units of speech. Rhythm (and the accents that punctuate it) is one kind of prosody in English; intonation (and the tunes that it composes) is another. Both involve pitch, and the two are the themes of Parts II and III of this book.

Full and Reduced Vowels

A preliminary to understanding the RHYTHM of English—and through rhythm the scheme of accents and the overall shape of utterances—is a grasp of the English vowel system. As we saw in Chapter 2, vowels come in two grades, full and reduced, of which only the full ones can be the bearers of accent. Following is a list of forms exemplifying the full vowels:

Word	Symbol	Word	Symbol
keyed	[i]	cod	[a]
kid	[ɪ]	cawed	[ɔ]
cade	[e]	code	[o]
Ked	[ɛ]	could	[ʊ]
cad	[æ]	cooed	[u]
cud	[ʌ]		

There are three reduced vowels, as in the last (always unstressed) syllables of the following:

Word	Symbol
Willie	[ɨ]
Willa	[ə]
willow	[ɵ]

The second of these, [ə], has the special name SHWA and is the most frequently occurring vowel in English, appearing with numerous spellings in such words as

*a*part	inst*i*tute	Tenn*e*ssee
c*o*llect	min*u*te (time)	synon*ym*o*us*

For convenience (the point is worth debating, but not in this context) we can also class as instances of shwa-plus-consonant the so-called "syllabic consonants" in which there is actually no clear vowel. Examples:

cotton	[katən]	more precisely [katn̩]
little	[lɪtəl]	[lɪtl̩]
otter	[atər]	[atɝ]
chasm	[kæzəm]	[kæzm̩]

The justification is that the syllabic consonants are phonetically similar to shwa-plus-consonant and they behave the same rhythmically as other reduced vowels.

   There are also three diphthongs, which are classed with the full vowels:

Word	*Symbol*
lied	[aɨ]
loud	[aө]
Lloyd	[ɔɨ]

As the symbols suggest, the diphthongs are made up of a full vowel plus one of the reduced vowels.[1]

   The status of the reduced vowels as a *mutually* contrastive set, individually marking differences among words as securely as the full vowels do, rests mainly on contrasts in the final syllables of words, as in the following sets:

tory	sallied	lassie	galleys
tora	salad	Lhasa	galas
toro	sallowed	lasso	gallows

Elsewhere, while reduced vowels still mark distinctions, they tend to do so as opposed to full vowels rather than as opposed to themselves, and the reduced vowel that is mostly involved is shwa, the vowel in the last syllable of the words *tora, salad, Lhasa,* and *galas* listed above. So *retire* 'to provide with new tires' with [i] in its first syllable (as in *read, ream*) is distinguished from *retire* 'withdraw' with shwa (symbol, [ə]), and *abjéct* with [æ] (as in *nab*) is distinguished from to *objéct* with [ə]. Though not necessarily entering into neat sets like those above, there are plenty of reduced vowels that are distinctive elements of words, including the interior of words. So we find the vowel of the top row above, symbolized [ɨ], in the second syllable of *polio*, the vowel of the bottom row, [ə], in the second syllable of *Maoist*, and the first syllable of *assert* contains another shwa. In all these cases the reduced vowel is STABLE, a set part of the word.

There are also words in which reduction is UNSTABLE, where speakers, occasions, and dialects may vary. The name *Maureen* may have shwa in its first syllable and sound like *marine*, or it may have [ɔ] as in *Maud*. This state of affairs has given rise to so much controversy that doubters of the approach adopted here are invited to consult Appendix A, where fuller explanations are offered. Meanwhile it should be borne in mind that just one thing counts in our later discussions of rhythm, namely the global contrast between full vowels and reduced vowels. The particular reduced or particular full vowel encountered in a particular word is of secondary importance.

Syllable Sequences and Timing

The combination and interspersion of syllables with full and reduced vowels are what largely determines the syllabic rhythm of English. There is a FOOT STRUCTURE, that is, a scheme of rhythmic measures, in which combinations of full syllables with or without reduced syllables following them serve both the prose and the poetry of the language.

The most consistent effect of ordering syllables one after another is that when one full syllable is followed by another, the first gets extra length. The result is that in an expression such as the Boraxo ad *Gets out dirt plain soap can't reach* there is mutual lengthening throughout. The words here all happen to be monosyllables, but words of more than one syllable will give the same result if all the syllables are full: *Attaché's chimpanzees don't dance fandangoes* (the speaker has to be one for whom all these syllables *are* full, of course). This even syllable-by-syllable beat has been called "syllable-timed rhythm."

The reason for the added length is probably once again accentual. If the speaker has reason to accent two such words in succession (the effectiveness of the Boraxo ad consists in doing so), the extra length provides for the pitch turn. As with other parts of the sound system, we do not wait to find out whether we need it; instead, we provide it consistently in case we might need it. An example such as the Boraxo ad does not actually require an accent on each word in order to retain its steady rhythm. One might respond to an objection like *I know you*

said that Boraxo gets out dirt that some kind of soap can't reach, but I didn't
hear just which kind with

pláin

It gếts out dirt

soap can't reach.

in which the last three words are deaccented but still keep their even
beat. The relationship between accent and rhythm will be discussed
in the next chapter.

When reduced syllables are interspersed with full ones, the rhythm
changes. Since a reduced syllable is not accented, whenever one is
present it provides a preceding accented full syllable with the material
it needs for the pitch turn, and the extra length is no longer needed.
The result is that a combination of a full and a reduced syllable (in that
order) may take no more time than one full syllable requires in utterances like the Boraxo ad. The ad can be reworded to show the
equivalence:

> Géts   óut   dírt   pláin   sóap   cán't   réach.
> Tákes a-wáy the dírt that cóm-mon sóaps can név-er réach.

The syllables *a-, the, that, -mon, can,* and *-er* are all reduced, and add
no extra length to the full syllables that precede them; the two-syllable
feet may thus be the same length as the one-syllable ones, and in any
case are less than twice as long as a one-syllable foot.[2]

Though the phonological conditions are the controlling ones and
the grammatical conditions are only incidental, sometimes the rhythmic differences can help in making a grammatical distinction. In a
sentence like *One was this year, two were last year,* the words *was* and
were are reduced (this happens to many function words, which are
low in information value, when they are not emphasized), and as a
result the preceding *one* and *two* acquire no extra length. But in the
sentence *All the beginning classes are trying to do it this year, but only two
were last year,* the word *were*—as normally happens when its complement (here, *trying to do it*) is deleted—is not reduced, and consequently the preceding *two* occupies a foot all to itself. The resulting
even beat in *two were last year* (all full syllables) is a help in interpreting
the sentence.

The lengthening effect is the same within words as between words.
A word consisting of two full syllables contains two feet of one syllable each. (The term *monobeat* will be used for a one-syllable foot, to
contrast with *iamb, trochee,* and *dactyl* in their conventional senses.) It
is longer than a word containing a full syllable followed by a reduced

one, which yields a single trochee; so we have contrasts such as *Agee–agy, Andes–Andy's, radar–raider, Curlee–curly, cónsole–consul.* In fact, the environment of the full syllables and the reduced ones— whether within a single word, between words, or even between grammatical constituents—makes no material difference, so long as the speaker does not intend a pausal break. Comparing two such sentences as *He's sad, you see* and *He's Sadducee* we find that they may sound alike so long as the speaker utters the *you see* as a run-on incidental remark: the reduced *you* adds no time to *sad* (the *sad you* even permits the palatalization of the [d] to [dʒ]) just as the reduced *-u-* adds none to *Sad-*, even though *you see* is a parenthesis, not connected grammatically with what precedes. Compare also *It's utter nonsense, if you don't mind my saying so* with *It's utter nonsense, all things considered.* (The intended pronunciation of *-sense* is with the full vowel [ɛ].) If the parenthetical second clauses are run on without pause, the reduced *if* may keep *-sense* quite short, while the full *all* lengthens it. In both, *non-* is lengthened by the following full *-sense.*

When—as happens in a good many words—speakers have a choice between using a full vowel in a given syllable and using a reduced one, there will be predictable effects on other syllables. The word *creativity* may, to preserve the connection with *creative*, be pronounced with full [e] in its second syllable (see Appendix A, p. 355). This will cause the first syllable, [kri], to become longer: it already has a full vowel and simply obeys the rule of extra length when a full vowel is followed by another full vowel. If the second syllable of *creativity* is pronounced with [ə], the [kri] will not take on extra length. If in the first syllable of *direct* the speaker chooses the diphthong [aɨ], that syllable not only will contain the full vowel but will have extra length because it is followed by the full syllable *-rect*; on the other hand, the first syllable of *dynamo* will not be lengthened, because of the following reduced [nə]. If one says *incantation* with a full [æ] in *-can-*, the result is extra length in both *in-* and *-can-*: full *-can-* lengthens already full *in-*, and is in turn lengthened by already full *-ta-*.

In most utterances, given the mixture of syllabic types within words and the mixture of words, we find a mixed rhythm: one-syllable, two-syllable, three-syllable, and occasionally longer feet are interspersed. The effect of full syllables remains the same: a full followed by another full has the predicted extra length. This happens with the *pon-* [pan] of *pontificate*, where *-tif-* is full, but not with the *pon-* of *pontiff*, where *-tiff* is reduced. It happens to *one* in *Ten times one makes ten* since it is followed by full *makes*, but not to *one* in *Ten times one is ten*, since *is* is reduced (and may be contracted, in which case the full *one's* again picks up extra length, since it is followed by full *ten*: *Ten times one's ten*). A longer utterance maintains the same relationships; in the following, the feet are separated by the diagonal and the syllables with extra length are marked with a plus sign:

> Quite / possibly / no / real / happiness can be / found in / all / these /
>   +   +   +   +   +
> struggles and / all / this / fan/fare.
>   +   +   +   +

(The plus sign under -*fare* indicates what happens when a full syllable precedes pause: it gets the same extra length as when it is followed by another full syllable. The two manifestations of extra length are probably related: in both cases the positions are where a pitch turn is most apt to occur.)

This example illustrates two additional points. One is the indifference to where the foot separation comes: it may be in the middle of a word, as with *fanfare* (two separate feet because two full syllables), as well as between words. The second is the generally irregular succession of foot lengths: here the syllable count is 1-3-1-1-5-2-1-1-3-1-1-1-1. We noted earlier that a two-syllable foot may have about the same length as a one-syllable foot, since the reduced syllable, itself short, induces no extra length on the preceding full one. But adding more and more reduced syllables to a foot cannot be accomplished by proportionately shortening the other syllables: *Hap* (as in *Hap told me*) and *happy* (as in *a happy girl*) are of about the same length, but *happiness* tends to be longer. While extremely long feet are rare, they can be concocted: for the speaker who says *fórmidableness*, this word constitutes a five-syllable foot, and in an utterance such as *The formidableness of the rebuttal was devastating*, the one-foot *formidableness of the* is eight syllables long; all but *for-* contain reduced vowels. (The first *the* does not count: a rhythmic measure normally starts with a full syllable, and *the* is reduced.) The effect of this possibility of constructing feet of various lengths is to make syllabic timing in English only approximately even (isochronous). It exists to the extent that one- and two-syllable feet may be fully isochronous and three-syllable feet are not too different from two-syllable ones—and to the extent that these three-syllable types make up the majority of syllabic rhythms. The poet of course gets around this mere approximation by choosing his words to fit a rhythmic pattern, and cheating a bit in compressing some of the syllables: in fact, by forcing an accentual onto a syllabic rhythm. The next chapter will discuss the relationships of these two types of rhythm.[3]

Other Manifestations of Length

What happens with English foot structure is the most important, but not the only, manifestation of variable length. A further instance of AUTOMATIC variation is the difference in length among the vowels and consonants themselves—the vowel [ɪ], for example, is shorter than [i], as can be detected by listening to the words *bit* [bɪt] and *beet* [bit]. But the most striking variations in length are at the word level or above, and involve usually some form of expressiveness, as the following examples show.

1. Inherent length in words. This quality adheres to words as a form of sound symbolism. Except for their initial consonants, *ball* and *drawl* contain the same distinctive sounds, but whereas in a sentence like *He's playing with a ball* we can shorten *ball* to the point of almost eliminating the pitch drop at the end, a similar treatment of *He's talking with a drawl* would probably be misunderstood—*drawl* is lengthened approximately as much as *-drawal* in *withdrawal*. Similarly *dawn* and *yawn* as in *It dawned on me* and *He yawned at me*. And similarly *side–sighed*. *Take the pine away* and *She'll just pine away* reveal the additional length in *pine*, verb. In street talk, *man* 'policeman' receives extra length.

2. Length for intensification. This too is expressive, and is applied most systematically as an intensifier on adjectives that express degree.[4] If in answer to *What do you think of it?* we hear *Queer!* with extra length, we interpret the meaning as 'very queer.' One can speed up *mean* in *I didn't mean that* to the point of distortion, but not *mean* in *a mean old man*. Other word classes are also affected to the extent that 'degree' is expressed—a lengthened *hate*, for example, in *How he can hate!*, or *intensity* in *What intensity!* (the stressed syllable is the one that picks up the extra length), or a lengthened *on* in *It goes on and on*. Exclamations make regular use of this form of lengthening; in the following, all the words are lengthened, *run* and *beautiful* especially: *Can they run!*, *Is she beautiful!* (See Deakin 1981a: 122.)

3. Whimsical lengthening. Length is used in various expressively imitative ways, increased for 'slowness' and diminished for 'rapidity.' Combined with monotone and low pitch, it is an ingredient of ghost stories.

4. Reduced length due to frequency and familiarity. The more an expression is used, the more its parts tend to fuse together and the faster it goes; the opposite is true of something newly introduced. This is ultimately a matter of pragmatics—the speaker can afford to put less effort into producing a signal that is easily recognized. We

adjust our speed to the estimated rate of comprehension of our hearer. Thus the speaker who said, by way of a translation, *Alameda de las Pulgas*—*it's a flea poplar grove*—*what do you make of that!* intentionally but without deliberation lengthened the word *flea*; had he not done so, the word would probably have been mistaken for *free*, as *flea* is unexpected in that context. At the same time, length-for-intelligibility may become a more or less permanent mark of the expression, particularly when a contrast depends on the difference between a longer and a shorter version. The term *way station* has been in American English at least since 1856, and admits more speed than the relatively recent *weigh station* (a place where trucks stop to be weighed). A *comforter* is a familiar item of bedclothing and may be pronounced faster than *Comforter* referring to someone who provides religious comfort. *To grow up* is a relatively fused phrasal verb applied to the maturing of a child, and is faster than *grow up* in a sentence like *The problem with that tree is getting it to grow up* (rather than sideways). The *mark* in the less common *bench mark* is longer than the *mark* in the more common *bookmark* (our writing and printing habits usually tell us something about the degree of fusion—the faster compounds are written faster, that is, without a space). The *choose* in the frozen expression *pick and choose* can be condensed more easily than the *chews* in the less frozen *nuts and chews* (candy). The word *awful* contrasts with itself in the sense that it is a very colorful adjective that can be lengthened for intensification (*It was a-w-w-w-ful!*) but is also so commonplace as a routine intensifier that it may be made shorter than average (*I don't care an awful lot for that*). In the latter sense it contrasts with the less colorful but also less usual *lawful*, which cannot readily be shortened. (*Jawful* is of course longer by rule, since *-ful* is a different suffix here; it has a full vowel, and that gives *jaw-* extra length. But *jawful* in turn may be shorter than *jaw full* as in *You shouldn't talk with your jaw full*; *full* is now an independent complement—'with your jaw being full'—which tends to expand things further.) The process of acceleration may lead to the eventual reduction of the vowel. An example is *by* in the spatial sense of 'beside' and *by* as a grammatical function word: *He lives by the store* tends to have an unreduced *by*; *He lives by the sword* may readily reduce the vowel. The *for* in *good for* is a stereotype and a sentence like *He will if he knows what's good for him* can reduce the last two words virtually to *f'rim*; that is less apt to happen in *What did you buy for him?* The *go* in *go on* is reduced to the point of being represented sometimes by the spelling *Gwan!* Compare the possibilities of speeding up in *I've gotta go home* and *I've gotta row home*, said by someone who lives on an island. All these gradations depend to some extent on one's intentions and one's experience with the expressions in question, and accordingly are not the same for all speakers.

Since particular sequences of monosyllabic *words* are by and large less fused than sequences of full syllables *within* words, examples like *Gets out dirt plain soap can't reach* may—contrary to what was claimed above—be longer than sequences with an equal number of full syllables not all of which are independent words.

The important thing for our purpose here is that none of the contrasts due to expressiveness or degree of familiarity just illustrated are part of the underlying system. They need not be present at all in any given instance. The extent of overlap is so great that a not overly shortened familiar form may readily have the same length as a not overly lengthened unfamiliar one. The differences are under the control of the speaker. This is not true of the lengthening keyed to the fullness of the vowel, which is part of the underlying system and occurs automatically.

5. The Shape of Utterances: Two Kinds of Rhythm

Any number of roads lead to analogies that will serve as models for the shape of a "normal" utterance, but one that appears promising on several counts is the conversational dyad in which one person asks a question and another answers it:

$$\text{Do you } ^{li}{}^{ke}{}^{\;it?} \qquad \text{I } l\acute{o}ve \;\; {}^{i}t.$$

Of course each of these is already an utterance in its own right, so "normal" seems to beg the question. Yet when we compare the dyad with what happens when we produce a longer utterance, we find that the two match up with surprising regularity:

$$\text{If you } ^{li}{}^{ke}{}^{\;it} \qquad \text{then } tr\acute{y} \;\; {}^{i}t.$$

In a sense, the second half "answers" the question in the first half: 'What about if you like it? Well, then try it.'

The Hat Pattern

Probably the majority of well-executed longer utterances have a shape and an organizational base that corresponds to some such question-answer pair. ("Well executed" represents an ideal: the speaker plans ahead and is not interrupted.) There's a part that lays the groundwork, that asks the question, that relates to what we already know or can guess, and a part that adds the figure to the ground, that answers the question, that supplies what was not already known. The first part is called the THEME and the second part the RHEME. (There are other terms, and distinctions have been drawn, but all we need here is something on which to drape our prosody.)

Since theme and rheme are fundamental to the meaning of the utterance, each is separately highlighted, and just as we are ordinarily limited, in highlighting a word, to one syllable (the stressed one) in that word, so it will be one word, hence one syllable in that word, that will serve as the peg for the accent in a theme and in a rheme. In our example the two words are *like* and *try*. It is no coincidence that they are also the words that carry the bulk of the information. ("Information" is too restrictive a concept, but it will do for the moment.)

In the original dyad, of course, there was only a single item highlighted in the question and a single one in the answer. So all we are entitled to say, really, is that the information we want to convey is what determines the highlighting. There is no information to speak of in *do you* or in *I*, and we can actually omit those words:

Even so, when a particular intonation is used over and over it begins to take on a reality of its own, and the two-accent shape is so typical that it has been designated the "hat pattern" (Cohen and 't Hart 1967) or the "suspension bridge" (Bolinger 1961)—shapes that usually turn out to be lopsided in practice but nevertheless exhibit the two corners of the hat or the two towers of the bridge:

The two figures represent the same ideal shape: relatively low pitches at beginning and end, flanking two higher-pitched corners or points. The middle level in the hat pattern and the sag in the suspension bridge are normal variants.

When things are put together one naturally expects them to affect one another somehow. In speech the togetherness produces two effects, both of which figure in the shape of the utterance as a whole. One is how each item affects its neighbors, the other is the nature of being first and last in a series.

A speaker must constantly adjust what he wants to say to the mechanism for saying it. Time is one-dimensional, and the only way we can string words or accents is end-to-end (though these two operations can go on simultaneously). Stringing the words together means that some successions will be easier for our speech mechanism than others, and this may cause us to seek the easier combinations or even to alter the harder ones to make them easier. In time we learn the tricks for this, which may be in the form of general rules as well as in certain more or less permanent changes that we make in our inventory of words so as not to have to resort to any special rules. (Since the problems are pretty sure to be the same for the majority of speakers, the solutions tend to be likewise, and this brings about the fairly regular changes that are observed in language.)

Stringing the accents together means that some will fall in a more advantageous position than others—advantageous psychologically, in that first and last are the positions of greatest impact. So the most effective places for the accents are initial and final, or as close to that as the more or less arbitrary rules of our syntax and the more or less arbitrary shapes of our words will permit. A trivial illustration can be given using a couple of compound words, *life-size* and *cross-eyed*. Suppose I ask you *How big is the portrait?* and you answer

```
                         lífe
           It's
                         size.
```

This would be a matter-of-fact giving of information. But now suppose that you do not know how big it is, and you look at it to see, and are surprised at how big it is—you will probably say

```
                    sí
              lífe
        It's
                  zeı
```

Similarly if I ask you *What's the matter with him?* and you reply

```
                  cróss
           He's
                  eyed.
```

—an unemphatic passing of information (unless the pitch goes too high on *cross*). But if you have to look to see, you may hit me with your surprise by saying

```
                  éy
            cróss
      He's
                  edı
```

(We must guard against being overspecific and saying that this intonation "means 'surprise.'" The high pitch means that the speaker is "keyed up," but its position—shifted to the right—suggests a buildup, or climax. From the hearer's standpoint there is impact by virtue of final position, on the psychological principle of last-heard-best-noted. The same intonation could be used if you and I had been arguing about whether the man is cross-eyed or not, and you were insisting rather than calmly stating.)

This explains in part why the last accent in an utterance—the one that tends to gravitate toward final position—is usually regarded as the most important one. It is sometimes called the "sentence accent," "sentence stress," or "nucleus." Our term for it, explained above, is RHEMATIC ACCENT. Languages of the most diverse kinds have such accents, so their presence may be some sort of universal.[1]

Though it is less striking, the initial accent has its own push, leftward. Suppose you ask me whether John swore on a particular occasion, and I reply

$$\text{He } ^{\text{nót}} \text{ only } {}^{\text{swó}}_{\quad\text{re}\cdots}$$

with the initial accent on *not*. This gives a matter-of-fact introduction to what I am about to add. But if I say

$$\text{Hé} \qquad {}^{\text{swó}}_{\text{not only} \quad \text{re}\cdots}$$

you know that I am about to impart the information as something out of the ordinary. The accent on *he* cannot be there because of any special focus on the person (as in *Hé won't but Í will*), but is there for the sake of the utterance as a whole. A similar but milder effect can be seen between the two utterances

$$\text{Not } ^{\text{ón}}\text{ly did he } {}^{\text{swé}}_{\quad\text{ar}\cdots}$$

$$\text{Nót} \qquad {}^{\text{swé}}_{\text{only did he} \quad \text{ar}\cdots}$$

with *not* performing the same office as *he* in the previous example.

The strongest evidence for the reality of this double-accent pattern is its ability at times to distort the stresses of words. (This assumes that stresses are fixed, of course—a point that will be questioned later.) The secretary, speaking in the motion picture *All the President's Men*, at one point says

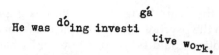

The normal stress is *invéstigative*, but accenting *-ves-* would have deflated the end too much to suit the speaker's purpose. Sometimes it is
the syntax that is altered. Colloquially, the word *yet* occurs after the
verb: *They haven't cóme yet* rather than the formal *They have not yet
cóme*. But even speaking colloquially one may resort to the formal syntax if by doing so it is possible to get the accent at the end in order,
say, to sharpen a warning:

$$\text{It } ^{m\acute{a}y} \text{ not be}\quad ^{t\acute{\imath}me}_{\qquad yet.}$$

is relaxed, but

$$\text{It } ^{m\acute{a}y} \text{ not } ^{y\acute{e}t} \text{ be}\quad ^{t\acute{\imath}}_{\quad m_{e.}}$$

puts the hearer on notice. The climactic effect of the end accent will be
examined more fully in Chapter 6.

The favored, typical, "unmarked" shape of an utterance containing
a theme and a rheme is to have two main accents, thematic and rhematic, one toward the beginning and one toward the end. These terms
can be used even when a given thematic accent is not strictly associated with a theme as such. Thus in the citation form *ónomatopoétic*
there is a "thematic" accent on the first syllable, and in answer to
What size is it? we can say either *Séven by twénty* or *Twénty by séven*,
with thematic and rhematic accents purely positional.

Other Shapes of Utterances: Interior Accents

So much for the "unmarked" shape, but the speaker is still free to
add more accents or even to put the "more important" accent first.
The occasions for doing the latter often involve some grammatical
shift such as putting the rheme ahead of the theme. Suppose a wife
has just been told of something she does not approve of, and she
thinks she knows who is responsible and says

$$\text{(1) I'm gonna } ^{h\acute{a}ve} \text{ to get}\quad ^{\acute{a}f}_{ter\ that}\quad ^{h\acute{u}s}_{band\ of\ mi^{n^{e\cdot}}}$$

Here the "main" accent is clearly in the middle, and reflects the speaker's wish to *do* something about the matter. The fact that the accent on

husband is at a lower pitch, and that the phrase *husband of mine* has a
terminal rise, reflects the thematic status of the last accent: 'husband
of mine' is part of the background. Had the wife said

```
                                       héar
 (2) That  hús
              band of mine is gonna
                                     from me.
```

the theme would be in its more usual place, at the beginning. On the
other hand, if the wife had said

```
                               hús
 (3) I'm gonna  háve to get  áf  ter that
                                           band of mine.
```

she would have been treating the 'doing something about it' as the
theme (as if to imply that her doing something about it is expected of
her) and the husband as the rheme (as if to imply 'You didn't expect
my *husband* to be involved in this').[2] In short, the balance of importance can be shifted and the last accent need not be either the most
important or the most prominent one.

　　As for the freedom to *add* accents, we have already seen examples.
The extra ones are fitted in as ripples on the hat or bridge rather than
as corners or towers:

```
                                                    dú
         ná
 The    tion exﾟécts év'ry mán to dó his
                                               ty.
```

The accents need not be rises, of course (though in a series the last
one almost always is above the reference line):

```
                                                  dú
 The   tion expécts év'ry mán to dó his
       ná                                      ty.
```

(with differences of mood). One would not ordinarily get this many
accents in a single utterance, but when there are fewer (given these
particular words) it is mostly because the meanings of one or more of
the words can be taken for granted. They may contain information already known, or information that can easily be guessed at. And since
accenting so many words is rather difficult to do in fluent speech, the
speaker readily adopts strategies that will excuse him from accenting
any more than he has to. A more usual form of the last example
would be

```
                                          év'ry man to do his
            ná                                               dú
   The      tion expects
                                                               ty.
```

in which only *nation, every,* and *duty* are accented. (The intonation
shifts the reference line upward in the last half of the sentence.) Du-
ties are done, so there is no need to accent *do*; and both *expect* and
man are highly predictable (hence unnewsworthy) in any context in
which this sort of sentence is apt to be uttered.

Even when some of the content words are quite informative, the
speaker is free to suppress accents if doing so fits the overall strategy
of the utterance. Givón has shown (1983) that the theme of a sentence
is the part that is easiest to reduce or even omit because it so often
expresses what we already know or can "get at" without much effort.
In commands we ordinarily omit *you* because it is clear that they are
addressed to 'you,' and themes have a greater tendency to be represented by such light elements as pronouns and inflections rather than
heavier and more explicit ones. The thematic accent is similarly subject to reduction. A speaker in the middle of a conversation has no
need to use an accent whose main function may be to imply, 'Pay attention! I'm transmitting to you!' The affective result of deaccenting
the theme is a lower degree of insistence, a greater casualness. So if
you say *I wish everybody wouldn't get irked at me all the time,* I can reply,
mildly, perhaps with a chuckle,

```
                              bóth
       Then don't go around        ering people!
```

with no pitch accent except the rhematic one on *bothering.* This same
suppression of the thematic accent is common in wh questions. You
say *John doesn't like it* and I respond with casual interest, *Why nót?,*
accenting only *not.* An eavesdropper who breaks into the conversation would say *Whý nót?*

Alongside the suppression of some of the accents we find the ma-
nipulation of others as a way of taking some of the strain off the vocal
organs. Producing an accent is a maneuver that calls for extra effort,
and the phonetic material that our choice of words delivers to the vocal mechanism is not always as propitious as it might be for forming
an accent. An example is the word *expects* in the sentence cited above.
The stressed syllable *-pects* ends in a cluster of three voiceless consonants which produce a quick shutoff of the vowel, in spite of the advantage that *-pects* would otherwise have by virtue of the lengthening
rule. The accent is supposed to go up and then down (or down and
then up), but there is not much leeway, and that may be one reason
why we prefer to ignore the accent on that word. But if another word

that normally does not carry an accent intervenes, it can serve as a foil; for example,

—the word *us* takes the downmotion that would otherwise have to go on *-pects*, and the maneuver can be carried out easily. The same is true (as we saw in Chapter 2, pp. 22–23) when the accented syllable contains sounds that are more easily prolonged, as in

where the second syllable of *requires* contains only voiced sounds.

The broad-gauge effect of this spacing out is a kind of mutual repulsion among the accents starting with the two main ones. Obviously if the tendency is to have the first one toward the beginning and the last one toward the end, that puts them as far apart as they can get. The principle is to make the best use of the space available, and here the space is the greater part of the utterance. At the level of the main accents the lesser ones do not count.

The narrow-gauge effect is to produce a kind of rhythm that seems to take on an existence of its own. If getting the accents where we want them calls for special arrangements like those we have described, then it is an advantage to have some ready-made scheme for fitting words together so as to have a few loose syllables in strategic places, and even for doctoring an occasional word so as to pry a loose syllable out of it.

How Loose Syllables Are Provided

Getting loose syllables where they are needed is not a trivial problem. It affects our choice of words and has permanent effects on the morphology and syntax of the language. A striking morphological effect is the backshifting of stress on nouns, most notably manifested in male given names, which have almost universally backshifted: *Théodore, Ábsalom, Mánfred, Rúdolph, Álbert, Áugust, Dávid*. A given name precedes a surname, and this pattern allows for buffer syllables between the accents. The preference for it can be seen in a name that still wavers, *Sinclair*. The preferred British pronunciation is *Sínclair* and the preferred American is *Sincláir* when the word is a surname (according to Kenyon and Knott 1953), yet when Americans make it a

given name, as in *Sinclair Lewis*, they usually stress the first syllable—
even when another stressed word does not immediately follow: *What
was Lewis's first name? — Sínclair.*

Where the language offers a choice between words that have approximately the same meaning, a speaker may unconsciously pick the
one that has a buffer syllable in the right place. An attested example is
I had to do the luncheon dishes, from a person who might have said *I had
to do the dishes from lunch* but would not have said **I had to do the lunch
dishes.*

Unlike nouns, verbs are not at a disadvantage if they have a terminal stress. They occur mostly toward the end of the sentence (see Appendix A, p. 351), often at the very end where the pitch turn can be
accommodated by a pause; and if not at the end, there is often an unaccented pronoun object following. So we sense a kind of spirited
verbness about a terminal accent.

Like nouns, adjectives favor stress before the end and usually
achieve it by the addition of unstressed suffixes: love*ly*, lis*som*, mush*y*,
work*able*, brok*en*, fruit*ful*, dar*ing*, care*less*—besides many borrowed
from Latin—poli*tic*, fat*al*, graci*ous*, pass*ive*. But where this tendency
in adjectives shows to greatest advantage is in the way the comparative and superlative degrees of adjectives are formed. The process is
half morphological (with *-er* and *-est*) and half syntactic (with *more*
and *most*): *wise, wiser, wisest,* but *intelligent, more intelligent, most intelligent.* English is an *analytical* language—it has lost most of the inflections on verbs, all of those on nouns except the plural, and all of those
on adjectives except *-er* and *-est*, and even these are confined to the
very common, mostly one-syllable, adjectives. Unlike the plural of
nouns, for which there is no readily usable substitute, the comparative and superlative could easily be handled with *more* and *most*, and
in fact we do use these analytical forms not only for the longer but
also for the less frequent adjectives (*plainer* but not **roaner, handsomer*
but not **gruesomer, narrower* but not **thorougher, lovelier* but not **poor-
lier*). So why have we kept the *-er* and *-est* suffixes—and in this rather
messy way, reflecting not only length but frequency, both of which
are relative? Just such an effect is predictable if we look at how serious
the rhythmic clash would be if the suffixes were not available. The
commonest position for an adjective is before its noun. The most frequent nouns in English are monosyllables (which are stressed by definition), and many of the polysyllables begin with a stressed syllable.
Forced to rely on *more* and *most* we would have to say things like *the
móst óld mán, the móre táll buílding, the móst déep ríver, the móre gréat
writer.* The *-er* and *-est* suffixes give a buffer syllable to help break up
those successive accents. We don't *have* to have them—there are other

ways of easing the clash—but it is most *useful* to have them precisely where we find them, with adjectives that are relatively short and relatively frequent. They are not needed in *a most informal occasion*, and an adjective such as *wan* occurs too seldom to make it worthwhile to retain *wanner* against the general tendency to regularize with *more*.

Syntax, too, is affected. One of the ways is the position and use of the indefinite article. People say things like *get a hold* of something rather than *get hold* of it. When the adverb *too* would give the unacceptable **It's a too abstract notion* we can move the article and get the normal *It's too abstract a notion*. The interrogative *how* as a degree adverb can be used in sentences like *How good a teacher is she?* and similarly *that* in *She's not that good a teacher*. But the plural is ruled out: **How good teachers are they?*, **They're not that good teachers*. Similarly with *as*: *Is John as old a man as Henry?*, **Are John and Henry as old men as Joe and Larry?* The article is a buffer in the singular, and some speakers go a step further and insert a fanciful *of* along with the article: *How good of a teacher is she?* This same *of* (or *'ve, have*) is used after the pluperfect *had* when it is accented next to *been*, in substandard speech: "I can't think somehow that Gandalf would have sent Mr. Frodo on this errand, if there *hadn't a' been* any hope of his ever coming back at all."[3]

In one instance the avoidance of successive accents makes it impossible to use a fairly common figure of speech when the words of our choice do not oblige by having their syllables arranged suitably. We can say *a not unusual (surprising, unexpected, extraordinary) result*, but we are not likely to say **a not strange result*, though we can avoid the conflict by inserting a qualifying phrase: *a not, shall we say, strange result* (see Bolinger 1980). Shifting the article accomplishes the same, but the meaning changes: *not a strange result*.

A further instance is the blocking of an auxiliary verb in precisely the construction where it would result in successive accents. We may say *Ought he do it?* or *He ought not do it* as alternatives to the same construction with *ought to*. But we cannot say **He ought do it*.

The Hat Pattern Within Words: "Secondary" Accents

The mutual repulsion that we speak of in macrocosm is that between the main accents; in microcosm it occurs between adjoining accents, and that—given the severely reduced space between them—is where one often needs the special means to separate them so that realizing a following accent will not interfere with realizing a preceding one.

One can illustrate by turning the microcosm into a macrocosm. Almost any content-bearing phrase can under some conditions serve as a complete utterance from which the theme has been omitted, and most noun phrases easily function in this way. If you ask *Who did it?* I do not need to say *The one who did it* [theme] *was John* [rheme]; I can answer simply with *John*. And if you ask *Where did he go?* I can abbreviate *He went* [theme] *to Cleveland* [rheme] to just *Cleveland*.

Here is where the melodic pattern of the utterance as a whole, which serves the separate needs of theme and rheme but is used over and over to the point of fixation in the hat or suspension pattern, asserts itself. If you ask me *What kind of figure of speech was it?* and I reply *Onomatopoetic*, my reply will probably sound this way:

```
              ét
  ón
      omatopo  ic.
```

—the full pattern exhibited on a single word, with the thematic accent on the initial syllable and the rhematic on the next-to-last. In our microcosm-turned-macrocosm, the thematic accent is the "secondary" accent, regularly occurring (when it occurs at all) on the first full syllable in the word unless that syllable is stressed, in which case there is no secondary (i.e., the secondary must precede the primary; see Appendix A, pp. 350, 356). The first full syllable need not of course be the initial syllable:

```
        á                        zá
Com^mis er ti_on.        Col^léc tivi ti_on.
```

If there are variant pronunciations, the rule still applies. A speaker saying *academician* as a citation form may hesitate between two pronunciations:

```
      mí                        mí
A^cá de ci_an.            Ác ade ci_an.
```

The first probably gets its secondary accent by analogy with *acádemy*, the second by analogy with *ácadémic*.

Most dictionaries mark a secondary accent (despite the fact that it is predictable if we know the nature of the vowel), and its location is usually termed SECONDARY STRESS, a term that we shall use to avoid circumlocution, contrasting it to (PRIMARY) STRESS. There is no need for a special symbol, since we know that the secondary comes before the primary, and the same mark will be used for both: *régularizátion*.

"Before the primary" calls first for locating the primary. It is the syllable that receives the rhematic accent in the citation form of the word: *onomatopoétic, regularizátion, amanuénsis, routíne*. When reference is made to "the" stress of a word, this is the one intended. In English its location is not entirely predictable from other formal characteristics of the word, though there are ways of making some pretty reliable guesses (in *-ation* words the stress will be *-átion*, adding *-dom* or *-ly* to a word stem will not change the stress of the stem, etc.).

The secondary stress, as explained above, is the syllable carrying the thematic accent in the citation form of the word. It normally falls on the first full syllable in the word when that syllable does not itself carry the primary, as explained above. In a word such as *ánalog* there is no secondary stress—the primary occurs on the first syllable and leaves no room for a secondary. In one like *perímeter* there is also no secondary—only one syllable comes before the primary and it contains a reduced vowel. But in *cálisthénics*, *détestátion*, and *procrástinátion* there are secondaries on the first full syllable, since the primary follows. As the examples show, there may be a reduced syllable preceding the secondary (*procrástinátion* for speakers who say [prə]) or an additional full syllable between secondary and primary (*détestátion*, with [tɛs]). In fact, there is no theoretical limit to the number of syllables, whether full or reduced, that may come between the secondary and the primary: *ántiphlogístine*, *írremediabílity*, *ródomontáde*, *gástroenterítis*. When a word has a variable secondary, as we saw with *academician*, the syllables are also variable, in such a way that the rule for the location of the secondary still generally holds: in *ácademícian* the second syllable is reduced, [kə]; in *acádemícian* the first syllable is reduced, [ə]; neither can therefore be accented. In *confábulátion* the first syllable is reduced, [kən], and cannot be accented; in *cónfabulátion* the syllable [fæ] is still full but the full syllable [kan] takes the honors because it comes first.

Not all words behave in this precisely regular manner. A few—mostly those with prefixes that have an obvious meaning of their own—allow the secondary to fall either on the prefix or on the syllable that would receive it if no prefix were present. The speaker may then choose more or less freely, but the choice is apt to be constrained by rhythmic regularity. For example, the word *reconstitution* may have its secondary on *re-* or on *-con-*. In an utterance like *The / réconsti/tútion was / scárcely com/pléte*, putting the secondary on *re-* produces a regular series of dactyls. Putting it on *-con-* in *The re/cónsti/tútion was / íncom/pléte* makes a better match with *incomplete*, which favors a trochaic rhythm. More discussion of this will follow.

Though to conform to the hat pattern the secondary and primary are the principal accents, any interior full syllable (before the primary) can be accented, just as it can be in a longer phrase. So a word such as *tintinnabulation* may take the shape

$$lá$$
tín
tin$^{\text{náb}}_{\text{u}}$
tion

with a minor prominence on -*nab*-. Emphatic speech tends to bring out the additional accents.

There remains the question of words in which the first full syllable is not separated from the syllable that carries the primary, for example *routíne, Chínése, órnáte*. It is sometimes argued that such words have no secondary, and it is true that the nearness of the primary deafens us to the prominence of the secondary; this has consequences in the evolution of words, since a full syllable in that position tends to be reduced eventually (see Appendix A, pp. 353–54).[4] But to avoid the problem by saying that the secondary stress (defined as a potential for accent in that position) "falls on the first full syllable in the word that is separated by at least one syllable from the primary" both makes the rule more complicated and fails to account for the fact that there is always the choice of accenting, for emphasis, any full syllable before the primary. An emphatic way of saying *Chinese* is as marked above, *Chínése*.[5] The same goes for a full syllable abutting what would otherwise be a sole secondary: we do not have to choose between *recónstitútion* and *reconstitútion* but may say, with emphasis, *recónstitútion*. Furthermore we need to retain a potential for accent on an unseparated secondary to account for the shift in prominence from primary to secondary in phrases. Examples include *Chínese chéckers, routíne óffer, órnate bálcony*, and more are given below. So we keep the rule in its simpler form.

Relative Prominence of Primary and Secondary

One other point regarding secondary ACCENTS (not secondary STRESS as a mere potential) is their prominence relative to the primary. It is generally claimed (e.g. Schane 1979: 589) that primary accents, that is, accents at the position of the primary stress, are more prominent, and this belief is sanctified in the other names that are often given to the primary accent: nucleus, intonation center, "sentence stress." As the chief accent in the rheme, the primary shares in the importance of the rheme (as we saw earlier, the theme is often simply omitted), and this gives it a psychological impact that the theme lacks, to which we can add the effect of climax (see the next chapter), which affects the primary especially. But the main reason for our impression of greater prominence in the primary accent is the fact that we implicitly appeal to the citation form of the word—as in the examples above—where the primary accent has a higher peak than the second-ary. This is because (see Appendix A, p. 356) the citation form of a word is an utterance in itself, answering a question about the word and using the intonation typical of answers to questions, e.g., answering the question *Where did you go?*—

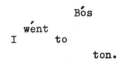

We could of course say

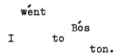

with the first peak higher than the second, but that might risk offense—it could be taken to imply 'What business is it of yours?' The former shape is the normal one to answer questions like *What word did you say?* or *How do you say this word?*—

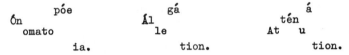

If the primary stress comes earlier, as described above, the primary accent will be the only one:

Ám

bulatory.

Cád

wallader.

This is the same as

Bós

ton was where I went.

—which is to say that the ends of such words are deaccented in the same way as the "old stuff" in a complete utterance. By this theory, if what marks the word as a center of attention is the accent it carries, then, by analogic fixation of the pattern, *within* the word the accented syllable is the microcosmic center of attention and the rest of the frame is fitted around that syllable, with following syllables deaccented just as following words in a sentence are deaccented.

But once we leave the domain of citation forms, relative prominence of primary and secondary accents becomes an open question. If I ask *What do you call those things that are just unsupported assertions?* you will normally reply with the citation form

```
              gá
         Âl
            le
                tions.
```

On the other hand, if I report hearsay reflecting on your character, you are more apt to say

```
         Âl
                 gá
              le
                  tions!
```

implying 'That's all they are!' Now it is the secondary that is more prominent (barring the addition of extra intensity on -*ga*-, which is possible but certainly not required). Similarly the citation form of *absolutely* is

```
                 lúte
         Âb
            so
                   ly.
```

But if I say something to which you want to give unconditional assent, you are just as apt to say

```
         Âb
             lúte
            so
                  ly!
```

Like the 'That's all they are' of allegations, this implies 'That's all there is to it, no more need be said.' This is a speaker-oriented intonation (see Bolinger 1972: 149, n. 8), an intonation of fiat rather than appeal.

Choosing Which Syllable to Accent

The secondary accent may thus outrank the primary in prominence. The effect where secondary STRESS is concerned is that it should rank as the equal of the primary under many conditions. This rather different view of secondary stress puts us in a better position to understand the so-called "shifts" of stress. If the secondary has about equal claim to prominence, nothing is lost, as far as accenting a word is concerned, if the secondary picks up the accent on that word *in the utterance*, with the primary getting no accent (or a reduced accent). It is not a matter of "shifting" the stress, since the stress, as a potential for accent, is already there; it is rather the *choice* of the secondary over the primary in a situation where some intonational advantage accrues.[6]

Three advantages follow from being able to choose the secondary over the primary. First is the simple separation of accents, which makes it possible to execute the pitch turn easily:

```
      ór      bál
        nate
              cony
```

If the accent on *ornate* is placed on the primary-stressed rather than the secondary-stressed syllable, the result is a difficult pitch turn on a syllable clipped short by a terminal consonant:

```
       ná     bál
     or   te
              cony
```

Second is the wider separation of theme and rheme, with their left-ward and rightward push respectively where accent is concerned. If *ornate* is thematic, it tends to be *órnate*:

```
                              wánt
    ór
       nate is  some thing I don't      it to be.
```

If rhematic, the tendency is toward *ornáte*:

```
                              ná
           wánt
   I don't       it to be so or
                              te.
```

Third is the advantage of evening up the rhythm:

The / néw one is / nót as or/náte as the / óld.
To / máke it as / órnate as / thát would be / bád.

Picking one or the other location for the accent in *ornate* makes it possible in both utterances to keep an even dactylic rhythm. Rhythmic regularity is something that speakers unconsciously strive for, though it seldom turns out so neatly as in these examples. And one can go against any of the trends outlined here without being judged "incorrect."

The three advantages will be taken up in turn.

1. Separation of accents. Avoiding an accentual clash—two accented syllables side by side—is the simplest case and has been thoroughly discussed in the literature on accent in English and other languages. The word *overséas*, for example (see Appendix A, pp. 350–51), has its primary stress on the last syllable and its secondary on the first. This means that in a phrase like *overseas voyage* there would be a clash if the primary were chosen for the accent, because the primary (and only) stress of *voyage* immediately follows. So we are allowed to choose the

secondary as the only syllable of *overseas* to be accented: an *óverseas vóyage*. Other examples:

the ínside tráck	the tráck insíde
a clóse-up víew	to sée close-úp
the áustere méasures	They're tóo austére.
thírteen chápters	chápter thirtéen
an írate cítizen	The mán was iráte.
an ídeal mátch	The mátch is idéal.
the cánteen cóok	He cóoks in the cantéen.
a néarby stóre	The stóre's nearbý.
an óbsolete wórd	The wórd's obsoléte.
I'll lámbaste Jóhn.	Jóhn I'll lambáste.

2. Thematic-rhematic repulsion. There is no clear dividing line between this phenomenon and the preceding one, just as there is none between that and the hat pattern applied to citation forms. If we answer *Who did it?* with *The cánteen cóok*, there is a good likelihood that we have already been talking about the canteen, which makes it the theme, and in any case the word *cook* supplies the main "point" of the rheme; so whether the separation is on the accentual or the thematic scale, the result is the same. The main difference is that accentual separation is satisfied with just one buffer syllable between accents. Thus *ímitation wálnut* could, as far as mere separation of accents is concerned, just as well be *imitátion wálnut*, since the syllable *-tion* would still divide *-ta-* from *wal-*. But the phrase as a whole calls for putting the secondary accent on the first full syllable (as if *imitation walnut* were a single word with primary stress on *wal-*), which in this case happens to be the secondary, not the primary, in the word *imitation*. The outcome is the same as if *imitation* were theme and *walnut* were rheme, even if the chief motive is only to separate the accents with a little extra buffer material. Other examples:

ácademic díscipline	thíngs académic
índirect líghting	You're tóo indiréct.
cóntraceptive píll	Trý contracéptives.

If the word is long enough to space out the primary and secondary stresses, it can easily happen—especially in careful or emphatic speech—that both accents will be retained:

an ímperféctive vérb	The vérb is ímperféctive.
a cóntracéptive píll	Táke a cóntracéptive.
óverindúlgent párents	The párents are óverindúlgent.

One finds this also in unusual words, which speakers tend to produce with care. Compare the fairly common word *diametric*, in a phrase such as *díametric méasure*, with the uncommon word *diapasonal*, in *díapásonal sóunds.* And *diametric* in the neutral context just cited can be contrasted with *diametric* in the emphatic context *She's the díamétric ópposite!*

3. Rhythm. Here the flexibility of accenting now this and now that syllable in a word comes into play in those longer utterances where stretches of several syllables can be grouped into accentual beats. The longer the utterance, the greater become the possibilities of suppressing this or that accent, not only because fewer accents mean less work but because the typical long speech is apt to be an argument or a narrative of some kind in which a number of secondary ideas are grouped around only a few central points, and deaccenting certain words is the way we show that they are taken for granted.

So we get a tendency not only to space out the accents but to do it more or less rhythmically. One can see here an analogy with breathing: it may be consciously controlled as when a diver holds his breath, or controlled by some other conscious act as when one takes breaths at pause points in a song, but most of the time, when our attention is elsewhere, it is relegated to a succession of more or less regular inhalations and exhalations which is fast or slow depending on the need for oxygen. Phased automatic activities are most efficient when they recur at regular intervals. This has deep roots in human physiology. A child from the day of birth is observed to phonate in rhythmically regular patterns, and speech rhythms are very likely grafted onto them as the child matures (Fridman 1980). "Infants from the first moment of life and even in the womb are getting the rhythm and structure and style of sound, the rhythm of their culture, so that they imprint to them and the rhythms become part of their very being" (Condon 1982: 66 quoted in von Raffler-Engel 1983: 303). "All behavior is a pattern in time: it cannot be random sequences because the observed versatility would require us to postulate memory capacities of a magnitude that is totally inconceivable. The only thing that distinguishes temporal *patterns* from temporal *randomness* is the existence of an underlying rhythm in the former and its absence in the latter. This, then, is a further reason for expecting the existence of rhythms in behavior." (Lenneberg 1971: 178–79.)

Syllabic Rhythm

The rhythmic patterns that concern us come in two layers, one based on syllabic structure, the other on accents. In the first, or SYL-LABIC, rhythm, what determines the "foot structure," as we saw in the last chapter, is the presence of a full syllable with its following reduced syllable or syllables if any. In the second, or ACCENTUAL, rhythm, it is the accented syllable plus its following unaccented ones. Though as we saw in Chapter 4 the syllabic rhythm has developed in a way that will support the accents (by providing room for the pitch turn), in speech the two schemes, syllabic rhythm and accentual rhythm, are independent. We can illustrate syllabic rhythm by speaking in a monotone and with even volume, to note the metrical structure that is still there. In the following, there is a successive increase in length of feet, but each utterance is isochronic, that is, all the feet (except the last) are of equal length:

> Let's / take / time / right / now.
> Let him / check the / timer / right a/way.
> Let him re/pay us the / time that he / rightfully / owes.
> Leave it as a / token of a / laughable re/spectfulness for / law.

One can also test the rhythmic shock of an abrupt change in the length of feet. In the following (still to be spoken on a monotone), the utterance starts with two-, three-, or four-syllable feet, and ends with one-syllable feet:

> Let him / check the / time / right / now.
> Let it be / tinted an / off-/white / gray.
> Leave it as a / token of an / out/right / fraud.

The independence of syllabic from accentual rhythm is best appreciated in utterances where some of the words for whatever reason have been deaccented. (See Chapter 7 for deaccenting.) Such a word, and by extension its parts, counts the same, accentually, as an unstressed syllable or syllables—if it occurs in the right place it will provide room for the intonation turn and no backshifting will be required. In the example

$$\text{wây}$$
$$\text{gót}$$
$$\text{You} \quad \text{ta} \quad \text{pút} \quad \text{a}$$
$$\text{junk like this.}$$

(which might be completed with *you can't just let it lie around*) the phrasal verb *put away* is able to accommodate the accent on *-way* because *junk* is deaccented. The reverse situation would be an utterance like

$$\text{jú}$$
$$\text{I'm} \quad \text{pútting} \quad \text{away}$$
$$\text{nk.}$$

in answer to *What are you doing?*—the accent on *put away* has now shifted to the secondary stress on *put* because *junk* is not deaccented and cannot serve as a foil for something else. In the former example, *junk like this* is monobeat as far as syllabic rhythm is concerned, because all three syllables are full, but accentually it is only an intonational tail for *awáy*.

The several types of rhythmic feet are manifested both syllabically and accentually. We look first at their syllabic manifestations.

Successive syllabic MONOBEATS depend on the rare type of succession in which there are no reduced syllables: *Pa made John tell who fired those guns*. For obvious reasons—the difficulty of even finding words to build such a sequence—the speaker will be suspected of arranging things deliberately.

Successive syllabic TROCHEES fare somewhat better but are still apt to be noticed: *I had to make an effort just to get a breath of air, He wants to ask you both the sort of thing you did before*. In each of these, regardless of the pitch accents, there is a definite beat determined by the alternating full and reduced syllables.

By the time we reach DACTYLS, a regular syllabic rhythm seems hardly strange at all: *He wanted to give them a piece of his mind*. There are of course fewer dactyls for a given number of syllables than of monobeats or trochees, which makes the dactylic rhythm less insistent, and that is probably one reason for its greater acceptability to our ear. Dactyls are ideal for the placing of accents, providing two reduced syllables to take the pitch turn after each potential accent.

Accentual Rhythm and Isochrony

We come now to accentual rhythm and its interaction with syllabic. The main difference between the two is that syllabic rhythm is structurally determined (by the arrangement of full and reduced syllables), whereas accentual rhythm is partly determined by, and must always adjust itself to, the accentual highlighting that the speaker imposes for the sake of his meaning. Since we imagine a meaning for everything we say, even the monotone examples cited to illustrate syllabic rhythm are "heard" with an accentual beat: *He wánted to gíve them a píece of his mínd*—the full syllables compel us to imagine accents on them, even though we know that in some contexts such a sentence might have only one accent, e.g. in answer to *Why did he give them a piece of his mind?*:

```
            wånt
    He
              ed to give them a piece of his mind.
```

The problem of course is that a sentence cannot be *uttered* without accents, and lacking pitch cues for them we fall back on other cues such as pitch and intensity. In fact, we probably impose, mentally, a pitch contour that would be appropriate to the context, especially if one can be used that is already of high frequency. Imagine that the example just quoted comes as a response to *What made him speak up like that?* The monotone would be normal at a low pitch and would come across as something like

He ᵂᵃ́ⁿᵗₑd to ᵍⁱᵛᵉ them a ᵖⁱᵉᶜᵉ of his ᵐⁱ́ₙd.

with each "content" word receiving a slight boost. It would not be heard as the version in which *want-* is the only thing obtruded. The monotone version could not be used to answer the other question, *Why did he give them a piece of his mind?*

But what we are interested in is what happens when pitch cues are actually present—and how the syllabic rhythms are manipulated by accentual rhythms.

The simplest case is that of concurrent syllabic and accentual rhythm: every full syllable gets an accent. With extended MONOBEATS this happens only in the sort of very emphatic speech that highlights every syllable: *Pá máde Jóhn téll whó fíred thóse gúns* (with a pitch excursion on every word). This sort of emphasis permits the speaker to replace reduced syllables with full ones so as to make them accentable: *Yóu táke thóse cháirs ánd sét thém dówn!*—here the usual [n̩] for *and* and [əm] for *them* are replaced with [ænd] and [ðɛm]. Concurrent TROCHEES are an invitation to scansion—fine for a poet but usually undesirable in prose: *I hád to máke an éffort júst to gét a bréath of áir.* The appearance of some kind of jingle is such that the speaker is apt to abort the succession before it carries him too far—perhaps by pausing after *effort* or by changing his already programmed *a breath of* to *some.*[7] Concurrent DACTYLS are less noticeable, for reasons given above.

These extreme cases do not describe the usual state of affairs, in which accentual rhythm diverges from syllabic. In one situation the divergence is compulsory: accents are normally only one per word, whereas any syllable can be full: *Sámpan hárdtack tástes like héll* has seven syllabic beats but only four accentual ones. An additional accent could be put on *like*, but none on *-pan* or *-tack* (except under the most extreme emphasis). Further, accentual rhythm counts syllables without regard for whether they are full or reduced. In *Sámpans are éasy to návigate, sír* the first dactyl has (after the accent) full *-pan* and reduced *are* [r̩], the second has reduced *-sy* and reduced *to* [tə], and the third has reduced *-i-* and full *-gate*. We thus have a regular accentual rhythm laid on an irregular syllabic one. Still further, a given set of regular syllabic feet may have more than one realization of regular accentual feet. The sentence *How John writes might seem too trite,* syl-

labically monobeat, may be accentually trochee in two different ways
(discounting the first or the last syllable):

> Hów John wrítes might séem too tríte.
> How Jóhn writes míght seem tóo trite.

The two versions respond to two different contexts.

But this degree of regularity at either level is still exceptional. For
the most part we find, at the syllabic level, the sort of mixture described on pages 41–42 made up of stressed monosyllables (e.g. *house*),
unstressed monosyllables (the personal pronouns, conjunctions, prepositions, etc. in their usual form), and polysyllables with varying patterns of stress. And at the accentual level the beats are at the mercy of
a throng of highlighted ideas that highlight their respective words in a
catch-as-catch-can of syntax. In any given utterance a regular accentual beat may be entirely lacking.

All the same, we do find a mild tendency toward accentual isochrony, perhaps favoring dactylic or slightly longer feet and taking
advantage of the flexibility of many polysyllables to adjust the length
of feet to that crude norm. Except in very slow or emphatic speech—
as we have already seen—or occasionally when a prefix gets a separate accent (e.g. *the prénátal examinátion*), a word in running discourse
gets at most one accent, and if there happens to be a secondary stress
the speaker has a certain play in fitting the accent to the rhythm.

We can illustrate with three sentences in which the words *counteract*
and *interfere* are differently affected:

> They were dóing it to counteráct the imprecísion of the vóte.
> They were dóing it to counteráct the interféring acceclerátion.
> They were dóing it to cóunteract the ínterfering fórce.

In the first sentence, *counteract* is under no pressure to choose the syllable *coun-* rather than *-act*. The first accentual foot technically has six
syllables but the function word *to* is cliticized to the verb—*doing it
t'counteract*—so in effect there are five syllables, followed by two feet
of four syllables each—5-4-4, not a bad match. In the second sentence
the same thing happens except that now the numbers are 5-4-5, still a
good sequence. But in the third, if one were to say *interféring fórce* the
third foot would have only two syllables, and then if the accent were
kept on the last syllable of *counteract* the result would be a succession
of 5-4-2: **They were / dóing it t'counter/áct the inter/féring / fórce*. To correct this, the speaker will probably take the first syllable of *interfering*
for the accent so as to get *ínterfering fórce*, and that in turn leads to
choosing the first syllable of *counteract* so as to get *cóunteract the ínterfering*. The result is the more nearly isochronous *They were / dóing it*

t'/cóunteract the / ínterfering / fórce, with 3-4-4 (or, with poetic license to count *to*, the even better 4-4-4).

Pressures from Right and Left

The backshiftings in the last example represent the domino effect noted by Thompson (1980: 116) in his example *Sán Francisco Gólden Gate Brídge*, where adjustments seem to be made from right to left: the main accent on *Bridge* is inviolable, and leads to choosing the secondary stress rather than the primary in *Golden Gate*, which in turn has the same effect on *San Francisco*. But more than mere separation of accents is involved. If that were the only adjustment needed, *San Francísco* could remain intact, since the accent on *-cis-* would still have *-co* as a buffer between it and the accent on *Gold-*. What we witness here is a pull from the left as well as a push from the right—the tendency to get the *utterance* secondary, the thematic accent, as far up front as possible, on the syllable *San*. Plus, of course, the rhythm: with *Sán Francisco / Gólden Gate* we get a 4-3 succession and at the same time satisfy both the separation of accents and the favored hat pattern of initial and final major accents, thematic and rhematic, on *San* and *Bridge*. On this latter point, a similar example is cited by the Merriam *Third New International Dictionary* (45a): *Bénefícial though it ís*, with *ben-* accented rather than the (primary-)stressed syllable *-fi-*, despite the fact that there are no fewer than three buffer syllables between *-fi-* and *is*.

It is also possible to demonstrate a force operating from the left in the *interior* of the utterance to compel a separation of accents and a better rhythmic succession. The sentence *The óne respónsible was his íllegitimate són* is fairly well balanced with its 2-5-5: the secondary stress is preferred to the primary on *illegitimate*—using the primary on *-gi-* would yield 2-7-3, an awkward succession. But if the word *own* is inserted to the left of *illegitimate*, the best choice is the primary: *The óne respónsible was his ówn illegítimate són*, 2-5-3-3. To retain *íllegitimate* would result in a 2-5-1-5 sequence. Some other examples of pressure from the left:

a hórizontal béam	a stráight horizóntal béam
the Pénnsylvania Ráilroad	the máin Pennsylvánia ráilroad
a cóunteroffensive móve	a nóncounteroffénsive móve
ábsolute jurisdíction	It conférs absolúte jurisdíction.

In the last pair, if *jurisdiction* is replaced with *power* the effect is to return the accent to the first syllable of *absolute*—*It conférs ábsolute pówer*—in spite of the succession *-férs áb-*. *It conférs absolúte pówer*, with its -*lúte pów*-, is worse. The stronger pressure seems to come from the right.

The strength of that pressure—the need we seem to feel to give a clear field to the rightmost accent—can be seen in the possibility of making a secondary out of a syllable that in the citation form of the word cárries a reduced vowel: a syllable can be chosen for the accent that did not bear a secondary stress in the first place. But the words in which this happens are a rather special class: for some speakers or on some occasions the syllable in question may have a full vowel. The oddity is that the speakers who do not ordinarily put a full vowel there still have the option of choosing that syllable for the accent (substituting a full vowel for their customary reduced one), as if they were selecting a feature that is not part of their own dialect but is probably something they recognize as in common use or remember having heard. Take the words *contrite, compact, obscene, contrary, complex* (adjective), *cannot,* and *mustache.* In all of these some speakers (or some styles) will use shwa as the vowel in the first syllable. This contrasts with such words as *bamboo, almost, recharge,* and *Osage,* which have only full vowels in their first syllables: [æ ɔ i o]. The latter can of course pick the secondary stress (on their first full syllable) for the accent: *bámboo cúrtain, álmost thére, récharged báttery, Ósage órange.* By rights the former—for the shwa-users—should not be able to, and yet they are: *a cóntrite héart, a cómpact cár, a cóntrary móod, a cómplex théorem, I cánnot gó* (compare *Gó I cannót*), *a mústache dýe-job.* Though *complex* with shwa in its first syllable compares with *complete* in sentences like *It's quíte compléx* and *It's quíte compléte, complete* follows the norm and accents only its second syllable, whereas *complex* permits the initial syllable to take over: *a compléte ídiot, a cómplex ídiom.* Similarly *obscure* follows the norm and thus contrasts with *obscene*: *an obscúre fílm, an óbscene fílm.*

The conclusion has to be that Jassem (1980: 9) is correct in saying that "In English, rhythm is . . . only tendentially, and not absolutely, present," and this raises the question of how strong the tendency is. A speaker catches himself saying *I séldom am áble to gó back to sléep* and wonders why he has said *I am* instead of the generally more colloquial *I'm*; on thinking it over he realizes that *I'm séldom áble to gó back to sléep* breaks the regularity of the dactyls. Nothing is lost here by using the regular rhythm. When a speaker garbles the syllables in an utterance, the error is apt to make the rhythm better; the following are among the examples cited by Cutler (1980):

what the spéaker thinks his ínterlocker knóws (interlocutor)
can nót be aprópally intérpreted (appropriately).

But generally, if accentual rhythm is mainly just an accommodation of the speech mechanism, then one expects it to yield to other parts of the prosody whenever the latter might conflict—from the nature of individual words to the overall buildup of the utterance.

Forces Opposing Isochrony

For the nature of individual words, we find instances of relative semantic colorlessness and relative richness that lead to emphasizing the latter by not suppressing any accents—Chapter 6 will show how far this can be carried in actually *adding* accents. A highly colorful word will keep an accent on the primary even if the result is juxtaposed accents—or actually in order to *create* a juxtaposition with its jarring effect. So whereas *éxtreme únction* is a possibility as a colorless technical term, there is no moving the accent in *extréme súffering*. Similarly, whereas a news report of the action of a board of censors might give the matter-of-fact *They were cóunting the atténdance at an óbscene pláy*, a moralizing citizen is more apt to say *It's a térribly obscéne pláy*. We would predict that a word such as *extraordinary*, given its meaning, would probably not yield the dispassionate **an éxtraordinary háppening*. And we would also predict that if a word has both a literal and a hyperbolic meaning, the latter would tend to keep an accent on the primary stress, as in *They gásped as they exámined his astronómical búdget* contrasted with *The astrónomer's táble was cóvered with his ástronomical gádgetry*. Likewise with the two senses of *comprehensive* in *Our service offers várious sorts of cómprehensive tésts* as against *It's a térribly compréhensive tést*. The matter-of-fact *a réady-made spéech* contrasts with the colorful *an órotúnd spéech*, where *orotund* accents both stresses. Similarly in *her óverwhélmed sénses* versus *an óverturned trúck*. There is an intonational peculiarity in these phrases that will be dealt with in Chapter 12—see especially pages 294–95—namely the tendency to say

in contrast with

From these fairly obvious cases we can turn to others that are more tenuous. Take the two verbs *understand* and *comprehend*, which, besides being synonyms, have the same stress pattern. Of the two, *understand* is the more colloquial and less colorful. We readily use it without the auxiliary in a question such as *Understand why?* ('Do you understand why?'), which would be unusual with *comprehend*. Its relatively neutral meaning shows up in the derived noun *understanding*, which—though it shares with *comprehension* contexts such as *It passes my understanding (comprehension)*—allows contexts like *The understanding was that. . . .* So it is not surprising that *understand* bypasses the primary stress in a sentence like *Do you únderstand whý?*, whereas *comprehend* is less likely to do so: *Do you cómprehénd whý?* This in spite of the fact that *-hend* is a lighter syllable than *-stand* (*-stand* has more consonants and a more open vowel).

A second influence comes from highly frequent cognate forms.[8] The adjective *expért* is closely enough related to the more frequent noun *éxpert* to be affected by it, with the result that even though the vowel of the first syllable of *expért* may be reduced, there is no difficulty in backshifting: *éxpert téstimony*. In fact, most speakers have now adopted *éxpert* as the normal pronunciation for both noun and adjective. Probably the adjectives *compáct* and *compléx*, already noted, are influenced by their cognate nouns *cómpact* and *cómplex*, again to the point that some speakers will say *It's quíte cómpact*. Similarly with *abstráct* and the noun *ábstract*.[9]

A third influence is that of contrast, which may at times be quite subtle. In a sentence like *I had thirty-three turnips and thirty-six carrots* we may pick the secondary in both numerals or neither or just in the first: the *six* in *thirty-six* contrasts with the *three* that has just been mentioned in *thirty-three*, and if the difference between the amounts is separately important, the corresponding syllables will be accented. Similarly with other compounds. We start out saying *He jóined the Boy Scóuts*. Then other groups are organized—*Gírl Scouts, Séa Scouts*— which carry a distinguishing stress on the first word of the compound. With their existence, there now comes pressure to do the same with *Boy Scout*, and this, coupled with the broad pattern of stressing the first element in noun compounds, results in a permanent shift for most speakers of American English: *Bóy Scouts*. It does not matter that *Were there mány Boy Scóuts in atténdance?* is rhythmically better than *Were there mány Bóy Scouts in atténdance?*—the latter will still be chosen.

A final (though certainly not *the* final) influence is the theme-rheme organization of the sentence. The rhematic accent always falls on a primary stress (except under climax—see Chapter 8), since the primary is to the right and the rheme is normally to the right. But sometimes theme and rheme are inverted (see pp. 50–51), and when that happens the rhematic accent still falls on a primary even when the result is two successive accents. Take, for example, an answer to the question *What's your next project?* in the form

$$\text{To} \quad \acute{o}ut_{do} \; J\acute{o} \atop ^{h}n.$$

Here the verb *outdo* has picked the secondary in the normal way. But in answer to *What are your plans for John?* one may have either of two arrangements:

$$J\acute{o} \atop ^{h}n \; I'm \; g\acute{o}n_{na} \; \acute{o}ut \quad d\acute{o} \atop o. \qquad\qquad I'm \; g\acute{o}n_{na} \; \acute{o}ut \quad {d\acute{o} \atop o \; _{h}n.} \; J\acute{o}$$

In the first, the theme, *John*, carries an accent to signify 'as for John' and is in the normal position for themes, at the beginning. But in the second that same accented *John*, theme, has been put at the end (its thematic status is partly cued by the terminal rise and by the lower pitch on *John* relative to *do*). It is allowed to do this, but it does not, in the process, alter the accent on *outdo* even though accented *John* follows. If the secondary were chosen here, yielding

$$I'm \; g\acute{o}n_{na} \quad do \quad {\acute{o}ut \atop} \quad {J\acute{o} \atop _{h}n.}$$

it would be taken to have a special purpose, perhaps to mean '*outdo*, not *underdo*.' [10]

This chapter has emphasized the rough and ready nature of the accentual rhythm that is grafted onto the much more predictable syllabic rhythm. The evidence is clear that accents do tend to group themselves into rhythmic feet, but equally clear that accentual rhythm yields to other communicative needs. How the ear seeks a rhythm can be seen in the treatment of two such sentences as *There ísn't a whóle lot you can dó* and *There's nót a whole lót you can dó*. In both, the phrase *whole lot* may, if the speaker wishes, be given equal prominence on both words. But this forces the insertion of a monobeat. The accents are more apt to be given as shown. And in the second example, even if the speaker says

$$\text{There's} \quad {n\acute{o}t \atop a} \quad {wh\acute{o} \atop le} \quad {l\acute{o}t \atop} \quad {you \; can} \quad {d\acute{o} \atop o.}$$

with an accent on *whole* as well as *lot*, the hearer has no difficulty in ignoring the resulting monobeat and "hearing" a succession of two dactyls, attending to the highest peaks (*not, lot, do*), as if *whole* had been leveled out—especially if *not, lot,* and *do* are enhanced with a little extra loudness. This sort of rhythmic adjustment of course is common in poetry. It quite easily produces—that is, we quite easily hear—a rhythm that is not actually present in the form of any real accentual prominence (see pp. 17–18). This is especially marked when the rhythm can be imagined on the basis of earlier prominences in the same utterance. Take an utterance with an early rhematic accent followed by a string of unaccented syllables. Reiterated material is apt to occur in postaccentual position. If someone wants to know why the Tennessee Waltz was not played at a dance, an appropriate reply is

<pre>
                ásked
        Nobody
                for the Tennessee Waltz.
</pre>

which is heard as *Nóbody ásked for the Ténnessee Wáltz*, with a 3-3-3 rhythm—the favored dactyls—even though as this would normally be said it is impossible to tell where the speaker intends the stress on *Tennessee* and the pattern could just as well be *Nóbody ásked for the Tennessée Wáltz*, with a 3-5-1 sequence. Our ear is prompted here not only by an extension of the pattern already begun but by our knowledge that if *Tennessee Waltz* were favored with accents, the word *Tennessee* would choose the secondary stress: *Ténnessee Wáltz*.

At this stage of our knowledge of rhythm in ordinary spoken language there is little that one can say except in general terms—to observe, for instance, that rhythm does exist in the two broad layers of the syllable and the accentual phrase, and to relate it to efficiency in communication. But RHYTHMS undoubtedly exist in specific forms for specific purposes. Successive monobeats we noted, with their ponderous emphasis. A later chapter (Chapter 10, pp. 231–32) will take up the regular accentual rhythm associated with terraced monotones. Very likely there are definite patterns of mixed rhythms in our repertory, some of them shared in part with music. One might look for them in playful forms of speech and verbal nonsense. Some examples of rhythmic chant were given in Chapter 1; nonsense sequences include things like *boop-boop-a-doop, dum-deedle-um-(dum)*. If rhythm can be exploited for its own sake in verse, the same thing must happen here and there in prose.

6. Accents of Power

Logical people like to view language as primarily the business of exchanging information. This view is reinforced by the importance we attach to writing: most of what we read is written to inform, either the mind or the imagination. But speech is different. It informs sometimes (as often inadvertently as by intent), but much of the time its aim is to cajole, persuade, entreat, excuse, cow, deceive, or merely to maintain contact—to let the hearer know that "channels are open."

Furthermore, even when we inform we are not above slipping in an extra message sub rosa: "The information I am giving you is important." The importance can be underscored by the words we choose (the windstorm was not merely *destructive*, it was *devastating*), or it can be underscored by the tone. And the main tonal means of infusing this importance, of stirring the hearer with the power of our message, is by the accents we choose and the way we arrange them.

Informing Versus Impressing

How information is conveyed by intonation is the topic of the next chapter. In this chapter we look at how intonation is used to IMPRESS. The two are not separable really, because information, like money, is power, and power, as the manifestation of feeling, is the motive force behind intonation. A monotone is powerless speech; departures from it convey greater or lesser IMPACT, and a speaker may use different forms and amounts to show different degrees of informativeness or interestingness carried by this or that part of the utterance. But there are also manifestations of power that affect messages as a whole, whether or not they are informative, and this purer kind of power is our concern for the moment.

At the beginning of the last chapter we saw how the hat pattern itself could be exploited for emphasis by getting the two main accents as far to the left and right as possible. It is as if we were hitting our hearer with maximum force at the beginning to get his undivided attention, and at the end to leave him with the strongest impression. Not only the location but the sweep and range of the accents are affected. We can say *No!* by rising to a higher pitch, or by taking longer to get to the highest pitch and back down again, or both, in order to heighten the effect. No more will be said on this point for now (see p. 225 for further comment); what we shall be looking at is where the accents fall and how many of them there are—matters of distribution rather than of the gradations within one accent. And we shall be speaking of just the major form of accent, the one that is made to stand out by having an abrupt drop after the accented syllable (or on it if no unaccented syllables are available to take the drop), e.g.

$$
\text{pre}^{\text{pós}}{}_{\text{terous}} \longleftarrow \qquad \text{pre}^{\text{pós}}{}_{\text{terous}} \longleftarrow \qquad \text{be}^{\text{ló}}{}_{\text{w}} \longleftarrow \qquad \text{be}^{\text{ló}}{}_{\text{w}} \longleftarrow
$$

(See Chapter 8 for the various patterns of accents. The one identified here defines PROFILE A.)

The simplest instance of power can be disposed of briefly. It is CARRYING POWER, and is simply the use of accent for audibility. The person at a distance who calls *Hallo-o-o!* is not necessarily himself stirred up or trying to arouse a listener. The rise-fall in pitch is just an attention-getter, as it is also in such expressions as *roger* and *over* used in communication systems. Audibility differs from other uses of accent in that a normally unstressed—even reduced—syllable is as apt to be made prominent as a stressed one. Thus we can say

$$
\text{Ro}^{\text{ger!}} \qquad \text{Hen}^{\text{ry!}} \qquad \text{Com}^{\text{ing!}}
$$

It is probably better to exclude this sort of prominence from the definition of accent.

Climax

As a rule, we expect more of our audience than mere attention, and accent invests itself with our feelings and the ones we hope to evoke in others. The most striking instances of accentual power are those referred to in earlier chapters as CLIMAX, where an extra degree of force is achieved by moving the terminal accent rightward. If the force of our message already depends to a great degree on having one of the two major accents near the end, then the nearer to the end we put it the more that effect is enhanced, and speakers quite readily "mispronounce" words to achieve it. What happens—and this is the justification for calling the phenomenon a mispronunciation—is that the accent is placed after the (primary) stress, which was defined in Chapter 4 as the position of the terminal accent in the citation form of a word. We saw that for rhythmic purposes a word might receive its sole accent at the position of the secondary: there was that much flexibility in choosing the syllable to be accented. But no accents were supposed to fall later than the primary stress. Yet they do, when speakers are keyed up. It is fair to call these cases mispronunciations, because now and then speakers realize what they have done and correct themselves. Two examples (the attributions are to show that careful speakers are just as prone to this as anyone else):

> I beliéve in coóperáting [pause] coóperating. (Strong second accent on *coóperáting*. Speaker: officer of New England Modern Language Association, Jan. 16, 1965.)

> . . . a pérson whose fúll-time jób was béing a secretáry . . . (Speaker: Prof. J. R. Ross, June 1, 1973; he hesitated at end of sentence and then reworded.)

For the most part, speakers are unaware of the shift:

> What yóu need is a líttle ádvertísing. (Thomas Mitchell, Jan. 29, 1955.)

> With the mícroscope we explóre the minútest organísms. (Truman Bradley, Apr. 3, 1966.)

> The réason for the íncrease . . . is temporáry. (Jimmy Carter, Apr. 14, 1977.)

> . . . that cénter around the sácrament of baptísm. (Prof. L. B. Kiddle, Jan. 29, 1964.)

> I thínk it could be tormént. (Prof. J. G. Redfern, Feb. 21, 1967.)

> Lét us not méasure him quantitátively . . . (Prof. Stephen Gilman, Feb. 26, 1967.)

> The bíll would have been aménded subsequéntly . . . (Justin Roberts, editor *Contra Costa Times*, May 14, 1979.)

Though it happens less often, now and then a reduced vowel is upgraded to take an accent:

> . . . was the enórmous and the enormitý of . . . (May 1964.)

> Hárdlý! (Author of this book, responding to question *You can't pass that [bargain] up, can you?*)

The same pronunciation as the one noted here on *hárdlý* is heard fairly often on other brief responses and exclamations such as *Bróthér*, *Prób-(ab)lý*, *Ráthér*, *Góllý* (with the folk spelling *gollee*), and *Cóuld bé* (though on this last example it does not qualify as a "mispronunciation").

While a climactic accent has the effect of floodlighting the whole utterance, it is not unusual for the charged meaning of some particular
word to be spotlighted at the same time. *Torment* and *enormity* are instances of this in the citations just given. Other examples

> . . . is a substántial incréase. (Administrative Board member, Har-
> vard Graduate School of Education, Mar. 20, 1964.)
>
> . . . to fóllow up their enthúsiásms. (Prof. Edwin Moise, Nov. 9,
> 1965.)

Radio announcers almost routinely mispronounce compounds in
the direction of giving them an extra punch:

> It úsed to bé that Dódge trúcks [were thought of just] as stúrdy *work
> hórses.* (KGO, San Francisco, Oct. 27, 1977.)
>
> Blánche . . . is expécted to réach *húrricane státus* today. (KCBS, San
> Francisco, July 27, 1975.)

(The *status* type—that of "empty words"—will be looked at in the
next chapter, pp. 120–21). But the most mechanical manifestation of
all is in what one might call the "reading stereotype": readers, including actors who mentally read their lines, often put the accent in the
supposedly most effective place regardless of the sense. An anecdote
from the *Pennsylvania Journal,* June 30, 1781, quotes a man who was
reading the Bible aloud and rendered one passage like this:

> And he spáke to his sóns, saying, sáddle me the áss; and they
> *sáddled hím.* (Mathews 1963: 37.)

Other examples:

> The Cóleman Report on *sécondary schóols.*
>
> I'm góing to go óut and gét a jób so wé can buíld a *fúture for
> oursélves.*

This last should have been *fúture for ourselves,* with *ourselves* deaccented.[1]

Permanent Effects of Climax

Up to this point we have drawn examples from what might be called
the pathology of climax. But as pervasive an influence as this was
bound to leave its mark on both the morphology and the syntax of
English, arranging the accents so as to obtain a climactic effect on
words and expressions whose emotive force calls for it. One even
finds minimal pairs, where the "same" word is differently stressed according to sense. In sports, one has an *óffense,* but one takes *offénse* in

the sense of psychological injury. (This doubtless originated in the sporting habit of using *óffense* and *défense* as a contrasting pair, but is now established and appropriate to the sense. One might still say, in a sport, *What sort of defénse did they put up?* But *What sort of offénse did they put up?* would be odd.) Speakers who distinguish two pronunciations of the noun *retort* will use *rétort* for the vessel and *retórt* for the sharp rejoinder. British speakers may distinguish between *dísciplinary*, for an academic discipline, and *disciplínary*, referring to discipline in the sense of punishment.[2] We also note, for example, the special piquancy in the contrasted senses of *gállant* and *gallánt* and the tendency of intensifiable adjectives and verbs to carry an end stress: *precíse, sevére, alért, exáct, robúst, insáne, galóre* (see Appendix A, p. 352). The fact that many more verbs than nouns are end-stressed points the same way— verbs are ACTIVE (and the exceptions among nouns tend to be likewise: *disgúst, replý, concérn, contémpt, disdáin, despáir, rewárd, contról, debáte*). Of course verbs and adjectives are a little more likely than nouns to have a larger percentage of their use at the end of the sentence (see p. 351), and this may well sway them in the direction of end stress; but as terminal accents are ultimately climactic anyway, it comes to the same thing.

Doublets such as *óffense–offénse* are a rarity, but words (and set phrases) that allow either of two syllables (or words) to receive the accent when in end position in the sentence are a little more common, and though there may not be two distinct senses attached to the two distinct forms, the one with the stress on or near the last syllable tends to be used for that extra punch. According to Kenyon and Knott (1953: xxv), adverbs such as *ordinárily, absolútely*, and *necessárily* tend to be accented as marked when they are emphatic. If we want to warn someone that a bottle containing a certain fluid is explosive, we are more apt to say *It's gasolíne!*, and to say *It's gásoline* merely to identify the contents. The same contrast can be observed in paired forms like the following:

Nonclimactic	Climactic
By áll means.	By all méans!
Good morning—how áre you?	Good morning—how are yóu? (as an opener, not as a response)
They were chóked to death.	They were choked to déath.
The signs are all óver the place.	The signs are all over the pláce.
He doesn't gíve a damn.	He doesn't give a dámn.
It's not mý fault.	It's not my fáult.
Are you ready?—Álmost.	Are you ready?—Almóst.
It's unwise in the lóng run.	It's unwise in the long rún.

Because I knów better.	Because I know bétter.
Not by a héll of a lot.	Not by a hell of a lót.
He's a regular hé-man.	He's a regular he-mán.
You didn't read the fíne print.	You didn't read the fine prínt.
See, it's a tángerine.	You're crazy—it's a tangeríne!
They're so fár-sighted.	They're so far-síghted.
His rule is ábsolute.	His rule is absolúte.
Just be résolute.	Just be resolúte.
It's illegal to ránsack.	That's a place I wouldn't dare to ransáck.
I don't like his pómpousness.	I don't like his pompósity.

Other expressions with the same dual possibilities: *in a fine fix, for God's sake, at a great rate, in jig time, for a long time.*

There are varying amounts of separate information in some of these phrasal examples—for instance, in *It's not mý fault* one can assume that 'fault' is understood from the context and therefore is deaccented, whereas in *It's not my fáult* 'fault' is newly introduced or reintroduced. But over and above the information content is the fact that the form with the terminal accent has an impact that the other lacks. And in many instances (including almost all those with variable stress on a single word) one would be hard put to assign any separate meaning to the separate parts—*means* in the first example of the list above is not separately meaningful, and the word *place* in the fourth example, though separately meaningful, is in the nature of a pro-form and is not normally accented by virtue of its own content (for instance, one would say *They are having tea in our gárden*, but *They are having tea at óur place*).[3] Putting an accent on *place* as a pro-form in *The signs are all over the pláce* compares with putting one on the manifest pro-forms *there* and *him* in cases like

> How do you know there was a fire at Elmo's? — I've just béen there (been thére), that's how.
>
> Í'll fix him (I'll fix hím)!

Not only may the accent—under the influence of climax—fall on a syllable for which there is no separate-focus reason to put it there, it may also fall on a syllable for which there is a positive reason *not* to put it there, given the literal meaning of the whole. A good example is the use of *I wouldn't* to give advice or warning. Literally, in an exchange like

> Should I tell Mom about it? — I wouldn't.

the *I* is in contrast and gets the accent: 'You might tell her but I wouldn't.' But it is common to say *I wóuldn't!* with the same intonation and meaning as *You shóuldn't!*, even when the now inappropriate *if I were you* is added:

> I wóuldn't, if I were you!

When a climactic accent makes as striking a difference as this in the overall meaning of the phrase, it is apt to become fossilized as a feature of the verbal formula. This is what seems to have happened with the cordial invitation *Help yoursélf!* used when offering something to someone, especially food. (The fossilization here can be seen in the use of the word *helping* to mean 'portion': *She gave them each a generous helping*.) Though the verb can be used in the ordinary way nonreflexively (*She helped me to a slice of the roast*), when reflexive it accents the reflexive pronoun:

> When the roast came by he helped himsélf.

If we were to say

> When the roast came by he served himsélf.

one might infer rudeness—he should have waited to be served, or perhaps should have served someone else. *To hélp oneself* has a different idiomatic meaning: *He tríed not to wéep, but cóuldn't hélp himself.* Two other stereotypes involving pronouns that are often accented climactically are *Excuse mé!* and *Believe mé!*

Climax and Style

Climax poses a question of style when by selecting a different word or construction one can augment the force of an utterance. Chiasmus is a figure of speech that depends on this:

> A superman in physique, but in intellect a fóol. (Merriam *Third* citation.)

Here we break the parallelism with the first clause in order to get the strongest accent at the end. The same purpose motivates the position of the verb in

> I did that, and a pretty tough job it wás.[4]

If *it was a pretty tough job* were substituted, the tendency would be to run down the pitch at the end. Another figure is the "Blockung-type" formation exemplified by

> He lay in his bed, sick and broken.

The more usual order, *He lay sick and broken in his bed*, puts a less emphatic element in terminal position (see Krasheninnikova 1976: 62).

The speaker who said

> I can't do it while I'm sick, and I'm still pretty íll, you know.

was able, by switching from *sick* to *ill*, to emphasize the last word in the phrase—had *sick* been repeated it would have been virtually necessary to deaccent it and put the accent on *still* or on *am*, farther back from the end. An example of the wrong stylistic choice in a similar situation is

> "Thirty?"
> "More," Robert said. "And there'll be even more."[5]

The word *even* has to precede *more*, but *still* is free to move, and the effective thing to say here would be *And there'll be more stíll*.

Anticlimax

If one can speak of climax, obviously one must consider the opposite possibility, ANTICLIMAX. Speakers are not always intent on plunging the sword up to the hilt. There are times when it is desirable to hold back. This should have been obvious in many of the examples cited up to now: the milder alternative is one that a speaker might well choose in order to seem more gentle, more reserved, or even— by the sort of turnaround that one often gets in maintaining good relations with one's interlocutors—more self-confident. A person who beats the drums constantly may seem to be covering up a sense of insecurity. (The best example of this reversal of strength and weakness is the use of PROFILE C, the low-pitched accent. See pp. 178–79.) So the person who responds to another's remark with *Ábsolutely* scores the last word of confident assurance. Further, a terminal accent may be inappropriate because it seems to give importance to something unimportant. Given the triviality of the state of one's beard, it probably sounds better to say

> This is the most hair I've had on my face for a lóng time.

than to put the accent on *time*, which presents the matter as something significant. Or one may use anticlimax to play down an idea, as in the following reference to an affliction:

> Until you are handicapped you don't realize what some people have
> to gó through. (KGO, San Francisco, Feb. 17, 1979.)

—*to go thróugh* would put the case more keenly. Playing down may amount to routine self-confidence on the part of the speaker—there is no need to be emphatic. So where one would expect

> He doesn't know his arse from a hole in the gróund.

with *hole* not receiving the main accent because it is presupposed in *arse*, one may hear the quietly confident *hóle in the ground*.[6]

Sometimes the intent of anticlimax is to avoid seeming querulous. In the following, A has said something to B, who is distracted and fails to answer. A complains, *Why don't you listen?*, and B replies,

> How do I know when to listen? The only signal I get is when it is being tránsmitted.

The citation form of the verb is *transmít*, but *transmítted* here would have sounded testy. In the following,

                             mȯst

    ɪ thȯught that thắt was

                                  ingenious.

the deaccenting of *ingenious* implies that it is a quality too obvious to need emphasizing—another instance of calm assurance. The same is true of the threat in

> We'll sée about that.

in contrast with *We'll see about thát.*

If climax often results in pushing a stress rightward, anticlimax may result in the leftward choice of a secondary as the main accent—as in the *transmit* example above. The rule of separation, as we saw in the last chapter, leads to choosing the secondary of *réady-máde* in a phrase like *réady-made spéech*. But we can also say

> The speech was so réady-made!

to damn it by understatement, even though there is no following word with an accent (such as *spéech*) from which the accent on the compound needs to be separated.

Climax and anticlimax are two poles of the same contrast. An early main accent is deflating, and may be avoided even when the speaker has no particular interest in being emphatic, as when a husband said to his wife, referring to a small household chore he had agreed to take on but had failed to do before she got to it,

> I was going to dó that, honey!

The "correct" accenting here would have favored *I* because of the contrast with *you*, but that would have taken the wind completely out of the rest of the sentence, and *do* was chosen as the next best place.

Exclamatory Early Accent

Anticlimax must be distinguished from another form of early accent, which comes from an effusion of feeling—Schubiger (1961: 258) calls it a tendency to "blurt out the idea uppermost in one's mind." It is usually at the beginning of the utterance, quite often on the very first syllable:

Néver had they seen anything like it!
I wísh I hadn't done it!
Whý oh why did it have to happen!

When this emotional accent occurs in the middle of the utterance, it is usually attached to some highly charged word:

```
                           tér
      wánt you to know
   I                       how
                              ribly sad we are for you!
```

In fact, it is likely that speakers sometimes deliberately put such a word in a strategic spot in order to get the emotional accent there. So it seems to be with the comparatively redundant *begin* in

I couldn't begín to tell you all the trouble I've been through.

or the intensifier and exclamation respectively in

He's súch a grand old fellow!
Gée I wish I hadn't done it!

What characterizes this early accent is the apparent overflow of feeling that engulfs whatever follows and more or less erases the accents that would normally appear. In the example with *terribly sad*, the word *sad* may be flattened completely into the level of *-ribly . . . you*, even though normally it would be the main terminal accent. In the following, there would more likely be reduced accents on *ob-* and *-lead-* (or the emotional accent may be put on *ob-* with *so* unaccented):

```
                   só
                    \    ób          léad
      But it's     o      viously mis    ing!
```

Similarly:

```
          ab
   It's    solutely pel  lú cid   réa soning.
```

A point that will be developed in Chapter 9 is the gestural interplay that accompanies intonation. The typical gesture with all these emotive backshifts is the headshake, which seems to imply 'This is simply too much for me, I can't adequately express my feeling.'

An early accent may occur not because of an access of emotion but because the speaker ideates a sentence wrong-end first:

> Cóusins I think they were. (Schubiger 1961: 258.)

Cumulative Accents

The discussion up to this point has concentrated on the terminal accent alone, as achieving climax by its rightward location (on the psychological principle of recency, "last heard best remembered"). But climax is also a cumulative phenomenon. One result of putting a primary farther to the right is that secondaries are freed to the left, to carry additional accents. Since the primary stress is the last position normally available for an accent, and the hat pattern decrees the same for the rhematic accent in an utterance, an early primary annuls further accents to the right (or drastically reduces them), but this does not apply to additional accents on the left. So a number of the examples already cited, if they had been more fully described, would have shown additional accents. Some selected instances:

> By áll méans!
> Nót by a héll of a lót.
> There'll be móre stíll.
> Excúse mé!
> Beliéve mé!

One also finds here the multiple accents on highly charged words that were noted in Chapter 5:

> díamétrically oppósed (versus diamétrically alígned)
> óverwhélmed sénses (versus óverturned trúck)
> írretríevable lóss
> péstiléntial íllness
> ábjéct póverty

In the last example, the separation rule would decree *ábject póverty*, but a climactic buildup favors the extra accent. The same is true with words that are not intrinsically loaded—the buildup is in the utterance, not in the word as such. The following puts an extra accent on *apple-pie*, disregarding the separation rule:

> Éverything was in ápple-píe órder.

Similarly in the choice of *róundabóut* rather than *róundabout* in

> Hé has súch a róundabóut wáy of dóing things.

The very existence of such a rule as the one calling for a separation makes breaking it more powerful, because the hearer assumes there must be a strong reason for doing so. Here the monobeat comes into its own: juxtaposed accents are *better* than separated ones, or, in general, more closely placed accents are better than more widely spaced ones. So the first member of the following pairs has more impact than the second:

If I ónly cóuld.	If ónly I cóuld.
Pút thát dówn.	Pút it dówn.
An enráged ádversary.	A fúrious ádversary.
A nót tóo háppy occásion.	Nót a véry háppy occásion.

One way to get extra accents is simply to lay them on, upgrading reduced vowels to full if necessary. In the following example the indefinite article may take either the spelling pronunciation [e] or a shwa upgraded to [ʌ]:

Don't try to burn wood treated with creosote. Ít mákes á méss!

Similarly with the definite article in the following, which was pronounced with [i]:

The one thing I like about it thé móst is . . . (ADP Computer Co. ad, KCBS, San Francisco, Dec. 13, 1982.)

The added accents go first on the full syllables, then on the reduced ones according to a rough implicational scale, with upgraded reduced syllables implying accented full ones:

A compléte fáilure.
A cómpléte fáilure.
Á cómpléte fáilure.
Á cómpléte fáilúre.

The form with the folk spelling *gen-tul-men* (*géntúlmén*) has been described as "an exclamation of surprise or dismay" (Ayers et al. 1950: 75; see also Bolinger 1955: 200). The pronunciations *évidéntly* and *pósitívely* also upgrade a reduced vowel, modeling themselves on *ábsolútely*.

Another source of extra accents is the addition of carrier words. They may be essentially nonsense, as happens in many exclamations:

Sákes alíve!	Góodness grácious mé!
Mércy mé!	Héavens abóve!
Jésus H́. Chríst!	Gósh áll físhhooks!

Or they may be simply redundant, as can be seen in the following pairs and triplets:

Belíeve mé!	Belíeve yóu mé!	
I will nót páy you a cént.	I will nót páy you óne cént.	I will nót páy you óne réd cént.
I díd it with my ówn hánds.	I díd it with my ówn twó hánds.	
It háppens that . . .	It júst háppens that . . .	It júst só háppens that . . .
He hátes évery óne of them.	He hátes évery lást óne of them.	

A further source is choice of an equivalent (construction, or synonym). *Bétter hád* both matches *bétter nót* and provides for the extra accent that is absent in *had bétter*. *Nó dóubt of it* has one fewer accent, and is less climactic, than *Nó dóubt abóut it*. And all this is of a piece with the infixing of words, as in *ábsoblóodylútely* (see McMillan 1980 and McCarthy 1982) or of nonsense syllables as in *críminéntly* (an expansion of the exclamation *crimine* invented by some wag) and the extra syllable added to *total* in *téetótal*.

Finally one can interpret the form of certain words as owing its existence, in part, to the provision it makes for an extra accent. An example is *cántánkerous*, with its successive accents.

Multiple accents are not confined to English. See Kvavik (1982) for the same phenomenon in Spanish.

Ascending Rhythm

In the earlier remarks on rhythm (Chapter 5), much attention was given to DESCENDING metrical forms (trochee, dactyl, and beyond), none to ASCENDING ones (e.g. iamb), where the accent is at the end of the foot rather than the beginning. Given the prevalence of downturns in pitch to mark accents, and the need for *following* syllables to accommodate the accentual turn, it seems that English must favor descending rhythms (see Thompson 1980: 14–15; Allen and Hawkins 1980: 234, 246–49). And yet the fact that climax builds *toward* an accent speaks for the opposite, at least where the final accent in an utterance is concerned. The very effort of stretching a syllable that must—when alone and accented at the end—be spread over a pitch turn adds to the force of the utterance: the terminal gains by being iambic if iambs are the marked rhythm.

And we unquestionably find expressions that are deliberately made iambic. The prefix *ker-* is added to many onomatopoetic words that denote a heavy impact, to get a running start and set off the terminal accent: *kerplúnk, kerwháck, kersmásh, kersplásh, kerflóp.* The same preparatory unstressed syllable is found in the resyllabification that can be heard in such pronunciations as *ga-ránd* for *grand, ga-lórious* for *glorious, puh-léese* for *please, Ca-ríst* for *Christ,* and similar hyperboles and exclamations. (When the initial sound is a continuant it may simply be anticipated: *N-n-n-n-o!; Sh-sh-sh-sh-it!* See below for *mess.*) And in context it is surely the iambic interpretation of the rhythm that conveys the emphasis in such things as

It néeds / no hélp / from mé!
I wíll / I wíll / I wíll!

Nor does the preparatory syllable need to be reduced; the only requisite is that the terminal be heavier—if two accents occur in succession, the result is cumulative as we have already seen. So one finds the extra syllable in *kée-ríst!* upgraded. Military commands take this form, and also have the special function of indicating the point at which the command is to be obeyed: *tén-shún!, abóut fáce!, presént árms!* etc. Ascending and descending rhythms may well be complementary in the language, corresponding to climax and anticlimax. If linguists have paid most of their attention to descending rhythms it is probably because they have focused on texts that are logical, reasonable, propositional, and unemphatic.

The discussion in this chapter leaves various aspects of climax untouched, but two important ones will be dealt with in later chapters. One is the overlaid climax or anticlimax of the accentual shapes themselves. That is, not only do we have a climactic buildup toward a terminal accent just by virtue of the SUCCESSION of accents, but the buildup can be further built up, or played down, by successively higher or lower peaks—as can be shown by an earlier example:

(there is a rise-fall on each accent, and *mess* is fortified in both versions by prolonging the initial consonant, *m-mess,* the same phenomenon as in *ga-rand*). The rising tangent of the accentual curves in the first sentence shows the speaker to be more keyed up for whatever reason: his own internal excitement, his eagerness to impress the hearer with the importance of the information, his angry rejection of someone else's statement to the contrary. The descending tangent of the second sentence shows the opposite: philosophical acceptance (of the nevertheless annoying fact), recognition that the hearer knows the fact already and shares in the amusement, dismissal of the fact in preparation for bringing up some other topic—any attitude that reveals itself in lowered tension without altering the underlying climactic nature of the statement. The rise-fall of the accents, itself a result of tension, is tempered by the rise or fall of the succession.

The other unexplored aspect of climax is its relationship to information and interest in general (see the next chapter). Intonation is useful not only to express the impact of the utterance as a whole but also to express the relative weight (importance) of the *parts* of the utterance. If a message has more impact as a whole when it builds up to a strong accent at the end, then it helps not only to put an accent there but also, when possible, to attach the accent to a part of the utterance that may be entitled to such a degree of highlighting. In the last example the word *mess* gets the terminal accent and itself is the most informative word: the "distribution of information" is ideal.[7] If we were to say *What a mess it makes!* normally we would still put the terminal accent on *mess*, but that leaves the exclamation deflated because *it makes* falls to a low pitch and *makes* can be unaccented: the effect is anticlimactic. (We might welcome the deflation, or we might not.) This can be remedied by going ahead anyway and putting an accent on *makes*, but that recourse calls for strong accents on *what* and *mess* as well, an extreme that may be undesirable. As a rule, the words are arranged to achieve a balance of relative importance without taxing the system too heavily.

7. Accents of Interest

Accents of power affect whole utterances. A climactic series of accents is intended to impress the hearer with the importance of the entire message. But speakers just as often need to underscore the importance of the separate parts, singly or in concert, and in relation to the parts that are viewed as less important. We can appreciate the distinction if we listen to the day-by-day blunders of radio and television announcers, when they resort to an automatic accent of power instead of thinking of what they are saying and adjusting the accents accordingly. Two examples:

> . . . celebrate the late for sómething day. (For *be láte for something day*, a compound that should be accented on its first element. KCBS, San Francisco, Sept. 5, 1976.)

> He appeared to have bled to déath. (For *bléd to death*, referring to a man known to be dead. Same station, June 4, 1975.)

Interest, Information, Contrast

Logical discourse—discourse that is intended to inform and must therefore adhere to certain conditions of truth and coherence—has such a hold on our minds that the "importance" of the parts of the message has come to be seen in terms of their contribution to the total of INFORMATION. A given word, say, is accented to show its informativeness, which in turn usually reflects its newness, its unexpectedness, its special contribution toward answering the question that usually lies back of the spoken sentence:

> Fréd did it. (Question: Who did it?)
> It's cóld in here. (Question: Why are you turning up the heat?)
> I hélped him. (Question: Why was he so grateful?)

The special status of the accented words can be seen in their indispensability as parts of the answer: sometimes nothing more is needed.

Thus in the first example the speaker might have said just *Fred*. And in the second, though the reply would be felt as incomplete grammatically, just the word *cold* would be enough. In the third, *help* is informationally central though not sufficient by itself—partly because we do not use inflected verbs without subjects.

But is "information" a proper characterization of accents that zero in on individual elements? Certainly not if we mean by it 'acquainting the hearer with facts not already in his possession,' 'drawing attention to something not previously in the hearer's awareness,' the something being that which is logically designated by the element that is given the accent. That may be the case with the majority of instances, but not with one like

Raw fish is good for you, but after all, who likes raw físh?

—since *raw fish* has already been mentioned in the early part of the sentence, this could "just as well" be expressed as

Raw fish is good for you, but after all, who líkes it?

There must be some other reason, then, for repeating—and accenting—the word *fish*.[1] The same happens in

Raw fish is good for you, but after all, who likes thát?

The accent here serves a kind of pointing function (a common gesture is holding one's hands up in mock horror at contemplating the object). Accordingly it requires either a pointing word such as *that* or a reidentification of the word itself. The accent is half reidentification and half exclamation. In both functions it shows something that the speaker is keyed up about, something of keen interest, real or pretended. The degree of interest is carried by the degree of prominence, the pointing is carried by the mere fact that there is an accent. So one might say, lackadaisically,

$$\text{Who}\ \text{likes}$$
$$\text{raw}\ \text{fí}$$
$$\text{s}_{\text{h}?}$$

with accented *fish* at low pitch—the accent is there, and points up the reidentification, but is scarcely exclamatory. At the same time it is a center of INTEREST, and this is a better cover term than INFORMATION for the various functions of accent focused on particular elements.[2] It will not be necessary to shun the term INFORMATION where it is appropriate (in a society that has business to transact this is the single most frequent manifestation of interest), so long as we recognize that there is a deeper reason for highlighting some things rather than others, and doing it to a greater or lesser degree.

The association of accents with interest is part of our cultural and perhaps even our biological heritage. In the exaggerated intonation used by mothers to their babies, the pitch peaks are found on items that are most apt to be interesting to the infant at various periods. "When you are six months old," writes Anne Fernald (personal communication), "the word most likely to occupy a maternal pitch peak is an attention-getting word, such as *hey!*, or a nonsense word that is in itself an interesting sound, like *Grrr!* or *Ooops!* These prosodic high-points are often accompanied by touches and tickles and other sensory delights, so that a pitch peak for a baby is often a multi-media event! By fourteen months, the picture has changed somewhat. By then, the words most likely to occupy the pitch peaks are the names of things. Instead of *The doggy goes RRRF!*, it's now *Look at the DOGGY!* I would argue that the early playfulness has provided the older infant with an excellent strategy for monitoring speech: pay attention to the pitch peaks and important linguistic information is bound to show up there." (See also Fernald 1984.)

A term often encountered in connection with accents that are especially prominent is CONTRAST, and it has even been supposed that there is a special subvariety that can be called CONTRASTIVE ACCENT. Examples usually cited are of cases where one or more individual items are singled out from a larger (but limited) set as being true as regards some relationship whereas others in the same set are untrue:

She líkes wíne but she hátes mílk.

Here liking and hating are contrasted within some such set as 'attitudes toward,' and wine and milk are contrasted within some such set as 'beverages.' There is no question that in this context these items are in a sort of *logical* contrast, but since the sentence can be said with no particular emphasis on the contrasted items, it is hard to claim that there is any special requirement of making them stand out accentually. The notion that there may be such prominence is probably due to the fact that logical contrasts are apt to be encountered in situations where feelings run high—if you say that John did it and I retort *No, Máry did it*, the mood of contradiction can easily raise the temperature of the accented word. But the identity of the accent whether contrastive or not can be seen by inserting the same sentence in two different contexts, one inducing a contrastive interpretation, the other not:

I suppose your back aches. — You're wrong. My héad aches.
You're looking depressed. What's the matter? — My héad aches.

Where we do occasionally find physical evidence of contrastivity is in the DISTORTION of a word to make it sound different. One reason for doing this is to suggest the idea 'This is not the same as that other word' which the hearer might be supposed to have in mind. We have already seen how climax can distort the pronunciation of a word by shifting the accent rightward from the normally stressed syllable. Contrast can cause a similar disruption, but what the nature of it will be is hard to predict. Here are some recorded examples:

> In a case of this kind, Mrs. Hall, our first concern is to persuade the patient that he is a stalagmíte. (*New Yorker*, Apr. 14, 1956, p. 36.)
>
> Natural régularity. (Carter's Little Liver Pills ad, WRCA, New York, Dec. 18, 1956.)
>
> The notion of length and unfamiliarity—or, to put this in reverse, condensation and famíliarity.

The first example is from a cartoon showing a patient standing upside down with his feet on the ceiling; the contrast is with *stalactite*, yet despite the fact that the normally stressed syllables -*lac*- and -*lag*- contain the contrasting consonants [k] and [g], the accent is moved to the right, probably for two reasons: the initial consonants in that syllable, [t] and [m], make a better contrast than [k] and [g], and the rightward shift adds the advantage of climax. The second example contrasts *regularity* with the unspoken *irregularity*, but now the accent is shifted leftward to get it closer to the position of *ir*-. In the third example the speaker had a choice, *fámiliarity* (to get the accent close to where the syllable *un*- would be) or *famíliarity* (which has the advantage of a full vowel to begin with), and chose the latter. If necessary, a reduced vowel is simply upgraded:

> [Though of the two plans (Plan A and Plan B) Plan A is in the minority in the department, Mr. X's candidacy is being advocated as if the opposite were true,] with Plan A somewhat the májority in the department. (Harvard adviser, Oct. 26, 1972.)

Here the syllable *ma*-, with its reduced vowel, is the only one available for the distorting shift that signals 'This word contrasts with its opposite, which you would expect under the circumstances.'

Another reason for wanting a word to sound different is to suggest that it has a different *meaning* from the expected one. Example:

> You don't want to use that -*ly* suffix twice in succession—nearly automatical*ly*! It should be almóst automatically!

Had the speaker used the more general pronunciation álmost, the hearer would have been left to infer that his mistake was in a wrong choice of meaning rather than in the wrong choice of word—shifting the accent on *almost* has a metalinguistic effect, pointing to the word as a word. A further example, this one from the "What's My Line" television program, August 16, 1964: one of the members of the panel said in jest that he had had an investigation made of one of the contestants (who happened to be a good-looking girl), to find out where she worked, and gave the address; at the end of that round of the program, the emcee, John Daly, remarked,

Who did the investigáting is what I want to know.

Had the normal pronunciation *invéstigating* been used, this would have sounded like a serious question about the investigative aspect of the preliminaries of the program (versus, say, the disclosing aspect) rather than a pure jibe.

There are instances of distortion that can be regarded not as just negatively marking the word as 'not the same as' some other word, but as positively highlighting the syllable on which they occur, for example,

This whiskey was not éxported from Ireland, it was déported.
The one I've been most dísappointed with is . . .

In the second example there is implied a previously understood situation of encouragement-discouragement, and though *appointed* is not the antonym of *disappointed*, the prefix *dis-* can be highlighted for its negative meaning.

So while we may speak of contrastive stress as signaling a contrastive accent under some conditions, it is better not to speak of contrastive accent as if there were some such entity clearly distinguishable from accent for interest in general. All the same, given a particular context, it is often impossible not to conclude that an accent is *used* contrastively, and this justifies keeping the term CONTRASTIVE ACCENT. An example:

They don't care about mý feelings.

The danger is in trying to relate the matter to some kind of grammatical rule. For instance, noting how common it is for the accented modifier of a noun to be used contrastively, as in the last example and in

He put on a réd shirt.
This job is for a yóunger person.

one might claim that all such cases are contrastive. That would be a mistake, in view of sentences like

Unexpectedly, in the dark, I heard a róbin's cry, and I knew that a cat must be on the prowl.

> How's Fred these days? — Well, I'm afraid old Fred has a médical
> problem.

in which the variety of cries and problems is unrestricted: there is no
contrast within a limited set.[3]

Nor are there intonational guarantees. It is commonplace to find a
rise-fall-rise on items that are in contrast, for example,

él

It ^{is}n't an ephant.

from which one is almost compelled to infer something like 'but it
could be a giraffe.' But a little testing suffices to show that the same
intonation quite readily occurs with items that are not in contrast, especially in affirmative sentences:

pól

They gave their a ogy.

—to which the speaker might add *What more can you ask?* The rising
intonation at the end in both cases suggests something unsaid, but
whereas in the first example it is the contrasting possibility that is left
unmentioned, in the second—as the added remark shows—it is something like 'conclusion left up to hearer.' Even with negation there is no
assurance of contrast. A common answer to *How did you do it?* is

éa

It was n't sy.

with the same intonation, again implying just 'I'll leave the conclusion
of this idea up to you.'

In one attempt to provide a grammatical underpinning for contrast
(Harries-Delisle 1978), sentences containing a contrasted item were
said to be—"underlyingly"—cleft or pseudo-cleft sentences. According to this theory, the following would all be fundamentally the same:

> Jóhn wrote the letter.
> It was Jóhn who wrote the letter. (cleft)
> The one who wrote the letter was Jóhn. (pseudo-cleft)

The study in question contains valuable cross-linguistic comparisons
but again assumes that "contrast" is definable both logically and grammatically. If cleft sentences are to be the proof of contrastivity, then
every sentence that answers an interrogative-word question is contrastive, because all can be converted to cleft:

Why did you slap her? — (It was) because I felt like it (that I did it).

What are you going to use the whip for? — (It is) to beat my chimpanzee (that I am going to use it).

Where does Jennie live? — (It's) in Baskerville (that she lives).

While given an appropriate context any one of these could imply a choice within a limited set, none does so necessarily. In an example like

What are you going to do? — (It is) write a letter (that I am going to do).

the "set" is an infinity: the hearer has no way of predicting what range of activities the answer may refer to. And this pretty well sums up the situation: accent does very often, perhaps most of the time, zero in or *focus* on something, but it is only incidental whether the item is part of a limited or an unlimited set. The wholly pragmatic nature of the question can be seen in a pair like

We have been talking about their customs, dress, ceremonials, marriage, etc. Now I'd like to know about another aspect of their culture: What did they éat?

They were forbidden pork, beef, cereal grains, and fruits?! What did they éat?!

In the first we have a contrast on food customs among other customs. In the second we are asking, in effect, 'How was it possible for them to éat?' There is a focus of interest on *eat*, but the contrast, if any, is with all other activities that the people in question might conceivably engage in.

Wh Words and Focus

When what is most interesting is also most informative, accent can be said to apply to information, and we can refer to "information focus." But it is also possible to have an utterance in which there is both an information focus and a separate focus of interest. This often happens with wh questions (*when, where, who, why* . . .).

Suppose A says either of the following to B:

I finally went out and bought something today.

Bill took me downtown to all the big department stores today.

To either of these statements B can pose the question

Oh yeah? Whát did you búy? (Culicover and Rochemont 1983, examples 16–18.)

In response to the second statement, *buy* is a focus of information: it represents one action from among infinite possibilities—*look at, shop for, see, try on, order,* etc. In response to the first, it repeats the *buy* that has just been mentioned, and B could "just as well" have asked

> Oh yeah? Whát did you buy?

deaccenting *buy*. From an informational standpoint the two questions ask the same thing, and yet they are different. In the question without accent on *buy* the speaker seems to be announcing a lack of interest in the activity of buying. With the accent, that interest is present, as can be seen by the kinds of things that can be added:

> Whát did you buy? (That's all I want to know.)
>
> Whát did you (have to) (go and) búy, (for goodness' sake,) (of all things to do)?

In the last example, each of the additions is a potential focusing device in itself—for interest, not for information. For instance, *of all things to do* shows that the speaker is reviewing the range of possible actions and expressing concern at the other person's choice of *buying*.

A *why* question shows the contrasts more clearly:

> John left early.
> Whý did he leave?
> Whý did he léave?

The latter question shows a focus of interest on leaving (why did he leave, when I expected him to stay?), whereas the former implies 'That's all I need to know'; the focus of interest coincides with the focus of information. In fact, this question is even more restricted than the simple question *Why?* Since the speaker does not need to add unaccented *did he leave* in order to get the information he wants (just *why* is enough), adding it has the effect of restricting the semantic range to precisely that narrow bit of information. With *why* alone the range is open to all possibilities:

> Whý? Thát's all I need to know.
> Whý? I expected him to stáy.
> Whý? What was the réal reason?

(Though the speaker is free to intone the *why* with almost any depth of terminal fall, the first of these three would tend to end at the lowest pitch; it is the most conclusive, since no extraneous interest is implied.)

Wh questions throw an additional sidelight on focus of interest when we look at what particular wh words can most easily express an interesting aspect of the *action*. It turns out that unless some such connection is established, the resulting wh question is odd when it retains the major accent on a repeated item. The following examples are responses to someone who has just said *I was talking a blue streak.* Only the major accent is marked; all have an intonation similar to the one illustrated for the first example:

Who were you tálking to?

```
                       talk

        Who
               were you
                          ing to?
```

Why were you tálking?
What were you tálking about?
How were you tálking? Extemporaneously?
What language were you tálking in?
ʾWhere were you tálking?
ʾWhen were you tálking?

It seems that the necessary connection can be established fairly easily except for 'time' and 'place'—most easily of all with *why*, probably because one is more often interested in inquiring into the motive for an action than any other aspect of it. Time and place are seldom of the essence in an action,[4] and that causes the last two examples to seem a bit odd, though they can be contextualized to make them plausible:

Where were you tálking? I thought you had been denied every platform and every outlet.

When were you tálking? I thought your schedule was too crowded.

Here the speaker has assumed the impossibility of the action; a possible time or place therefore becomes relevant to its occurrence. What counts is a mutual relevance of wh word and verb. The verb *run*, for example, does not very strongly imply a destination—one may be running from rather than to a place, or running in circles; the verb *travel*, on the other hand, does imply destination. Accordingly we get

They were running.
ʾWhere were they rúnning to?
They were traveling.
Where were they tráveling to?

But the speaker can take care of the ambiguity of *running* by specifying his interest in the destination:

Where were they running tó?

The case relations of several wh words permit this sort of analytic rather than synthetic expression:

> John did it.
>> Whý did he do it?
>> What did he do it fór?
>
> John broke the vase.
>> Hów did he break it? — With a hammer.
>> What did he break it wíth? — With a hammer.

Similarly the substandard *where . . . at*:

> Where ís everybody?
> Where's everybody át?

The accent points up the aspect of the action that the speaker is most interested in.

In the preceding examples the wh word is accented, even though it does not always carry the major accent; it is a focus of information, which is normally a focus of interest. But it may be fully deaccented if it ceases to be a focus of interest, even though it remains a focus of information. This happens when it is repeated:

> Whén did you sée your bróther? (= Náme the tíme you sáw your bróther.) — I saw him yésterday. — When did you see your síster? (= Name the time you saw your síster. = What about your síster? = And your síster?)

In the latter question *when* is still a focus of information (it controls the answer, e.g. *Yesterday too*), but it is "old stuff" that no longer needs pointing up.

Many other elements besides accent—gestural, phonetic, lexical, and syntactic—are specialized to a greater or lesser degree as focusing devices. Among the lexical are the wh words, by definition. Also used in questions and statements—and focusing on the truth value of the utterance—is the auxiliary *do*: *Do you confess?*, *I do believe you*. Most of the lexical focusers also attract the accent—this is pretty uniformly true of *do* in affirmative statements but not necessarily in questions or negative statements (see pp. 128–30). It is especially noticeable with words such as *even, actually, only, just*:[5]

> Éven Pául was unable to do it.
> It will show you how to dó júst thát (precísely thát, thát véry thíng).

The chief syntactic devices are the cleft and pseudo-cleft sentence types; they too attract the accent as a rule:

> It was Pául who did it.
> The one who did it was Pául.

But clefting is basically independent of accent, as can be seen in cases of repetition (like the brother-and-sister example above). In the following conversation,

> What does John have to do with the affair of the letter? — It was
> John who wróte the letter.

John in the answer can be completely deaccented, since it is a repetition, and yet it is focused on. In this sentence there are two foci, one syntactic, the other accentual. The only new and interesting item in the reply is the fact of writing.

Pointing gestures, pauses, etc. may also be focusers. But English uses accent more than any other one thing.

Deaccenting and the "Neutral" Sentence

Now that we have seen what motivates a speaker to give a separate accent to this or that part of a sentence, we come to the reverse question: what is the motive for deaccenting?

At first sight the question looks superfluous. If we know why an accent is given, all we need to do is subtract that reason and the result is deaccentuation. But things are not that simple. For one thing, a sentence with zero accents is hardly normal; there is still the pattern that—for the sake of the sentence if not for the sake of any of its segments—tends to put a major accent at either end. For another, as we saw in the last section it is normal under some conditions not to accent something even when there might be a reason for accenting it. So we have to look for a balance between accenting and deaccenting. Either can be done with a purpose.

From one standpoint, deaccenting is a more "positive" act than accenting: this is the standpoint of the neutral or "unmarked" sentence. There have been a number of attempts to identify this baseline sentence, mostly stemming from some such notion as that of the hat pattern, or at least to half of the hat pattern: the presence of a "sentence" or "nuclear" accent, with its position defined in some syntactic or lexical fashion. Probably the commonest definition is that a neutral sentence has its main accent on the last "content" word; nothing is stipulated about other accents.

In our terms this would have to be expanded to include at least one more accent, the annunciatory one at the beginning. But what of intermediate accents? When a speaker utters a word at *any* position in a sentence, are we not to assume that it carries sufficient interest to be accented? Otherwise, why say it? A neutral sentence then would be one in which *all* words, or at least all content words, carry an accent, and a non-neutral or marked sentence would be one in which one or more words have been deaccented. Putting it another way we can say that the neutral sentence makes no assumptions about what can be played down because the hearer is supposed to know it already; everything it says it *tells*.

This is the "destressing hypothesis" (in our terms "deaccenting hypothesis") proposed by Bing (1980).[6] Bing's proposals are preferable to those of D. R. Ladd, the intonologist who has done most to promote the idea of deaccenting, in that Ladd does not attach importance to medial accents. In his discussion of "breadth of focus," for example (1980: 77–78), he gives examples like the following (cited, p. 75, from Chomsky and better for our purposes here than the examples on pp. 77–78), in answer to the question *Was he warned to look out for an ex-convict in a red shirt?* The range of answers goes from the narrowest focus, such as would occur with

> No, he was warned to look out for an ex-convict in a red tíe.

to the broadest, as in the two following:

> No, he was simply told to be more cáutious.
> No, nothing was said to ányone.

The problem is that this recognizes only the terminal accent. Unless the original question carries a full range of accents, that is, unless it takes the form

> Was he wárned to lóok óut for an éx-cónvict in a réd shírt?

then at least some of the answers become inappropriate. For instance, if everything is deaccented except *shirt* in the question, then the first answer is appropriate but the others are not.[7]

Bing correctly recognizes accents other than the terminal one, but limits them to nouns. That limitation must be dropped: a neutral sentence accents all content words, if it is to be defined as a sentence that makes no presuppositions. Suppose, for example, that the verb is deaccented in the sentence

> The Chicágo políce confiscated a cáche of drúgs.

—the effect is to presuppose confiscation, by prior mention, by obviousness under the circumstances, or whatever.

One way of testing for a neutral sentence is to see whether it is a normal answer to the general question *What happened?* This is just a way of determining whether the sentence is one that could come out of the blue. But it is not an entirely reliable test, because there can be presuppositions and "givens" even then. Modifying our last example slightly we might get

What happened? — The Chicágo políce found a cáche of drúgs.

with *found* deaccented. Finding is presupposed on the strength of the mere mention of police and drugs—it would almost be the same to omit the verb altogether and say

What happened? — The Chicágo políce! A cáche of drúgs!

Unless the speakers themselves come out of the blue, they are bound to share varying amounts of information and expectations and then may deaccent the referring words. One might thus greet a friend with

Hi there, Jack—I see you're not góing to the office these days.

with *to the office these days* deaccented, when there is prior knowledge of Jack's office-going habit. (See pp. 111–26 for this and other motives for deaccenting.)

What Is Accented

Phonetically speaking, what is accented is a particular syllable of a particular word. If we want to make the word *Caligula* stand out, we emphasize not the entire word but the second syllable. (As we saw in Chapter 5, sometimes more than one syllable is accented, but that is usually for some purpose other than to highlight the word.)

Semantically speaking, we accent a word because its meaning is of particular interest. But meanings are complex, and it may be only some part or aspect of a meaning that we intend to highlight. This can be seen most readily with words whose meanings are rather sharply divisible. An inflected verb gives the best illustration, because it is a composite of such things as tense, mode, number, and person, besides the lexical meaning. Some of these may be highlighted with the rest not counting.

1. Tense: He used to sell those products regularly, didn't he? — He sélls them. Still.

2. Mode: So you insist that he sell those products, eh? — No, I insist that he sélls them. He does it already. There's no need to require him to.

3. Lexical meaning: Why doesn't he buy those products any more? — Because now he sélls them.

4. Activity: How come I can't buy those products in his store? — Because he rarely sélls them. Now he handles a competing line.

5. Actuality: Why doesn't he sell those products any more? — He sélls them! What ever gave you the idea that he had stopped?

Examples 1–3 are self-evident. Example 5 is similar to 2, and both could be paraphrased with *do*: *I insist that he dóes sell them (not that he dó sell them)*, *He dóes sell them!* (opposed to the question with *doesn't sell*). Example 4 does not imply that he gives them away or hoards them; this is an establishment whose business is selling, and the component that the accent emphasizes is simply that activity as such—it is the dynamic component of the verb's meaning, and is paraphrased by *handles* in the next sentence.

A speaker may also foreground the *durative* aspect of a verb. An attested example is the following. The conversation was about the best place to feed a cat with an annoying habit of regurgitation. Indoors was a problem, but she was occasionally fed a snack outside with no difficulty. The speaker said *Maybe we should féed her out there*, meaning 'Maybe we should make that her regular feeding place.' Since feeding was already the topic, there was no need to underscore the lexical meaning of the verb, and in fact the verb would be deemphasized if the durative aspect were extracted so as to carry the accent explicitly: *Maybe we should feed her out there régularly.*

Highlighting person and number in this way is more difficult, since these aspects of meaning, when highlighted, are generally shifted to the noun or pronoun:

> Two are coming? — No, óne is.
> Two are coming? — *No, ís.

But it is possible to have something like a contrast of person read into a verb, as can be seen in the following (the arrow signifies that the pitch of the first word on the next line remains the same):

This was intended to mean 'When yóu are the one to do it, you usually remember, but when someone élse does it, you are liable to forget.' If the speaker had actually emphasized *you*, he might have seemed to be extolling the efficiency of the person as the performer, whereas the intent was only to point up where the responsibility for the *action* lay—the interest is sufficiently in the latter to allow the neighboring verb to absorb it (and *put* can be prominent anyway because it is in contrast with *take out*). But the meaning could be dissected to extract 'responsibility,' in which case the accent could go there:

```
              spón              pút

When you're the one re    si ble for    ting...
```

With other less clearly composite meanings, such as one usually finds with nouns, it is not quite so easy to illustrate the highlighting of one aspect of the meaning with others in abeyance, but a certain amount of dissecting is still possible. A noun includes its grammatical number, and sometimes that is highlighted:

The forest was devastated. Not a trée was left stánding.

Since forests are trees, the word *tree* here does not acquaint the hearer with the fact that trees are present, but only with the fact that none could be counted. The 'quantity' factor can be teased out by using *one*: *Not óne trée was left stánding.* (The most likely intonation here is

```
              trée was left
                               stánd
       Not a                       ing.
```

in which the accent on *tree* is marked by a jump up but no jump down. This is typical of quantifiers. See pp. 169–72.

A noun may also designate some quality of what it names as well as the individual bearing the quality. If we say

Who came? — It was the sáint.

the reference is to an individual. But if we say

It's enough to make a sáint swear.

saint is generic and refers to the quality of sainthood.[8] The same is true of the simple descriptive sentence *He is a sáint* ('He is saintly'). The quality may be quite specific to the context. If one takes a sentence like *Fóllow mé* in isolation, it seems as if it must mean 'Follow me rather than John' etc.—me in my individuality. But in an exchange like

How can I get there? — Just fóllow mé.

the reference is to me as guide: 'Adopt my direction of motion.'

Here is an anecdote to illustrate the ambiguity that may result from the possibility of using the same accent for either quality or identity. Three persons at table were discussing whether a certain loaf of a bakery product was bread or cake. The price marked on the package seemed to indicate that it was cake, and the three more or less agreed. Later during the meal, one of the three, on tasting it, said

<pre>
                 bré
      This
           is
              ad.
</pre>

The two others understood the statement to mean 'This is wonderful stuff (bread of the quality that bread should be),' but it turned out that the speaker meant 'bread, not cake.'

These examples show that as a rule it is necessary to highlight an entire word (through its stressed syllable) when only some part of its meaning is in focus. Again, an illustration from verb inflections:

> You say it blasts easily? — No, it blásted easily.

Here the focus is on the tense, which is also physically manifest in the suffix *-ed*, and yet it would ordinarily seem out of place to accent that syllable: *blastéd*. On the other hand, many words contain some rather transparently distinct affixes, and the less bound these are, the easier it is to accent them separately, especially for contrastive focus. This is not usually done with suffixes:

> Was she careful? — No, she was cáreless (*careléss).

But it can be, especially if instead of, or along with, the implication 'You have the wrong meaning' the speaker implies 'You picked the wrong word (or the wrong pronunciation)':

> We got the information from your informer. — You mean from my informánt.

English has an easier time with prefixes:

> I'll bet they overbíd you. — No, they únderbid me.

> Your country peddles offénsive weapons. — Our weapons are all défensive.

The question of what can be accented affects not only what meanings are focused on but what classes of words are able—by reason of their meaning or their grammatical status—to be accented as centers of interest. We noted in connection with the neutral sentence that content words in the middle of the utterance do qualify. Is it possible for any given content word to be focused as well, that is, to be a main center of interest? And what about function words?

Of the grammatical classes in English, nouns are undoubtedly the most consistent bearers of accent. This is invoked by Bing (1980: 125–40) as the basis for her "noun phrase prominence principle" according to which nouns are always accented unless they refer to previous discourse (p. 126), and also by Gussenhoven (1983: 391) for his accent assignment rule. The claim is too strong, but as we look at the functions that the parts of speech perform, it becomes clear why nouns are nevertheless preeminently accented. Nouns designate the *entities* that we talk about, the objects of prime interest. Here is an example of a word, *own*, that can be either an adjective or a noun. The writer notes that scholastic logic borrowed its categories from the natural languages; then later,

> When logic and metaphysics were used as the basis of grammar, language was, as it were, only getting its ówn back. (Robins 1951: 87. Accent supplied.)

The word *own* is here a noun and must be accented; as an adjective it would not need to be.

In addition to the inherent preeminence of nouns, a quirk of English sentence order frequently forces a verb or an adjective into a position that is normally deaccented. More will be said on this later, but a couple of examples will serve. The problem is the "canonical order" of English sentences, subject + verb + object, which generally— unless there is a change in syntax—forces the agent to take initial position and the predicate to follow. If the interest is focused on the agent, the main accent then is compelled to occur initially, and all succeeding accents are either wiped out or drastically reduced. (This is the "no secondary after the primary" rule discussed on pp. 56–60; it usually applies when the rhematic accent comes first.) In the following, the accent on the verb completely disappears:

> Why are you in such a hurry? — My móther's coming.
> (My móther's visiting us today.) (My móther just phoned.)

These actions are rather highly predictable as causes of the focus of interest on the agent (what counts is the agent's *presence*), and the accent can accordingly be sacrificed. If English had the flexibility of word order that one finds in Spanish, the first example could be worded

> Is cóming my móther.

and the accent on the verb would be preserved, just as it can be, though somewhat awkwardly, with a change in syntax:

> The cóming of my móther.
> A vísit from my móther.

Since technically both *coming* and *visit* are nominal subjects here— hence "nouns"—we note again how much more readily the noun carries an accent.

The other side of the coin is that the parts of speech whose members are commonly referred to as "function words" may, if they are informative or otherwise interesting enough, carry accents. In the following,

> There's a lot more tó it than that.
> We don't know enough abóut it.

the prepositions carry the main information, as can be seen by paraphrasing them with content words:

> There's a lot more that it can cláim (what is *to* it).
> We don't know enough of its partículars (its aboutnesses).

The reason for the more usually subdued condition of prepositions is that their meanings are generally subordinate and more easily inferred from context. They are, in fact, very much like affixes.

There are also differences among individual function words, even within a single category. Take the two prepositions *on* and *upon*:

> The rhythm is already *in* the airstream, in fact, before the actual vowels and consonants which make up words are superimposed on it. (*Linguistics* 6 [1964]: 6. Italics in original.)

As written, this could be *superimpósed ón it*, but would more likely be *superimpósed on it*. If *upon* replaces *on*, it is more apt to be accented: *superimpośed upón it*. While this may in part just be because *upon* is a "heavier" word (as maintained by Thompson 1980: 127), it is also a matter of the greater specificity of *upon* as a spatial and not merely relational and abstract particle. *Upon* has the advantage here, but *on* has it in comparison with *to*, which is still more abstract and dative-like in the following:

> Ón the ríght was a hígh wáll.
> To the ríght was a hígh wáll.

—*on* can be deaccented here, but it would be unusual to accent *to*. As Sweet (1898: §1909) notes in connection with *under*, a similar distinction may be made between concrete and abstract senses of a single preposition:

> Únder the táble. (Jóhn was únder the táble.)
> Under an obligátion. (Jóhn was under an obligátion.)

—the second *under* adds little to the sense: 'John was obligated.' Similarly *by*:

> Bý the táble is a lámp.
> By a líttle before síx they were fínished.

Likewise *with* in the concrete sense of 'accompaniment' versus the more abstract one of 'mutuality' in the phrase *to fight with*. When we say *They are fighting* the word *with* normally adds nothing—the same meaning is expressed by *They are fighting with each other; with* only makes the mutuality of the fighting explicit. But in the less usual sense of 'fight on the side of,' *with* is normally accented. An example of both greater concreteness and greater syllabic weight is *after* versus *for* in

> They wént áfter it.
> They wént for it.

After gives a direction of motion; *for* is an abstract purposive.

A further reason for deaccenting is that in order to get the accents distributed in a sentence to the best advantage, some things have to yield to others, and the function words are more easily sacrificed. This extends to words that are logically quite important. Vanvik (1961: 93) notes the deaccenting of *no* in the phrase *no lónger*, and the same goes for *no sóoner* (*no sooner had he spoken than he realized . . .*); such expressions are a sort of compound, a class of words that normally have only one peak of prominence. (The same principle of sacrifice-for-the-sake-of-prominence applies here as within polysyllabic words, except that there, for the most part, the syllables are relatively mean-ingless and it makes less difference which ones are played down so that one can stand out: in *hórripilate* the syllables *-ri-*, *-pi-*, and *-late* are all sacrificed for the sake of *hor-*.)

We can illustrate the relative sacrificeability of prepositions with ex-amples using the simple *of* and *about* and the compound *because of*. Take the sentence

> He's déad and I'm glád.

This expresses, paratactically, the reason for my feeling glad. There is no need to be specific about 'reason' or 'cause,' and that explains why, if we include a specific reference to causation, it is readily deaccented:

> He's déad and I'm glád of it.
> He's déad and I'm glád about it.
> He's déad and I'm glád because of it.

But if we want to point up 'cause' we may do so:

> He's déad and I'm glád óf it.
> He's déad and I'm glád becáuse of it.

This has the double advantage of explicating 'cause' and adding em-phasis: the extra accent so close to the end (especially in *glád óf*) is climactic. One might think that given the unimportance of *of*, empha-sis is the only reason for putting the accent on that word, and yet if we try to do the same with *about* the result is not very good:

> ?He's déad and I'm glád abóut it.

Our sensation here is much the same as if we had tried to say

?He's déad and I'm glád where thát's concérned.

—*about* and *where that's concerned* mean roughly the same, and they add almost nothing to the sense, whereas *of* and *because of* name the source or cause, and stand in opposition to *in spite of*. There is a stronger contradiction in

*He's dead and I'm glad of it even though I regret its happening.

than in

He's dead and I'm glad about it even though I regret its happening.

The tables are turned, with *of* and *about*, in the expressions

No dóubt about it.	No dóubt abóut it.
No dóubt of it.	?No dóubt óf it.

Now it is *about* that more readily takes the accent. 'Where x is concerned,' our gloss for *about*, is the relevant sense, whereas *of* has no obvious meaning apart from the purely relational one. (For the same reason, *of* is normally the deaccented member of the compound preposition *becáuse of*: *because* is more specific to 'causation.' It would be unusual to say *He's déad and I'm glád because óf it.*)

All this seems to show that we prefer to put our accents of power where they might go anyway as accents of interest. The same modicum of interest and its usefulness to power can be seen in the accenting of nouns that, within their noun phrases, are comparatively redundant. Suppose we say

John is a níce mán (sórt, féllow, gúy, cháp, pérson).

The fact that John is all those things is foreknown, and yet that shape of the sentence is more usual than

John is a níce man.

with *man* deaccented.[9] By accenting *man* we make the statement more powerful. At the same time there is justification from the interest standpoint in that a sentence like

John is nice but he's no good as a husband.

may sound a bit contradictory, and we are apt to prefer something like either of the following:

John is nice in some respects but not as a husband.
John is a nice man but he's no good as a husband.

—'nice as a man.'

Grammar gets involved in this to the extent that there is a difference in behavior between nouns preceded by descriptive (intensifiable) adjectives and nouns preceded by classifying (nonintensifiable) adjectives. The latter are freely deaccented, especially when their contribution to the meaning of the phrase is relatively slight—the similarity between such phrases and noun-noun phrases is obvious:

> This method won't work because of the calóric résidue.
> This method won't work because of the héat résidue.

In both instances the accent on *residue* may be dropped. (This is the basis of "compounds" such as *fát lady, wórk permit, hótfoot, wíldlife,* etc.) The former—nouns preceded by descriptive adjectives—are almost routinely accented (the pattern is sometimes referred to as a "phrasal stress" in contrast to "compounding stress"); they are deaccented as a rule only when the meaning of the noun is already given:

> John wears a cólorful tíe. — Looks more like a fláshy tie to mé.

In both cases of deaccenting, if the speaker wants either to point up the meaning of an otherwise deaccented noun, or to gain power, he may add the accent:

> What does John know about treating these diseases? — My friend,
> Jóhn is a médical mán!
> John wears a colorful tie. — It cértainly ís a fláshy tíe!

The gain in power is most evident with a fully redundant noun, and the same is true of the place-holding pronoun *one*:

> I wasn't aware that John was a member of the club. — My dear fellow, Jóhn is the óldest mémber (óldest óne)!

When a descriptive adjective is used merely to classify, it behaves like a classifying adjective:

> John is a crázy mán to act like that.
> John is a cŕazy man ('lunatic') and should be locked up.

Interest and power may compete in a speaker's decision to accent this or that function word. The following is the legend under a *New Yorker* cartoon depicting a Canadian Mountie at the door of a snowbound cabin with a single row of tracks leading toward it:

> Come on out, Batiste. I know you're in there.

The second sentence virtually has to have the main accent on *in*—it is the more informative locative word, and 'thereness' is given anyway.[10]

Function words may compete with one another. In the following, the rival forms are the copula *be* and the preposition *with*:

> It looks as if it were going to be with us for a while.

As originally spoken, the main accent was on *be*, as if *be* were more or less equivalent to *stay*. But it could as readily go on *with*, emphasizing the 'accompaniment' aspect and at the same time picking up a little more power by virtue of the position of *with*. The same happens in the following, where the rival forms are the comparative *more* and the preposition *of*:

> That sugar's all right, but you have to use a lot more of it.

As originally spoken, the main accent was on *of*. Here it is the admonitory effect of the climactic accent that seems to have swayed the choice. If *it* is replaced with *the stuff*, an accented *of* becomes less likely; the accent is backed farther away from the end, and too little of the power advantage remains to offset the scant information value of the preposition.

Other function words too may come to the fore when their meanings are essential:

> Did John do it, or James? — John ánd James did it.
> Everything was fine, bút . . .
> What's shé doing here?

The last example, an accented pronoun, is typical of the deictic or pointing use of that part of speech: if it comes out of the blue it requires a gesture indicating the person in question, who could as easily be identified as *Sálly* or *thát pérson*.

Enough has been said to show that while some loose generalizations can be made about this or that part of speech, the question is really tangential to what controls the placement of accent: the item to be accented, and power to the utterance.

What Is Deaccented

Deaccenting puts sharply the question of what is done because it is done and what is done because it is intended. This line between the arbitrary and the meaningful must be drawn at every level of language, but it is nowhere more wavering and indistinct than in the placement of accent.

In an ordinary word such as *cameo* there is no question about the status of the individual syllables. *Ca-* gets the accent if there is one, *-me-* and *-o* are not only not accented but the vowels are reduced as well. We can speak of the "stress of" *cameo* because its pronunciation allows no choice.

In the phrase *happy couple* we may accent both words (*háppy cóuple*) or deaccent either or both (*happy cóuple, háppy couple, anóther happy couple*). We are free to choose and do so in accord with our meaning. It would be incorrect to speak of the "stress of" the phrase *happy couple* (though we might speak of the "stress of" either of the two words that make it up) because there is no predetermined location of stress. We may only speak of the "accent(s) on" the phrase.

But what are we to make of the title of a 1959 movie, *A Hóle in the Head*, so pronounced in the advance trailer, with no accent on *head*? Or the indecorous use, in various longer expressions, of *a hóle in the ground*? If our notions of the neutral sentence mean anything, something must have acted to *remove* accents from *head* and *ground*, causing a shift toward the arbitrary side of the line, enabling us—almost—to speak of the "stress of" such phrases.

An even more striking example, because it affects a particular word in all its occurrences and not just in particular phrases, is the pronoun *it*. The shape of the word itself tells a story: *it* rather than *hit* (a dialectal form that is still heard), unlike *'im*, *'er*, and *'is*, which still have their undiminished forms *him*, *her*, and *his*. Though we can accent *it* if we must, as in

If I have a clean shirt I'll wear ít rather than thís one.

we are uncomfortable with this pronoun when it is heavily accented:

As between Jill and John, give me hér.
*As between John and his dog, give me ít.

It is somehow stigmatized as relatively unaccentable.

The first observation about deaccenting—if we assume that accents are given with a purpose—is that it depends on the lack of such a purpose. In terms of "accents of interest," the lack of an accent on an accentable word should signify some kind of lack of interest. There is nothing in it to get keyed up about. The most obvious motive for this is simply that the referent of the expression has already been mentioned:

What's your policy toward Israel? — I've álready tóld you about that.

Although we are free to accent the word *that* (using the rise-fall-rise intonation typical of "reversed themes"—see pp. 50, 182) and would normally do so if *that* began the sentence (*Thát I've álready tóld you about*), we are not required to accent it, because it repeats the sense of *policy toward Israel*. (One often finds cases of elegant variation here, resulting in a flabby style because the subsequent mentionings are de-accented; for instance, in

> Latin America is increasing its population at the rate of three million a year, while the U.S. is growing by about two million annually.

annually repeats *a year* and must be deaccented, thus deflating the end of the sentence.) This kind of coreferentiality is what accounts for the normal deaccenting of personal pronouns; their referents are generally also their antecedents. The same is true of other coreferential expressions, whether epithetical, legalistic, or whatever:

> I gave the book to someone. — Who did you gíve *the stupid thing* to? (Who did you gíve *the said book* to?)
>
> Did Ernest get away? — No, they cáught *the nincompoop.*

On the other hand, deaccenting does not depend on such near-total inconsequentiality. One could never determine when something is totally inconsequential anyway. *Relative* inconsequentiality affects not only meanings that have gone before but also meanings that are already implied in the context, meanings that are so ubiquitous that we can take them for granted, meanings that we share so intimately with our interlocutor that they need no emphasis, meanings that are less important than some nearby focal meaning and must be sacrificed to it, and meanings that we simply feel like playing down at the moment. (The question of whether they need mentioning at all is another matter.) In the following examples, the deaccented expressions are shown in smaller type.

Meanings already implied in the context

Context here refers to verbal context or situational context or both:

> She got most of the letter all right, but she skípped a line. (*Line* could be accented, but in the context of a letter no accent is needed.)
>
> One problem about summer is that it's so hard to keep fóod from spoiling. (If you keep it, the object is to keep it from spoiling.)
>
> If heavy débt payments are weighing you down . . . (TV ad. Heaviness weighs one down.)
>
> You can't place a bet unless you're eightéen or over. (*Or over* could be omitted and *eighteen* as 'a limit' would still be implied.)
>
> Why don't you like fluorescent lamps? — The húm annoys me. (Annoyance is expected in the context of not-liking.)
>
> If you try to avoid any shield at all (in riding a motorcycle), the force of the rain is like sánd thrown in your face. (Under the circumstances the natural place for this to be felt is in the face.)

They strángled him to death. (Strangulation normally implies death. Contrast *They hóunded him to déath.*)

No dúmping allowed. (*No dumping* suffices. Contrast the less expected *Dúmping allówed.*)

Lie down! Put a píllow under your head. (The normal place for a pillow is under the head.)

An áccident happened. (There is little else that an accident can do. But contrast the more or less definitional *Áccidents just háppen.*)

Why are you so resentful of him? — Because he fíghts against me.

In the last example, fighting is normally 'against' (compare *Because he fíghts me*), so *against* can be deaccented, though it would be equally correct to accent both words or just *against*. But if the sentence is *Because he acts against me* it becomes virtually necessary to accent *against* (and possible to deaccent the colorless *acts*), because *against* is the only word carrying the needed sense of 'opposition.'

Ubiquitous meanings that can be taken for granted

Since ubiquity is 'context' in a very broad sense, there is no real separation between this subclass and the preceding one:

When will it happen? — About an hóur from now.

How far is it? — About a míle from here. (In this and the preceding example, the axis of orientation is the speaker, whose location in space and time is assumed.)

What happened to Jóhn? — He broke his lég. (A common accident involving a leg. Contrast *He scálded his lég.*)

I'm going to have to have my wátch cleaned. (Cleaning, repairing, adjusting, and the like are common operations with mechanical devices.)

Pánts pressed. (Sign on door of cleaning establishment, normal reading. But *Pánts cléaned and préssed*—the balance of information shifts.)

I don't know whether I féel better because I get up earlier, or get up earlier because I féel better. (*Feel* introduces the notion of health, within which, given the circumstances, 'better' is expected. But *féel bétter* is equally possible.)

What's the matter? — My héad aches. (Common complaint where heads are concerned. Contrast the more emphatic *My héad is kílling me.*)

You won't catch me going anywhere in thís weather. (Weather is always with us; the word could be omitted here. Compare the use of *it*, for the ubiquity of weather: *It's hot, It's windy, It's wet.*)

Meanings intimately shared with the interlocutor

Among family members, friends, and acquaintances there is much
that can simply be taken for granted, for example:

> Hi, George! I héard you were going to be around a couple of days. Wélcome
> báck!

> Let me apologize for my brother. He knéw he should have asked your per-
> mission first. He was júst thóughtless.

> What's new? — I had a date with the líghthouse-keeper's daughter.
> (The interlocutors know the daughter through her relationship to
> her father. Contrast the unexpected *I was bitten by the líghthouse-
> keeper's dóg.*)

> We're lost. — It's not mý fault. Í'm not responsible. (Both speakers recog-
> nize the imputation of fault. Accenting either *fault* or *responsible*
> would present the idea of fault as not previously shared.)

> I'm surprised that Zák hasn't asked to come in. (This was a casual re-
> mark, out of the blue, referring to a cat with a well-known com-
> ing-in and going-out habit.)

Meanings sacrificed to a nearby focal meaning

Again, this subclass overlaps with the preceding ones: in any bal-
ancing of interest, if one is favored another is disfavored. We saw this
earlier in connection with examples like *Why are you in such a hurry? —
My móther's coming*, where one might under the same conditions find
a somewhat different conversational exchange: *Why are you in such a
hurry? — My móther. — Oh, is she coming? — Yes.* Here the primary
answer is 'It's on account of my mother'; the *coming* is important only
so far as it puts her on the scene. Still, it is possible to deaccent things
that are important in their own right, only less important than the
item carrying the accent, as we saw in the sentence *It's enough to make a
sáint swear* (p. 103). Examples:

> Look at Sandy! Her páws are even dry! (Surprise at the paws overrides
> the evidence of dryness.)

> Mommy, mommy! A béar came and bit me!

> I have to hurry along. My cóusin's having breakfast with us. (Speaker ex-
> pects hearer to accept the mere presence of *cousin* as explaining
> the haste; it could be any other action that puts him on the
> scene.)

> Stand aside. Jóhn's taking this turn.

Indefinites that signify 'approximate identity' are eminently sacrificeable, and are routinely deaccented:

He has to gó somewhere. (Contrast *He has to go hóme.*)

Come óver sometime.

What repels me about Georgette is that she hátes everybody. (She is a hater.)

Stáy a day or two. (Contrast *Stáy tén dáys.*)

This applies also to indefinite nouns especially when indefiniteness is reinforced by some such formula as *or other*:

Where's Jim? — He's out páinting some building or other. (It would be unusual to deaccent *some building* if *or other* were not added.)

Where's June? — She's in the kitchen cóoking God knows what.

The indifference to the identity of the object makes the action central:

What's he doing? — He's attáching some gadget, I guess. (Spoken of a person seen puttering around his car. The word *gadget* is inherently indifferent to identity.)

Where's Joe? — He's in the living room réading his usual trash.

Meanings the speaker simply chooses to play down

There may be nothing in the text or context to suggest or induce a deaccentuation, yet deaccenting suits the speaker's purpose. (It always does, of course, but in other cases we have textual or contextual clues to what the purpose is apt to be.) In the following, the first and second answers show what is apt to happen with an indefinite object—the interest shifts to the verb; but the third shows the same answer as the second with everything softened except the drumbeat of power at the end:

Why did you clam up all of a sudden? —
Because I didn't want to embárrass anybody.
Because I didn't want to embárrass any of the people.
Because I didn't want to embarrass any of the péople.

In the following, the speaker has decided to make everything subordinate to the central idea of gambling:

What's Larry been doing lately? — Just gámbling every nickel he could lay his hands on, thát's all.

A similar case in which the centrality depends on the emotional impact of the accented word (see pp. 83–84):

It's áwful the way they manipulate the people of this country.

And a similar one in which shared knowledge adds a motive to the deaccenting—a policeman is talking to his wife:

You won't belíeve the things that happened on the beat today.

One may even find a positive reason for giving an accent, which the speaker ignores. In the following, there is an implied contrast between *did* and *didn't*, and yet the speaker was heard to deaccent *did*:

Did I lóck that or dídn't I?

As locking a door was just being brought up, it would have been odd to deaccent *lock*, and *did* was sacrificed to it. Probably accenting both words would have seemed too emphatic—the power aspect is also a factor.

We come now to the *hóle in the head* or relatively fixed-accent types, where it is possible, or nearly so, to speak of the "stress of" the expression. There is always some degree of stereotyping, which is manifested in several ways, including the tendency to restrict the position of the accent. This frequently means the loss of an accent position, most often the one toward the end, resulting in the typical shape of the English compound with its leftward stress, as in

He was sent to the eléctric chair.
Let's go get our Chrístmas tree.
It's about time for them to repaint the cénter strip.
They were looking for légal advice.

Compounds assimilate themselves in this respect to independent words, which have a virtually fixed stress. Depending on the degree of fusion, a compound may or may not allow an accent on the element that does not usually receive it. The three forms

éyeglasses   réading glasses   dístance glasses

go down from highly to slightly fused, and this accounts for the freedom felt by the speaker who said

I didn't bring my dístance glásses.

to convey the point that glasses as such were the problem, not just the kind of glasses.

Degree of fusion can be tested even with unit words:

I'm not compláining, I'm just expláining.

Here, despite the fact that the two verbs are cognates, fusion has gone so far that we are not apt to express the contrast by accenting the prefix,

*I'm not cómplaining, I'm just éxplaining.

though as we saw on page 104 above this can readily be done with less fused derivatives:

He didn't próclaim, he déclaimed.

Give me a lemonáde, not a lemon píe. (The speaker is one who normally says *lémonade*.)

Most compounds, as might be expected, are unfused enough to allow a separate accent when there is a shift of interest, and some still waver—there are speakers who say *ápple pie*, *íce cream*, *oátmeal*, and *eléctric chair*, and others who continue the older "phrasal stress" with *apple píe*, *ice créam*, *oatméal*, and *electric cháir*.[11] Examples of shift of interest:

This knife is so dull I can't tell which is the cutting édge. (The idea of 'edge' was new to the context, and important.)

How do you manage to hold the bottom of the coffee pot without burning your fingers? — I use my fingernáils. (The fingers are held so that the nails, not the flesh, are in contact with the hot surface; further, *finger* has just been mentioned and is redundant.)

She always comes in the áfternoon. (Twelve-year-old, speaking of someone who always comes 'later'; probably no direct contrast with *forenoon*, which is not likely to be part of the child's active vocabulary.)

Soon the young [mink] become keen hunters, sometimes taking on such unlikely customers as snapping turtles. (*Reader's Digest*, Mar. 1958, p. 110. Could be read either as *snápping turtles* or as *snapping túrtles*, the latter if it is sufficiently remarkable that turtles of any kind are the victims.)

You should have heard yourself grumbling away. — No, you should have heard yóurself.

Although compounding is not strictly a matter of affixing a satellite word, like a kind of suffix, to a main word, there is something of this in the kinds of nouns that make up the second element in the bulk of our compounds. They tend to be rather general in their meaning, hence less informative than the grammatical "modifier" they are attached to, and this in part explains their deaccenting.[12] The word *street*—in the context of a city—is more general than *avenue*, *boulevard*, *lane*, *road*, *way*, *court*, *circle*, or *crescent*. Looking down on a city from a height one can speak of seeing its streets, but not its avenues, lanes, and so on unless specificially those *kinds* of streets are meant. Accordingly, *street* is deaccented, whereas the other names ordinarily are not:

Élm Street   Fírst Street   Birch Láne

(This does not mean that we could actually have predicted that *street* would be deaccented in such names, only that there existed the greater likelihood that it would be.) Similarly the word *magazine* is more generic than *journal*, *review*, or *monthly*—the average person is more apt to say *Look at all the magazines on that rack* than to say *Look at all the journals* (*reviews*, *monthlies*) *on that rack*. Accordingly we get

Hárper's Magazine	The Atlantic Mónthly
The Ladies Home Jóurnal	The Saturday Revíew

Other contrastive pairs and sets:

line vs. *railroad*: the Rock Ísland Line; the Rock Island Ráilroad

building vs. *palace*: the Góvernment Building; the Government Pálace

foundation vs. *endowment*: the Róckefeller Foundation; the Carnegie Endówment

engine vs. *locomotive*: a stéam engine; a steam locomótive

chief vs. *princess*: an Índian chief; an Indian príncess

solution vs. *emulsion*: an óil solution; an oil emúlsion

concert, program, performance vs. *opera, symphony, ballet*, etc.: the Póps concert; the Metropolitan Ópera

time, tide vs. *equinox, solstice*: súmmertime; summer sólstice (but a choice between *súmmer season* and *summer séason*)

port vs. *harbor*: Néwport; Bar Hárbor

group, association vs. *league, alliance, party, bund*: Ross Loos Médical Group; the Epworth Léague

house vs. *capitol*: státe house; state cápitol

drops vs. *kisses*: lémon drops; lemon kísses

joint vs. *café*: Jóe's Joint; Joe's Café

So when we find things like

Gúlf Stream (contrast *Japan Cúrrent*)	sénsitive plant
búsy work	júry trial
búsiness district	cómfort station
líght year	Húntington's disease
chúck wagon	(contrast *Huntington's choréa*)

we assume that there are other kinds of streams, work, districts, years, wagons, diseases, etc.; the contrastiveness of the first element of the compound is probably the chief determinant of the stress of the compound when it is first created. One example, *Boy Scóut* versus *Gírl Scout*, was discussed on page 71. Besides such individual cases there are also some broader generalizations of less interest to us here because the study of compounds involves much more than the vagaries of accent placement: the general tendency to backshift the stress (see pp. 351–52), the institutionalization of the referent, the category of the head word (noun, adjective, etc.), the category of the modifying word, and so on. On the latter point there is a loose tendency for adjective-plus-noun phrases to retain the "phrasal stress" on the second element but noun-plus-nouns to move the stress to the left. So, while we speak of

the hóusing shortage

we also say

the Presbyterian Chúrch	short círcuit
the Republican Párty	sacredców
scarlet féver	collective bárgaining

But this is more attributable to the dynamics of the particular combinations than to a grammatical rule.[13] We say *disappearing ínk*, but *vánishing cream*, probably because vanishing cream has been institutionalized as part of a battery of cosmetic creams that are referred to in comparison with one another. So we find adjective-plus-noun compounds that stress the first element (and usually employ nonintensifiable adjectives):

márital problem	matrimónial agency
bláckbird	experiméntal farm
yéllow streak	ráwhide

and noun-plus-noun compounds that seem to contradict one another:

a séa voyage, an ocean vóyage; a séa trip, an ócean trip
lima béans, líma beans; kídney beans, pínto beans, etc.
ólive oil, castor óil, cástor oil; míneral oil
Báptist seminary, Baptist séminary[14]

Why, for example, the inconsistency in *jélly beans* and *candy córn*, both naming kinds of candy? Perhaps because jelly beans are more detectably jelly than beans, whereas candy corn imitates exactly the shape of a grain of corn—or, if we are looking for a grammatical explanation, because *candy* is more often used as a modifier—*candy cáne, candy cóne, candy Sánta Claus*—just as *chocolate* is in the parallel inconsistency *chocolate cáke, spíce cake*.

To add more complications, there are also dialectal differences—the reader will probably not agree with all the preferences indicated above. The one thing we can say, in spite of the historical drift that alters these forms as the separate meanings are submerged in the whole (thus becoming "opaque"), is that at *some* point the choice of an accent or a deaccent was dictated by the same principles that operate in less stereotyped cases.

But it is true nevertheless that there are words—the pronoun *it* was one example—that appear to be formally and arbitrarily less accentable than others. They are apt to be words of inherently low semantic content and therefore relatively predictable and uninteresting. The sacrificeability of prepositions has already been discussed; but even nouns are involved. Consider the noun *sake*:

> They did it for Jóhn's sake.

As this says little more than 'They did it for John,' the accent on *sake* can be sacrificed. In fact, it would rarely be accented except with an accent of power, in exclamations like

> For Gód's sáke!

The same is true of the noun *behalf*, and here we see an odd tug of war between that word and a preceding possessive. A speaker on radio was heard to say

> . . . on its behálf . . .

deaccenting and reducing the word *its*—not surprising in view of the usual treatment of *it* and *its*, but doubtful here. We can appreciate the difference better using the possessive *his*, which in its full form requires aspiration of the *h*. Thus whereas *He rode in on 'is horse* is normal with reduced *his*, in a conversation like

> What about John, where carrying out this action was concerned? —
> My friend, I did it on his behálf!

the *his* must take its full form even when not pitch-accented (the main accent on *behalf* points up the notion of 'beneficiary'). But like *sake*, *behalf* tends to be sacrificeable, as in

> Why did they do it? — They did it on Jóhn's behalf.

Other examples of "empty words":

> The orange had a sóft spot (vs. a soft blémish).
> He gave me a 25-cént piece (vs. a 25-cent cóin).
> They went down the róad a piece (a little way).
> Afterwards we had a ráiny spell (vs. a rainy dáy).
> They brought me some réading matter.
> Look at those cráwling things! (vs. crawling ínsects).
> Come over to mý house (vs. my stúdio).
> Give him his móney's worth (vs. his money's válue).

He was up on a pérjury rap.

They have a good stock of sóftware.

The fact that *software* is written solid testifies to the degree of fusion, and underscores the fact that there is no dividing line between the "words" that make up such compounds and the "formatives" that were once words and are now lost, though some can still be identified. We can see *-ware* in *tinware, hardware, silverware*, etc., and *-goods* in *drygoods*, and we still coin with them: *Fárber ware, plástic goods*. But others are more or less lost: *-land* [lənd] in *Iceland, -ton* (= *town*) in *Bremerton, -forth* (= *ford*) in *Danforth*, etc. Many are submerged and unrecognizable.

Now we are in a position to move afield from compounds and look at deaccenting in a broader framework, for relative "emptiness" is found everywhere and is keyed to the drabness of familiarity as well as to the indifference of overbroad meaning.

First, there is the general tendency to stereotype commonly used phrases, whether they are precisely like "compounds" or not, and part of this stereotyping is the freezing of the accent. The following are regular enough to enable us to speak of the "stress of" the phrase:

> They had a regular frée-for-all. (Contrast *It was free for áll.*)
>
> He ran like a hóuse afire. (Contrast *like a soul in ágony.*)
>
> It contains garlic, thyme, sage, and só forth (and só on). (Contrast *and so fórward, and so ónward.* See Jones 1956: §990.)
>
> Stop trying to pull the wóol over my eyes!
>
> If you do that I'll knock the stúffing out of you.
>
> It looks like something the cát dragged in.

Others are less fully stereotyped:

> You can express yourself until you're blúe in the face. (WEEI, Boston, May 29, 1969, Jim Westover, talkmaster, speaking.)
>
> I guess I didn't, áfter all. (An accent of power would have made this *after áll.*)
>
> What happens when they change the bíll of fare? (Jack Benny, Apr. 15, 1962.)
>
> It all depends on whose óx is gored.
>
> I can do it with my éyes shut.
>
> She has a good héad on her shoulders. (Compare *a good head for búsiness.*)
>
> Sit down! Take the lóad off your feet!
>
> For goodness' sake! What tóok you so long? (An accent of power would give *took you so lóng.*)
>
> [If I kiss him] he'll give me a big sóck in the nose. (Nine-year-old.)

The last example seems to be modeled on the fully stereotyped *stíck in the mud, hóle in the head* examples cited earlier.

In other cases the familiarity of the deaccented words seems to be a stronger factor than stereotyping—added of course to the relatively greater importance of the accented word:

> Look at you! You've got múd on your hands!
> Would you lóok at this thing!
> Wait till I put some móney in the drawer or we'll run short next time.

Some deaccented words are like certain of the compounding forms such as *street, -man* [mən], *-town, -dale,* etc.—deaccented most of the time, as in *They live in Fóstertown* (versus *They live in Foster Cíty*). Examples are *man* [mæn], *place, spell,* and the epithetical nouns that are often used coreferentially as noted above:

> Why don't you show Martin aróund the place? ("Masters of Mystery"
>   program, WABC, New York, Sept. 27, 1956.)
>
> He was jailed because he shót a man.
>
> Come over and stáy with us for a spell.
>
> How did you happen to stop? — I saw a couple of guys pláying.
>   (Contrast *I saw a couple of bóys playing.*)

One can predict with a fair degree of safety that such words will be deaccented much of the time. But there is no difference, in principle, between such more predictable deaccenting and the less predictable deaccenting that depends more heavily on context. In both cases what decides the question is the focus of interest. In the following, *right* is not as predictably deaccentable as *place, spell,* etc., yet in its context it adds less to the overall meaning than *ripe* does—we could say *Wait for conditions* and imply that they must be *right*:

> Wait until condítions are right.
> Wait until conditions are rípe.

Up to this point nothing has been said about the *position* of the deaccented item, but in nearly all the examples cited it has come at the end of the utterance or at least just before a pause or major syntactic break. This biased attention is a shortcoming of most studies of deaccenting: the deaccent position that is most often discussed is the "post-nuclear" one, the one directly after the final accent in the utterance. The explanation no doubt is the striking difference between the accent pattern we are most accustomed to, with a major accent at or near the end, and the pattern that shows a backshift. It is easier to hear the difference between *They jáiled him because he shót a man* and *They jáiled him because he shót an ófficer* than to hear the difference between *They cáught a man stéaling* and *They cáught an ófficer stéaling.*[15] Nevertheless, given the notion of "neutral sentence" in which all content words are accented, if a word that is correctly deaccented when it comes after the last accent is instead encountered earlier, it should (assuming an equivalent message) be deaccentable there too. In the sequence

> . . . unless you enter at mid-year. In thát case you have to wáit a semester to cátch úp.

semester can be deaccented because academic time is so often expressed in semesters; the important thing is the waiting. It makes no difference what the reason is for deaccenting. In an example like

```
        nóugh
You've done e
                                      hé
              harm not to want to hurt   r.
```

harm and *hurt* are deaccented probably because of some immediately prior reference to harming and hurting, *want* probably because of a presupposition. In the exchange

> When did it happen? — Well, maybe around the first of September. But I know it was in the early fall.

one may distribute the accents as in

```
      knów
                   ín      éar   fá
But I      it was     the     ly
                                11.
```

with *know, in, ear-,* and *fall* all getting them, or as in

```
      knów
                                  fá
But I      it was in the early
                                11.
```

in which everything in the middle is deaccented. The first pattern may imply that the information is all relatively new (though it could be "interesting" merely from an argumentative standpoint), whereas the second may imply a repetition of the idea—the other speaker perhaps has questioned the fact, and the present speaker repeats what he has said before.

To return to more or less routine deaccenting, it is not merely a question of individual *words* being more familiar or more exiguous in their meanings, but of contexts being so commonplace as to make some of their component words redundant. For example, in expressions like

> Whích ánswer is corréct?
> Hów hárd did you trý?

the interrogative word is accented, but in more hackneyed expressions like

> Which ís it?   What fór?   How cóme?

the interrogative word is often deaccented to the point of being devoiced or otherwise deformed; *Which is it?* may become *Chisit?*

The same thing happens with verbs. In expressions like

> light a fire   open the door

the verbs may be deaccented: a fire is always lighted and doors are regularly opened; but a case like

> change one's mind

is different—in changing one's mind what counts is the change (see Sweet 1898: §1904). A routine verb such as *get* is often deaccented:

> Téll 'im to get lóst.
> I've gótta get on the tráin.
> Trý to get a pícture of him.

How regular deaccentuation is with *get* can be seen in the folk spelling *giddap* for *get up* (to a horse), and in the need that most writers feel to put the verb in quotation marks when it has its full transitive value:

> Since the government abandoned its attempt to "get" him on perjury charges . . . (*I. F. Stone's Weekly*, Dec. 19, 1955, p. 3.)

The verb *go* also has a folk spelling, *gwan*, for its deaccentuation in the phrase *go on* (see p. 355) and a similar deformation occurs in

> [gə] 'wáy! (*go away*)
> [gə] hóme! (to a dog)

But a less routine use is not deaccented:

> What did you do [as a result of not being able to get in the toilet on the ferry], "gó" on the train?

Incidentally, this is not restricted to the sense of 'defecate'; one may easily have

> Can you gó ['get where you're going'] on the tráin?

Compare also *see* versus *spot* and *catch* versus *capture*:

What happened? — Tómmy saw a béar!
Tómmy spótted a béar!
Tómmy caught a béar!
Tómmy cáptured a béar!

(These are not required choices, only likely ones.)

Verbs in final position may of course be deaccented too, though this is not the commonest spot for a verb; an example already cited:

Why are you in such a hurry? — My móther's coming.

But there is one construction that has occasioned much dispute, mainly because investigators have tried to impose a syntactic rather than a prosodic explanation on it. The typical contrast is exemplified in

John has órders to léave.
John has órders to leave.

The first signifies 'John is supposed to leave,' with focus on his leaving; the second, 'John is carrying orders (to be turned over to somebody),' with focus on the orders. At the same time, there is a difference in the syntax: in the first, *to leave* is intransitive, and modifies *orders*; in the second, *to leave* is transitive and takes *orders* as its implied direct object. (There are more involved statements of the relationship, but this will suffice.) That is, such is the syntax so long as nothing is contextually presupposed. The syntax takes a 180° turn if we supply the following:

I thought that John was supposed to take his orders with him. — No, John has órders to léave.

I thought that John was merely obeying a requést to leave. — No, John has órders to leave.

So the syntax explains nothing, and we come down to a relative weighting of interest. It is obvious why *leave* is highlighted in the first sentence. It is almost as obvious why it must be less highlighted than *orders* in the second sentence, and its position does the rest: the usual thing is to accent nothing after the last main accent (this much *is* syntactic). Relative weight can be readily seen as we substitute verbs having different degrees of interest within their contexts:

John has bréad to eat, móney to spend, a jób to do, a bóok to read, stóries to tell, whéels to grease.

John has a pálimpsest to decípher, a stúdent to díscipline, a cáncer to éxtirpate, a wáll to undermíne.

As soon as one gets away from conventional objects having conventional actions tied to them (bread is naturally to be eaten, money is for spending, etc.), the action takes on more importance. And it may have more importance than the noun even in some conventional settings:

> John has tíme to búrn.
> John has lóts to dó.
> John has sómething to sáy.

And the weighting may easily vary:

> (1) John has a lífe to líve.
> (2) John has a lífe to live.
> (3) John has thíngs to dó.
> (4) John has thíngs to do.

In (1), the interest is in the verve of living; in (2) it is assumed that living is what one expects of a life. In (3), the interest is in John as a doer; in (4), things are weighing on him.

Playing Down at the End

Enough examples have been shown to demonstrate the possibility of deaccenting before as well as after the last main accent in a sentence. Yet deaccenting at the end has a particular effect, probably because it goes against expectations: the rhematic accent is usually close to the end and usually is carried by some focally important word. Deaccenting that part deflates the utterance—the reverse of power. A speaker may choose the resulting anticlimax for reassurance or courtesy. Compare

> I'm giving you this wristband for your watch because I don't want you to be lósing it all the time.
> . . . because I don't want you to be áll the tíme lósing it.

The second is suitable for a reprimand—the donee may be notoriously careless; the first is gentle and perhaps humorous. Similarly in

> What's wrong here? — Your employee John Smíth made a slight miscalculation.
> ?. . . Your employee John Smíth made a miscalculation.

The downplaying in the first (whether to reassure the person spoken to or not to lay too heavy a blame on the culprit) is seen in the wording—a *slight* miscalculation; the second sentence is less likely because a miscalculation, unqualified, is too serious a matter to be played down.

Deaccenting for non-power thus accords intonationally with deaccenting for real or pretended lack of interest, and the two so often go together that we come to expect everything to be at a flat level following the final major prominence in the utterance. Or at least linguists have allowed themselves to come to that expectation. Some analysts (e.g. Daneš 1960: 46; Bing 1980: 31) have argued that no prominence at all is to be found on the terminal level, at least for some syntactic types. But that is an overstatement (see Chapter 12, n. 4). It is not purely a question of deaccenting, but is to some degree a question of the RELATIVE HEIGHT of the accents, a point to be developed later (see pp. 237–41). It will be enough here to give some illustrations of slight bumps on the landscape alternating with a prairie-like flatness. We note that although absolute flatness is always possible, when a terminal level runs to greater length the temptation to add small rises becomes greater. In the following the grave accent is used for such prominences within the overall flattening indicated by smaller type:

> What are you doing there? — I'm putting away some of the júnk
> that's been lýing aròund since last Jànuary.
>
> Oh, I want that new CB! Can we get it? — Well, it depends on
> whether you've got any móney in those wèll-prèssed, wèll-tàilored
> brìtches of yours.
>
> You aren't interested in telling us the truth! You're only interested in
> quieting us down so we won't tróuble you while you procèed with your
> nefàrious plàns!
>
> You look worried. — I ám worried. My móther's going in for an operàtion.

In the first example, a dead level would be about equally likely. In the second the speaker is apt to underscore the irony not only by slight pitch prominences but also by lengthening *pressed* and adding other forms of non-pitch accenting such as voice qualifiers and facial gestures. The third example is to be imagined shouted by an angry housewife at a Nuclear Regulatory Commission official suggesting the venting of krypton gas at Three Mile Island; the accents are unmistakable, but do not reach the height of the one on *trouble*. In both the third and the fourth, a flat level is unlikely, because of either strong feelings or essential information or both. This is the opposite of what happens when the speaker seems to throw in unimportant material just to get the deflating effect of the dead level:

> You want me to listen? Then stop pontíficating all over the place.

Though the differences between degrees of accentuation in the terminal level are great enough to leave no doubt that significant accenting does occur there, studies are needed to show to what extent speakers and hearers may imagine there are accents when there are none physically, or imagine there are none when an instrument would show otherwise—that is, the extent to which the detection or non-detection of accent is a perceptual problem.

Affirmation and Default

On page 101 above, the example

> Why doesn't he sell those products any more? — He sélls them!
> What ever gave you the idea that he had stopped?

appeared as an instance of how a verb can be dissected into several components any one of which may be accented—here it appears to be the 'actuality' or 'truth' of the event, which we more often extract using the verb *do-does-did*: *He dóes sell them!*

This general mode of AFFIRMATION is a neglected subject in syntactic studies, perhaps because there is no commonly used function word on the affirmative side equivalent to *not* on the negative side,[16] and means of affirming are accordingly more diffuse and harder to detect. Yet they are there, as one can see even in the affirmative parallel to "*not*-transportation":

> I believe he doesn't like it → I don't believe he likes it.
> I believe he does like it → I do believe he likes it.

One can argue that the affirmative, just like the negative, is "raised" from the subordinate clause to the main clause.

It is at the point of accent-for-affirmation (as in *sélls*) that the closest convergence of accent-for-power and accent-for-interest is found. When we are emphatic in our utterance it is usually to insist that what we say be accepted, and if what we say is intended to inform, this means, indirectly, that the information be regarded as *true*. An accent of power therefore is in the particular case quite often an accent that affirms. We are quick to recognize this where the auxiliary *do* is concerned, since English has grammaticized it as an affirmation-carrier (actually affirmation-negation carrier, since the negative is attached in *doesn't, don't,* and *didn't*).[17] In fact, we extend *do* sometimes beyond its grammatical limits: *Let's do plan to see each other.* It is also generally recognized that accent on other auxiliaries has the same function, as in

> Why haven't you done it? — I háve done it.
> Get busy and study. — I ám studying!

But that is as far as recognition usually goes. Yet the fact is that other elements may be accented for the same purpose, as Sweet pointed out in 1898 (§1896):

There are some formal connecting words, such as *be*, which have little or no meaning in themselves, and are therefore incapable of independent emphasis. Hence a strong—that is, in this case, an extra strong—stress on such words is felt to be equivalent to emphasizing the whole sentence:

What áre you doing?
What dóes he know about it?
You are late. — I ám rather late.
He will be angry. — Lét him be angry.

We may call this **distributed** stress. The positive emphatic non-interrogative forms of the verb . . . always have distributed stress: *I díd say so.*[18]

Sweet's examples are only of verbs, but other parts of speech are affected also. Relative pronouns, for example:

That's precisely the sense in whích I meant it!

Women whó examine their breasts. ('Who do examine their breasts.' Dr. Dean Edell, KGO, San Francisco, Aug. 8, 1981.)[19]

Or a preposition:

My real secret is what's at the other end. — W'l what's át the other end? — United Airlines cargo. (United Airlines ad, KCBS, San Francisco, Apr. 14, 1981. Could have been *what ís at the other end?*)

I maintain that there are no entities, of the kind which he alleges, fór me to recognize.[20]

As Vanvik (1961: 93) notes, the *to* of the infinitive is a favorite for this purpose—as if it were felt as an additional verbal auxiliary:

I'm not sure about what tó review and what nót to review. (An explicit affirmative-negative contrast. The accent could go on *what* instead of *to*, or on both at once.)

This gives the members a chance to do something about it íf they want to, and leaves room for their consciences to make them miserable enough tó want to.

An instance with a colorless verb:

Oh, but you must come! We're only <u>háving</u> people who hate New Year's Eve parties! (Underscoring in original. Cartoon in *New Yorker*, Dec. 26, 1959, p. 19.)

It appears that when a verb complex consists of an element that normally gets the major accent plus a companion (and usually, but not always, preceding) element that is unaccented or less accented, affirmation shifts the major accent to the companion; we have observed this with auxiliaries, *to*, and prepositions preceding *to*. It is also true of phrasal verbs, in which the adverbial particle normally receives the major accent, e.g. *come ín, make úp*:

Why didn't you come ín? — I cáme in!
I wish they would make úp. — They máde up!

There is also the more usual option, of course, using *do-does-did*: *They díd make up!*

Here is a miscellany in all of which one can read the intent to say 'Note well this fact!':

1. I've been by your house every Sunday for a month, but couldn't raise anyone. — I'm usually not át home on Sunday.

2. That's the area of the subject that we want to work ín.

3. How that cat chews the cereal. — It's something tó chew on this time! (Tough morsel.)

4. Having this schedule does not relieve the student of knowing the precise assignment made by the instructor, since circumstances may compel a class to deviate slightly fróm it.

5. The bills were not large but there were a great many óf them. (Jones 1956: §998.)

Example 1, slightly altered, shows what might be done in another dialect, accenting a different function word·

I usually don't bé at home on Sunday. (See Putnam and O'Hern 1955: 20.)

Example 4 could logically have the accent on *deviate* with everything after that deaccented, since *deviate* implies 'from'; but the accent on *from* points up the fact more sharply. Example 5 likewise could have had the accent just on *many*—in fact, that is the natural point of contrast (*not lárge, but mány*); but the accent on the preposition has an effect analogous to the one on *did* or *were* in the two following:

6. The bills were not large but we díd have a lót of them.

7. The bills were not large but they wére númerous.

Example 7 shows 'affirmation' most clearly, as it is a counterpoise to the *were not* in the prior clause.

The word to receive the accent need not be inherently colorless; it can be rendered colorless by its obviousness in the context, e.g. through repetition, and is then normally deaccented. Then, under the conditions described here, it can be *re*accented, for affirmation. This is especially true of verbs:

The Bureau of Study Counsel wants this bulletin posted. I guess we'd better put it on the board. In fact, it's exactly the right time to pút it up. (The accent could just as well go on *to*.)

Go ahead. Téll him you think I'm a liar. He isn't going to believe you. (Telling has been under discussion.)

Suppose you fínd (= dó find) him there at nine o'clock—what will you do about it?

OK, OK! Let him márry the woman if he wants to. He'll find out soon enough.

Bé an ass! See if I care!

The reaccenting is usually with an extra boost in pitch, surpassing what would be there if the accent were for the sake of the word's content. Looking back at one of the examples on page 129, we see that in place of putting the accent on *to*, we could keep it on *review* with the extra boost:

I'm not sure about what to revíew and what nót to review.

—*review* is assumed to have been mentioned already.

More than verbs are affected in this way. Other words too—redundant within their context—can carry an accent for affirmation. Here is a conversation between two people looking for the sales counter atop the Empire State Building—the last word, *side*, had a high rise-fall:

It isn't here—it's on the óther side. — All right, let's go to the other síde.

Given an accent on a function word, one is entitled to wonder whether it goes there because of any particular attachment to that spot, or, as Sweet implies, because there is no other place for it to go without suggesting a wrongly placed focus. Perhaps we are dealing with a kind of "default accent," and in fact as Ladd (1980: 81) uses this term, it covers cases like the ones just cited:

I can't imagine what it would be like to be a dentist—but I'm awfully glad there are guys who want to bé dentists.

On the other hand, as we noted earlier in this chapter, speakers seem to prefer having accents of power where they would go anyway as accents of interest—this is the "convergence" referred to above—and it is not likely that the particular accent of power that interests us here, the one used for affirmation, will be one that falls entirely by default. The closest we can come to pure default would be a modification of the *entities* example (p. 129 above), taking the accent off the preposition *for* and putting it on the last syllable of the verb: *there áre no [such] entities for me to recogníze.* Since the syllable -*ize* has no meaning of its own in this context, the accent there is as close to pure default as we can get. (It could also go on *to*, but *to* has some content.) The fact that -*ize* is also the last syllable in the utterance gives the bonus of climax, an obvious advantage to affirmation that shows up further in the possibility of accenting more than one function word at a time:

He actually máy háve béen a doctor once, but . . .

Here we can accent any one of the three words separately or *máy háve* without *been* or *máy . . . béen* without *have*, all to much the same effect, but the more accents there are, the stronger the affirmation.

But most of the time there is some residue of sense in the accented word that is appropriate in the context. The *entities* example has *for* (or could equally have *to*) roughly in the sense of appositeness or purpose. One can paraphrase with any of several content words that are loosely synonymous and that would then receive the accent:

> . . . no entities that I would féel like recognizing.
> that I would have any inclinátion to recognize.
> that there is any úse in recognizing.
> that one cóuld reasonably recognize.

When we compare contexts with *to* we find, as with *for*, that a residue of the primitive 'direction' or 'purpose' sense remains:

> I didn't do it because I was never determined tó do it.
> *I didn't do it because I was undecided tó do it. (Normal with the accent on *undecided*.)
> Why did you ever buy a thing like that? — Because I was forced tó buy it.
> *. . . because I was begged tó buy it.

Determination and being forced propel one *toward* the action; indecision does not, nor does being begged, at least not directly. The same 'to-ness' kind of push, and the lack of it, can be seen in the following:

> Would you refrain from buying it if you were really eager (keen, crazy, anxious, inspired, encouraged, in the mood) tó buy it?
> ?. . . if you were willing (ready, allowed) tó buy it?[21]

Phrases consisting of verb and preposition make a good test case for the accent of affirmation falling on the low-content member of the pair. Take two such expressions as *get through* (an opening) and *look through* (a telescope). In the first, the preposition is the weightier element, and normally gets the accent of interest:

> Was that the opening you got thróugh?

This means that *get* will be favored for affirmation:

> How come you didn't get through the door in back? — Because it was too damned hard a place to gét through!

But *look through* is the opposite; here the verb is the important part and the telescope is only an instrument:

> Was that the telescope you lóoked through?

Now it is the preposition that is favored for affirmation:

> No wonder you couldn't see anything through this telescope. The
> lens is dirty. — But that's not the telescope I looked thróugh!

See Bolinger 1983 and 1985 for additional examples.

How does one explain the wide latitude that speakers have in choosing more than one spot—sometimes several spots, alone or in conjunction, as with the *may have been a doctor* example above—to receive
accents of affirmation? The reason seems to be that by affirming one
part of an utterance (like negating one part of an utterance) by implication one affirms all the relationships that that element contracts
with the other parts. So if you say *I arrested John yesterday* I can question and you can affirm each part of it:

> Arrested? — Yes.
> John? — Yes.
> Yesterday? — Yes.

Further, just uttering the item in question, accented, can be an affirmation of it:

> I arrested John yesterday. — John? — John.

It follows that to express the contradictory of the negative *hasn't* in the
following sentence, one has the choice of any or all of the words
carrying the accent marks before *whó hásn't*:

> I can't remember whó's béen tóld and whó hásn't.

—in addition to separating and accenting the auxiliary *has*:

> I can't remember who hás been told and who hásn't.

The best argument for "default" is that the sheer unexpectedness of
an accent on a low-content item makes it more suitable for the intent
not to highlight the lexical content of the word but to affirm it in its
relationship to the whole, and it is precisely with relational words like
auxiliaries and prepositions that the involvement of the sentence as a
whole is at the fore. The sense of the individual word is not in most
cases entirely lost; it is just that the dual purpose of accent—power
and interest—is biased in favor of power when the word in question
has little claim to interest, and power in turn is so often "power to the
truth" of what is said.

So much for default in its relationship to affirmation, which is essentially a relationship with accents of power. There remains the
question of default in connection with accents of interest. Are there
times when for whatever reason an accent that would fall on a partic-

ular element because of its lexical contribution to the utterance, instead falls elsewhere?

Earlier we saw instances of a main accent moving to an unexpected position *within a word* (see pp. 68–70, 91–93). The first instance was in connection with the "rhythm rule" whereby instead of *comprehénsive tést*, with the "normal" position of the stress as would be encountered in *The test was comprehénsive*, we say *cómprehensive tést*, to space out the accents. But we saw that when attention is directed more closely to the meaning of the word, the "normal" position is retained: *What a comprehénsive tést!* The adjective here is as if predicated of the noun, even though it occurs in an attributive phrase. So it appears that there is considerable justification in referring to a "shift" of the main stress from the third syllable to the first, just under those circumstances that tend to obscure the meaning of the word and fuse it in the larger phrase. The stress moves off the syllable *-hen-* and falls—in a sense by default—on the syllable *com-*.

The second instance was the distortion of normal stress with the intent to imply 'this is not like that other word.' To accomplish the distinction, the stress is moved away from its normal position (if it fell there it would be too much like "that other" word) and placed on another syllable—to say again "by default" is more or less justified by the fact that it often makes no difference which of two or more positions it takes (e.g., *fámiliarity* or *familíarity*). The same in fact would be true of the *entities* example (pp. 129, 131). We noted that the final syllable of *recognize* could receive the accent of affirmation, which was also potentially on either *for* or *to*. Imagine that *psychologize* is a synonym of *recognize*. If that word were employed in the same context, there would be a fourth possibility for the accent: *psýchologize*. This distortion of the stress is like the others: the word is not being singled out for its lexical content but for another purpose, so it is simply made to sound different, and for that purpose the accent can go on any convenient syllable except the normal one. ("Convenient" usually means a syllable containing a full vowel. See p. 85.)

With accents of interest, we find the same two possibilities of shifting the accent away from a repeated or otherwise redundant item—which by its redundancy is rendered unsuitable for expressing the interest that is still lodged in some part of its semantic structure—or, as an alternative signal, keeping the accent on the redundant item and augmenting it. An example of shift:

> The Prosecution argued that he should be denied entry back to the U.S. because he had worked for the Communist government of Rumania, but the Defense maintained that everybody ín Rumania worked for the government.

Rumania is deaccented because it is repeated, and the accent shifts to *in*. But we note that if *there* were substituted for *in Rumania*, no shift would be needed, since *there* is already a "different" word from *Rumania*:

. . . everybody thére worked for the government.

Since *there* embraces the entire phrase *in Rumania*, it is reasonable to say that the unit locative as a whole has kept the accent but merely moved it to another syllable, exactly as with the *psýchologize* and *recogníze* examples above, but with the added advantage that *in* does have a content of its own (*in Rumania* versus *of Rumania*), satisfying our preference to put accents on content whenever we can.

Another attested example:

The only thing Yvonne has learned to make in cooking class is créam sauce. — That's nice, then she can have cream sáuce while you're gone.

Here *cream sauce* is directly repeated. If *créam sauce* were used in the response (and not given an exaggerated accent on *cream*), it might suggest 'new idea' or 'contrast,' which would clash with the fact that the item has just been mentioned. (The accent on *sauce* also adds a certain piquancy to the remark: imagine eating only cream sáuce!) A similar case is the following, which differs only in that what is repeated is a fact of interest that has been discussed many times before, not something mentioned in the immediate context:

He's sure an alley cát, isn't he? (Rise-fall on *isn't he*.)

This was said in reference to a mongrel cat's fondness for catnip, a sign of low breeding. The compound *álley cat*, like *créam sauce*, has its stress normally on the first element, but to have put the accent there in this instance would have made the utterance sound as if it were intended to be new and informative (the content of *alley cat* would then be in focus). A similar case, this time involving direct repetition:

If there are minimal pairs in Swedish, then why isn't Swedish a tone lánguage?

Tóne language is a compound, but if the normal stress had kept the accent in the context of this utterance, it would have sounded as if the subject of tone languages were being introduced, whereas it had already been under discussion. To have put the accent on *isn't* would have implied an immediate contrast to the stated opposite view, as if someone had said *Swedish is not a tone language*; but that was not the case. The only alternative was to distort the stress of the compound.

Or to exaggerate the pitch on *tone*, which we don't usually prefer if there is a convenient loose syllable to accent instead.

Here is such an exaggeration on a conjunction:

> I can't understand why this femme Kerrie Shawn hasn't answered the personals I've published. . . . Unless she's left the United States, or is dead. As far as that's concerned, there's been enough newspaper publicity to call her back from Africa, ór from the dead.[22]

In the most likely reading of this passage, *dead* is deaccented and *or* gets an accent with a boost. If content-ful *dead* were accented, it would appear to be newly introduced, but it is repeated, so *or* inherits the accent, partly on the strength of its own content, 'choice.' But *or*, too, is repeated, hence the boost. The same idea could be expressed using an accent without a boost if a different word expressed the 'choice':

> . . . there's been enough newspaper publicity to raise éither possibility.

Finally, an accent of interest on a colorless verb:

> Why don't you take the bus all the way to Gaviota instead of just to Santa Barbara? — That bus only góes as far as Santa Barbara.

The accent here could instead fall on *far*, and, less likely, on either *as*: 'There is no more going (no more far-ing, no more as-ing) than to Santa Barbara.' Each point represents a shift away from the noun in that verb phrase, but also onto an item that has some small claim to an accent in its own right.

Part III

MELODIC PROSODY

8. Profiles

In Chapter 1 it was explained that pitch accents are set out by jumps from a relatively uniform line. The jumps can be either up or down, and though upward jumps are more frequent, downward ones are perfectly capable of marking an accented syllable:

```
      Í                                        bláme
  Am                              Am I to
          to blame for that?                       for that?


                                      thá
                  Am I to blame for
                                           t?


  Am    to blame for that?         Am I to          for that?
     Í                                      bláme


                  Am I to blame for    t?
                                    thá
```

In the first three instances, the words *I, blame,* and *that* are accented by upward obtrusion; in the second three, the same words are accented by downward obtrusion.

Profiles as Accent Configurations

These shapes, and other shapes determined by how the pitch jump cuing the accent is realized, will be referred to as the PROFILE of the accent. The first three examples above, in which the accent is at a relatively high pitch followed by a jump down, illustrate Profile A. The second three, in which the accent is at a relatively low pitch reached by a downward jump with no further drop, illustrate Profile C. (See

Chapter 10, n. 11 for the correspondence between Profile C and the "low rise" that British intonologists recognize in their analyses.) The particular manifestations of these two profiles as just shown, with a leap away from a reference line and then a return to it, are the easiest examples to grasp because of the striking contrast between figure and ground. But there are other kinds of obtrusion, in addition to modifications of these two.

Given the fluid nature of intonation, how is one to determine the scope of a profile, or even to know that a division into this sort of accent-centered unit is the analysis most likely to succeed when longer stretches are addressed? On the latter point, it is obvious that there are successions of accents, and that when an accent is suppressed the effect seems to be that the degraded material is subordinated to a remaining accent, with certain rhythmic adjustments. And we have seen the importance of the initial and final accents in the template of the utterance as a whole. Most accents are self-evidently separate; if it is legitimate to attach neighboring material to them, they make natural division points. Further, the profiles have functional roles, described later in this chapter, which permit the grouping of variants around prototypical shapes: an A profile, for example, has a meaning that remains constant despite variations that contribute secondary meanings. It is not easy to draw the line between profiles (the minimum MORPHOLOGICAL units of intonation) and contours (the SYNTACTIC units), but without some such segmentation the analyst is left with an unmanageable complexity.

The profile-as-unit agrees in the broad sense with other current approaches to intonation. According to Ladd (1983b: 54–55) "the tonal segments of which phrase-length and utterance-length contours are composed . . . [are] PITCH ACCENTS, distinctive configurations or prominences accompanying major stressed syllables; some such unit . . . is a part of virtually all current models of intonation." Where the profile analysis differs from others, including Ladd's, is in looking to meaningful gesture rather than to abstract phonology in carrying the analysis to deeper levels.

Another reason for giving the accent a pivotal role is simply the weight of the accented syllable. A large part of the emotive force of an intonation resides in how much material is *down* with reference to the rest, and how much is *up*. An accented syllable counts more heavily in this balance than an unaccented one (because of its usually greater physical impact in terms of full vowel and added length and intensity, plus the simple fact that we *know* its importance to the discourse). But the unaccented syllables may sometimes be weighted to the point of rivalry with the accent. The result is that the primary profiles, A, B, and C, are conditioned in certain ways that seem to entitle the modifications to status as separate profiles. For practical reasons, they are given that status here, though it would be possible, by complicating their descriptions somewhat, to continue using just those three.

As for the scope of a profile, the working principle will be that it is the limit of intonational movement that can occur on a one-syllable word. If we can posit that a single word represents no more than a single accent, this allows us to demonstrate how much intonational ornamentation, so to speak, can surround one accent. Take the word *John*. The commonest shape is a relatively high pitch followed by a quick drop:

$$\text{It's} \quad \overset{\text{Jó}}{\underset{\text{hn.}}{}} \qquad \text{(Profile A)}$$

An almost equally common shape starts higher than a preceding pitch and does not fall:

$$\underset{\text{It's}}{} \overset{\text{Jóh}^{n \cdot}}{} \qquad \text{(Profile B)}$$

A less common shape is approached from above, and does not fall:

$$\overset{\text{It's}}{\underset{\text{Jóh}^{n \cdot}}{}} \qquad \text{(Profile C)}$$

A still less common shape starts at a relatively low pitch, goes up, and abruptly comes down again:

$$\text{It's} \quad \overset{\text{h}}{\underset{\text{Jó}}{}} \underset{\text{n.}}{} \qquad \text{(Profile CA)}$$

A somewhat commoner one is like the first one above (Profile A) but ends in a rise:

$$\text{It's} \quad \overset{\text{Jó}}{\underset{\text{h}^{n \cdot}}{}} \qquad \text{(Profile AC)}$$

The least frequent of all is a sort of combination of CA and AC, and is the limit of what one normally encounters on a single syllable.[1] It has the shape of a tilde; the *o* is repeated to show the display:

$$\text{It's} \quad \overset{\text{o}}{\underset{\text{Jó}}{}} {}_{\text{o}} \text{h}^{n \cdot} \qquad \text{(Profile CAC)}$$

While the single-syllable illustrations are useful to show the scope of a profile, multi-syllable illustrations are needed to show the location of pitch obtrusions and, later, the overlap between the complex profiles and combinations of profiles. In the description that follows, the profiles are necessarily treated concretely—that is, as actually spoken contours each consisting of one profile (a contour, that is, a spoken manifestation of intonation patterning, may consist of any number of profiles). A linguistic description is always plagued by this divorce between abstraction and reality: in order to exemplify, one has to utter, and utterance occurs at a time and a place. The result is that a good deal of what is set forth at this point will anticipate the chapter on contours.

Profile A

"Accent at a relatively high pitch followed by a jump down" is the specification for Profile A: the downward jump is the obtrusion necessary for the accent on this profile. But what about the syllables that flank the accent to the left? Why should differences in their patterning not suffice to distinguish more than one profile, instead of being lumped together? The answer lies in how best to organize the data. The various approaches to the accent make less difference in our overall impressions of an utterance than do the shapes that are identified with other profiles; it is a matter of the degree of concurrent similarity of form and meaning. For example, in answer to *How on earth are you able to do it?* one may say *It's easy!* with any of the three following shapes:

There are intonational differences here—the first might be called 'matter-of-fact,' the second 'Why should anyone think otherwise?,' and the third 'Not worth fussing about'—attributable to the relative tension of *It's* and *ea-* in the pattern as a whole. But the differences are substantially less than one finds between any of the three and either of the following:

The first might suggest 'No reason to be concerned' and the second leaves the matter open. But the three instances of Profile A are all a frank answer, one that leads most naturally to the explanation that the question *how* calls for: *It's easy! You just arch your back and lift with your leg muscles.* There are many other situations in which A profiles can be shown to cluster semantically and differ from C and B. (Halliday 1967 seems to make the same distinction. His Tone 1 corresponds to our A.)

An A profile can be realized in a variety of ways. The three illustrated above are only a sample. The movements in the unaccented syllables on either side of the accent, and within the accented syllable itself, are important in their own right, and will be looked at in Chapter 10. Here are some of the possibilities.

1. Fall within the accented syllable versus fall from the accented syllable to the next syllable. If there is no following syllable, that is, if an A profile occurs on the last syllable before a pause or before a B or another A profile, the fall must occur within that syllable:[2]

```
         wí                          mú   knó
  I                        They
         11.                         st    w.
```

But if there is a following unaccented syllable, the speaker has a choice. For example, either of the following is normal:

```
  He's a nó                  He's a nó\
         body.                      obody.
```

Putting the fall within the accented syllable is more emphatic (see Pike 1945: 74, 86), as a combined result of the 'separateness' conferred by the movement and the extra length required to carry it out. Sometimes the extra emphasis is merely that, as in

```
       fár                           fá
  It's                vs.     It's
        too big.                  r  too big.
```

But at other times the emphasis lends itself to different interpretations, in such a way that grammatical distinctions may be partly based on it. For example, the more independent, morphologically or syntactically, a word or word-like element is, the more it is apt to carry the fall within the syllable. Thus

```
                      whí
  He lives in the
                   te
                     house.
```

is almost certain to be taken to mean 'the house that is white,' whereas

```
                  white
  He lives in the

                    house.
```

can as easily be *White House* (where *white* is separately meaningless) as *white house*. Similarly

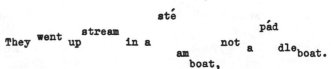

```
                    sté
            stream                        pád
They  went  up        in a        not  a    dle
                          am              boat.
                        boat,
```

is possible, but a similar treatment of *steam* in *He lives in Steamboat Springs* would be most unlikely. In a case like

```
              ár
     His  name  is    is
              totle.
```

(where *Ar-* again is separately meaningless) the fall would not occur within the accented syllable except perhaps to correct someone who has mispronounced that syllable and needs to have it emphasized to get it correct. One might conceivably say

```
          flá                  tél
It's not a    g   le,  it's a    e      pole.
               po            phone
```

because *flag* is more or less independent, but one would hardly pronounce *tel-* with a falling pitch. The rhythm rule (pp. 53–58) owes itself mainly to the need to avoid unnecessary pitch movements within syllables—of the two versions

```
                           én
    It  ón   oc cúrs  on the
         ly                  d.
```

```
                           én
    It  oc cúr   ón   on the
             s     ly        d.
```

we prefer the first because it does not require putting the Profile A drop within the syllable *-curs*—the syllables *on the* are there to take the drop. (So much for the "rules" often quoted that govern the position of words like *only*.)

If *flagpole* is not apt to have the downmotion in *flag-* because of the cohesion—nonseparateness—of the compound, a phrase in which there is a potential disjuncture (point of separation) may require, or at least benefit by, having the downmotion of the A before the disjuncture. A sentence like

```
    Why's        dárk
         it so
                   in here?
```

may be as diagrammed, or may have the drop within *dark*—there is hardly a detectable difference. But if there is an additional profile,

```
Why's      dá      hé

          it so    rk in   re?
```

'Why is it so dark, and in here, of all places?' with *in here* a separate item of information and the possibility of pause before that phrase, the fall within *dark* is virtually necessary if its profile is to be an A and not a B, as would be the case with

```
Why's      dárk      hé
          it so      in   re?
```

Without the drop within *dark*, the sentence is equivalent to

```
Why's         dárkness      hé
        there such              in   re?
```

rather than

```
Why's         dárk          hé
        there such   ness(,) in   re?
```

In other words, if the condition for the A profile—an immediately following drop—is not satisfied, the result is a B. Occurrence before the disjuncture is like occurrence in final position: the fall must occur before the break, and if there is not an extra syllable to take it (as there is in *darkness*), then it must occur within the accented syllable. (Both forms are perfectly good sentences, but the implications are different: the A+A may refer to two separate items of information; the B+A suggests that the first has already been introduced: 'I'm not surprised at the darkness, but why in here?')

The experiments carried out by Cooper and Sorensen (1981: 134–41) show clearly the effect of disjuncture on the drop in pitch within the accented syllable. The stronger the disjuncture the greater the tendency to manifest it in that way. Examples (their p. 138):

> Janet made prune juice the day before yesterday and *grape* juice last week.

> Janet made prune juice the day before yesterday and *grape* just last week.

The pitch on *grape* in the first example—a compound—was virtually level; the *grape* before the adverbial clause dropped from 150 to 125 hz.

At times the location of the drop may be more a matter of the phonetic flow. In a sentence like *I wás wóndering about it*, with A profiles on both *was* and *wondering*, the uninterrupted sequence of voiced sounds in *was wondering* makes it difficult even to hear the difference between two such realizations as the following:

```
    wá   wón                          wás
                      it.                   ᴧn              it.
  I   s     dering about            I     w°  dering about
```

2. Delayed fall. Speakers sometimes fail to "turn off" an A profile right at the transition between the accented syllable and the following unaccented one. This may be due to speed or to emotivity. Take the following answer to the question *How did you learn about the latest Cabinet shakeup?*

```
                    pápers
         The
                         told the story.
```

In this context an A profile is expected because 'papers' is a newly introduced idea (see p. 166); yet there is little or no contrast in meaning between *papers* at a level pitch and *papers* with *-pers* at a lower pitch. Delayed fall is most apt to happen when the syllable or syllables following the accent are reduced and therefore brief. Tests have shown (Lehiste 1972) that a word such as *shadiness* is not much longer when spoken than the cognate *shady*, with the result that it is difficult, except in deliberate speech, to hear or produce a contrast such as the following:

```
         shád                    shádi
             iness                    ness
```

Delayed fall is not apt to extend beyond a single syllable after the accent (the "one syllable leeway" principle becomes important in the CA profile, described below), but it may do so with an increase in emotivity. This might happen in choosing one of the following in answer to *Just how bad was it?*

```
       tér                   térri                  térribly
It was               It was                 It was
        ribly bad.            bly bad.                   bad.
```

Since accents ultimately respond to our feelings of importance and excitement, it is only to be expected that at times a speaker will be carried away in this fashion.

3. Truncated fall. This is found under three conditions: intentional truncation, truncation due to insufficient syllabic material, and truncation due to insufficient intonational space.

As with most melodic movement, more represents more of what it signifies, less means less. In other words, intonation is gradient. A fall after an accent signifies 'finality' in the broadest sense, and the deeper the fall, the more final it is. The description of Profile A calls for a fall after the accent; nothing is said as to how deep the fall needs to be. The fact is that it can be reduced to a bare hook and still suffice to mark the accent; and that is a choice open to a speaker who wishes to state something in a more or less offhand or tentative manner. Suppose someone repeats to you some grievous fact that you are already aware of. You may reply

$$\text{I} \quad \text{kn\'o}_{\text{w.}}$$

After saying this you may shake your head and continue, *It's a shame, isn't it.* If instead of just agreeing with the other person you want to assert your knowledge of the fact in a positive manner, you will use a deeper fall.

Insufficient syllabic material is responsible for the truncation of the fall in an utterance such as

$$\text{You} \quad \text{m\'u}_{\text{st.}}$$

Here the syllable is closed with a voiceless cluster [st], and unless the speaker lengthens the vowel (which would be appropriate for slow, emphatic speech but not for average conversational speed), the downturn may all but vanish. But since the loss is automatic, and makes no difference as far as there being or not being an A profile is concerned, listeners probably compensate by being more or less deaf to it, crediting the speaker's intention to hit a low target rather than his unintentional failure to arrive there. (The notion of "target" is Ladd's, supported in this instance by the research of 't Hart 1981, which showed that listeners are poor at discriminating the depth of a fall.)

Insufficient intonational space results in a truncated fall when the start of the A profile is already so low that there is little if any room for any further drop. Since the A can be approached from a higher pitch and there is no rule limiting the width of the drop *to* the accent, that drop can go practically to the lower limit of the voice; for example, in the third *It's easy* above:

$$\text{It's} \quad \text{\'ea}_{\text{sy.}}$$

When the profile consists of a single monosyllable, and the speaker seeks the emotive effect of a very low pitch, the downturn of the A may flatten completely. Thus the last three words of the sentence *If it keeps you from collecting your graft I consider it time well spent* may come out like this, with a flattened A profile on the last word:

wéll

time

spént

This is gestural, and is apt to be accompanied by parallel head and eye movements: the head goes up and the eyebrows are raised on *well*, and both are lowered on *spent*. The emotive effect of the low pitch can be seen in an episode from the Jack Benny television program (aired Oct. 28, 1956). Mary says to Jack, using a glide down to a very low A profile accenting *that*,[3]

Are
you going to be on television

thát often?

Jack then admonishes her to repeat the lines as they had rehearsed them, with a surprised and cheerful B on *that*:

Oh,
you going to be on television thát often?
Ja
ck. Are

Truncation may occur at higher pitches when the overall array of profiles makes it difficult to execute a drop. In the following attested example, the result was the actual substitution of a B profile for an A. The speaker was remarking about a research course of extraordinary length, and said

That's
two units more than an
MÁ
thé
sis.

Both elements, *MA* and *thesis*, were in contrast with the point of reference, yet the only A is on *thesis*. To make the double contrast explicit, there would have had to be an A profile likewise on *MA*, with the syllable for *A* starting at the level of *M* and then falling. For lack of syllabic material the A profile was sacrificed—to force it here would have seemed to add an undesirable degree of emphasis. Had it been *doctoral* rather than *MA*, no sacrifice would have been called for:

the
dóc
more than a toral
sis.

4. Glided peak. The almost-never-steady movement of pitch inevitably produces some gliding of the accent on the A profile, though

when minimal it is probably heard as level. On the other hand, a marked movement either up or down will affect the mood of the utterance (see p. 225). In response to *Who will do it?* one may have

í

will.

If the *I* is glided up, the response might be taken as an eager offer; if glided down, it sounds self-confident, perhaps excessively so.

5. Gradient heights and slopes. These are alterations found among all the profiles. It will suffice to illustrate them just with Profile A.

In the following series of three sentences, spoken in the order given, there are three A profiles, with accents on *yesterday*, *before*, and the first *before* respectively:

> One day ago is yesterday. Two days ago is day *before* yesterday.
> Three days ago is day BEFORE day before yesterday.

The compounded contrasts build up the Profile A peaks: "the greater the contrast the higher the peak."

The fall after the peak can go to any depth (that is, if truncated it can be truncated high or low), and may go fast or slow. If the distinction is important, we can refer to these styles of movement as DOWNSKIP (no appreciable glide), DOWNDASH (rapid downglide), and DOWNTILT (gradual downglide). In addition the speaker may lengthen at will. The following instances of *Sure!* represent the same profile with different expansions:

Sú   s-ú-ᵘ-ᵣ
                                        ᵣ
   re.   e.

Profile C

Profile C is the mirror image of Profile A: the obtrusion is down instead of up. The accent is marked by "downward to" rather than "downward from." It presupposes a higher preceding pitch: the "pitch goes up in order to come down" (Gårding 1981: 153). Here is a series of three C profiles, with accents on *just*, *said*, and *mo-* respectively:

That's
        júst what I
                    sáid to your
                                 móther.

Compare this with the same sentence using A profiles:

                                    mó
            júst what   sáid to your
   That's   I   ᵗʰₑᵣ.

(The accents on successive C profiles tend to have a descending tangent. Those on the A's often rise. Neither direction is essential.)

The chief variation in shape with Profile C is in the motion following the accent. Generally it is up, as in the next-to-last example. But it may be level or even slightly falling. The gradient difference between rise and level can be seen by comparing the following successions of three C's:

```
It's                               It's
      néver too                          néver too
            láte to                            láte to
                  ménd·                              ménd.
```

And the gradient difference between rise, level, and downtilt can be seen in the following, with B profile followed by C, accenting *mean* and *all* respectively:

```
          méan to say that
   You
                      áll of them are like that?

          méan to say that
   You                áll of them are like that?

          méan to say that
   You                áll of them are like that?
```

(The example with level pitch has a special "stylized" use. See pp. 226–37). The essential characteristic of the profile is the skip down *to*, and what follows, provided there is no abrupt fall and the terminal pitch is well above the lower limit of the voice, is optional for marking the accent. There are, however, considerable gradient differences, as one can see by comparing the uptilt and the downtilt following the accent in

```
      you think that
   Do              Í would do a thing like that?

      you think that
   Do              Í would do a thing like that?
```

The latter, in keeping with its incurious downmotion, is more apt to be a rhetorical question.

If there is a marked drop rather than a downtilt after *all* and *I* in the last two sets of examples, those accents will be heard as part of an A profile. The difference can be tested contextually, as the A profile is more appropriate to the introduction of a new item, the C to the repetition of an old one, though this distinction is not absolute. For example, in a discussion of satchels, after the topic has been introduced, one might ask

```
      ́anybody ever carry a
Does                        sátchel any more?
```

(B on *an-*, C on *satch-*)—a question expressing casual interest. But in a discussion of luggage, when 'satchel' has not been mentioned and is now being introduced, with more than casual interest in the new topic, the intonation is more apt to be

```
      ́anybody ever carry a sátch
Does                            el any more?
```

Although this utterance would be more apt to end at a lower pitch than the preceding one, they could be the same in that respect; the critical difference is that the downskip is from rather than to the syllable *satch-*, and this defines an A profile.[4]

The commonest shape of C is with a preceding downward B profile and a following upward tail, for example:

```
                              Gíve it a
Dón't be so un                          trý.
               réasonable.
```

```
Whére did you put the
                     bróadcast manual?
```

```
Dó they be
          líeve all that nonsense?
```

But as preceding examples have shown, there are many possibilities in what precedes and what follows the accent.

There are also the same general alterations in C that were observed in A, depending on the amount of syllabic material, the choice of whether to put a post-accentual rise within the accented syllable or on the following one, differences in rate of speaking, etc. We can illustrate what happens when the amount of syllabic material is slight with a contrast that one often hears on the word *yes*. A very sprightly (or 'yes-but') *yes* takes an A profile with a following rise (identified below as AC); a patient-restrained-condescending *yes* takes a C, either with the initial drop reduced almost to zero or with the sound of the consonant *y-* uttered at a relatively high pitch followed by a quick jump down:

                Yé
                  é   Y
                e^s.   (AC) $_{ée}$s.   (C)

(Imagine these spoken in answer to a summons, or as affirmative responses to a question.)

For choice of where to put the rise we can illustrate with *all*; in the first example the rise is on the syllable following *all*, in the second it is within *all* itself:

    Are they   Are they
           áll like that?   áll like that?

As with Profile A, the accent is more emphatic when it incorporates part of the subsequent movement. (Profile C and Profile B correspond to differing interpretations of Tones 2 and 3 in Halliday 1967.)

Profile B

In Profile B the accent is jumped up *to*. (If the accented syllable is initial, there will be nothing to mark the upward jump except the fact that the accent will be at a fairly high pitch: there is an "up to" in the speaker's range.) Examples, with various treatments of the syllables following:

       thát the best you can do?   thát the best you can do?
    Is   Is

              thát the best you can do?
          Is

The end of the profile, from accented *that* on, is respectively rising, level, and falling, but with no abrupt change such as might signal an additional accent, as would be the case in the following, with an added B profile and A profile respectively:

                          dó?   dó
       thát the best you can   thát the best you can
    Is   Is   o?

This situation can be illustrated more clearly with a compound in contrast with a phrase. Take *móving van* and *móving ván*, with one accent and two respectively, all manifested by B profiles:

                                                        ván?
              móving van?   móving
       Is it a   Is it a

(See Pike 1945: 61 for "slight tendency to drift upwards or downwards.")

As with the other profiles, a deficiency of syllabic material may force an intrasyllabic movement. In the following, we have an A profile (for comparison), a B profile, and a succession of two B's:

```
   thát                thát you?              thát yóu?
Is                  Is                     Is
   you?
```

Imagine, for the first, a context in which a guest has been shuffling through a set of old photographs looking for the likeness of the host; after two or three unsuccessful guesses, he thinks he has found what he was looking for. The downmoving pitch of the A profile suggests 'end,' which here would be taken as 'end of search.' For the second, the same situation applies, but there is no hint that the search is over. The third requires no presuppositions: *that* and *you* are equally new to the discourse—the guest has perhaps been looking idly at the set and is struck by the resemblance in one of the photos. In completing the first B in the third example, the speaker drops the pitch slightly at the end of *that* to make room for the second B on *you*. A second (or later) B is apt to force that sort of adjustment rather than just to continue up—it is as if we were afraid of running out of space to reach higher, or perhaps reluctant to display the degree of tension that higher and higher pitch might suggest. The danger is greater when the first of two successive B profiles has a fairly long tail (the part that comes after the accent); one may then find a DROPBACK embracing more than one syllable—the tail may gradually fall, or rise and then fall:

```
            móre than they're really gonna néed?
Will they have
```

```
            móre than they're really gonna néed?
Will they have
```

Without the dropback, even with a fairly appreciable extra jump up on *need*, this is apt to be heard as a single B with accent on *more* and everything following that word, including *need*, merely part of the tail—this would be appropriate if their need has already been introduced and 'more' is the only new idea. The same holds even with a dropback, if it is slight—that is, the cues in this upmoving direction have to be pretty conspicuous to be effective. We can show this with an utterance in which the context makes a second B unlikely, and there nevertheless may be a small dropback and resetting of the upward motion. Take the sentence bóoks

They gave us

and things.

It is pretty clear that *and things* is unaccented, a mere tail for the A profile, and it should also be no more than a tail in the following B profile:

give

What did they   bóoks and things?

you,

The B tail here could rise continuously, but the interruption saves space, always an advantage if the speaker overshoots the B rise in the first place and might otherwise have to go too high. (Other test sentences give the same result, e.g. *When you asked for offprints and papers, shouldn't it have been bóoks and papers?*, where *and papers* is a repetition and hence unaccented.)

Perhaps for the same reason of space, a rising terminal, when there is one (as there is more often than not), tends to have the greater part of the upmotion on the last syllable, where the speaker is in the best position to judge how much room is left:

ágonizingly?

Did they need to struggle so

And this is a further reason for a dropback when a second B follows—if the greater part of the upmotion is on the last syllable anyway, an upskip without a preceding dropback is not an effective way of signaling a second B at that point.

On the other hand, a dropback may signal a fresh start, and this has syntactic uses. It creates a break that may be used to separate constituents. In the following, the two nouns are given separate importance:

pásteurizableness   bílity?

Does it refer to   and refina

The break not only makes room for the rise on *-bil-* but cuts *-ness* off from what follows. Similarly in the next pair, both containing successive B's, the first is precoded and the second is afterthoughtive:

Does it refer to yóu or your bróther?

Does it refer to yóu? or your bróther?

In contours containing series, where the B profiles are of equal importance to the discourse and consequently tend to be of equal height, words with initial stress not connected by a conjunction may be forced to incorporate their own initial dropback in order to provide the lower pitch for the upskip to the accent. Compare the following at the point where the second example omits *and*:

```
                cóffee       sándwiches
  They bought          and              and ice  cré
                                                     am.


                cóffee,
  They bought          sándwiches,  and ice  cré
                                                 am.
```

In the second example, *sand-*, for lack of a preceding unaccented syllable (such as would be available, e.g., in *tomatoes*), incorporates its own dropback and the upskip characteristic of B turns into an upglide. (The same problem affects successive monosyllables when all are B's, whether series or not; see p. 291 for the example *In one ear and out the other*.) The difference between the dropback and a downskip to *sand-* from *-fee* that would establish a C profile is that in the latter, *sand-* would tend to be level. But this is a zone of potential·ambiguity. Here is a setting in which the difference would be audible. The speaker starts out by saying

```
                cóffee...
  They bought
```

and seems on the point of forgetting the next item. His hearer interrupts with *Sandwiches?*, and the first speaker accepts the addition, repeating it with a C, and nodding:

```
              wiches,
  ...sánd           and ice
                         créam.
```

(See Appendix B for this and other problems related to B and C.)

Profile CA

The profiles described thus far may be said to have a single effective position: the accents in A and B are *above* certain other material in their configurations, C is below. We come now to profiles that combine more than one effective position. First is Profile CA, which embodies the characteristics and positions of both C and A. It has been identified in some other treatments (e.g. Bolinger 1965: 49) as a variant of Profile A, because of similarities in function; but here we follow

Halliday (1967: 16) and Deakin (1981*b*: 63) with their "Tone 5," in recognizing it as a separate profile in spite of similarities to A. At the same time it is necessary to recognize that the border between the two is uncertain. If the accent in A is approached from below, there may be enough upglide to give the impression of an intended lower pitch before the peak. One then gets a graded series like the following:

why
But I want to know   But I want to know   why
y.   y.

y
But I want to know why
y.

The middle term is midway in its insistence between the first and the third, A and CA respectively.

Typically, in CA, the accented syllable is at a low pitch, and the peak is then taken by the immediately following syllable, after which there is the drop characteristic of A:

Oh,   tur
ná   ally.

The following, with CA on *get*, occurred as the final turn in a conversation in which it was preceded by *Don't we have any more blankets? — No. —*

Well   then   let's   some [sm]
get
more, then.

But—as with the other profiles—if there is insufficient syllabic material, the upmotion will occur within the accented syllable, and, again as with the others, the speaker has the choice of putting it there anyway, for greater emphasis. The complete rise-fall is very common in emphatic pronunciations of *yes, no, so, how?* (e.g., when the speaker doubts that the action in question is possible at all), *ah*, and other frequent carriers of emphasis. There is increasing emphasis in the following, all with CA:

ways   l
It's   ál   It's   á   ways   like
like that.   that.

```
     1
         1
It's  ,   ways
      a       like
              that.
```

In the last example, the syllable *al-* takes the full rise-fall. All three have the essential ingredients of low start, immediate rapid rise, and immediate rapid fall.

More than the other profiles, it is difficult to discuss CA without referring to its gestural motivation. The speaker at first "holds back," but then his tension is such that it breaks the bonds of the earlier restraint. This in turn means that when the force of the rise is so great as not to be able to spend itself by the time the first postaccentual syllable is reached (assuming there is enough syllabic material for a full display), the rise may continue a syllable or two farther. In the following, you have asked me *Was it cleansed or contaminated?* and I reply, quite exercised at your question and alarmed at the possible consequences of the contamination and therefore inclined to warn you of them,

```
                    ted
              ina      is
Con   in             what
   tam                     it
                              was!
```

Slightly less tension would bring the pitch down on *-ed*, less still would bring it down on *-nat-*; more could conceivably hold the high pitch through *is*. Other indicators of high tension tend to accompany utterances like this. It is common to find a skip into falsetto on the last syllable of the rise; in the last example as diagrammed, this would be the syllable *-ed*.

The literally or figuratively uncontrolled burst of tension after the initial low pitch makes CA powerfully emphatic. It may be used ironically, e.g. to exclaim

```
             er
      Clév      )
           r!
```

for a pretended outburst of admiration. The controlled initial pitch also makes a striking difference in the interpretation of *Ah!* as uttered on CA by comparison with A: CA generally means 'the truth should have dawned on *you*'; A generally means 'the truth now dawns on *me*.'

A virtually uniform feature of CA is the reduction of the syllable at the peak. If that syllable were not reduced the effect would be that of an accent *at* the peak, resulting in an A profile. For example, suppose that somebody is claiming that no one ever swam the Hellespont and puts his claim as a question: *Who ever swam the Hellespont?* You know that X person did, and you want to remind the other speaker of the fact in no uncertain terms. If X's name was *Byron* you have no trouble—the final syllable is reduced:

ron

Bý

did.

But if the name is *Falstaff*, the result is the unsatisfactory

staff

Fál

did.

with a syllable containing a full vowel at the peak, and seeming then to be accented, though -*staff* is not stressed in *Falstaff*. (This is evidence that high pitch takes precedence over low as a manifestation of accent, and explains why more cooperation from other cues is required to mark a low-pitched syllable as accented.) The remedy is to spread *Fal-* from the low beginning pitch through the peak. An example of how the presence of a full syllable at the peak can be confusing when the speaker intends a CA profile is the following, spoken by Eddie Albert (U.S. Steel Hour television program, Oct. 31, 1962). Albert had just been given a necktie as a present, and was affecting surprise:

ti

A

néck

e!

The first impression was that he meant to imply that he had expected to receive, say, a *neckbánd* rather than a *necktíe.* Sometimes the speaker can avoid the impression of an accented peak by putting a reduced variant there. In the following,

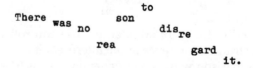

if the full variant of *to* is chosen, the sentence will be heard as *There was no reason tó disregard it* (see p. 132 for accent on *to*); with the reduced variant [tə] it is heard as *There was no réason to disregard it.*[5] A number of the function words offer this possibility, e.g. *can* in

```
              can
        You

              do it.
```

—with [kæn] this is an A profile, *You cán do it*; with [kn̩] it is a CA, *Yóu can do it*. But *can't* is like *Falstaff*, because it has no reduced counterpart (phonetically we depend in part on the full vowel in *can't* to distinguish it from *can*), and the result is that

```
              can't
        You

              do it.
```

is apt to be heard as an A: *You cán't do it*. But such ambiguities are usually cleared up by the context. If you say *Ánybody can do it!* and I retort *Yóu can't do it!* using this intonation, the intended CA will be obvious.

The low pitch of the accent need not be the lowest pitch in the first part of the profile. It needs only to be appreciably lower than the peak. So we have the following (from a radio dramatization of Dickens's "The Poor Relation," WABC, New York, Dec. 24, 1956):

```
                         of
                     óut
        I am seldom
                          my
                            castle.
```

The accent is on *out*.

The CA profile figured prominently in the oratorical style of Winston Churchill and can easily be detected in recordings of his speeches.[6] It is much used in English where German would favor certain modal particles (see Schubiger 1979: 279–98).

Viewed as a variant of A, the CA profile shows the freedom that the speaker enjoys to improvise by "holding back." An even further elaboration is possible, to show extreme emphasis. Someone who is thoroughly exasperated at another person's failure to respond to a request might say

```
                             it
                       i
                      g   e
             Then      v
                     i
                          to him!
```

with the monosyllable *give* prolonged onto a rise-fall-rise, the entire profile then becoming rise-fall-rise-fall. The restraint of the low pitch is now augmented by higher pitches on either side: "See how hard I am trying to control myself!"

Profile CB

Profile CB bears the same relationship to B that CA bears to A: the accented syllable is held down, after which there is an immediate jump up. Whereas CA has a downskip immediately after the peak, with CB the pitch of the tail remains high, on a downtilt. CB is not common as an independent contour, but may be heard as a kind of perfunctory pronunciation of *yes*:

$$\text{Ye}^{\text{´eees?}}$$

With a better display of syllables:

$$\text{It's un}_{\text{cón}}{}^{\text{scionable!}}$$

Usually CB leans on a following A or C, for example this CB+C:

$$\text{But }_{\text{thát}}{}^{\text{doesn't make any}}\text{ difference.}$$

The accented syllable, as with CA, may be relatively high, but must be lower than the peak, e.g.

$$\text{But thát }^{\text{doesn't make any}}\text{ difference.}$$

If the upskip puts the accented syllable at the level of the start of the tail, the result is no longer CB but B:

$$\text{But }^{\text{thát doesn't make any}}\text{ dífference.}$$

And if the upmotion after the accented syllable is not a skip, the result is C, as in the following C+C:

$$\text{But thát }^{\text{doesn't make any}}\text{ difference.}$$

What stands out most in BC is the contrary motion of the upskip and the downtilt. The upskip alone is not enough to characterize the profile and leave it free to have a tail that is level or upmoving as well as downtilting. This can be seen by testing utterances like

$$\text{doesn't make any}$$
$$\text{But}\ \text{that}$$
$$\text{difference.}$$

The result is that the upskip between *that* and *does* is virtually indistinguishable from a smoother upmotion; in either case we have a B with a rising tail. This is the same difficulty noted above with successive B's, where a dropback to reset the B was called for.

There is a strong possibility that CB should be regarded as a subtype of C, and not as an independent profile. It is as close to C as CA is to A.

Profiles AC and CAC

Profile AC embodies the characteristic peak of A and the characteristic trough of C—the resulting movement is fall-rise. As with other profiles, AC may be found on a single one-syllable word, on a polysyllable, on a phrase, or on an entire sentence provided only one syllable is accented. In the following, a speaker's turn contains three utterances, all AC:

$$\text{Pá}\qquad\text{Cón}\qquad\qquad\text{Théy}$$
$$\text{u}\ \text{l?}\qquad\text{stan}_\text{ti}\text{ne?}\qquad\text{wouldn't}\ \text{do}\ \text{it!}$$

(Though *do* in the third utterance is not intended to be accented—it refers to something previously mentioned—there is an obvious resemblance here to an A+C succession. See pp. 191–92 for a further treatment of this uncertain borderline.)

Profile CAC embodies the low pitch plus abrupt rise of CA with the same following C characteristics that entered into the compounding of AC. Here are two CAC's in succession:

$$\text{i}\qquad\qquad\text{would}$$
$$\text{Ál}\ \text{n}\text{y?!}\ \text{Théy}\qquad\text{n't}\qquad\text{it!}$$
$$\text{mo}\qquad\qquad\text{pay}$$

Here is a CAC on a single syllable, in response to *Too bad you didn't do better*:

$$\text{I}\quad\text{í}$$
$$\text{tr}\ \text{d!}$$
$$\text{e}$$

'so what more can you expect?'

The extra emphasis in CAC by comparison with AC can be appreciated in echo questions, which are often incredulous. To a question like *What foolishness did he say?* one may react with AC:

```
        fóol

   What
            ish
               ness  did he      y?
                              sa
```

or with CAC:

```
                ish ness

   What
        fóol          did        y?
                         he   sa
```

The first might call just for a confirmation that that was indeed the question that the other person had asked; the second would suggest 'How could you ask such a question?' At the same time, the restraint of the low pitch is evident in the reproach embodied in the following (from Schubiger 1958: 36):

```
                           ten
      You might have

                   writ        him.
                          to
```

If the highest pitch were on the accented syllable *writ-*, the effect would be one of petulance approaching rudeness. (The flexible scope of the profile can be seen in the possibility of preserving it even when the utterance is reduced to *You might have written*. The syllable *-ten* is manifested only by the sonorant [n] and yet is stretched to cover the entire rise-fall-rise—a phonetic feat that speakers manage more or less well despite its difficulty.)

The uncertain border between CAC and the combination CA+C is discussed in Chapter 12 (pp. 316–17). Profiles AC and CAC correspond to Tone 4 in Halliday (1967).

Unaccented Syllables

In this discussion of profiles, unaccented syllables have been looked at mainly in their role as determinants of configurations. The important thing about a B tail, for example, is that it sustain a high pitch long enough to distinguish B from A; if the pitch drops too soon (generally if it drops even on the first unaccented syllable after the accented one) the result is an A. But unaccented syllables carry a great part of the emotive force of a profile—easily as much, sometimes, as the accented syllables, partly because there are usually more of them.

And the speaker may also give them extra weight, in sweep or intensity or both. In the example on page 161 that goes *They wouldn't do it*, the speaker has the option of sliding the unaccented syllables to right or left, so as to have as much or as little as desired on one side or other of the trough—even of stretching *they* to cover the downskip as well as the accent, thus freeing all the remaining syllables for the upglide (we can add an initial *but* to get a better display):

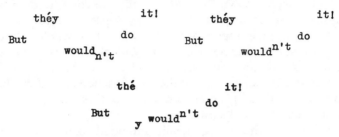

—these plus the arrangement diagrammed on page 161. (And if, to express greater astonishment, the speaker intensifies *do*, the result might be taken as an A+B contour. Compare the following A+B:

The same tension, interpretable as astonishment, is present in both— which points to the ultimate role of pitches and their successions, over and above accents, as the determinants of emotive effects.) Even the one-syllable *Paul?* (p. 161) can be given the same rightward weighting, with the final [l] segment carried to the upper reach of the voice and made quite loud.

This flexibility of fitting syllables to tonal segments and expanding or contracting the segments is found with all the profiles, but is most notable on terminal rises. When combined with certain kinds of utterances in certain contexts, the effects are striking enough to tempt the observer to read syntactic distinctions into them, but this is likely to be a false trail. Take the contrast of low rise and high rise:

On casual inspection the first invites the interpretation 'statement' (e.g. as in answer to *Why do you keep on using it?*), the second that of 'question' (as in response to *I'm going to use this old pump for the job*). But the first can be a question, though an incurious one, and the second a somewhat exercised statement (again to answer *Why do you keep on using it?* but this time implying the continuation *So why shouldn't I?*).

Uses of Profile A

Chapters 6 and 7 dealt with accents of power and accents of interest. The shapes of those accents were, by and large, variants of Profile A, which were shown to have a double function: to demarcate and emphasize separate portions (usually separate words) of an utterance, and to give impact to the utterance as a whole. On the latter score we saw a number of cases in which otherwise redundant elements might be added mostly because they were handy carriers of extra accents. We also saw that the two functions could not be readily separated: a "default" accent tended to come on an element that had a certain claim to it in its own right.

Profile A is the one generally intended, consciously or unconsciously, in most discussions of accent and intonation, and with good reason. It, along with its congeners CA, AC, and CAC, figures as the ASSERTIVE profile par excellence, and when a linguistic description leans heavily on propositional logic, as most such descriptions do, assertion plays a central role. The assertiveness of A is evident in its physical shape: the accented syllable is, more often than with any other profile, at the highest pitch, where it has greatest impact. One might say that it dominates the landscape.

In Chapter 5 we examined the double-accent or "hat" pattern, and we shall have occasion to study such combinations of profiles in Chapter 11. For the moment the question is relevant to the uses to which the profiles are put. Take an utterance like

<pre>
                péo   háve
       But   ple don't be
                                      that wa_y.
</pre>

This is clearly a contour composed of two A profiles, with accents on *people* and *behave*, respectively. It is easy to see that 'behave' is somehow the "point" of the utterance: it is the important fact in challenging what someone else has said. But what about the first profile? Does it signify that 'animals might, but people don't'? That is one possibility, but if we had the full context we might readily discover that there is no suggestion of non-persons.

In such a case, the accent is not on *people* to single people out in a special contrastive way, but is there for the sake of the utterance as a whole—not exclusively, because *people* is an important word, but mainly. In the same context one might shift the accent to *don't*, which is equally important, or (for less impact) eliminate the first A profile altogether:

```
                    háve
     But people dón't be
                           that wa y.


                    háve
     But people don't be    that way.
```

The hat pattern is a strategy that recalls a maxim offered to public speakers who want to ensure that their words remain in the minds of their audience: "First tell them what you're going to tell them, then tell them, then tell them what you've told them." The initial accent is in a sense annunciatory, the final one terminative: 'Listen' and 'I'm finished.' At the same time, both contribute to the assertive power of the utterance.

The 'assertiveness' of the A profile links up with 'separateness,' probably through some kind of metaphor of iteration. The same metaphor is present verbally in *He told me that five different times*; it would be strange to think of being told something five *same* times, so that the only gain in using the word *different* is to suggest that if one repeats the stimulus it will be more effective. The downmotion of the A profile marks it off more distinctively from its background than the upmotion usually associated with B and C, with the result that when a succession of A's is encountered, the power of iteration can be felt. But separateness has another use where A is concerned, as Pike was careful to note (1945: 62). Take a noun phrase consisting of an adjective and a noun. Two common ways of handling it are with a B profile plus an A, and an A plus an A:

```
           éxcellent mán              éx        mán
She's an                  She's an        cellent
                a ger.                             a ger.
```

Though physical gesture and other qualifiers may level the difference, the first is a bit more perfunctory. In the second, the adjective is made important separately, not just as part of the phrase.

The same 'separateness' is found where the speaker makes one sentence virtually the equivalent of two. In answer to the question *What happened?* or *What was wrong?* one might have

```
          hús                   ác
     Her
               was in an
          band            cident.
```

If the separation is clear enough—that is, if the drop in pitch on -*band* is deep and makes a sharp demarcation—this can imply something like 'Her husband is what's wrong—he was in an accident.'

Further, separateness can signal the introduction of a new entity into the discourse. This may be seen in the way the A profile sorts with an indefinite noun in a presentative sentence such as

```
          súddenly    nói
Then            a    se  bróke  the  ní ght.
```

Here we have a B+A+A+A succession, with the main A on *noise*, the new thing that is being introduced. It would sound odd to say

```
          súddenly    nóise broke
Then            a                the  ní ght.
```

with *noise* on a B profile and not separated by a drop in pitch from what follows. (For a discussion of the accents on *broke* and *night*, see Appendix B, p. 369.)

Finally, separation tells us something about compounds in English. Compare the following:

```
          Jóhn        yóung man    twén
When            was a          of      ty...
```

```
          néed
We        yóu  mán
            a   ng    for the job.
```

In the first, *young* with its B profile is back to back with *man* and its A profile: *young man* is a compound, equivalent to 'youth.' In the second, *young* has its own A profile, which separates it from the noun: two qualifications are sought, man *and* young.

Uses of Profile B

Profile B differs from A along the dimension of 'connectedness-separateness' and all the semantic inferences that can be drawn from this. Where A singles things out, B ties them in (see Pike 1945: 39),[7] and the physical trait mainly responsible is the absence of an abrupt drop *after* the accent; as we saw, that drop in A acts as a sort of cutoff.

It follows that B is most in evidence where things are predictable, where there is no need to single them out for separate attention (see Bolinger 1965: 57–66). It may be that an expression is predictable by reason of being some kind of stereotype; or it may be predictable because some part or all of it has been previously introduced in the discourse—it contains nothing new.

Here are examples of stereotyped sentences using B+A:

```
        wóuldn't do it for a mín
  I                           ute!


        thát was  thá                    sháme on
  And           thá.          Why                  hé
               t.                                  r!


        whát do you knó        Jó
  Well                   It's
                    w!            hn!
```

There is a sort of singsong effect here, appropriate for a ritual expression. Contrast the "uncombined" and more "sincere" A+A:

```
        thát    thá                 sháme    hé
  And        was                Why       on
              t.                            r!


                 knó
         whát               much,
  So      do you     Not          sure^ly.
               w?
```

B profiles are plentiful in recited poetry, which is ritual utterance elevated to art.

Connectedness is easiest to exemplify in compounds (such as *young man* already cited) and other close-knit expressions that might be called intermediate compounds. Compare the following instances of B+A contrasted with A+A, as answers to *What did you see?*:

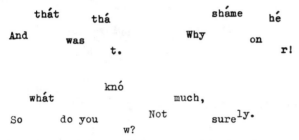

```
          tórney at lá                        tór       bréak
  I saw an at                  I saw an at    ney at
                 w.                                      fast.


         póstmaster gén                    póst      éat
  I saw the                    I saw the    master
                 er al.                               ing.
```

These are appropriate to the question—and it would also be appropriate to have A+A in all four (as we saw above, A's can be iterated for emphasis); but it would not be appropriate to answer that question with the second member of either pair using B+A instead of A+A:

```
                    póstmaster éat
        *I  saw  the
                              ing.
```

This would be normal if the question were not *What did you see?* but *When did you see the postmaster?*, with 'postmaster' previously introduced and therefore not in need of separate and independent treatment.

Other examples of intermediate compounds, B+A:

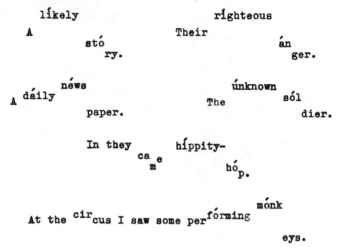

```
        líkely                      ríghteous
    A                        Their
              stó                            án
                ry.                            ger.

              néws                    únknown
    A  dáily                     The          sól
              paper.                            dier.

        In they        híppity-
                  ca  e
                    m              hó
                                     p.

                                          mónk
    At the   cir cus I saw some per fórming
                                            eys.
```

In the next-to-last example, *hippity-hop* is typical of reduplicative compounds. The last example is normal for 'monkeys trained to perform.' An A+A would be expected for the meaning 'monkeys that happened to be performing'; compare

```
        cir                    odd-áct    mónk
    At the     cus I saw some  ra ther    ing
                                              eys.
```

—in this last example, *acting* is not a stereotyped member of a phrase *acting monkeys,* and accordingly takes the A profile; it is a separate and independent bit of information.

Earlier (p. 56) we saw that utterances whose main constituent is a single polysyllabic word are often matched to the hat pattern in such a way that the word carries both accents of the pattern. When this happens, since the item in question is a unit word whose halves are naturally in tight association with each other, the first of the two accents is apt to be carried on a B profile:

```
                    ínterfer óm
        It's an
                            eter.
```

Similarly, in response to someone's objection one may say

```
              dém                        áca
         áca                        It's      dém
    It's                                              
              ic.                              ic.
```

—two instances of B+A, with different implications of mood due to the relative height of the accent (see pp. 237–44). One can also, for less emphasis, have a single A, or for more, two A's:

```
         dém                          ác dém
    It's aca                     It's    a
         ic.                              ic.
```

Although the relative height of the B profile is important in other respects, it is not relevant to the tying-in effect, which remains the same whether the B is higher than the following A or lower. In answer to *What's that water in the distance?* either of the following is appropriate:

```
                          Rív
              mérican
    That's the A
                          er,  you  idiot!
```

```
              mérican
              Rív
    That's the A
                          er,  you  idiot!
```

Also, the tail of the B (*-rican*) may have an uptilt or a downtilt without affecting the relationship. *American River* is a compound. On the other hand, if someone has been looking at a map and has remarked about how straight the river courses are, a hearer might respond with A+A:

```
                                        rív
              character is         mér
    That's                                 
                      tic of the A    ican
                                          ers.
```

—*American* is important in its own right. But if things American have already been under discussion and only 'rivers' is new, *American rivers* may again have B+A.

Profile B is common in expressions that do not *inform* so much as they *enhance.* Typically these are quantifiers or affective modifiers, especially epithets. Examples of the latter:

```
         rótten                 dástard    són of a
    You're a     lí        That               bí
              ar.               ly              tch.
```

The second example has a succession of B's (accented on *das-* and *son*) followed by an A (accented on *bitch*). A's could be used throughout for more impact (as if to imply 'I'm really informing you about that fellow'). If A replaces the B on *rotten* in the first example, yielding

```
                    rót
                          lí
          You're a
                    ten
                          ar.
```

the suggestion is 'You are not very good at telling lies'—*rotten* becomes informative rather than epithetical. Some enhancing expressions other than epithets:

```
                                            bú
          whóle thing        ástronomical
    The                was an
                                        st.

        répresents      índivisible
    It              an              fór
                                          ce.
```

Astronomical does not refer to astronomy but to magnitude. We could of course use A's here to suggest that we are "informing" rather than "commenting"; what we cannot as easily do is the opposite—replacing the A in the following, which is verbally informative, with a B:

```
          bú                  nóm          lá
    He's    sy with his astro  ical calcu
                                      tions.
```

Similarly *indivisible* signifies more than 'not subject to division'—it implies 'powerful.'

An example from Schubiger (1958: 102) illustrates the enhancing use of *more*:

```
          móre quarrelsome péo
    There were                             day!
                           ple there yes ter
```

This signifies 'What a lot of quarrelsome people there were.' To make a literal comparison of how many there were yesterday with how many there were some other time, it would be more appropriate to put separate A's on *more* and *quarrelsome*.

The quantifiers that favor B are generally those that also enhance. It follows that smaller amounts are more apt to favor A (though what really counts is the speaker's intent). The first example below answers the question *What have you got in that basket?*:

```
          ́on
It's                  ́doz   ̓e
          ly  a      en   gg s!
```

```
          ́liv                                        ́fin
They  ́did n't de    er  it  because it was no  ́more  than  ́half
                                                              ished.
```

Larger amounts are more favorable to enhancement. *All* and *every* are typical:

```
          ́all of them        ́every
I've got            ́fin              ́o
                    ished,            n
                                       e.
```

Similarly with synonyms of *all*, such as *full, solid, undivided,* etc.:

```
               ́undivided at
     ́gave  them
I        a        my              ́ten
                                     tion.
```

(We note the rhythmic shift of the accent here to the syllable *un-*, which takes the upward jump of the B profile.) Contrast the following instances of *solid* in the figurative sense of 'complete' and the more nearly literal one of 'firm':

```
                 ́ho
        ́solid
I  ́spent  a         ur
                       on that cold street corner.
```

```
                ́rea
          ́sol
I  ́need  a more     id
                      son for firing the man.
```

Numerals and kindred amounts also fall into line. The following answer the question *How fast were they going?*; the first implies 'They were going very fast'; the second gives an informative estimate:

```
          ́hundred miles an
They were  ́going a              ́ho
                                   ur.
```

```
                   ́twen  ́miles  ́ho
They were  ́going about     ty       an
                                     ur.
```

Contributing to 'enhancement' is the sustained high pitch of the B in a number of these examples, particularly where the B is higher than the following A.

The quantifier *single* has an intensifying sense, implying 'even,' in sentences like *It didn't have a single one.* This favors the B profile, and one can discern a potential contrast in meaning between the following, with B and A, respectively, where *it* refers to 'egg' and *one* refers to 'yolk':

> It ^{dídn't} have a   síngle   ,   ón   e.   (That's why I didn't eat it.)

> It ^{dídn't} have a   sín   gle   one.   (That's why I didn't eat it.)

In the first, the egg was not eaten because it had no yolk at all. In the second, it was not eaten because it had a double yolk. The first example illustrates another rather frequent trait of the B profile when quantifiers are used on it for enhancement—they tend to be lengthened: *Not a sin-n-ngle one; Do it an-n-y way you please.*

Profile B has its uses also in a broader syntactic sense. We look first at medial positions, that is, B within rather than between clauses. In keeping with the fact that B does not separate its content from the rest of the phrase, clause, or sentence, we expect to find it on terms that are less new and less contrastive in the discourse. Suppose a speaker is reassuring the recipient of a gift about what his intentions were, and says

>   Í   máde it for   yó
> didn't make it for ^{jóhn,} I   u.

Here *made it for* is important enough to be accented, but is not new to the discourse, and receives a B; an A profile,

>   yó
> I ^{máde} it for   u.

while possible, is less likely—it would be as if the information had to be introduced anew, and could be taken to imply 'Another time, don't forget.'

The same old-versus-new distinction can be observed even when the verbal material itself is skewed in the direction of 'contrast.' A good test is with those forms of the auxiliaries that are used for contrastive purposes: *do* and its various tenses, and the unreduced forms of other auxiliaries, e.g. *can* instead of *c'n* and *is* instead of the contraction *'s.* In the following examples, the full form of *is* is used and is prolonged:

                Ís cóm   í cóm
    (1) He   ing,   he?   (2) He s   ing,   he?
                       isn't   isn't

The most likely use of the B in (1) is for confirmation—the speaker is assuming an old fact and asking to have it verified. The A in (2) is more likely for bringing up a new thought, one that might be introduced with *by the way*. A similar distinction can be heard in

              ís há   í há
                        mí
    (3) It   d, I ad   (4) Howév   it   s
           r   t.   er,   rd.

We 'admit' to something already introduced, hence the B in (3); but *however* indicates a contrary—therefore new—point, hence the A in (4). (There is no hard and fast attachment of either locution to either profile, but the tendencies are as indicated. Since intonation is relatively independent of grammar, the speaker is free to pretend that the old is new and the new is old.)

We can use tag questions like those in (1) and (2) to illustrate not only the hint of something already in mind but in addition a further manifestation of the connecting-up effect of B. Compare:

                        dón't belíeve
            (5) You
                                     me,
                                         do you?

                    dón't   líeve
            (6) You   be
                                     me,
                                         do you?

With its A's, (6) is appropriate as a joking remark after the speaker has told a tall story that the hearer has apparently taken seriously: the idea of not believing is newly introduced. But (5) reveals not only a repetition—the speaker has already heard or inferred that the hearer does not believe him—but also the amalgamation of *don't believe* into 'disbelieve': it is more readily interpretable as 'You disbelieve me, do you?' in which there is no reversal of polarity. It is thus logically the same as *You don't believe me, don't you?*, and probably represents a conclusion. This can be tested by attaching *so: So you don't believe me, do (don't) you? So* is more difficult to add to (6). As usual, these interpretations are only probabilities. In some contexts the meanings of (5) and (6) can be turned around.

A further phrasal syntactic use is to express a kind of casual observation—we might say that it *comments* rather than *tells*. It is common after the word *just*, as if to imply 'no great need to tell you this'—the speaker may be downplaying it or may feel that it is too obvious to view as a matter of information. Compare the use of *killing* in the following, with B+A and A+A, both in answer to *What are you doing?*

```
         kílling                           kíl
    I'm just    tí            I'm              bú
                                       ling
                  me.                        gs.
```

Or the B+A in the following, where the speaker feels the hopelessness of saying anything:

```
                    dó the whole bit a gá
        He'll just
                                        in.
```

Though there is no *just* in the next example, it is implied. The first part of the sentence is *If this snow keeps up*:

```
                  ríght around and go back to Flór
    the  bírds will turn
                                            ida.
```

(Here the B profile has a downtilt, which adds to the casualness of the remark.)

Profile B is also common on certain adverbs—typically those of time and place—when they occur in initial position. They are the same adverbs, as Ladd notes (1980: 66), that are normally deaccented when they occur at the end of the utterance; the reason is the same: they are regarded as incidental to the main content. So, in answer to *What are your plans?* we may have either of the following:

```
    Well,
           morrow        stáying
        to       I'm            hó
                                  me.

         guéss        hóme
    I          I'll stay
                         tomorrow.
```

—the B on *tomorrow* in the first compares with the deaccent in the second on the same word. If in either case *tomorrow* were given an A profile, the hearer would probably infer a contrast: tomorrow but not the day after. The adverb *soon* behaves similarly:

```
        sóon to                        léave
    He's       lé          He's góing to
            ave.                        soon.
```

Profile B is common in listings where the speaker is mainly just reciting the list and not focusing on individual items:

$$\text{She bought } \overset{\overset{\text{ar,}}{\text{súg}}}{} \quad \overset{\overset{\text{toes,}}{\text{tá}}}{\text{po}} \quad \text{and } \overset{\text{rí}}{\underset{\text{ce.}}{}}$$

An A profile on the first two items (the third already has an A) would make the choice of sugar and potatoes sound very dramatic.

In successive CLAUSES, a B on the early clause is the rule for gnomic stereotypes—the speaker is not revealing anything new:

$$\text{Easy } \overset{\text{cóme,}}{} \quad \underset{\text{easy}}{} \quad \underset{\underset{\text{gó.}}{}}{}$$

$$\text{Now you } \overset{\text{sée}}{} \overset{\text{it,}}{} \quad \text{now you } \overset{\text{dó}}{\underset{\text{n't.}}{}}$$

$$\text{Ask me no } \overset{\overset{\text{tions}}{\text{qués}}}{} \quad \text{and I'll } \overset{\text{téll}}{} \text{ you no } \overset{\text{lí}}{\underset{\underset{\text{s.}}{\text{e}}}{}}$$

$$\text{Give him an } \overset{\overset{\text{ch,}}{\text{ínch,}}}{} \quad \text{and he } \overset{\text{tákes a}}{} \overset{\text{mí}}{\underset{\underset{\text{e.}}{\text{l}}}{}}$$

$$\text{What goes } \overset{\text{úp}}{} \quad \text{must come } \overset{\text{dó}}{\underset{\underset{\text{n.}}{\text{w}}}{}}$$

Unstereotyped clauses are found too, and here the speaker may be suggesting that he doesn't care. This often contributes a flip tone, especially with conditional clauses:

$$\text{If you } \overset{\text{líke}}{} \overset{\text{it,}}{} \quad \overset{\text{éat}}{\underset{\text{it.}}{}}$$

But the place where B is most conspicuous and has been most discussed is its SENTENTIAL use in utterance-final position, where because of the fact that there is no cutoff (in the form of a drop in pitch) and the pitch usually remains high, the effect is that of 'something unfinished.' Here we find the prototypical instances of noninformativeness, namely yes-no questions:

$$\text{You're } \overset{\text{stáying are}}{} \overset{\text{you?}}{}$$

Likewise complementary questions:

$$\text{His } \overset{\text{réason be}}{} \overset{\text{ing?}}{}$$

Noninformativeness is of a kind with incompletion: the information comes in the answer, which completes the conversational exchange. This can be illustrated by adding the answer, *He was too busy*, to the last question, and then combining them into one sentence:

```
        réason being               tóo  bús
His                   he was
                                             y.
```

We see here the kinship between questions and nonfinal clauses within sentences: both expect completion, and neither need make any assumptions about the facts.

It is necessary to emphasize "need make" in this context because there is a possible choice between B and any of the other profiles with a rising terminal. The choice affects yes-no questions less than complementary questions or nonfinal clauses—the latter have the choice, but yes-no questions do not, or at least not at all on the same terms. Take first a question with a B:

```
                        táste a little of it?
Would you like to

                        táste?
Would you like to
```

Put these on an AC profile:

```
                    táste
Would you like to
                               a little    it?
                                        of
                    tá
Would you like to        te?
                       s
```

This is rather unusual for American English, except in echo questions—if for example a speaker muses to himself *Would I like to taste?* and someone else repeats the question (changing *I* to *you*), surprised that the first person has asked it, then the AC profile is normal for both British and American English; but as an original, not an echo, question, it sounds too insistent to American speakers.

But it is perfectly normal in complementary questions,

```
                    réa
        His
                son  being?
```

and in nonfinal clauses:

```
                    tél              cáll
As  sóon  as you get a      e
                      phone,
                                  me.
```

One could use a B here, but that would not "make a point" of the
condition:

```
                          telephone,  cáll
As soon as you get a
                              me.
```

B thus shares 'incompleteness' with AC and CAC, because of the
rising or nonfalling terminal; but it lacks the assertiveness, separate
pointing, etc. of the profiles that contain A.

A final B in an utterance that is not a question is similar to a clause-
final B as far as 'incompleteness' is concerned—that is, more is expected to be said or done, either by the speaker or by the hearer when
it comes his turn. Also in regard to 'not making a point of it': the
speaker is observing or commenting more than informing. In the following B+B+A we get the impression that everything has been said
before:

```
    told you to do it.                  lis ten.
                                                   What ⟶
  I              You wouldn't

                          pé

    reaction did you ex
                          ct?!
```

If AC is used, the speaker is probably reminding the hearer of the
facts, not merely voicing a kind of exasperated lament:

```
    told                            lis
  I      you to do it.  You wouldn't   ten.  What etc.
```

The terminal rise on these B examples is, of course, not part of the
definition of Profile B, and one may have a terminal level or a downtilt
with the same 'everything has been said before' implication. The difference is along another dimension: the rise is prodding, the level and
downtilt suggest boredom or pointlessness (see pp. 226–37). When
we examine B's in the form of commands, these differences stand out
more sharply:

```
                        leave it alóne!
            Just
```

A person disregarding this command invites trouble: the prodding is extreme. With a level or downtilt the prodding is diminished but given other signs of tension the effect may still be menacing. One way or another, the B profile leaves things in suspense.

Uses of Profile C

Profile C was described above as the mirror image of Profile A, in its shape. It is also, in most ways, the mirror image—that is to say, the opposite—in its functions. Where A tends to play up, to emphasize, to suggest contrast or newness, C plays down, deemphasizes, and often implies foreknowledge. If to accent something is to give it force, then the accent in C can be thought of as a reverse accent (see Bolinger 1945): the speaker needs to make the item stand out—figure against ground—but has opposite feelings about it. This rough description accommodates many special uses and meanings depending on context.

The C profile is inherently contradictory, for it "deaccents an accent," and if it were not the fact that intonation abounds in similar modulations, in simultaneous tuggings in more than one direction at a time (especially when combined with physical gesture), it might seem to be an impossibility. Yet there can be no question of its use as a pitch movement to make the syllable on which its accent falls stand out for importance. The following can be uttered with uniform timing and volume, and the syllables *an-* and *new* will still be the focal ones:

```
Have you   y new ones?            Have you any     ones?
         an                                   new
```

At the same time, the anomaly of C's self-cancellation does create problems for the system, as will become clear in later discussion, and probably explains its apparent rarity in languages with restricted intonation, in particular the tone languages where pitch plays a different and sometimes conflicting role.

Perhaps the commonest use of C is for reassurance. It has a soothing quality that fits it for use with infants and small children, and this is carried over into the classroom where some teachers tend to overdo it, especially in asking questions. Some B+C's:

```
There        Don't                        your
       there!        cry!  Give   mummy
                                              bottle.

What's       Isn't it         Tell me how you
       that?          nice?                 did it.
```

But it is common enough in speech with adults. To show reassuring approval of someone's action one may say (to the person),

$$\text{Thá}$$
$$\text{t's}$$
$$\quad\quad\text{my }\text{Dó}11\text{y}^!$$

with A+C; a B+AC is more apt to be a disapproving comment:

$$\quad\quad\quad\quad\text{Dó}1$$
$$\text{Thát's my}\quad\quad\text{1y.}$$

C is the profile that is least restricted as to the syntactic type that may be used with it. Although there is no absolute restriction in this respect with any of the profiles, B is found on questions more than A is, and A is found on statements and commands more than B is; but C is impartially used on all—any of them may at times need to be played down or softened in some way.

As the diagrams above suggest, probably the commonest contour on which C is encountered is B+C. There is probably a good phonetic reason for this. Since C is approached from above, the handiest way to gain the prior altitude is by way of a B profile. But it is possible to stretch the accented syllable leftward so as to get a dip without any earlier profile. Compare the following questions, the first with B+C, the second simple C, each containing a politely repressed reprimand:

$$\text{yóu trying to}$$
$$\quad\quad\quad\quad\text{me?}\quad\quad\quad\quad\quad\text{me?}$$
$$\text{Are}\quad\quad\quad\quad\quad\quad\quad\quad\quad\text{Thréatening}$$
$$\quad\quad\quad\text{thréaten}$$

There is no lack of combinations with other preceding profiles. The following are A+C, CA+C, and C+C:

$$\text{Jóhn}\quad\quad\quad\quad\quad\quad\text{ny}$$
$$\quad\quad\quad\quad\quad\quad\quad\quad\quad\quad\quad\quad\text{isn't}$$
$$\text{ny isn't}\quad\text{zy.}\quad\text{Jóhn isn't}\quad\text{zy.}\quad\text{Jóhnny}\quad\quad\text{crázy.}$$
$$\quad\quad\text{crá}\quad\quad\quad\quad\quad\quad\text{crá}$$

Profile C can be used, as A is, to bring in new information, but usually not *as* new information (but see p. 317 for A+C and CA+C with accents of power). That is, it suggests familiarity of some sort or other. It is no coincidence that the expression *You know* when used as a crutch always occurs on Profile C. In the following, the 'scary place' is new to the context but the speaker suggests either 'You might know she would react that way' or 'I thought you knew, so why do you ask?' It answers the question *Why didn't she like the book?*

$$\text{There was a}$$
$$\quad\quad\quad\text{scáry place in it.}$$

In the next example, a contour consisting of B+C+C+B+A, the interior C's refer to a bothersome trifle that is of regular occurrence:

```
        júst as I'm about to       off——→
 So                          dóze
```

```
    to                              póp
           sléeᵖ the  thíng starts
                                    ping.
```

In the next example, getting one's glasses is a routine or expected thing. It comes in response to *Shall we go?*

```
                    gó get my
    Yé
        ah. I'll           glásˢᵉˢ·
```

The speaker here could add another B+C:

```
        Júst
            wáit a minute·
```

The next example was a comment made as a motorist passed two pedestrians on a rainy day and was careful to drive slowly through the puddles so as not to splash water. One pedestrian said to the other,

```
        Thát's
            conˢᶦᵈᵉʳᵃᵗᵉ·
```

The fact was obvious to both pedestrians. An A profile would have suggested some need for the speaker to *inform* his companion. The same utterance with the C could have been used ironically had the pedestrians been splashed—a fact equally obvious to both.

   Though both profiles ordinarily end with a rise, C differs from B in being more subdued. In the following, the first sequence, with its successive A+C contours, is more subdued than the second, where the accent occurs on the rise rather than at the trough:

```
    Nó                      ít's
        body's blaming  u,     ⁿoₜ        fault.
                       yó          yóur
```

```
    Nó                      ít's
        body's blaming yᵒu,    ⁿoₜ yóur fault.
```

(The accents in question are on *you* and *your; blaming, not,* and *fault* are unaccented.)

The "held-down" accent of C and CB has the same inhibiting effect, as can be seen in the following succession of C+CB+C:

```
        n't it awfully      cy in view of the
   Is
                 chán                    rísks?
```

Uses of Profile CA

Of the complex profiles, CA requires little discussion since, as earlier examples have shown, it is a sort of intensification of A, common in emphatic discourse, e.g. in exclamations, vocatives, etc., such as *God!, Johnny!* (respelled below for display):

```
         o                     ny
     Gó                   Jóhn
        d!                      y!
```

One occasionally sees the folk spelling *NevER!*, in which the capitals represent the highest pitch of the CA, exaggerated for emphasis:

```
       er
   Név
       r!
```

Uses of Profile AC

Profiles AC and CAC share a terminal rise that adds 'incompletion' to the overall effect of A. It is enough to consider AC, of which CAC is then an intensification.

The various uses of AC conform to those of A plus the 'incompletion' of the rise. Following are some of them:

1. Salutations and farewells. This seems to answer to the association of such utterances with CALLING, which is often done across a distance and employs a sustained final pitch for audibility or as an attention-getter:

```
      ló-                          bý-
         o-o!                          e-e!
   Hel                       Good
```

The final sustained pitch shades into a final rise, as may be seen when there is enough syllabic material to make the movement apparent:

```
      ló                         bý e
   Hel                       Good
        there!                       now!
```

2. Selective contrast. AC is used to point one thing up against other possibilities. In answer to *What would you like for breakfast?* one may reply

I like wáf fles.

to suggest one possibility—the rise seems to ask 'Is that OK?' or (in Ladd's terms) 'Does that count as an answer?' If we are speaking of Mary's qualities and say

She wrítes well.

we leave the door open to other things that she does or does not do well. If we are wounded by someone and say

Not yó u!

we express our astonishment that you of all persons should be the one.

3. Theme particularization. If you ask *What happened?* and I answer with A+A, as in

Your bró lé ther broke his g.

I report two items of interest, the person affected and the part injured. But if you ask *What happened to my brother?* and I reply

Your bró lé ther broke his g.

I imply 'As for your brother, he broke his leg.' In fact, that wording would also take Profile AC. (It might take B, but that would seem to be dismissing the matter as of little importance.) The AC may be used for theme particularization at either end of the utterance. In answer to *Why do you use a hammer?* one may say either of the following:

With a hám éa mer it's sy.

It's éa sy with a hám mer.

4. Emphasis. When an AC profile is non-final, it is often truncated, and is then indistinguishable from a truncated A. Since the terminal rise of AC signifies 'incompletion' and interior position is by definition non-final and therefore 'incomplete,' the rise is absorbed in the rise that may come anyway with the next profile. By carefully including it, the speaker makes the separation more striking. This may be used for emphasis, including ironic emphasis, as in the exaggerated

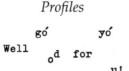

5. Admonition. The shape of the profile preceding the AC may influence the interpretation of the AC. With A+AC the interpretation is apt to be "logical"; thus in

<pre>
          thá
Dón't
      do
         a^t!
</pre>

one probably implies 'It's OK to do the other thing'—the speaker is keyed up only about the identity of the thing. But with B+AC, especially if the B has an upglide or uptilt, the interpretation is more apt to be 'emotional':

<pre>
               thá
  Dón't do
               at!
</pre>

The speaker need not be implying anything about the permissibility of other acts, only about the impermissibility of this one. The emotivity is also apt to raise the pitch of the final fall-rise, reducing the fall. Warnings and cautionary statements are common with this overall shape, rising B plus AC:

<pre>
              cáre   gó
     bétter be   ful.   wón't do any   od.
You'd   It
</pre>

Uses of Profile CB

The commonest use of CB is as the initial profile in one of the following contours: CB+C, CB+B, CB+A, and CB+AC, probably in that order of frequency. Three of these—all except CB+A—are manifestations of the so-called "contradiction contour" (see pp. 245–52). An example is this CB+C:

<pre>
       n't it strike you as
Dóes
                        stránge?
</pre>

Ambiguity

Speaking of an apparent shift of word stress, Classe writes (1939: 46–47):

It happens that a word becomes accented initially (even though the normal word stress is on some other syllable) where there would appear to exist no compelling rhythmical necessity for doing so. Thus the word *however*, when not used initially, is *always* stressed on the second syllable. But I have occasionally heard such forms as: *However* . . . (with the stress on *how*) although it cannot be said that this shifting of the accent is in any way due to the necessities of rhythm, since this form is usually heard by itself in the sense of 'however that may be.'

What Classe heard as a shift of accent is actually a change of profile from A (or AC) to C: the stress remains at the normal place, on *-ev-*, but the accented syllable is at the trough rather than at the peak. Other words similar in function to *however* are often treated in the same way, e.g. *besides*:

$$\text{Be} \qquad \text{whó would really} \qquad \text{cá}$$
$$\text{sídes, } \qquad \qquad \text{r}_{\text{e?}}$$

What's more, moreover, unless, and yet, etc. likewise are fairly common on the C profile. But it is especially appropriate to *however* because of the adversative sense of the word and the need, for purposes of courtesy and restraint, to play it down.

But this does not explain why Classe "heard" the *how-* part as accented.[8] Other tests have shown that hearers tend, when their attention is directed to "stress" or "accent" (which cues them to listen for loudness rather than sense), to identify the high-pitched syllable as the strong one; and physical measurements sometimes agree. This gives us one more reason for assigning greater importance to pitch prominence than to other cues of accent. Profile C "plays down" the accented syllable, and in that sense deaccents it; but in the definition of *accent* followed here, the syllable is still accented. It is more useful to keep that dimension constant, and to treat the effects of playing up and playing down as superadded. (Furthermore, as we recall, the low-pitched accent often retains other cues of accent such as extra length and delayed release.)

An incidental question is whether the prominence of such items as *how-* is exploited in some way. As part of a C profile, *how-* is ground to *-ev-*'s figure; but it is a noisy piece of background, and since speakers are seldom inclined to let anything go to waste, it may well be utilized as some kind of attention-getting signal, especially as under the conditions described it is apt to be initial in the utterance. Speakers may readily exaggerate it, and in so doing might be said to create an additional profile, a B in this case, preceding the C. An illustration of how this can come about is provided by a passage from an Erle Stanley Gardner novel:

"That's right. Come to think of it, I've seen you there."
"I know almost everyone that passes."
"Oh," Bertha said, "*I see*," and laughed.[9]

Gardner italicized the pronoun *I* to indicate that he "heard" it as accented. Yet in the more usual pronunciation of *I see* meaning 'I understand,' there is a single A profile with accent on the verb and no accent on the pronoun. So it is fair to assign this to a C profile, with accent on *see* but with an extra prominence on *I* perhaps amounting to an added B profile (with too little material to reveal a clear tail). The same kind of shrewd or knowing observation can be expressed with

$$\text{Éverybody}$$
$$\text{knów}^{\text{s}\,\cdot}$$

with a manifest B on *everybody* (and *ev-*, like *I*, tending to be prolonged). One speaks of a "shrewd look" accompanying remarks of this kind, especially noteworthy in

$$\text{Yóu'll}$$
$$\text{sée!}$$

with the speaker prolonging *you'll* and perhaps shaking a finger at 'you,' and with a strong suggestion of a B profile there.

If the *I* of Gardner's

$$\text{I}$$
$$\text{sée}\cdot$$

is to be counted as an independent B profile, then we have a case of the accented syllable of one profile serving as ground to another's figure, since *I* establishes the higher pitch for the downskip to the accent that defines the C profile on *see*. There is thus a zone of uncertainty between "mere ground" and "accented syllable as ground." In the normal pronunciation of *however*, in which the diphthong of the first syllable is more or less reduced, the *how-* is best regarded as mere ground. (See p. 39 and Appendix A, pp. 353–58, for such cases of unstable reduction.) There are many other such instances in which vowel reduction is an indicator of whether an extra profile may be intended or not. The word *it* comes as close as one can get to an inherent lack of stress, and it is often encountered as ground in a C profile, not infrequently reduced virtually to zero in a sentence such as *It's nothing* spoken to reassure someone. It then comes out as '*Snothing*, with the initial fall of the C profile taken by *-no-*, which spreads over both the fall and the trough. But the speaker is also free to exaggerate *it* in both length and volume, as if to imply 'No matter how serious this may seem' (= arousal on first part) 'we can still play it down' (low pitch in last part). Existential *there*, as in

$$\text{Th\'ere wasn't any tr\'ouble.}$$

has the same possibilities as *it*, and this example gives a better display of the B profile. The initial high pitch can readily be taken by shwa, as in

$$\text{A g\'ain?!}$$

and the shwa can be exaggerated as in the other cases, becoming a lengthened $[\Lambda]$.[10]

We find the same uncertain status of the initial B profile before an A as before a C, thus:

$$\text{How\`ever.}$$

As with the C, the *how-* can be reduced or it can be exaggerated.

A different sort of ambiguity is found not between the presence and absence of a B profile before a C or an A, as in the above examples, but between whether to interpret a preceding profile as a B or an A. As might be expected, the ambiguity arises from an insufficiency of unaccented syllables to serve as ground, so that the configuration, like the reversible staircase, can be "seen" in either of two ways. Take a sentence like *John was sick*, with accents on both *John* and *sick*. In the shape

$$\text{J\'ohn was si ck.}$$

where the speaker has been careful to stretch *John* onto the fall, there is no ambiguity; the utterance is A+A. But with the shape

$$\text{J\'ohn was si ck.}$$

one cannot tell whether to regard *John* as A or as B. As A, it relies on *was* for the downskip required by A. But that fall in pitch could as readily be a dropback from a B. A better array of syllables brings out the contrast:

```
 líz            sí           lízabeth      sí
E    abeth was               E        was
              ck.                          ck.
```

These are unambiguously A+A and B+A. In the latter, *was* is not needed to support the B profile, which already has enough material in *-abeth* to establish the ground for the accent on *-liz-*; it is a surplus syllable available for emotive purposes. If it remains high, the speaker is revealed to be quite exercised—the tension is sustained for a space of five syllables; it is enough for the pitch to drop on that one syllable to relax the tension markedly. As for the contrast between the two figures as they appear above, the A+A is equally appropriate as an answer to either *Why weren't you able to come?* or *Why wasn't Elizabeth able to come?*—there are potential "new information" points on both *Elizabeth* and *sick*. The B+A would not be appropriate to the first question; it is rather like *Elizabeth?—well, she was sick*; Profile B is less suitable for new information. As for the example with *John*, since it is ambiguous between the two figures it can be taken either way.

Still another kind of ambiguity involves identifying a profile as AC or as C. The problem again arises when there are too few syllables to make figure and ground unmistakable. Take an utterance such as

```
 I
   will.
```

As far as the pitches are concerned, this could have either *I* as figure with *will* as ground (*I* is dropped down from), or *will* as figure with *I* as ground (*will* is dropped down to). In response to *Who will do it?* the first interpretation applies; in response to *You haven't done it yet!* the second applies. The context clears up the ambiguity and the hearer is almost certain to get it right even if other cues are absent, though more likely they will be there—extra length or intensity on the accented syllable.

This same kind of ambiguity may embrace conditions that make it possible to have a phonetic equivalence between one profile and two. Take the utterances

```
                                      pút it
  There's certainly nothing adequate to
                                            on.

    pút it
                                       fi
Just          Then we can see how it
       ón.                             ts.
```

The first has *put it on* as a single AC profile with delayed fall (the *it* would normally take the greater part of the fall). The second has *put it on* as B+C, which can be shown by its equivalence to

```
              pút the damn thing
      Just
                        ón•
```

which has a better array of syllables. The two instances of *put it on* may be phonetically identical, though the second can be distinguished by more length or intensity applied to *on*. (It is the particle of a phrasal verb, which normally carries a stress; for example, *chóp dówn the tree*. A preposition, such as *on* in the first example, is normally unaccented.) [11]

Ambiguities also result when content words—which are important enough to claim an accent in their own right—are arrayed in competing positions on a configuration. Take an utterance like

```
      I'm
                          milk for that!
         not going to
                    buy
```

in a discussion of bathing, including possible bathing in milk. After the A profile with accent on *I*, the next is either a C with accent on *buy* (the lowest pitch, jumped down to) or a B with accent on *milk* (the first pitch jumped up to). Either one makes sense, the first to imply 'I don't mind your bathing in milk if I don't have to pay for it,' the second 'I don't mind your bathing, but not in milk!' Again, the two may be phonetically identical, though the key words are apt to be distinguished by other cues of accent. (By shifting the words a short way along the legs of the fall-rise, one can make *buy* an accent on a B profile, or *milk* an accent on a C. It is only by testing this way, e.g. *milk* first as a C and then as a B, that one can appreciate the contrast in meaning—the toning-down of the C, the arousal of the B.)

The identical problem can be seen playing on a verbal ambiguity in the following, in answer to *Is it scarred?*:

```
      Júst on the
                      óutside•
```

If the last two syllables represent *out side* ('the side that's out') then we have a C profile with accent on *out*, which is in contrast with *in*. But if the syllables represent *outside*, with normal stress on the second syllable, then we have a B profile with accent on *-side* ('nowhere else but on the outside,' with no specific allusion to 'in'). In both cases there is an initial B with downtilt.

A similar ambiguity can be found between CA and B, conditioned by failure to carry out the falling movement of CA as abruptly as that profile normally calls for. In the following attested example of CA+C, the speaker intended *we're* to be contrastively accented, making it part of a CA:

```
        not
            doing any
Wé're
                  móuntain climbing!
```

The degree of indignation was just sufficient to keep the pitches after *not* fairly high, bringing the shape close to that of a downtilted B, which would have been more faithfully represented by

```
        nót doing any...
We're
```

in which *we're* is unaccented and *not* is the accented syllable of a B profile. The main trouble is the unreduced form of *not*, which so readily makes it appear to be accented even when, as intended here, it is only part of the ground for the accented syllable *we're*; the ambiguity is unavoidable because the only reduced form of *not* is the fully reduced contraction *n't*, which cannot be used here. (The same hitch also makes it possible to take the example as representing an A on *not* with *we're* again unaccented—the drop in pitch after *not* is just enough to define the A.)

A simpler case of ambiguity comes about through the problem of successive B's (pp. 153–54)—when to regard a rise as merely a tail, and when as containing an additional B profile. In the following,

```
        yóu be staying here?
Will
```

with a level tail, there is manifestly only one profile. But B's more often have rising tails, with the greatest amount of rise at the end:

```
                            e?
        yóu be staying her
Will
```

It is not difficult to read a second B into *here*: 'Will you, of all people, be staying here, of all places?' The second B would be virtually unambiguous if there were a dropback on *-ing*:

```
        yóu be staying hére?
Will           ing
```

The problem with *not* underscores the complexity of cues and the reliance that has to be placed on other prompters besides pitch. The presence of reduced forms such as *n't* for *not* makes it possible at times to be a bit careless in delineating an intonational profile, but when that assistance is gone, there may be confusion. Here is a further instance where the normal contrast between two forms of a function word, *some* and *s'm*, might have helped. The contrast was unavailable (either way, *some* had to be emphasized), and the hearer was at a loss to interpret:

<pre>
                    s^{om}e
    I thought   cat_s, you have to ———►

                          mouse
        pro^{tect} them from the
                            trap.
</pre>

The confusion was between A with accent on *some* and *cats* serving as ground, and B+A with A represented by *cats* (see pp. 147–48 for such low-pitched A's). Punctuation and paraphrase bring out the difference: 'I thought that sóme (but not all) cats have to be protected from the mouse trap' versus 'I thought, "Sóme cáts! (What ridiculous cats!) They have to be protected from the mouse trap!"'

It might be thought that if such ambiguities are to be found, the notion of figure and ground is itself invalidated, and that, inasmuch as length and loudness are going to be relied on anyway, pitch as a cue to accent could be dispensed with or described as secondary to other factors that condition it. (Pitch accent was once viewed in this way by American structuralists.) As to the first objection, it would equally invalidate figure and ground under all circumstances where cooperating cues are stripped away and the viewer (or listener) is left with only part of what is needed to identify a configuration securely. The classic example is the reversible staircase. If the picture is completed with even a few of its natural details—a figured carpet, a hat rack on a landing, or whatever—the reversibility disappears. It is the unnaturalness of the examples cited above—their separation from context—that makes them "reversible." In order to describe the profiles it is necessary to strip them bare, but that does not mean that they will carry their nakedness into normal discourse.

As to the second objection, it leads to the chicken-and-egg question of what cues are so important that other cues can—in the sort of "economical" description that linguists favor—be regarded as merely ancillary to them. We saw the futility of this in Chapter 2. The capacity of pitch to override other cues can be illustrated using a fully displayed Profile A, with flanking syllables on both sides:

I said it was fester^{i}ng, not that it ^{hád}festered.

The pitch configuration marks -*ing* as accented, even if the first syllable of *festering* is given more volume, and despite the fact that -*ing* is a most unlikely candidate for an accent.

How Much a Profile Covers

The domain of a profile was defined (p. 141) as the limit of movement that can occur on a one-syllable word, referring, of course, to an ACCENTED word. But we have noted certain complex shapes that seem to be able to claim now one accent and now more than one. An AC, for example, with its fall-rise, executes the same turn as a contour consisting of two profiles, A+C. And one can imagine the AC taking A+C as its model. Compare the following, in which an AC imitates a succeeding A+C and both seem to be conveying the same intonational message; the speaker has been misunderstood to imply something to the detriment of his hearer, and speaks emphatically and reassuringly:

Not thá t! I don't want / yóu to have to súffer!

Similarly

Not mé e! I didn't hít him! I'm not to bláme!

Is the AC "really" A+C, with a single one-syllable word carrying more than one accent? Or is the A+C "really" just a protracted AC?

A yes to the first question is possible if we accept the idea that a single syllable can carry more than one prominence. This apparently can happen with successive A profiles, as in an emphatic negative, *Nó-ó-ó!* But in that case all three accents are marked by peaks of intensity as well. In the present case, the *me* in *Not me!*, for example, has only one such peak; the pitch turn is there, but other prominence is lacking.

The possibility of a yes to the second question is planted by the fact that nothing in the respective utterances after *you*, *I*, and *I'm* reports anything new. All those syllables can count as unaccented, functioning as a tail to the accent. In this view, the pitch turn on *suffer* has no more significance than the total lack of pitch prominence in a terminal level such as in the following:

```
                              yóu

          júst that I don't want
    It's
                                 to have to suffer.
```

Here the material after *you* is the tail of an A profile; in the case we are examining it would be the tail of an AC. So interpreted, it makes no difference where the trough comes on the tail, whether on *to*, *have*, *to*, or *suf-*, with whatever is left carrying the terminal upmotion. The more syllables there are on that final upglide, the more keyed up the result, but it is the utterance as a whole that is affected, not some individual portion of it.

The AC illustrated here could also be ambiguous with A+B, if for example the word *suffer* were sufficiently prominent on the upglide:

```
              you

    I don't want                    suffer.
                    to have to
```

There are other pairings that reveal a close kinship between AC and A+C. Take the expressions that inquire the purpose of something. They can be used together, as in the following three-part question:

```
    Whý?    Whát            Whát's
        ⌣          fór?        the      réason?
```

The second and third would carry A accents on the last word if the speaker were not playing down:

```
             fó                   réa
    Whát                Whát's the
          r?                        son?
```

So we have some justification for assuming that *for* and *reason* are accented in the other case as well, matching an A+C there to an AC on *why*. (The relatively wide downskip *to* the C strongly suggests that solution; see pp. 272–73.)

To sum up: We have a zone of uncertainty,[12] a pattern that does not mark pitch excursions so unmistakably that one can be reasonably sure about the presence or absence of an accent, and must then rely, at least in part, on other cues. But the emotive recipe remains constant: all three ways of asking 'why' in the example above have the same mollifying effect.

In order to analyze, one must either discover structure or impose it. In this case, the identification of the profiles involves a degree of imposition. Nevertheless, from the speaker's standpoint there is no ambiguity, in so far as the location of the accents is concerned: he knows where he wants to put them. And they form our safest organizing principle, because they are "the most actively programmed attribute" of the pitch curve (Cooper and Sorensen 1981: 98).[13] If intonational morphs are to be anchored anywhere, the accents are the most logical place, and we have to do the best we can.

9. Intonation and Gesture

To analyze intonation—which will be the undertaking of the next chapter—we need to know the nature of the units. Are they, as some claim, the same kind of relatively meaningless articulatory integers that we find in word-based grammars, where a phoneme /n/ in contrast with an /r/ makes a workable distinction between a gnat and a rat even though /n/'s have nothing particular to do with gnats and /r/'s are scarcely symbolic of rats? Or do their meanings in some way reflect their own inner nature, as the order of the clauses in *John came in and sat down* reflects the order of the events?

The Symptomology of Up and Down

The position adopted here is that intonation—meaning strictly the rise and fall of pitch as it occurs along the speech chain—has its symbolizing power thanks to a primitive drive mechanism that raises pitch as tension rises and lowers it as tension falls. The communicative use of this, to quote Tronick et al. (1980: 271), follows "the Darwinian principle . . . of antithesis: opposite emotions are expressed by opposite behaviors." The opposition is already systematic in infancy: "The infant in Play sits up straight, raises his head and 'up-lifts' his face into a smile. In Protest, the infant looks away, turns his body away and 'drops' his face into a frown." Adults react in characteristic ways to the ups and downs of pitch: "up contours produce ratings of highly pleasant, active and potent emotions such as happiness, interest, surprise, and also fear. Down contours have similar effects but do not seem to contain elements of surprise or uncertainty" (Scherer 1974: 251).

The ability to read symptoms is a matter of life and death in the animal world, and it was to be expected that some symptoms—and the ability to read them—would be specialized and built into the biological design. It could be fatal if one needed to depend on the gross ability to read a bulging seam on a boiler as signifying the imminence of an explosion; instead, we attach a pressure gauge and let the "bulge" show up there. It could also be fatal if one were able to predict the onset of an attack only by the bulging eyes of a potential aggressor; by then it might be too late to avoid harm to the victim and perhaps to the aggressor. There had to be some gauge for assessing the varying states of the organism as they might affect other organisms of the same or different species, one that would be sensitive enough for timely reaction.

The answer to this was the development of particular assemblies of highly detectable symptoms as specialized indicators, coupled to the organism as a whole and responding to its overall emotive temper. For the most part, highly detectable signifies—when tailored to the most generalized sensory systems—highly visible and highly audible. The visible has come down to us chiefly as the ability to make and to read faces and poses; the audible, as the ability to produce and hear the changes in fundamental pitch and voice quality overlaid on vocal mechanisms that seem to have had an emotive function from the start.[1] Though it has been specialized, symptomatic communication of this sort is PRESENTATIVE rather than REPRESENTATIVE: like the pressure gauge it is *part of* the system on whose states it reports. In this respect it differs from those communicative acts whose meaning-carriers bear no natural relationship to their meanings—the distinctive sounds ([t] of *time*, [l] of *lime*), the arbitrary words (why are cats called *cats*?), and the fossilized arrangements (*Dogs bite cats, Cats bite dogs*). Intonation is EXPRESSIVE, and, to some degree at least, spontaneous.

Intonation and Emotion

Intonation is part of a gestural complex whose primitive and still surviving function is the signaling of emotion. Its ties to human physiology can be seen in the evidence coming from neurolinguistics and allied research. This has been summarized by R. D. Kent (1982) and is pretty persuasive in the connections it makes between intonational disorders and damage to the right hemisphere of the brain: "affective and prosodic processing" take place in the same areas. The same patients who have trouble with intonation also have trouble with emotional gesturing. And we learn from a brief summary by Ekman (1982: 172–73) that recognition of faces is better when emotion is displayed than when the faces are affectively neutral. The relationship of the *articulate* parts of language with the opposite hemisphere has been known for more than a century—the delicate phonemic contrasts are localized, as far as anything can be strictly localized, in the left hemisphere, and it is at least suggestive that intonation should be mainly on the other side, with communicative functions that seem to relate to emotion.

Next a curious piece of evidence from psychology, with a bearing on our earlier discussions of accent as a sign of "interest." It is well known that young children are able to produce contrasts in pitch that they attach to "new" information and that adults interpret as normal accentuation. Weeks (1982: 165) reports a study of five children aged 1:9 to 2:5 all of whom managed this well. Cutler and Swinney (1980) have found the same, but their word-recognition tasks produced the quite unexpected finding that those same children were not helped in performing the task by the presence of the normal pitch accent in the test sentence. They did just as well without it, in telling the difference, for example, between a sentence like *The nurse brought a cléan towel and took away the dírty one* and one like *The nurse brought a clean tówel and took away the dirty one*. It seems that production precedes recognition, the opposite of what is usually expected, and one wonders why. A plausible answer is that innate mechanisms of emotional arousal are involved. The child knows the meaning of the sentences and the meanings of the individual words—otherwise the tests would have given no results at all. Now imagine a child producing a sentence in which one word is more important—more interesting and more exciting—than all the other words; nothing more natural, then, than to go up on it.[2] The child knows how he feels about the word, but has not yet learned how to interpret the signals coming from other people. The same is apparently true of pitch in its function of marking the ends of sentences and clauses: whatever ability children have to produce appropriate falls and rises at separation points is not reflected in their understanding of sentences: they are not confused, as adults are, by inappropriate contours (Bosshardt and Hörmann 1982).[3] Lock (1980: 103) makes a similar observation about manual gesture: if a child "points at something the mother will (usually) give it to him, but if she points at something he will not give it to her." It is difficult to understand the child's use of pitch if we do not accept some kind of "built-in tie between intonation and affective state" (Pye 1983: 601, writing of accent in the speech of Maya children).

All this accords with what we know about communicative behavior among man's closest relatives: "facial displays and vocalizations take place when the sender is in an emotional state. (Thus, a call does not *represent* 'fig,' but the animal may become highly aroused when it beholds a fig)" (Redican 1982: 269).

Though it is indirect, the evidence for innateness is also impressive on the linguistic side. When we compare the descriptions of intonation from language to language, we find resemblances that far surpass anything that could be attributed to chance, and so widely separated in space that they could hardly be the result of diffusion. Among kindred but mutually unintelligible languages, say between English and Romanian,[4] one finds highly similar intonation systems, and something approaching these same resemblances turns up in native American languages and languages of Asia and Africa (see Bolinger 1978).

The same universality is found in the expression of emotion through physical gesture. Ekman and Oster (1982: 148) report experiments showing that members of preliterate cultures (specifically the South Fore of Papua New Guinea and the Dani of West Iran) "chose the same facial expressions to describe particular emotions as members of literate cultures." Though it remains to be shown how much these actual expressive movements have to do with those of intonation, it is clear that the two modes share both a source and a goal.

Cultural Adaptations

And yet—does the case we have made for the commonality of the gestural complex extend beyond the manifestation of emotion? Do the emotional correlates of intonation—high pitch for excitement, low for boredom, wide-ranging for fluctuations of feeling—really have anything to do with the properly linguistic role that intonation appears to play? It is not unthinkable that some kind of emotional drive at one time did and even today at certain stages still does prime the system, without our having to assume that a mature adult speaker is in any way emotional when he uses intonation to discriminate a compound or a nonrestrictive clause or a postposed theme. That being the case—unless it can be established that facial and other physical gestures deserve their own place in the grammatical scheme—the whole notion of a gestural complex that includes intonation becomes a mere reflection on man's antiquity. Even the striking similarities among languages could be due to the relatively brief time since the linguistic function of intonation emancipated itself from the emotional, providing too little opportunity for languages to evolve away from one another. The evidence points both ways: the similarities suggest a common origin, and the differences suggest a level of independence that has perhaps attained something of the arbitrariness that is found in words and in grammar. And of course we know all too well that arbitrary uses of pitch have come about in the many tone languages of the world.

The difference between intonation-turned-arbitrary and intonation that still maintains its ties with emotion can be illustrated by the techniques of two different drama coaches. The first coach might tell a student, "Make what you're saying a command, not a question: begin at mid range and go steadily down." The second coach might say, "You must imagine yourself in control: give that command as if you expected to be obeyed." The first coach looks to an analysis of intonation to give instruction *about*; the second coach follows the advice of the actor Konstantin Stanislavski to re-create the emotion from which the right intonation will *emerge*: intellectual versus emotional, arbitrary versus expressive. How far has intonation come on the road to the arbitrary and conventional?

It seems hardly likely, if the emotional origin and a surviving emotional matrix of intonation is granted, that any neat evolutionary separation has occurred. What is much more likely is that physical gesture has conventionalized grammatical uses that have not been hitherto appreciated, and that both intonation and gesture, like Antaeus, cannot survive without contact with the earth. In other words, we have a mixed system, expressive at base but with adaptations that differ from culture to culture. Even if gesture and intonation were totally expressive, they would not need to be spontaneous: they can be deliberately posed. From there it is but a short step to stereotyping and RITU-ALIZATION. A ritual is arbitrary to the extent that the performer does not sincerely "feel" the message he conveys. And yet the ritual is still close enough to the erstwhile reality it enacts so that it cannot be understood without reference to that reality. That appears to be the stage at which the supposedly arbitrary uses of intonation and its gestural counterparts have arrived. The most revealing insights on the grammatical applications of intonation are gained from the perspective of grammar as one autonomous system and the gestural complex of which intonation is a part as another, with intersecting lines. Each has its more or less invariant meanings, and "generates its own contextual meanings" when in contact with the other.[5]

A different form of conventionalization is found with combinations of gestures that have been frozen in place to serve as what Ekman (1979) calls "conversational signals." A particularly complex one is the 'I don't know' act. You ask a question and I preface my answer by raising my eyebrows ('up-in-the-airness'), compressing my lips with mouth corners down ('no answer coming out'), head facing slightly down and sidewise with eyes "looking out of the corner" ('I'm away from you on this'), shoulders up in a shrug (this may have started as a protective gesture in case you retaliate for my noncompliance), and possibly hands held palms up and out below the level of the waist ('hands empty, no information'). One can speculate on the interpretations, but the complex is now quite automatic in our culture. It may be coupled to the 'I don't know' tune described below (p. 211), but either can be used by itself.

The concepts of adaptation and ritualization of biologically "given" responses are familiar ones in anthropology, and anthropologists also have an answer for the "cultural relativists" who would deny the universality of emotive expression by appealing to the obvious differences between cultures. To the extent that any gesture conveys feelings, it is sensitive to what Ekman and Friesen call the DISPLAY RULES that govern what feelings and what intensities of feeling a given culture will allow the performer to parade before his fellows (see Ekman 1979: 179). Ekman and Oster (1982: 149) report an experiment in which Japanese and American subjects were shown a neutral or a stress-inducing film. In one test the viewers sat alone, and then the Japanese and the Americans showed the same facial actions. In another test a person in authority was present; then, "as predicted by knowledge of display rules in the two cultures . . . , the Japanese subjects smiled more and showed more control of facial expression than did the Americans." All bodily functions are subject to infinite forms of socialization and conventionalization without ceasing to be what they are. Self-presentation signals, as Scherer (1984: 17) points out, "cannot afford to stray too far" from their base lest "they should quickly lose their adaptive value": "There must be a valid underlying relationship between signal and referent."

The Coupling of Intonation and Gesture

Noting how the speech stream and the gesticulatory stream are coordinated, Kendon (1980: 211) concluded that "it is as if the speech production process is manifested in two forms of activity simultaneously: in the vocal organs and also in bodily movement." Von Raffler-Engel (1983) comes to the same conclusion. We turn now to observations about those two forms of activity and how they often reveal themselves to be a single form in two guises, one visible and the other audible. They need not go on at the same time, but when they do they tend to be synchronized—even eye-blinks are timed to occur at definite points with reference to speech (Condon and Ogston 1971).

Synchronization does not necessarily mean unison. The gestural scheme is orchestrated in ways that permit the "voices" to move in one direction or several at the same time. Parallel movements are COUPLED: the hands and shoulders, say, move up and down together. Nonparallel movements are uncoupled. An illustration of the latter is our freedom under some conditions either to shake or to nod the head without changing the overall effect of the message. A speaker wishing to agree with what an interlocutor has said may say *Absolutely!* and, to underscore his agreement, may wag his index finger forward and back at about the level of the chin; the meaning of the latter is something like 'Note well.' At the same time he may nod his head, or shake it. The nod is a further intensification of the affirmative; the shake is aimed at all opponents of the view expressed: 'Let no one say the contrary!' This sort of counterpoint is typical of gestures that are mainly EMBLEMATIC, in the sense of Efron (1941)—they are rather sharply defined in both movement and meaning and are likely to be holistic. Thus a nod of the head is well delineated and is stereotyped as signifying 'yes,' and is not made up of smaller movements that have independent significance. Other such gestures include nose-wrinkling for disgust, fist-shaking for defiance, and a variety of sexual and scatological signs, all expressive in some sense and to some degree.

More interesting from an intonational standpoint are those gestures that are regularly coupled with intonation, exhibiting the same ups and downs as those of pitch.[6] It should hardly surprise us that head and face gestures are typically affected, given their proximity to the vocal mechanisms. Easiest to observe is the coupling of pitch with head movements. When a speaker says

I

w_il^l·

using a C profile with a terminal rise, the head—if it moves at all— will move in parallel; to make it do the opposite requires practice. Similarly with the more complex CA,

I   w

knó

w!

where the head easily follows the movement of pitch, but only with great difficulty opposes it.

One frequent exception to this covariation is the use of a downward thrust of the jaw to mark an accent, which in turn may be paralleled by a downward jab of the fist for the same purpose. Since intonation marks accents much of the time with a rise-fall, pitch and head movement may go in opposite directions, e.g. in saying

knó

I

w.

But it is appropriate even here to let the head take the parallel movement, and that is probably the case in general: not inappropriate to move in parallel, often inappropriate to do the opposite.

Other up-down gestures can be carried by the eyebrows, the corners of the mouth, the arms and hands, and the shoulders. Motion in parallel with pitch is again the rule. The entire system may often be seen working in unison. When saying

shée:r

It's   nón

sense!

with the topmost syllable lengthened for emphasis, one may observe the eyebrows, corners of the mouth, hands, and shoulders moving up on that syllable and then coming down forcefully on *non-*. (The mouth takes a "forced smile," with teeth approximated, perhaps clenched.)

The mouth gesture deserves special attention. For Ohala (1983) the smile is an evolutionary product of high pitch as the sign of helplessness: high pitch relates to the small size of infants and defenseless animals and enables them to claim protection. The acoustic effect of smiling is to raise the second formant of voiced sounds, particularly the vowels. The opposite gesture, that of lip-rounding, has a lowering effect. The smiling speaker imitates the high register of the infant's voice and signals nonaggression. Ohala relates this to a panzootic frequency code "whereby vocalizations consisting of high frequencies signal the vocalizer's apparent smallness and, by extension, his non-threatening, submissive, or subordinate attitude and by which low-frequency vocalizations signal apparent largeness and thus threat, dominance, self-confidence." The code "is an inherent part of human vocal communication (and probably has been for millions of years). . . . The frequency code explains the similarities in cross-language and cross-cultural use of the pitch of the voice to mark questions vs. non-questions, to signal different social attitudes . . . , and to refer to things small and large using sound symbolic vocabulary." Things may not be quite as straightforward as this—Ekman and Friesen (1982) show that smiles come in several varieties and involve more than one set of muscles; but smiling could have been simple in its beginnings.

The dynamic unity of up-down motion suggests a system in which processes bind together in their bearing on goals: the same goals can be achieved by different parts of the system, different neuromuscular assemblies. Kelso and Tuller (1982: 43) describe it like this:

Within limits, people (and animals) can achieve the same 'goal' through a variety of kinematic trajectories, with different muscle groups and in the face of

ever-changing postural and biomechanical requirements. This phenomenon—variously referred to as motor equivalence . . . or equifinality . . . —has
been demonstrated again by Raibert . . . , who showed writing patterns to be
characteristic of the same individual even when produced by structures (such
as the foot or mouth) that had never previously been used for the act of
writing.

Kelso and Tuller conclude (p. 52) that "speech and limb movements
are dynamically alike in sharing a common solution to the equifinality
problem." We can go a step further and say that "speech and limb"
is an artificial separation to begin with, and that the overintellec-
tualization of speech by casting all its manifestations in the mold of
syntactic and morphological abstraction has obscured the true nature
of intonation.

The Metaphor of Up and Down

Dynamic unity and equifinality require an organizing principle.
This is to be found in the imagery to which up-down movement lends
itself. Lakoff and Johnson (1980: 57) include up and down among "the
central concepts in terms of which our bodies function." Pitch can do
little else but rise and fall, or stay high or low, but "by extension," as
Ohala says, that simple opposition can perform in limitless ways as it
plays on ever-changing contexts, supported by the same and other
symbolic acts in the gestural complex as a whole. There is an upness
of effort and tension associated with getting up, lifting, reaching a
high place, getting the upper hand, and in general escaping the pull
of gravity that decrees that states of rest must somehow be down.

It is not necessary, for the intonational part of the metaphor to
maintain itself, that high pitches be tense on all dimensions and low
pitches relaxed. Once the metaphor has been established and a gradient of high-low related to a gradient of tense-relaxed, it is normal
even for a lower pitch that involves the tensing of certain muscles—a
"reaching for" the low pitch rather than a mere "letting go"—to be
interpreted as 'more relaxed.' For this to happen it is essential only
that high-low be more obviously associated with tense-relaxed than
with the opposite.[7]

We have already seen the importance of the up-down metaphor to
accent, where what is most interesting and exciting is "up." But it extends to all the manifestations of vocal pitch, and here we see how
difficult it is to separate the expression of emotion and affective state
from the speech acts and the grammatical contrasts to which logicians
and linguists have tried to confine their interest in intonation. An intonation that leaves the hearer up in the air, for example, is the typical

one for incomplete clauses and for many questions; one that comes to rest at a low pitch is typical of utterance that is either literally final (e.g. the end of a sentence or a paragraph) or figuratively final (*He spoke with finality,* implying that his was the last word on the subject). This opposition of high and low for suspense and conclusion is a device that speech shares with music. One infers it from the more fundamental connection between pitch and tension, according to which excited speech (the speaker is "keyed up" for whatever reason) is expected to be at higher registers. What is still in suspense—namely the end of some discourse unit—is not at rest; it may not be precisely "excited," but it will be more in the "keyed up" than in the "keyed down" direction.

A more immediate expression of excitement is found in emotional speech in general; but that too has extensions in the form of higher pitch for greater cordiality and lower pitch for greater politeness, for showing that we are "in control" of our feelings. If this line of reasoning seems facile—after all, given high pitch for excitement, low pitch ought to be for indifference, even boredom, so how can it be that and "control" at the same time?—we must then appeal to the configurations in which the pitches occur. One example will show how 'control' rather than 'indifference' is conveyed. In a contour such as

<pre>
I'd
     nev_{er}
              say
                  tha^t!
</pre>

the main accent is at the lowest pitch and is flanked by higher pitches, especially at the beginning. The pattern is one that suggests that the pitch has been *brought* down, hence that the earlier excitement is being controlled. Something approaching a mid-low monotone would be a more likely candidate for boredom, and monotone patterns do have such an implication (see pp. 226–37).

The up-down metaphor is encountered in other forms of gesture as well, whether or not coupled with intonation. If we want to calm someone "down," we may extend the hands in front of the body and make two or more downward movements with the hands terminating in a lower position. (See Meo-Zilio and Mejía 1980: 34 for this gesture in the Spanish-speaking world.) A downmoving pitch has the same function, e.g. in

<pre>
Thére,
       thére!
</pre>

and this intonational gesture may be coupled with the manual one, the latter usually repeated on each word. If we want to summon a person from a distance, we want both "high" visibility and "high" audibility, so we wave or beckon with hands held high and call out in a high-pitched voice. The up-down in various gestural modes may be uncoupled, however, which allows us to present our hearer with a richer choice of responses. For example, an utterance like

<pre>
    Nóbody be
                líeved
                      it,
                         then?
</pre>

in which the pitch goes down to signify a conclusion of sorts, but (and this is the gestured counterpart of the question mark—see Ekman 1979: 185 for references) the eyebrows go up—the speaker manages to assert and ask at the same time, which is taken to mean 'assertion presented for confirmation.'

Reading Gesture into Intonation

If the up-down scheme and how it is embodied in various forms of coupled and uncoupled movement—of pitch, mouth, hands, shoulders, eyebrows—were the limit of our interest, we could halt the discussion here. But we shall do well to expand our perimeters a bit, not only to get a better grasp of the total contribution of gesture to every communicative act but to put ourselves in a position to separate intonation from other gestural factors, not necessarily because intonation deserves a special place but as a form of self-discipline. It has been too easy for persons examining intonation to assume the stance of a given gesture and read its meaning into the intonation. Imagine a situation like the following: John's mother wants John to eat his spinach and takes John's father to the room and points to John and says, *I told John to eat his spinach, and look!* If the father takes the mother's statement as a complaint he may say,

<pre>
He's
            it!   why are you complain
    éating   (So   ing?)
</pre>

to quiet her protest. But if he takes the remark as expressing satisfaction he may use exactly the same intonation, which now affects surprise and is intended as a rhetorical question:

<pre>
He's
            it?   darned if he
    éating   (Well   isn't!)
</pre>

The analyst confronting that utterance out of context is tempted to adopt, unconsciously, the attitudinal stance appropriate to a given interpretation—if the second of the two suggested, there will probably be (actually or implicitly) the raised eyebrows of the understood question plus a smile ("lips up") that is both questioning and expressive of satisfaction. The intonation then may be labeled 'delighted surprise,' when actually all that it contributes is the general 'controlled' response of the low-pitched accent, which in the first instance is intended to calm the mother and in the second is a figurative restraint in which the father pretends to be controlling his enthusiasm (it is "all bottled up"—hence is powerful enough to *need* control). Fónagy (1980) describes similar differences of interpretation due to the background of a sound rather than to the sound itself.

What the linguist does in adopting the gestural stance is of course exactly what a skilled reader does when reading aloud and adding an intonation that is appropriate to the interpretation given to the passage read. The reader, too, may be tricked into asserting that his interpretation is what the passage has to mean, because the intonation is added unconsciously. Someone more accustomed to talking about intonation is aware of other possibilities. Physical gestures are at a still lower level of awareness and linguists are liable to miss them and overinterpret the intonation.

The self-deception is aggravated by the fact that it can easily be transmitted to subjects in a test. Our putative intonologist pronounces his example with the desired intonation and with the unconsciously adopted smile and perhaps also a forward thrust of the head suitable for the simulated question. The effect on the resonators is audible.[8] The subjects then react to the whole gestural complex, not just to the intonation. Visible gesture is never totally excluded from the sound wave. If it were, the telephone would be a poorer instrument than it is.

Blends of Intonation and Gesture: Syntactic Effects

So it is worthwhile to look at some instances of richer blends. Take the following, which involves gesture at five levels besides intonation: head, eyes, eyebrows, mouth, and hands. The speaker is in an argumentative and rhetorical mood, and asks the B-profile question

$$\text{Does he } \overset{\displaystyle \quad\quad \text{it}^?}{\underset{}{\text{ne}{}'\text{ed}}}$$

with *it* rising to falsetto. The hearer is expected to be compelled to say *no*, and that is supposed to clinch the argument. The rising intonation insists on a reply, and the concomitants are: (1) eye contact; this "holds" the listener to making the reply that the intonation insists on; (2) eyebrows raised; this is coupled to the intonation: high pitch, high eyebrows;[9] (3) mouth left open, corners upturned; (4) hands out-flared, palms up: 'Everything is in plain view,' hence nothing is concealed, the case is obvious; (5) head shaking: 'The answer is *no*.' (The fact that the gestures are available does not mean that they will necessarily be used. Individual habit or social custom may decree that one or more be omitted. And some depend on others—without eye contact it is less likely that eyebrows will be raised.)

Each of these components contributes to the question and one can play with various combinations to test the contribution of each. First, with everything else the same, change the intonation from rising to a uniformly falling A:

$$\text{Does } \text{he} $$
$$\text{né}_{\text{e}_{\text{d}}}$$
$$\text{it?}$$

The speaker now probably looks for an easier agreement from the interlocutor—what is expected is a confirmation more than an answer. Next, close the mouth at the end of the utterance; this builds in still more confidence. Next, replace the smile with a "shrewd look"—the eyebrows are lowered and the nose is slightly wrinkled, removing the "openness" from the face; now the speaker is sharing a confidence: 'Knowing what you and I know, do you really think he needs it?' Finally, replace the outflared and palm-up hands with hands held palm forward and slightly down, and rotating in opposite directions from the wrist; the hand gesture is now coupled with the head-shaking gesture, and the negation is reinforced.

Other hand gestures also conjugate with intonation. Consider the proffering hand. If I ask you

$$\text{Do you } \text{líke } \text{it}^{?}$$

and extend my hand with fingers also extended and with palm up but tilted slightly to one side, my question becomes an invitation for you to take some. The tilt seems to be essential—it is as if one did not mind spilling out whatever the hand contains. It is not appropriate to hold the hand straight out with palm upturned and level—that is too much like 'fill it up,' and might be called the "gimme" hand. But neither can the tilt be brought all the way around to the vertical. That is, it can be done, but the meaning changes to something like 'I am directing this question to you,' much like simply pointing with the index finger. The difference in hand gesture can be tested by using a neutral sort of question like

$$\text{Was it } \overset{\text{r\'aining yesterd^{ay}?}}{}$$

The vertical (pointing) hand is appropriate if the question is supposed to get immediate attention. But the proffering hand is a bit out of place, and so is the gimme hand. Of course receivers[10] will give the benefit of the doubt to any reasonable interpretation, and if your proffering hand looks anything like the outflaring hand, the question may be taken as argumentative. Ambiguity in gesture is resolved like ambiguity anywhere else.

Complementary questions give a good setting for another contrast of manual gestures, two kinds of waves but with a different shape. Suppose someone says—using a downtilting B profile—

$$\overset{\text{t\'old me yesterday}}{} \text{that it was for...}$$
$$\text{You}$$

along with the gimme gesture but with fingers waving rather than held stiff. This is to beckon the information in from the receiver. But if the proffering position of the hand is used, with its sidewise tilt, and the same finger-wave is performed, then the beckoning is being aimed at the producer's own recollection—the answer has been forgotten and must be summoned back. It would be nice for the receiver to supply the answer, of course, but the request is not direct. It would be appropriate to add a memory-searching click or headshake, and the eyes are averted. (So is the hand, with its tilt.)

There is also a type of complementary question that is used for prompting and shows the interplay of facial gesture. The discourse function is to cue the receiver to get on with the business. There are no syntactic cues, and the interrogativeness depends as much on gesture as it does on intonation. Suppose you are in a restaurant and you call *Waiter!* and the waiter comes up and says *Yes, sir.* If the pitch rises, and you were writing down what he says, you would probably punctuate with a question mark: *Yes, sir?* The loose interpretation is 'What can I do for you?' If the pitch falls but the utterance is accompanied by raised eyebrows and open mouth, it will probably again be felt as a question. But if the pitch goes down and the eyebrows are not raised and the mouth is closed at the end of the utterance, the impression given is that this is a kind of reporting statement: 'Here I am at your command.'

Every syntactic type reacts similarly with the gestural complex.

A wh question can be shifted from one asked purely for information to one asked with puzzlement or one asked rhetorically. Take the question *Why go?* as a response to the statement *He'll go*. With raised eyebrows, open mouth, and slight smile, this asks essentially for the person's reasons for going. Substitute a frown and you get something like 'I don't understand; relieve me of my perplexity.' Replace that gesture with shoulders raised, mouth closed over a lip shape that parallels the shrug, and head inclined slightly to one side, and you get a rhetorical question: 'What's the use of going?'

Even wh questions that appear to be only for eliciting information are affected by gesture to the extent of being more question-like or more command-like. Wh questions straddle the line between interrogative and imperative: they use interrogative inversion but freely use an intonation that is more typical of commands—continuous downmotion plus a terminal fall. So if a speaker asks,

Whére did you

　　　　Pút
　　　　　it?

with nothing arched up ("with a solemn expression") and with lips tightly closed at the end of the utterance, the assumption of authority is manifest. But if the usual question cues are added—smile, raised eyebrows, and mouth open at end of utterance—the authority is softened. This is not to say that the syntax is affected to the point that the utterance is no longer a "question," but there are other cases where the syntax is affected to the point of making us wonder whether we really know what a question is. Or a command. Take certain utterances that appear to have imperative structure and are subjected to changes of intonation and gesture. The continuous downmotion mentioned above applied to

Téll me how you

　　　　díd
　　　　　it.

yields what we would probably regard as an imperative regardless of facial gesture. We might waver between "command" and "request" if the usual question gestures were added, but would not go so far as to label the utterance a question. On the other hand, if a rising intonation is used,

　　　　　　　díd it·
Téll me how you

the result becomes very much like

How did you dó it?

even with a straight face. And if question gestures are added, one gets the impression of a shift of syntax toward a truncated yes-no question used as a request,[11] as in

(Will you) téll me how you díd it?

A syntactic effect may also be observed when an apparent imperative is used with a stative verb. Such instances are often put down as ungrammatical: *Be tall. But whether they are or not may depend on gesture. Suppose you ask me, *What can I do to impress people?* and I say, with a straight face,

Bé táll.

The effect of this is apt to be surprising—the utterance is matter-of-fact but the recommendation is scarcely achievable matter-of-factly. *Be firm!* with the same intonation is an achievable recommendation and is therefore "grammatical." But if *Be tall* with that intonation is said with lips and nose puckered, eyes squinted, and head nodding (the gesture *introduces* the utterance and continues through it, except that the lips must be disengaged for articulation), then it comes across as a suggestion or confidential hint in the form of a "conditional imperative"—'If you are tall you'll get that result.' The gestural pattern is rather equivalent to the word *just*, which can, in fact, be added: *Just be tall—that's all it takes,* or *Just being tall—that's enough.* (With *just* added, the utterance is "grammatical," or at least normal, without the gestures.)

Finally, a syntactic effect can be observed in two types of negative statement that have been presumed to be transformationally equivalent, e.g. the sentences *It has no purpose* and *It doesn't have any purpose.* We can make a wide choice of intonations and gestures, but there is one configuration for each that has a slight edge. Both use B+A contours, but the heights of the profiles are reversed. The first has a higher B and a lower A:

It hás no púrpose.

and the gestures include head slightly bent and eyes cast down (eye contact may be made initially, but is broken off at once, as if to signify that communication on the matter is ended). The intonation and the gesture combine to shut off debate. The second has a lower B profile and a higher A:

```
                                 púr
        It dóesn't have any
                                    Pose.
```

The likely gestures are eyes on receiver, eyebrows raised but not quite arched to a questioning position, mouth slackly closed at end, and possibly a faint smile. The intonation and the gestures combine to embed a statement that comes out as an appeal for acceptance. The intonation, in fact, is one that is commonly found on yes-no questions in a number of languages and dialects, including some dialects of English; and a question, after all, tends to be an appeal for information. The syntax in both these forms of negation is appropriate to the intonational-gestural complex. *It has no purpose* affirms a negation—the verb is affirmative and its effect is conclusive. *It doesn't have any purpose* denies an affirmation: *any* is "open" to all possibilities.[12]

Though syntactic effects like the three cited here are in no way exceptional, the usual thing is for the gestural complex and the syntax to relate in a free-wheeling way, with either side capable of wide variation while the other remains constant. Here is an example of constant gesture-plus-intonation with syntax that varies through all the major categories:

Declarative: They're nót going to beliéve you.
Yes-no question: Ís it a prómise?
Wh question: Whére did you pút it?
Alternative question: Wíll you or wón't you?
Imperative: Gíve me the móney!
Fragment (exclamation): Nót by a júgful!

The contour is B+AC, the implication is 'admonition' (see p. 183) and the first example would look like this:

```
                          líeve
   They're nót going to be      you.
```

The gestures consist in turning the head slightly to one side and drooping the eye on the opposite side but continuing to look at the receiver unsmilingly while shaking the head rapidly in a very narrow arc—vibrating it, so to speak. The appearance is referred to in the folklore as "looking at someone out of the corner of your eye." The intonation carries rising tension, a climactic accent, and a suspenseful ending—all in keeping with the sense of threat.

Variable intonation and gesture but constant syntax are nicely illustrated by conducive questions with reversed tags. These are qualified intonationally by the choice of profile—C versus A—on the tag. (There are other possibilities, but those two are the main ones.) The falling-rising C is used when the question really seeks information,

```
        cóm
He's                    he?
    ing,  ɪsn't
```

the rising-falling A when an answer would be practically superfluous:

```
      cóm
He's            ís
    ing,   n't  he?
```

Accompanying gestures may be reinforcing or qualifying in various ways up to outright contradiction. Arched gestures increase the interrogativeness of the fall-rise, the opposite gestures increase the confidence of the rise-fall. But if the fall-rise is spoken with a straight face, the interrogativeness is reduced and the question is apt to be one that is asked to put someone in the wrong: *He's coming, isn't he?— so why are you complaining about his having been a little slow in answering your invitation?*

Not only are syntax and gestural-intonational complex free-wheeling with respect to each other, but, as we have seen, parts of that complex may themselves be mutually free-wheeling. Intonation can be uncoupled completely. If you ask a question of someone and receive no more than a hummed response with the following tune,

—
___   ___ —   —

you will interpret the response as 'I don't know'—the intonation is what would be used on those words if spoken. This is an analog of whistle speech in Tepehua and Gomera Spanish (cf. Cowan 1972). Likewise, gestures may function separately, in or out of concert with one another. The standard gestural sign for 'I don't know' goes like this:

Lips pursed: 'No comment.'
Eyebrows arched: 'I'm wondering too.'
Shoulders raised: Same.
Head tilted sideways: 'Evasion' (?).
Hands held slightly forward, palms up: 'Empty, no information.'

The gesture and the tune may be performed together.

Gradience: "Amounts" of Up and Down

Nothing has been said up to this point about the relative EXTENT of a gesture, whether physical or intonational. If upward movement contributes an "up" sense to an utterance, increasing the movement ought to make it "more up," and this should be especially noteworthy when two or more such movements are close enough to one another to invite comparison. Take the clause junctures that have been identified as major and minor continuation (cf. Delattre et al. 1962). These may be marked intonationally as in the following (compare pp. 26–27):

Even without pause, the relative height of the pitch maxima (higher for the major continuation, lower for the minor) makes it clear that these are to be interpreted, respectively, as

> If he calls you when you get there, let me know.
> If he calls you, when you get there let me know.

Facial and manual gestures if any will normally parallel the line of pitch: eyebrows will be arched highest as the highest pitch is approached; and if the hands gesticulate and the utterance is spoken deliberately enough for separate positions to be marked, the heights will correspond at three points: *you*, *there*, and *know*. The tightness of the coupling can be tested by trying to reverse the relative positions of the hands in the first two positions of the first example, moving higher-lower rather than lower-higher: it is more difficult not to follow the line of pitch than to follow it. There are limits to the dexterity of these larger muscles, of course: a gesture "fades" more slowly than an intonation. But the collaboration is unmistakable, and the relative fixity of the gesture may be an advantage: it can precede the utterance and set the stage for it.

Though both intonation and physical gesture are capable of expressing varying extents, the advantage here is all with intonation. We know too little about the gestural complex to say for certain that the raising and lowering of the eyebrows, head, shoulders, etc. is less able than that of pitch to express varying amounts, but we know that the sensitivity of the human ear is such that a difference of less than a semitone is quite audible. Physical gestures have the advantage in different MODES of movement—say, where the arms are concerned, backward and forward or open and shut as well as up and down—but in the up-down dimension pitch seems to be supreme. We may not use all the degrees we are capable of hearing, but we exploit contrasts of a high degree of delicacy. If 'end of sentence' can be signaled by a low pitch, 'end of paragraph' can be signaled by lowering the pitch of the whole last sentence. If a jump up on a given syllable shows that the word containing it is important, a higher jump shows that it is more important. The lavishness of the range makes it possible to do more than one thing at a time without departing from the basic up-down metaphor, even to play the metaphor against itself. The configurations that we have labeled profiles remain intact when moved up or down as units. An A profile can express the same contrast at a low or a high overall pitch. For example, in answer to *Who was it?*

<pre>
                        Jó
    It was   It was
         Jó
       hn.   hn.
</pre>

both have the downskip that defines the A, and both express the contrast (John versus someone else) better than does either of the following instances of C:

<pre>
                     It was
    It was   Jóhn.
         Jóhn.
</pre>

—which in their turn preserve the C configuration though widely separated in overall level. Overall level is thus left free to express wider variations in mood. This trait of pitch of course is what makes it possible for intonation to be preserved in tone languages—the tone contrasts ride on the larger wave just as the accentual ones do. The difference is that the tonal contrasts are arbitrary[13] whereas accentual contrasts obey the up-down metaphor by marking what is interesting and exciting or what is unbridled as against what is subdued.

Relative Advantages of Intonation and Gesture

There are other ways besides gradience in which one part of the gestural complex may have an advantage over other parts. A physical gesture is not tied directly to the stream of speech and may accordingly be posed before speech begins, serving as a kind of illocutionary announcement: 'question about to begin,' for example. Similarly a gross body movement detached from speech is apt to be more decisive than an intonation: an annoyed interlocutor who gets up and walks away writes a categorical finis to a conversation. The same detachment permits attitudinal displays that the sender can deny verbally—irony and other forms of deception have wider play than the vocal stream alone will permit. But the reverse is also true; by its attachment to the speech stream intonation is able to "cut in" at precise points within an utterance, which makes it more useful in its intersections with grammar.

Intonation acts in concert with the rest of the gestural complex and to be understood it must be seen in its proper setting. But it does not lose its identity in the process.

10. Parts and Their Meanings

For some, the term INTONATION covers all the expressiveness of the human voice, whether contributed by pause and rhythm, by depth of resonance, by weak or forceful articulation, or by the levels, ranges, or ups and downs of fundamental pitch. The previous chapters have taken for granted a single vista in this wide panorama, that of the fundamental pitch and its variations of high and low and what they signify.

The Fundamental Pitch and Its Variations

Not all the variations of the fundamental pitch need concern us. The pitch varies in other ways than up and down, some of which have a closer bearing on the patterning than others do. A conspicuous example is the interruption of what would otherwise be a steady tune by other events in the speech stream, particularly the voiceless consonants. In a word such as *coattail*, for example, the double [t] stops the vibrations of the larynx and produces an interval of silence. Because of these interruptions, intonation comes to us in snatches of voiced sound (on the vowels and on consonants such as [r l n m z v] and to some degree on others such as [b d g]), and we have to reconstruct it. Fortunately the interruptions are brief enough as a rule not to cause trouble.

Changes in the tune caused by these articulated sounds are mostly automatic and unavoidable: no one except perhaps a poet chooses words that will avoid the interrupting consonants; but there are other effects that are more or less controllable and that lend certain qualities to the voice whether they ride in on a surge of emotion or are put in for effect.

The most striking is the simple abolition of the fundamental. We call this whispering, and our first impression is that if the fundamental goes, all intonational patterning must go with it. Yet some intonation remains, and is carried chiefly by two elements of the sound wave: volume and vowel height.[1] One can whisper a sentence and still make the important syllables stand out by whispering louder. And a pitch pattern of sorts emerges as the whisperer distorts the vowels, skewing the second formant up for higher and down for lower. (The sound of this formant is what we are most conscious of when we whisper *ah-ah-ah-eh-eh-eh-ee-ee-ee* and feel that we are going "up.") To make *I will* sound as if it had a rising pitch we whisper something like *I weel*; to make it go down we whisper something like *I wool*.

Whisper need not concern us further; its intonation patterns are merely reflections of the normal ones. Nor are we concerned with other disturbances such as tremolo, choked voice, and husky voice. All make potential contributions to messages—tremolo for uncontrolled emotion,[2] whisper for confidentiality, husky voice for sexual appeal, etc. They might be called QUALIFIERS. The term is not intended to sweep them under the rug. They deserve attention, but there is no room for them here.

Register

Something that is like those qualifiers but comes a little closer to the heart of intonation is known as REGISTER. As one hums upward, and again as one hums downward, there comes a point where one can hum no further without a striking change in the quality of the voice. Going upward it is particularly noticeable in the male voice (and is unstable during adolescence, as any youth whose "voice is changing" can testify). The two breaking points divide the scale into three ranges: the mid range is MODAL, the top is FALSETTO, and the bottom is VOCAL FRY or CREAK.[3] Though for the purpose of most intonational description it is enough to assume that the modal range is the one being used, the two others have important limiting and expressive effects. It is natural that the mere fact that they represent extremes of some kind should have been seized upon to carry meaning. Whereas the modal register offers great possibilities of inflection, falsetto has less and creak has less still. The main significance of the two extreme registers is a speaker's electing to use them at all, regardless of actual pitch, though the latter does make its independent contribution.

Since creak is the range a speaker reaches as the voice is lowered to the extreme, it becomes the sign par excellence of whatever it is that being "down" signifies. A downglide that stops at any level above creak is to some degree ambiguous (though least so toward the bottom of the modal range): did the speaker intend to arrest the fall, or to go all the way? A downglide that ends in audible creak is 'finished.'

Though creak is less usual in other positions than at the end of a unit, it sometimes is heard initially or medially. Some male speakers affect this sort of "glottalized speech" as a badge of masculinity, and a very few use it virtually to the exclusion of other registers,[4] but it is available to any speaker for the strongest manifestation of the sorts of things that low pitch in general conveys, as a sort of intensifier. For example, in *Ah, well,* with *Ah* at mid or higher level and *well* at creak, one has the ultimate in conclusive resignation or dismissal. Similarly *Why bother!* with *bother* at creak. William James reportedly said of his brother, *Henry's all right, but hell!,* using this high-low on the last two words, with *hell* at creak—a total negation of the concern embodied in the earlier high pitch. A *Nah!* at level creak is total rejection. A *Yes!* or a *Yes?* starting at creak and then rising sets the 'arousal' of its rising pitch against the initial lack of arousal—the creak is interpreted in the context of the rise; the effect is one of controlled arousal. If the creak occurs between higher pitches, the effect is that of *bringing* the arousal under control—one senses something closer to 'restraint.' So with

s.
Yé

one might readily have a thoughtful *I guess you're right* as sequel. But with

Yé s.
e

the sequel is apt to be a more unwilling *But. . . .* These patterns do not differ, except in degree, from similar ones entirely in the modal register.

Falsetto plays a more curious role. The obvious analogy is with the scream, and in many of its uses it does convey this extremity of arousal. A *What!* entirely at falsetto is surprise unbounded. A warning such as *Watch it!, Careful!, Easy!* may have its first syllable at low mid pitch and its second at falsetto—the element of the scream overrides the normal accent pattern in these expressions and puts the greatest prominence on the otherwise reduced syllable, where it will have the most impact. But in its more general uses this height of emotion is harnessed to lower pitches that modify it in various ways. Coleman (1914) cites the example

It's like

súm
mer!

(with *It's like* in falsetto) as signifying 'despair of adequate description,' and this can be shown more directly in a sentence like

```
        I just can't describe

                    it!
```

In these examples one has, so to speak, 'high arousal brought under control.'

Reversing the order has the opposite effect, that of breaking out of control. The speaker who in place of

```
               him
        tóld           it.
   You            about
```

with everything in modal register, says

```
               him  about it.
        tóld
   You
```

with *him about it* in falsetto, changes the implication of the CAC profile to something like 'no remedy now, it's his funeral.' In fact, *It's his funeral* may carry the same terminal falsetto on *funeral*.

Falsetto has another side, seemingly the contradictory of the one just described. It probably has the same biological source as the one that Ohala assigns as the origin of the smile (see p. 201), namely the primitive association between small size and high pitch, exploited by infants and other small creatures as a bid for protection or nonaggression. The infant's voice is naturally high-pitched. The effect, at low volume, is disarming. This is the "cooing" side of the protection appeal; it *coaxes* protection, carrying a nuance of sweetness. High volume presents the "screaming" side of the appeal: it *demands* protection. Van Hooff (1962: 110) describes the "scared threat face" of the higher primates in terms that suggest the kinships proposed here:

> *The mouth* is opened, usually widely.
> *The mouth corners* are retracted completely.
> *The lips* are completely retracted vertically. . . .
> *The vocalisations* which accompany this expression movement may vary from a high-pitched, staccato barking to a more prolonged high-pitched screaming. . . .
> A peculiar property of this posture . . . is the fact that, when the scared threat response is performed by an animal living in a group, other animals, not immediately engaged in the encounter that caused the display, "come to the rescue" of the performer by attacking the animal which is threatening it. . . . As the rescuer . . . may appear from a place where it could not see the performer, it is likely the high-pitched scream is one of the main features which elicits the response.

We see here both the analog of the smile, in the grin that accompanies the scream, and the analog of the high volume that pertains to the demanding falsetto. The 'appeal' remains constant in its relationship to the high pitch; the difference is in the *type* of appeal, carried by the contrast in volume.

Feminists may dislike the reminder, but if this theory is correct it describes the female as well as the infant voice as the product of millennia of evolution in which women and children required protection and mewled or screamed to get it, while adolescent males acquired the gruff voices that signaled their fighting role—a sexual dimorphism that characterizes many species besides man (see Ohala 1983: 13–14). The falsetto remained available to males as a sign of nonaggression— the whine of submission or cowardice.

However one may view these theoretical speculations, it is a fact that an unsustained falsetto terminal at low volume is unaggressively appealing. Asking

it?
Do you líke

with *it* at falsetto, carries the appeal of delighted surprise, and shows a cordiality lacking in the same profile with a modal ending. An AC profile, as in

tháₜ I
Don't do

is pleasant, even playful, when the last word is at falsetto, by comparison with the more or less stern warning when the top pitch is in modal register. A B+B contour with continuous rise, e.g.

thát I

f wouldn't say

may be sweetly cordial disagreement with *that* at a soft falsetto. Nonterminal falsetto may have the same effect, though it is more apt to be overridden by the following lower pitches. A denial or rejection of the form

Nó

o I

with a soft falsetto followed by an immediate drop to creak, may be sweetly reasonable by comparison with the same pattern when the first pitch is high modal.

If the volume is increased in any of these, the touching quality of the falsetto easily shifts. It is noteworthy that volume affects the physiology of falsetto as well. At the lowest volume, falsetto extends as much as an octave into what is normally the modal range; at high volume, the modal range pushes into the falsetto. This can be demonstrated by humming the gamut at high and at low volume and noting where the break between modal and falsetto occurs. It can also be demonstrated by humming a steady pitch at low volume just high enough for it to be in falsetto, and then increasing the volume without readjusting the vocal tension. The effect is to "break" into modal at a lower pitch.

Falsetto thus acquires some of its gentleness from the fact that the milder the volume, the more falsetto there is. It is a more relaxed form of phonation than modal in terms of the subglottal pressure and airflow required. The fact that it can be attained at fairly low pitches when not overloud makes it useful especially for the terminals of yes-no questions, which are essentially an appeal for information. But it must be used in small doses. Otherwise it too readily becomes—regardless of volume (or *because* of volume if one views a succession of low-volume elements as adding up to a high volume)—a scream. The question terminal is fine when limited to the last syllable, but compare the following two questions:

```
                 some?                     some of this pudding?
Would  you               Would  you
       líke                      líke
```

Most uses of falsetto are probably one-syllable excursions—brief up-skips rather than long glides—regardless of position. The profiles most affected are B and C (with falsetto terminal), as illustrated above with questions, and CA or CAC, as in

```
          the                     don't
      thát
   Is                         Í    want to      yⁿ•
      ʷaⱼ?                               hurt
```

Here the accent is at the lower pitch (*that*, *I*), and the unaccented following syllable takes the falsetto. The falsetto may occur on the accent, but there is again in that case the same danger of overextending it.

We find here a tie-in with gesture that seems to confirm Ohala's thesis. When you say

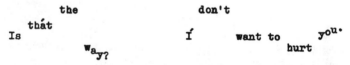

```
                                             it?
            ásked you  to,              dó
   If I                        would you
```

it is easy and normal to accompany the rise on *do it* (with *it* at falsetto) with a broad smile, widened eyes, and raised eyebrows. If the terminal is at a lower, modal pitch, the eyebrow gesture is still easy to manage, but the smile is less so. The same is true of nonquestions, e.g.

<pre>
                                                          it.
    I'll   to,   ,   round   to
          be   when I gét a
          glád
</pre>

with *it* at falsetto. (The speaker may accompany the smile with compressed lips at the end to signal 'conclusion,' as the high pitch suggests the opposite—the lip gesture helps to mark the nonquestion as such.) There is a similar coupling with a smile when the falsetto is initial, as in

<pre>
          Yé   Nó

          es.   o.
</pre>

With both the affirmative and the negative the smile is normal, though it is less likely with *No*. With *Yes* it is easy to have everything "up" (though the pitch falls—now it is pitch direction that tells us something like 'nonquestion')—high initial falsetto, broad smile (that is, corners of the mouth up), and raised eyebrows. With *No* the gestural intersections are more complex:[5] the smile, to the extent that it can be managed, is more apt to be accompanied by puckered brow and eyebrows—the gestural complex exhibits a BLEND (Ekman, Friesen, and Ellsworth 1982: 19). (We are assuming that this *No* disagrees with the interlocutor. If it agrees, then everything can be up again.) But the most remarkable fact is that if one uses modal register and tries to say a firm *No* on that profile and smile at the same time, the "smile" is seen as a grimace. Interpreting the gesture as a smile depends at least to some extent on the falsetto.[6]

The paradox of high pitch for sweetness is thus partly explained. Excursions into falsetto and smiling go together much of the time. Both are affectively "up."

Binarity of Up and Down, with Qualifications

The theoretical position of this book is that intonation is fundamentally the opposition of up and down, with meanings clustering around the poles of the opposition in accord with metaphorical extensions (see pp. 202–4), also that intonation shares with physical gesture the manifestation of this opposition—up and down are carried by the facial muscles, shoulders, etc. In spite of its myriad ramifications, the system is coherent, to the extent that most if not all manifestations can be ultimately traced to the primary metaphor, and the arbitrary segmental (phonemic) use of pitch, such as is found in tone languages, is excluded.

The imagery of up-down may symbolize height or movement directly, e.g.

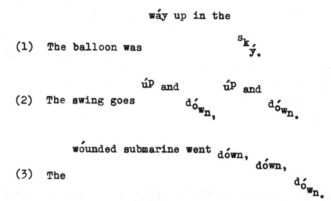

In (1), the highest pitch is apt to be at falsetto; in (2) and (3), *up and down* and *down, down, down* are in rhythmic succession in their respective sentences.

Mostly, up-down is not quite so literal, as we saw in the last chapter. Down may be for "playing down," which can be for calming someone, as in

Thére,

thére.

or for minimizing the importance of something, as when the pitch of an entire parenthetical remark is lowered. Or for minimizing to the point of denying, as when low pitch is associated with negation— ironic expressions like *in a pig's eye, a likely story*, or *I'll bet* or *sure,* when used ironically, are apt to stay low.[7] Or it can be the down of 'rest' or 'completion' or 'closing off,' which is the way we end most utterances and (lower still) practically all discourses. (*Open* and *closed* are the tags used by Hultzén 1962, Gantzel 1967: 104–5, and Cruttenden 1981.) Up may be for liberation, freedom from being "held down," as in

Wheéeeeeel   I'm fréeeeeel

Or for non-rest, for being "left up in the air," as with the ends of most yes-no questions and most non-final clauses. Or for being emotionally keyed up, as when we express indignation:

$$\text{I } \overset{\text{wíll}}{} \overset{\text{nót!}}{}$$

Or for being "up" in importance, as when a word is given a high accent to make it stand out. These manifestations are not prohibited from occurring together. An accent is a relatively grammaticized phenomenon: it normally occurs on the stressed syllable of a word; the other syllables may then indicate, by their height, some level of emotion. We saw this in the example *Elizabeth was sick* (p. 187), where if *-beth* was kept high the speaker was shown to be emotionally keyed up.

Not to confine the metaphor, but to have a mnemonic peg on which to hang its nuances, I offer ± AROUSAL as the interpretation of ± up.

But intonation would be impoverished if it were limited to the metaphorical associations of up and down. What we find instead is that the simple opposition is enormously enriched by the modifications that play on it. Following are some of the important ones.

1. Glide versus jump. Though the physiology of the vocal organs does not permit very sharp transitions from one posture to another, with the result that in moving up from P to Q or back from Q to P there is always a certain amount of glide, nevertheless speakers are free to make an effective jump in contrast with an effective glide.

2. Monotone versus rise or fall. The pitch may hold steady at a given height, with marked effects if it lasts long enough. A monotone may of course be combined with movement, to or from or both.

3. Intensity of segment. Speakers do their profiles freehand, so to speak, and can make any portion louder or softer than the rest. To express angry rejection, one may say *No!* starting at mid-high pitch and ending at a level only a few semitones down, with a drawl between and a final level, heavily intensified and breathy:

$$\text{Náwwwwwh!}$$

A vocative such as *Daddy!* or *Alice!* on an AC profile may have the rising terminal lengthened and intensified, as a sort of playful protest—'How could you do such a thing!' Without this treatment it is merely a call for attention.

4. Length of segment. There is the same freedom to stretch any portion. This may be done to achieve a rhythmic succession, as in the *swing* and *submarine* examples above. Or it may be done for exaggeration. An example famous at one time was the one-word speech of the stationmaster in the Jack Benny television program, who—as acknowledgment of someone's expected request—would say *Yes?*, starting a C profile at falsetto, sweeping down to the lowest pitch and prolonging it, then rising in another long sweep. The effect was one of exaggerated courtesy laced with ridicule.

5. Relative height. A given pattern may start higher or lower (including falsetto and creak), and may move a greater or a lesser distance in either direction, without ceasing to be the "same" pattern. There is some dispute about "low rises" and "high rises" as being essentially different; the point will be discussed later.

6. Sequence. Patterns may go from low to high or from high to low.

7. Combination. A pattern may be combined with itself or with another pattern, indefinitely, and this involves again the features of intensity, length, height, and sequence. It makes a difference, for example, whether a contour containing two profiles each with high pitches has the first higher than the second or the reverse; or whether a combination of an A profile with a C profile, for example, is permuted as A+C or as C+A.

Two of the modifications listed, intensity and length, will not concern us further as topics in their own right. The others, especially the last three, must be studied, particularly as they apply to contours, that is, combinations of profiles serving as complete utterances, for the reasons already stated under point 7.

Glides and Jumps

In the form in which it was stated above, point 1 prejudges an issue: it says that glide and jump are not necessarily variants of each other but may be in contrast. Yet there exists some experimental evidence that listeners have difficulty perceiving the two as distinct. Greenberg and Zee (1979) report that very short dynamic sequences are perceived not as moving but as static, or as very minimally moving. Longer sequences are perceived as moving but in terms of the initial and final portions of the glide. A downward movement from P to Q is thus a jump down, not a glide down. Only much longer sequences are perceived in detail, that is, in such a way that one senses the actual rate of change. One can infer from this that we favor jumps over glides, as the latter are perceived in terms of the former.

This provides an opening for the theoretical stance touched on in Chapter 3, which sees intonation in terms of LEVELS. If P to Q is heard as a jump from P to Q, then P and Q may be significant in themselves, and since P is "at a certain level" and Q is "at another level," up and down can be analyzed as a succession of levels.

The problem with levels is partly terminological. Being at a level is not being a level—P and Q are points, and are levels only to the extent that we treat our coordinates as if they were real and not merely fictions useful for measurement—a horizontal line from left to right across a graph and passing through P is a "level" in one sense, but the actual movement from P to Q is not level if P and Q are "at different (fictional) levels." The trouble is that we do have level intonations, in the sense that they continue without rise or fall—and do so with a very strong effect on meaning, as will be explained in the next section.

But the real difficulty is the practical one of whether jumps and glides differ semantically. The Greenberg and Zee experiment suggests that they do not, but its relevance is unclear. The listeners were asked to react to pitch changes as such, not to react to contrasting patterns in terms of their meanings. It is well known from experiments in categorial perception that these are two quite different tasks. Glides and jumps do seem to differ semantically, as we saw in Chapter 3. Take a simple A profile and vary its slopes (compare the *I will* example, p. 149):

(1) Tᵉˡˡ   (2) Téll   (3) Tᵉ́ˡˡ

   me.   me.   me.

All three have the downward jump that defines A and is common on such commands, but the pitch of *tell* rises in (1), holds level in (2), and glides down in (3). If one were to ask "Which expresses greatest urgency, which is most neutral, and which is most confident or reassuring?" there can be little doubt that the answers would be (1), (2), and (3), in that order. The skip portion (or motion as close to a skip as one can manage) is essential for defining the accent, but the glide provides the affective nuance which—beyond the general assertiveness of the A profile—is the main part of the message. It is pointless to insist that in (3) the phonetic glide on *tell* is "really" a jump from a higher to a lower pitch. Its gliding nature—and that of *tell* in (1) also— can be made apparent by slowing it down: the 'urgency' of (1) and the 'comfortingness' of (3) are increased proportionately. Similarly an up-glide is more rousing than an upskip. Compare

The potency of the glide can be seen in its use in nonverbal alarm systems, e.g. the call to battle stations on a warship. In the gradient world of intonation, *everything* that is detectable is potentially significant. (See pp. 152, 156–57 for the increase of emphasis on an accent when the accented syllable incorporates part of the succeeding movement that might otherwise be realized as jumps to succeeding unstressed syllables.)

To the extent that intonation is dynamic, it makes no difference, in describing a movement, whether one says "first you are going to be up and then you are going to be down" or "you are going to go down." But the first is a better description of a jump and the second is a better description of a glide. We need them both.

Monotone Versus Rise or Fall: "Stylization"

The direction of pitch may be up or down, or horizontal, that is, sustained. For the latter the term *monotone* will be used, to avoid the ambiguity of *level* mentioned above. It refers not to a uniform pitch throughout an utterance but to a succession of syllables (or a prolonged syllable) without up or down variation, alone or in combination with another monotone or a variation.

The fullest treatment of monotone is in Ladd (1978), which identifies a consistent meaning in monotone utterances that conform to certain patterns. In keeping with the viewpoint adopted here, which is that intonation as a whole hinges on a scheme of tension and relaxation, Ladd's views will be modified, but the essential outlines of his work remain.

Absolute monotone is rare—that is, a single level throughout, rather than terraced levels or levels with other variations. But as we saw in Chapter 3 it does occur, e.g.

<u>That old story again!?</u>

Further, the mood is not essentially altered when such a monotone is terraced:

<u>Télling me</u>
    <u>thát old story again!?</u>

As in these two examples, the monotone parts will be underlined in what follows. Further, a colon will be added to show prolongation,[8] so that an utterance scored

<u>Jó:</u>
    <u>ohn:</u>

is to be taken as a succession of two monotones (one syllable here is prolonged at each of two heights), such as one might use in calling someone.

Ladd notes that in utterances like

<u>Dáddy forgot his bríef:</u>
    <u>case:</u>

with *brief* and *case* both prolonged, the implication is that daddy is habitually absentminded or generally maladroit. The action is 'one that can be expected of daddy'—something routine, commonplace, everyday. If we are told

Lóok out for the broken sté:

                                ep:

with *step* divided between two monotones, we take it as a reminder of something already known. If instead we hear

                óut for the broken sté
      Look

                                p.

we might assume that there is a danger of which we had no previous knowledge.

The preceding examples add monotone to contours ending in AC. It is just as common with B and C. Suppose you are jogging with a friend over a route that you both know well, and you begin to feel winded, and say

          thrée
                  blócks to   (B+C+C)
    (1) Just   gó.

You will be "making conversation"—offering an obvious remark that gives no information and does not need to be "finished" (it ends well above creak). But if your hearer does not know the route and your remark is intended to inform, you will probably say

          thrée
                  blócks to   (B+C+A)
    (2) Just   gó.

Or you could add something to the first example by way of finishing it:

      thrée
               blócks to   (B+C+C+A)
                      gó, and we're
    (3) Just   thére.

Examples (2) and (3) are a "mix"—they are part routine and part newsworthy. There is something "expected" about referring to distance in the context of jogging, which makes the monotones normal. Otherwise what are now monotone would probably be uptilted.

More examples of B+C or B+C+C:

Yéah,   ('We've been over all this
    yéah.   before.')

Gó   ('I'm tired of your continually
    'wáy!   bothering me.')

    álways
He's   ásking for   fávors.   ('and I'm getting fed up.')

Wóuldn't you

        knów!   ('That's exactly what you could
                            have predicted would happen.')

Díd you

       héar me?   ('I shouldn't have to repeat
                            this another time!')

The following B+C came in response to a spouse's question *Are we walking now?*

   Yes,   pút my

        I'll   shóes on.

'as I always do when we go for a walk.' In the next examples we have something repeated, hence routine, predictable:

    báck: and   báck: and

It goes   fórth,   fórth.

       ó:ver and

They did it

             óver.

The monotone is sometimes able to specify, almost unambiguously, which of two meanings of an expression is intended. If we hear

    Í:

     shówed him.

we are apt to infer 'I put him in his place.' It is a routine boast rather than a reference to how something was done. Similarly

         sée?

    You

is more than likely a question calling for a response of some kind, whereas

    sée?

   You

is most appropriate in an 'I told you so' sense.

Ladd allows for an indefinite number of descending monotones, though for practical reasons there are not apt to be more than three or four:

   Éasy

      cóme,

         éasy

           gó.

(Aphorisms—*It's never too late to mend, Old soldiers never die, Pretty is as pretty does*—are highly predictable and readily take the monotone.) Ascending monotones, however, he limits to a single level pitch (p. 531), citing as typical the series intonation in cases like the following, which answers the question *What did you have for dinner?*—

```
Oh
‾‾    the usual      bróccoli,   mátoes,      óli,  you
           thing--              to        ravi        know.
```

With the dropback and resetting, all the items on the list are at approximately the same pitch; a gradual descent would be equally possible, but a rise would be quite unusual. It is understandable that rises should be less frequent than falls, simply from the semantics of monotone utterance: what is routine is not what one is apt to be aroused about. But successive rises are nevertheless normal if circumstances warrant. One can have a "stylized" admonition, for example:

```
I                         thát!
                  súre of              (C+B+B)
wóuldn't be so
```

```
Don't                 wáves, my lad!
                máking                  (C+B+B)
       álways be
```

Or question:

```
          álways     bóre    lísten to?
Is he           such a     to         (B+B+B)
```

The last example could have the last two monotones reset to the same level as the first, or they could descend. Rise and fall thus intersect with monotone, and contribute what we expect of the semantics of rise and fall. In the following, the rise to the monotone on *eyes* keys up the first part of the utterance—the command is a little more insistent by virtue of it—but this is tempered by the fall to the monotone on *sleep*, as part of a command that might be used to reassure a child—'everything is routine, everything is under control':

```
          éyes        to
      your        gó              (B+B+B+C)
Shút         and      sléep.
```

The entire utterance has this reassurance when both monotones are reached by a drop:

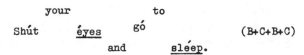

How close does 'routine, ordinary, everyday' come to characterizing the meaning of the monotone? Certainly it fits the examples cited thus far, and if the notion of metaphorical extension that we have been developing applies here, the fit may be unexceptionable. But metaphorical extension of what? We must take a step backward to the primitive senses we have been trying to ferret out. There may be other extensions, better described in different terms. Take a command such as

```
        Dón't
                  máke a              (B+C+C)
                  fúss.
```

which seems intended more to restrain the hearer by emphasizing the fact that there is nothing to get excited about, than to express some such idea as routineness. Of course if the reason for the fact that there is nothing to get excited about is the predictability of the course of action in question, then one can infer routineness, but it is not the primary extension of the primitive meaning.

Possibly a step in the right direction is to note the almost invariable pronunciation of *Ho, hum*: two monotones, descending. Gantzel (1967: 106) points out that his subjects with a high degree of consistency labeled a low flat monotone as 'tired,' 'sad.' Taking our cue from this we can say that some such extension as 'boredom' is more inclusive than 'routine' etc., and yet handily covers 'routine'—when we say

```
                 sáme
        It's the        óld
                           thíng.
```

we imply 'routine' by the fact that we are bored with the subject.

On the other hand, 'boredom' also seems a bit too specific. Take a conversation in which A says to B *What's this I hear about Llewellyn?* and B starts his reply with

```
                sád,
        It's a       sád
                        stóry.
```

Gantzel's 'sadness' seems to apply. Similarly

```
        Móther,                    áll
              síster,
                      fáther--    déad.
```

In the case of

Whát

difference does it make?

or

Nóbody

cáres any more.

we might understand 'discouragement.' In a rather different vein we have

Thére,   pút your head on daddy's

     thére,   shóulder.

Táke it   nó

    éasy,   húrry.

Júst this little   féel

     swállow and you'll   fi$_{n_e}$.

These carry the same 'gentleness' and 'reassurance' that we noted in the *shut your eyes* example. Similarly, 'playful reproof':

náughty,

      náughty

You're a

         gírl!

To subsume this range of possibilities we need once again something as general as 'nothing to get excited about.' Whether one is depressed or restrained, solicitous or bored, the monotone conveys the same emotive flatness that its shape suggests. The impression it creates is undoubtedly reinforced by the striking musical nature of the sustained tone—successive monotones make an utterance sound almost as if it were set to music, and a musical tune is designed to be repeated, and hence is, in a sense, routine. "Musicality is directly proportionate with redundancy and inversely proportionate with information" (Fónagy 1981: 128n). We earlier noted the 'everybody knows' implication of the chant, e.g.

Súsie   ª táttle

   is   tale.

The rhythmic nature of the chant is its most salient feature next to the tune, and we note a tendency toward equal time in utterances containing successive monotones—each "terrace" takes the same amount of time. The tendency to isochrony is strong enough to cause syllables to be tightly compressed when one terrace has more than another:

<pre>
        hárdly an
                  tícipated such a
We   fáilu
                                          re.
</pre>

Here the six syllables of *-ticipated such a* take no longer than the three of *hardly an-*. Remove the monotone terraces and the isochrony goes with them. A further analogy to music with these terraces is the sensitivity of the ear to small changes in pitch. If we say

<pre>
   Páy no at
             téntion to such   trí
                                  fl
                                    es.
</pre>

the terraces may differ by as little as a semitone, yet we are conscious of the difference and weigh its effects against those of wider intervals—'tension' can be delicately adjusted.

Whether the music or the conversational monotone came first there is no way to tell, but the two undoubtedly reinforce each other. Of one thing we can be fairly sure: though utterances intended to inform do not, as Ladd points out (p. 531), use the monotone, it is not directly because they are informative but because having real information to impart is one of the things that enliven our speech.

Thus far we have not examined the monotone in the light of the profiles on which it is carried out. Most of the examples cited have had either a B or a C profile—a B in the few instances where the monotone has been at a higher pitch than what preceded it, a C in most of the rest. Particularly in the latter, the 'restraint' attendant upon having the accented syllable pushed *down* in pitch has been the major ingredient of the overall emotive effect. (The rest is due to the lack of a terminal rise, which, in the case of the B profile, is the only sign of restraint in addition to the monotone itself.) The 'restraint' of the C profile was noted in the general discussion of the profiles. If the speaker desires it, along with this effect of restraint, he may distort the pronunciation of a word in order to get a terrace. In a Perry Mason television program (aired Oct. 28, 1961) the judge before whose bench Perry is trying his case says at one point,

<pre>
        Pró:
               céed: (B+C)
</pre>

converting the first vowel from reduced to full and treating its syllable as, in effect, an accented one.[9] The boredom of the routine was self-evident, and more striking than in the more normally terraced

<pre>
     Yóu may pro
                  céed.   (B+C)
</pre>

One can appreciate the difference between a B or C profile with monotonic tail and an AC with monotonic tail by manipulating the broken-step example (p. 227) so as to contrast the original B+AC with a B+C:

```
       óut for the broken sté:              óut for the broken
Look                           ep:   Look                        stép:
```

Although the first is routine enough to suggest 'step known to be broken,' its A profile still conveys a genuine warning; the second, with its depressed accent, can be taken as virtual indifference—perhaps the warning has been issued so many times that the speaker is bored with giving it.

The B+AC contour is one of the most frequent in English, probably used more than any other for issuing warnings, e.g.

```
                            ló
            léave me  a       ne!
      Just
```

especially when the tail is at a relatively high pitch. The variant we encounter in this section, which has a monotone tail (its ambiguous status is discussed below), is a good testing ground for the effect of monotone at various positions in the contour, as well as for the contrast with B+C. Take a locution such as *Give him his money* on the B+C contour:

```
Gíve him his
                móney.
```

One infers something like 'Don't be tiresome.' With a B+AC and monotone we have

```
Gíve him his món
                ey!
```

This carries a note of warning, which can be rendered sharper by replacing the first monotone with a rise:

```
                 món
      Gíve him his
                   ey!
```

and sharper still by replacing the second monotone as well with an equally prolonged rise:

```
                 món
      Gíve him his
                    ey:
```

Finally, we find the modification noted earlier, which consists in prolonging the terraces. It augments the sense of a final AC profile, but not a C. Thus

<pre>
Gíve him his   Gíve him his
        mó:ney: mó:
                                               ney:
</pre>

would be odd, but

<pre>
                        mó:
        Gíve him his
                        ney:
</pre>

is often heard. (We note, incidentally, the change in syllabification with this lengthening: *mo-ney* rather than *mon-ey*.) Just as often, one finds this same device used in calls, where B+C would be inappropriate (at least for calling someone by name), with or without prolongation (see p. 181):

<pre>
        án: *Álex   *Álex
            der: án: der: án:
        Alex   der:
</pre>

Whether calls have any special relevance to the import of monotone AC would be difficult to prove, but one might reason as follows: A call is an attention-getter. If your listener is so unaware of his circumstances that you have to shake him up with a call, the obvious or the commonplace is implied: you are saying, in effect, 'Wake up! This should be plain to you!'

Calls may or may not be part of the source, but we do know that they share in the outcome—that is, a call may itself be modified by the type of profile it occurs with. Compare the following ways of saying *Hello!*, with B, AC, and C profiles, respectively:

<pre>
        ló: | ló: Hel:
    Hel   Hel   o: | ló: |
</pre>

Either the first or the second would be normal for attracting attention. The third would not be used for that purpose. It is most apt to occur in a stereotyped situation: in answering a telephone (though most likely without prolongation unless the speaker means to be exaggeratedly cheery) or as an exclamation of feigned surprise.

All things considered, it seems beyond dispute that the profiles retain their identity in a monotone or a polytone context.

Ambiguities of Monotone

The discussion thus far assumes that we know when we have a fall to a monotone and can tell it apart from a truncated fall (see pp. 146–48). The difficulty here is that a downmoving pitch has four possibilities in the way it ends: it may level off at a monotone, as in the preceding examples; it may descend more or less smoothly and terminate at a relatively high pitch without prolongation (truncated fall); it may do the latter but fade into voicelessness (breathy voice) at any pitch—this usually at a rapid rate of talking and with an overall impression of breathlessness; or it may go all the way down to creak. One possibility of confusion arises between the first two of these. If a truncated fall is not truncated abruptly, that is, if there is a slight prolongation of the last audible pitch, that prolongation may be heard as intentional, i.e., as a monotone. There is thus a potential ambiguity between what the speaker intends as a fall cut off at a relatively high pitch—we can refer to this as a TONAL ENDING, to distinguish it from an unintended cut-off—and a monotone, which is intentional by definition. A second possible confusion is between intended and unintended truncation, between a tonal ending and an ending that, for whatever reason, is cut off when it might as well have gone lower. The premature cutoff may be due to speed of utterance or to some interfering consonant. The sentence *It's a hack* spoken rapidly on an A profile may have only the slightest downturn at the end and yet be heard as quite conclusive, comparable, in fact, to *It's a hag* with fall to creak.[10] If the speaker strives for the effect of a clear tonal ending in *It's a hack*, he must prolong the vowel.

We can dispose of the contrast between tonal endings or between tonal ending and creak by simply pointing out that any audible difference in the depth of the fall can be heard as a greater or lesser degree of finality. A speaker who says *I can't* with a half fall may leave the impression that an explanation is in order (or that some other continuation is to be expected). If the pitch is dropped to creak, the impression will be that no explanation is necessary, though the speaker might still give one out of courtesy; the subject is closed.

The difference between a tonal ending and a monotone is more subtle. Take the answer to the question *When shall I do it?* —

No
w!

Said rapidly and with a tonal ending, the "up-in-the-airness" might imply urgency. If the one being urged failed to respond, the speaker might repeat and drop the pitch to creak; this is more likely if he feels that the hearer has failed to understand. But if the hearer has failed to pay attention, then the speaker is apt to produce a terminal monotone:

No: [na:
w:!   =   o:]

The problem of tonal ending versus monotone does not arise with Profile C, for the simple reason that the drop is taken by the accented syllable which must then be heard either as a monotone or as a low-plus-rise. This can be seen in a more subtle context in an example such as

^{I} told him where to get
off.

'I gave him what-for, I put him back in his place.' We know that *off* is accented. Here it levels out (and could be stretched to a monotone), but it might also rise at the end. If it falls even slightly, the profile will be heard as A, with a possible drastic shift in meaning: 'I told him where to dismount.'

The three-way contrast—between tonal ending and creak on the one hand, and between those two and monotone on the other—can be illustrated by an A-profile example such as

prés   sáy
Thát's up to the   Wé don't have ánything to
ident....
about it.

The message is essentially the same with tonal ending or with creak, though tonal ending might suggest 'I could go on' whereas creak would probably settle the matter. But if the terminal pitch goes up just a little bit, the final profiles in the two halves will be heard as AC rather than A with tonal ending, and the impression will be quite different—a sharp reminder, perhaps, or a mild warning. The difference in the first case, between tonal ending and creak, is gradient; the difference between tonal ending and rise is all-or-none. A monotone is ambiguous between the two, and requires lengthening to establish itself.

Monotone is neither fall nor rise, and reasons have just been given for distinguishing it from a tonal ending, that is, from a truncated fall. But there remains the counterpart question: should it be distinguished just as categorically from a rise? The description of Profiles C and AC in Chapter 8 has already given an implied no to this question, in allowing the terminal pitch to level off as well as to rise, and the discussion in the present chapter has assumed the same basic identity between a monotone and a rise. This is the position adopted by Ladd (1980: 265—"there *are* no plain level tones, but only stylized rises") and is similar to that of Hultzén (1957: esp. p. 325), who uses "not low" to subsume both monotone and rise. It is natural for us to react this way: a monotone is appreciably above creak, and the higher it is, the more it resembles a rising pitch in the tension it conveys. The B+AC contour spoken rapidly and with high pitches on the AC part may have a terminal rise or a terminal monotone with hardly an audible difference. Furthermore, the successive C monotones in the earlier examples in this section can all be slightly rising, e.g.

```
          always
He's            ásking for
                           fávors.
What
      dífference does it make?
```

(The second of the two examples is dispirited enough to allow a slight downtilt—very slight, for otherwise the utterance would be heard as having an A profile with its characteristic drop after *dif-*.) In fact, just as we noted above (p. 229) a possible resetting to get a better contrast on successive B's, so we can have a resetting with C, in this case, naturally, with the extra syllable at a higher rather than a lower pitch. So we can have

```
He'll
       téll you if he's
                      áble to.
```

with two C's and a "wild" *he's* which does not have the effect of turning the first monotone into a rise, but gives a better contrast for the second monotone. It could remain on the same level as *tell you if* (but the effect would be less "up," less "bright").

All this is just to say that within both the C and the AC profiles—as happens within other categories—the variations are gradient. Slow it down and the difference between monotone and rise becomes fully audible and quite significant in the degrees of tension conveyed. But even there, the difference between monotone and slight rise is comparable to the difference between slight rise and greater rise—monotone is on the same scale as rise.[11]

Relative Height

Whether by skips or by glides, the chief way of expressing amount in intonation is by going farther in a given direction. We saw in the last section that slowing the movement down, making it more appreciable, produced an augmenting effect; a higher rise or a deeper fall does the same. Referring to the latter, an early work on intonation, Coustenoble and Armstrong (1934: 10), stated correctly that "The depth [of a final fall] depends on the degree of finality intended." Similarly the higher a rise the greater the arousal, for whatever reason.

The effect of relative height is clearest in two circumstances. The first is a simple glide up or down, e.g. the sentence *You will* uttered with *will* moving up higher and higher or down lower and lower. The higher the rise the greater the exasperation if the utterance is a statement, and the greater the surprise or curiosity if it is a question (the intonation is the same either way). The lower the fall, the greater the certainty or finality if the utterance is a statement, and the greater the confidence if it is a question. This is purely a matter of gradience, and all degrees are possible, from creak to falsetto. It is not just the terminal pitch that counts, but the extent as well: a sweep that is longer (in duration, not just in frequency) is in some sense "more" than a shorter one, given the same terminal pitch.

The second circumstance involves two (or more) successive profiles. Take first two successive rise-fall A's. The effect of having the second higher, or lower, than the first is similar, despite the intervening drop, to that of a simple rise or fall. Compare the following, in which the tangent to the peaks is falling, level, and rising:

```
       (1)                      (2)                       (3)
    cán't                    cán't  má                            má
            má                                         cán't    
  You        i            You        i            You           i

         gine.                       gine.                      gine.
```

The greater "keyed up" effect of (3) is apparent; (1) is less exercised, more inclined to dismiss the matter. The accents do not necessarily pick out separate words. They may, as we saw in Chapter 6, fall on the secondary and primary stresses of a single word. The power play is the same:

```
          ín
                fér
        The   ter
                  ence we had to put up with!
```

```
                fér
          ín
        The   ter
                  ence we had to put up with!
```

Similarly the double accenting of *hélló*, with variation in height of peak: the double accent in itself conveys extra warmth (or surprise), and when the higher comes last, the warmth (or surprise) is augmented. The same is true of *shalom* in Hebrew.[12] This is simply the phenomenon of climax that was noted on page 87: a succession of rising-falling A profiles is in itself climactic, and is rendered more so when each is higher than the last.

Consider next two successive B's. We saw earlier (p. 212) that the relative height of a terminal rise cued the hearer as to where the major break was supposed to come: *If he calls you(,) when you get there(,) let me know.* The higher of the two rises corresponds to the comma and tells whether *when you get there* modifies the *if* clause or the command. This shows intonation in the service of grammar, and we might conclude that here at least intonation is simply grammatical—that speakers have some sort of underlying sense of grammatical subordination (and sub-subordination), and have adopted the height of the clause-final rise to convey it.

It is possible that the intonation in this case has become conventionalized and is used with no particular attitudinal stance or sensation on the part of the speaker. It would be hard to prove the opposite. But it would be wrong to conclude that clause endings are instances of a divorce between intonation and the underlying metaphor. For one thing, even if the intonation here is arbitrary it is too fragile to withstand an emotive push in the opposite direction. Suppose the speaker is aroused about the clumsiness of an employee, and says

```
                           blúnders
                 ány more
 If he makes                       while he's ──→

   emplóyed here,  fíre
                       him.
```

In this example the blunders are a source of such tension that the usual sequence of the rises is reversed. (The ambiguity, if any, can be cleared up by a pause in the right place.)

Such being the case, we are entitled to suspect that the (only partially?) conventionalized use is still tied to the up-down metaphor. The main part of a sentence is the part that the speaker will consider most important, that will be foregrounded intonationally. As we saw with accents of interest, it is the part that is most worth getting excited about. It is the "point" of what the speaker is saying, as can be demonstrated by extending the sentence:

> If you decide to go ahead, when you get there call me; but don't bother if you change your mind.
>
> If you decide to go ahead when you get there, call me; but don't bother if you make up your mind sooner.

Exchanging the *but* clauses between these two sentences would be anomalous in the first and at least a bit odd in the second.

Intonational subordination has no necessary connection with grammatical subordination. In the following,

```
            er
        s ú m m
                        bírds are singing
  When it's      and the                   I'll be

                                        háp
                                           py.
```

the second clause (*and the birds are singing*) is subordinated intonationally to the first—we are allowed to infer that the singing of the birds is a consequence of its being summer. But if the two rises are reversed, the second clause becomes relatively independent: it reports a bright new thought—'When it's summer and (just think!) the birds are singing. . . .' The effect is enhanced by lengthening *birds*, and rising facial gestures are almost certain to accompany the rising pitch: smile, widened eyes, and raised eyebrows.

It has been noted for many languages that by and large height diminishes as an utterance progresses. Coustenoble and Armstrong (1934: 82) describe this tendency for French, noting that in a succession of grouped phrases the highest pitches form a descending sequence. Thorsen (1983) notes the same for accented syllables in Danish declarative sentences. The term *downdrift* is sometimes applied to this supposed universal.[13] And it may indeed be a universal in the sense that as initial energy is expended, utterances tend to be more and more deflated toward the end. This in turn may underlie the "down = finished" metaphor. There have been proposals—for example the "topline rule" of Cooper and Sorensen (1981)—to use this descending pitch as a norm for measuring deviations up or down, on the theory that an upward jump of a given extent toward the end of an utterance should count as "more" than one of equal extent coming earlier, since the overall pitch is expected to be lower. One might hypothesize a descending mid-line from which the speaker "reaches for" either a higher or a lower pitch. The mid-line would represent the progressive positions of least effort, the neutral pitch at any given point in the utterance, from which it requires more effort to produce either a higher or a lower pitch.

Apart from the possibly universal tendency to slide down toward the end, variations in height are exploited in numerous ways. We saw in Chapter 7 (pp. 126–27) that when there is an early peak on the most interesting word followed by markedly lesser peaks on following words the latter tend to approach dead level. The extra boost in pitch for the affirmation accent was noted on pages 130–31. But the form of exploitation that has been most discussed is relative height as a distinguisher of how speakers and hearers present and interpret INFORMATION. In essence it is no different from the manifestations that relate to arousal in general; it merely specializes arousal in terms of what kind of information we are more likely or less likely to get excited about, and uses the audibility of that excitement as a sign of the nature of the information. This is probably a universal phenomenon (see Bearth 1980).

Key

A useful term here is the one adopted by Coulthard and Brazil (1982, esp. pp. 103–5), namely KEY. High key is 'contrastive,' mid key is 'additive,' and low key is 'equative.' One can appreciate the difference between high and low by testing the opposition between *and* and *but*. The following are to be taken as continuations of the sentence beginning *Everyone is crazy but thee and me*:

```
                      thée
        sómetimes  I think
and                             is a  líttle  quéer.
```

```
                          qué
        sómetimes        thée
but                I think   is a  líttle
                                         er.
```

And shows the relation of inclusion: 'queer' is included in 'crazy,' and the pitch of *queer* stays low, since it only repeats a meaning already expressed. *But* shows the relation of exclusion: 'queer' is contrasted with 'crazy,' and *queer* goes to high key. (Actually the whole phrase *a little queer* is affected: lower with *and*, higher with *but*; but the main accent carries the bulk of the contrast.)

The difference between high and mid can be illustrated by the following:

```
        énd
     pláy
The                          The    pláy
                                       énd
        ed     ilУ•                ed     ilУ•
          happ                       happ
```

The first is more apt to carry the sense 'to have a happy ending'— 'end' is contrasted with 'beginning' or 'middle'; the second is more likely as 'we were happy that the play came to an end,' but since all plays end and 'end' is not in contrast with 'beginning' or 'middle,' 'end' is only additive. It is possible for these to be reversed, more readily the second than the first (high key for 'end' would be unlikely when not contrastive, for the reason just given—all plays end). If the second is taken in the sense 'to have a happy ending,' the specific meaning is probably 'For all its faults, the play at least had a happy ending'—'end' is informative, hence additive, but is not in specific contrast with 'beginning' or 'middle.'

For all three levels of key we can use a park sign as illustration: *Area bounded by walks reserved for children and escorts.* The first part, *Area bounded by walks*, takes high key—it contrasts with other areas. *Children* likewise has high key—'children' are in contrast with other park-goers. *Escorts* is ancillary to *children*, therefore is not contrastive (as *young adults* might be); but it is nevertheless additive, and takes mid key, just as *and persons escorting them* would in this context. If the sign were to read *for children and the like* or *for children and such*, the last word would be at low key, for its meaning is more or less equal to that of *children*.

Key has important practical applications in elocution, particularly for people who recite information in which they are not personally involved and to which they often give a false intonational interpretation. Coulthard and Brazil (1982) offer an example of a political announcement made on the BBC:

> and tomorrow Mrs. Thatcher will make a considered statement on immigration.

The announcer pitched the syllable *-sid-* too high, making the insulting suggestion that Mrs. Thatcher's earlier statement on immigration had been thoughtless. An example from an American announcer is *It melted telephone lines in the area*, with *area* not only accented but at high key, as if *in the area* had some special significance beyond being a mere equivalent of *there*, to which no one would think of giving any prominence. The announcer's unreflecting habit is to make the last noun prominent whether it deserves to be or not. We have seen other instances of this sort of treatment of "empty words" (pp. 77, 120–21). (Both accent and key are involved: the word *area* in the above example may be deaccented or accented at low pitch, but an accent at high key is misplaced.)

One difficulty with assigning the term *contrastive* to the concept of key is that it has already been attached to accent, especially that of the A profile. Since profiles intersect with relative height, one can then get something that is contrastive in terms of one but not in terms of the other. The following illustrates the problem:

```
    múr                                    thá
A      derer wouldn't do a thing like        t.
```

—'although a pickpocket might'—a contrast between 'murderer' and 'other miscreants,' but not a shift to high key: murderers have probably already been under discussion. On the other hand, in

```
      múr
A     derer wouldn't do a thing like  thá t.
```

we have 'even a murderer' as a very likely interpretation—contrast, plus high key for intensification. In the following,

```
                              rí
       Hey,        Tóm was
            dad--
                       ght.
```

the mid pitch of *Tom* suggests that Tom has recently been mentioned, whereas with high key on *Tom was* one might be recalling something discussed several days earlier, hence more in need of a forceful reminder. In both cases we have B profiles with *Tom was*, signifying that Tom is not being singled out from other persons. But such a contrast can be added by a change in profile, to A, as in *I don't know about George, but*

```
                    rí
          Tó
            m was
               ght.
```

Now we do have Tom versus others, but *Tom* is still at mid key; if set at high key, the reference to Tom would be understood to be surprising in some sense.

So we seem to have two kinds of "contrast." One is configurational: Profile A separates an item from its context horizontally, cutting it off by the abrupt drop that characterizes that profile. The other is dimensional: high key separates an item vertically, by degree of height. We might say that one marks identity while the other marks importance (what one gets excited about). We tend not to discriminate them because Profile A so often has high key, and when it has low key, as it typically does after the main accent in an utterance, it alternates with a total absence of accent.

A further problem with key is the limitation to three levels. If height is relative, any number of levels should be possible—within the powers of the hearer to discriminate, of course. In answer to the question *Who was responsible for this atrocity?* we might have the following, in which higher numbers stand for higher pitches:

```
         2        3      4        1         6
The man who did it was John, but the man who profited by it was
      5
George.
```

The heights correspond to relative importance or unexpectedness. The notion of profit is the most striking fact; the person most responsible comes next, etc., and the least important is the second instance of *man*, which has already been mentioned (see Bolinger 1957: 303).

Given these difficulties, we will retain *key* for informal use referring to pitch height that corresponds to being keyed up for whatever reason (informational or other), but not in a technical sense. The role of mere excitement in key can be shown in the impatience speakers display when they have to repeat a response that they feel is superfluous, as with the following affirmation accents:

> Are you writing him? — I wróte him, I wróte him!
> Come along. — I'm cóming, I'm cóming!

It would sound odd not to have these at high pitch. The fact is that for every informational instance of key one can find an emotional one, which suggests, as has been emphasized in this book many times, that the emotional thrust is basic and that informational emphasis is a case of being excited over what is important informationally. We use emotive strategies for logical and grammatical purposes.

Sequence

In sequence, the primary metaphor holds: low to high is increasing arousal, high to low is decreasing. This is true both within and between profiles. In the description of profiles we saw that an A with its fall symptomized relaxation of tension, hence finality, assurance, and the like. The more complex profiles achieve their effects not only by the pitch movements themselves but by how the movements are arranged. The CA profile, for example, represents a sort of breaking free of prior restraint, embodied in the initial low followed by the quick upward jump, plus a reimposition of control in the immediately following return to a low pitch.

It would be impossible to do more than give a sample of the effects that are achieved by varying the direction, extent, slope, and arrangement of the component movements of pitch. A linear analysis is implied, one that takes into account not only the accents and their profiles but also the behavior of more or less free unaccented syllables and the gradience of the whole.

There have been attempts to do this scientifically by applying a sort of yardstick to intonation contours, the most widely accepted ones being in terms of accent and terminal. A contour is said to consist, say, of a pre-head (the material before the first major accent), a head (the first major accent), a body (the material between the first and the last major accent), a nucleus (the last major accent and the most important of the contour), and a tail (the pitch movement after the nucleus).[14] Though this has certain advantages—it is not a bad description of the hat pattern that we observed in the chapters on accent—it tells us nothing about the differences between one accent and another (on the A and C profiles, for example), the contribution made by unaccented syllables at various intervening pitches (higher or lower than an accent peak, for example), or the accenting or deaccenting of material between the major accents.

On this last point in particular much is left unsaid. Suppose we have a B+B+A contour such as the following, in answer to *What was the trouble?*

```
                                            gó
     wóuldn't let me téll him where to
     He
                                      o.
```

The "head" in this case is doubled—the syllables *would-* and *tell* are equally accented. Or take one such as this, an A+AC contour in answer to *Does Joe prefer the tall one?*—

```
          jóhn
                            táll
     Noo'        prefers the
                            one·
```

Here the nucleus would be on *John* if defined by height, on *tall* if defined by position. Actually it is an inversion of the AC+A

```
                    jóhn
          táll
     The       one
               préfers.
```

—a matter of relative position of theme and rheme (see pp. 50–51, 111, 182). The description in terms of profiles, A+AC versus AC+A, makes the inversion explicit.

A Sample Analysis: The "Contradiction Contour"

To understand the resources that are available to speakers we have to take a microscopic view to see how each succeeding movement qualifies the preceding ones and contributes to the ensemble of effects. Every utterance produces a prosodic impression on the hearer. How is it achieved? Is it some more or less arbitrary message that the whole pattern conveys, so that one could have a complete description of intonation by making a list of whole patterns, tracing their gross shapes, and defining their meanings—a sort of intonational logo-graphy? Or are the individual parts of the tracing meaningful? Or do we find patterns that become to some extent arbitrary while still re-sponding to the meanings of their components, on the principle that the whole is always more than the sum of its parts?

The view that an intonologist favors is influenced by where his alle-giance lies in his general view of language. If it is a view heavily swayed by logic, then the notion of the arbitrary whole made up of meaningless subunits is apt to prevail. If it is a view embedded in af-fect and metaphor, then the subunits will take on meaning of their own and the whole will reflect the meanings of the parts, though some arbitrariness is not excluded. The latter view is the one adopted here, and is the one that must be favored if one is to explain universals of intonational meaning that go beyond vague resemblances that could be traced to anatomical similarities or common origin and that include supposedly grammaticized phenomena.

An example that will serve for illustration is one that has been of-fered as a case study of holistic—that is, unanalyzable—contours.[15] Though we shall not be concerned with contours as such until the next chapter, the one in question involves only two profiles and its main characteristics—specifically the "whole" meaning that has been assigned to it, namely, CONTRADICTION—can be seen in terms of its separate pitch movements. What makes it especially interesting is that it is not a single contour but a family of three contours with an overall similar shape that produces a similar meaning that overarches the meanings of the separate contours.

The overall shape is rise-fall-rise, and the three contours are CB+C, CB+AC, and CB+B. There is range for wide variation in the pitch treat-ment of the unaccented syllables, but the three shapes that accord most closely with the description as originally proposed (in Liberman and Sag 1974) are the following:

```
                  nóbody's blaming the Ca
CB+C:    But
                                           nádians.


                  nóbody's blaming the Caná
CB+AC:   But                                 dians.


                  nóbody's blaming the      nádians.
CB+B:    But                           Ca
```

In all three the unaccented syllables following the accent on *no-* move gradually down (after the upskip from the accent) to the point where the accent on *-na-* takes over. None of these movements are essential except the ones that define the profiles, and we can test a few other possibilities after looking at what these three have in common and how it affects the interpretation assigned to utterances that employ them.

First the question of holism. Is the meaning 'contradiction' one that, however loosely understood, applies to all utterances that use these contours? It is certainly appropriate to a great many. Take the following, which, to save space, we will consider only on the CB+C contour and will mark with a circumflex for the highest syllable and a grave for the lowest (the first shape above would thus be marked *Nobôdy's blaming the Canàdians*):

> I dôn't have to take that from yòu.
> It's the verŷ least that they can dò for us.
> I'll nevêr be able to fàce them.

One can readily imagine these sentences occurring in the context of an argument. But now we must ask whether changing the syntax results in a "different" intonation, despite the identity of shape. 'Contradiction' can refer only to statements; when one issues a command or asks a question (other than a rhetorical one) there is nothing to contradict. The following have the same intonational shape just described:

> When dô we get to go hòme?
> Is ît far from here to Èlm Street?
> Tell mê what you're thìnking.
> Just give ît the best you hàve.

And even statements need not relate in any obvious way to contradiction:

> I think Î can dò it.
> That'd be fùn.
> Funnŷ you should àsk.

If changing the syntax does not change the intonation, and if intonation is meaningful, then all such statements, questions, and commands must have a common intonational meaning. It cannot, for obvious reasons, be 'contradiction,' but it must be of such a nature that contradiction can be *inferred* from it. And also that the 'considerateness,' 'deference,' etc. of questions like the *Elm Street* example or the perky, cheerful prodding of the commands can be inferred as well. It hardly seems that any sense assigned to the configuration as a whole will give us a basis for inferring such disparate meanings. We must look at the components, which tell us something about the emotive interplay. If from a high pitch one can infer, given a context, either anger or enthusiasm, and not be guilty of any inconsistency, perhaps the more elaborate display of ups and downs that we have here will lend itself to a similar consistent interpretation, regardless of the syntax.

Assume that the following gives an approximation to the meanings of the components of this contour:

1. Initial rise cueing the hearer to the concern, interest, etc. of the speaker.

2. High pitch on an unaccented syllable, marking the concern, interest, etc. as nonselective, that is, as applying to the utterance as a whole.

3. Immediately succeeding stepped or gradual fall, showing the tension to be under control, and therefore intended.

4. Accented syllable at low pitch, deemphasizing the referent of the word and contributing to the restraint of the downmotion.

5. Terminal rise, leaving the utterance "open" to further comment or to continuation within a larger utterance. The gradient extent of the terminal rise augments the effect of the initial rise.

Point 3 relates to point 2 in that the relative gradualness of the downmotion helps to eliminate the possibility that the contour will be heard as having a CA profile. For the latter to be possible, there would need to be a relatively abrupt drop, but instead, the initial CB has its customary upward jump and gradual fall. The difference can be seen in the following pair:

```
           kins wouldn't tell a
       Háw
 Miss
                                    lıfe·


           kins
       Háw
 Miss
                 wouldn't tell a
                             lıfe·
```

The first, with its CB+C, leaves open the likelihood of further comment about the whole matter; the second, with its CA+C, leaves open the likelihood of further comment on who else besides Miss Hawkins might tell a lie.

"Leaves open the possibility" is our cue to interpreting one of the segments of the contour, the final one. The rise leaves matters up in the air, for whatever reason. A terminal fall would destroy this "openness," though not in a logical sense—the speaker is free to continue but the expectation is that he does not need to. The latter of the two examples, given a terminal fall, would be most likely in a context such as *You thought it was Miss Jenkins who wouldn't tell a lie; you were wrong—Miss Hawkins wouldn't tell a lie* ('Miss Hawkins is the one who wouldn't . . .').

The openness or inconclusiveness of the terminal rise can be clearly seen in the earlier examples of the CB+C contour, whether they are questions, statements, or commands. *That'd be fun* on this contour is a prelude to adding (or implying the addition of) *Come on, let's try it!*, or *Don't you think?*, or *I don't understand why I didn't think of it before*, or any other such continuation that might sensibly be led up to. *Funny you should ask* can hardly be left without some such sequel as *I was just about to bring up the subject myself* (though the words by themselves, regardless of intonation, are stereotyped in that direction—a perfect example of how hard it is to isolate the meaning of the intonation alone). *I'll never be able to face them* uses the inconclusiveness to imply ineffability—the speaker suggests that more needs to be added but he is unequal to the task of putting the experience into words. In an example such as *There's nô need to be rùde about it* the inconclusiveness is a matter of courtesy, as can be readily seen in the contrast with the extremely cutting CB+A

<pre>
              no need to be
  Thére's   rú
                            d
                             e
                               about it.
</pre>

with terminal fall. (N.B.: *There's* is accented, *no* is not.)

By manipulating other segments as we manipulated the terminal one, we can test their contribution likewise to the overall impression. The next segment to the left is the accent on the C profile. It can be modified in either of two ways: by shifting it rightward, which changes the contour from CB+C to CB+B, or by giving it a low rise-fall, which changes the contour to CB+AC. These three contours, as was noted at the beginning, bear a sort of family resemblance. As long as everything else remains the same, the implications enumerated above are not affected except in so far as the change of profile affects point 4. If the final profile is B, the terminal upmotion is augmented, since now it includes the accent as well as the tail. The effect is predictable: if the utterance expressed more or less restrained anticipation before (as with *That'd be fun*), now it expresses enthusiasm. What was a polite or restrained question now becomes a surprised or querulous one. What was a milder command is now an insistent one. The command *Give ît a little more of a shòve for Christ's sake!* is a bit odd; the insistence seems to call for moving the accent on *shove* to the right:

<pre>
  Gíve it a little mo
                     r
                      e
                       of   shóve for Christ's sake!
                          a
</pre>

To make a concession like *Anỳthing you wìsh* under some conditions might sound too condescending. Changing the C to a B increases the cordiality:

$$\text{Án}^{y}\text{thi}_{ng} \; \text{yo}_{u} \; \text{wìsh.}$$

In all these cases the 'restraint' associated with having the accent at the lowest pitch gives way to a greater arousal, whatever the reason may be. (The arousal is gradient, and can be achieved to some extent even with CB+C, by simply moving up farther on the terminal glide. But it is arousal still tempered by the restraint of the C, as can be appreciated by contrasting two such instances as the following:

$$\text{Wóuld}^{n't} \; \text{yo}_{u} \; \text{like to} \quad \underset{\text{trý}}{\quad} \text{at least?}$$

—this request has the restrained courtesy of the C on *try*, but becomes more insistent as the terminal rise goes higher.

$$\text{Wóuld}^{n't} \; \text{yo}_{u} \; \text{like} \; \underset{\text{to}}{\quad} \; \text{trý at least?}$$

Here—with the B on *try*—courtesy gives way to impatience, which easily turns to exasperation as the terminal rise goes higher.)

CB+B offers a further possibility in that tail following the accented syllable. If it levels off, we get the "stylized" effect noted earlier. Modifying an example from Liberman and Sag (1974), we might have, in response to a request to drop a friend's pet whale off at the aquarium,

$$\text{Théy} \; ^{\text{don't}} \; \text{want him at the} \; \underset{\text{a}}{\quad} \text{quárium!}$$

with the last three syllables level. The implication is boredom at something that should be a foregone conclusion: 'It was foolish of you to ignore such an obvious fact.'

A change from CB+C to CB+AC adds the nuance of the latter profile, notably the possibility of contrast. An example like

$$\text{í} \; ^{\text{don't have to}} \; \text{ta}_{ke} \; \text{th}_{at} \; \text{from} \quad \overset{\text{yó}}{\underset{u^{u}}{\quad}}.$$

is appropriate in a context that implies my possible willingness to take it from someone else. The higher the pitch on the upward *you* jump, the more emphatic the contrast becomes, and at the same time the more exercised the utterance as a whole. This is just to say that the effect of upmotion is the same, no matter which of the three possible positions it occurs on in this family of contours. If in addition to the upward jump of the CA, the amount of terminal upmotion is varied, one can express any degree of arousal, from slight uncertainty to exasperation.

The next segment to the left in our original CB+C contour is the gradual downmotion of the CB tail. Since a downtilt is one of the defining characteristics of CB (see pp. 160–61) not much can be done by way of manipulating it except to vary the steepness—the less steep the fall, the more keyed up the utterance will be. More striking changes can be seen if a B profile is substituted for the CB, since the tail can then be up, level, or gradually down—anything other than the abrupt drop that characterizes the A or AC profile. These different directions contribute in proportion to their tension and relaxation. If the pitch of the B tail goes up instead of down, e.g.

$$\text{But} \quad {}_{n\acute{o}body's}\ blaming\ the\ ^{Ca}{}_{n\acute{a}dians\cdot}$$

the effect of 'control' set forth in point 3 above is lost: the speaker is astonished, indignant ('How could you be so stupid as to think that?'), or whatever. The only control is the violent reversal of pitch to the accented syllable itself (-*na*-), which comes into play only after the full upglide has run its course, and suggests the difficulty the speaker is having in restraining his emotion.

The remaining segment to the left in the CB+C is the upskip from the accented syllable of the CB profile to the immediately following syllable which starts the downtilted tail. As we saw (p. 157) regarding CA, increased tension may delay the drop on the tail, and the same can happen with CB, with the result that an extra syllable can intervene in the upmotion between the accented syllable and the rest of the tail. The effect is to increase the initial arousal that was interpreted in point 1 above as concern, interest, etc. A masher making his first move says, using the normal CB,

Haven't I seen you before somewhere?

The warmth of interest here is just the right degree for an opening. If he increased the initial upmotion by saying

Haven't Î seen you before somewhere?

he might seem to be overdoing it (this would be normal as an expresion of lively concern—something serious may be involved). But to eliminate the upmotion altogether, as would happen with a down-tilted B profile,

Háven't I seen you be
                    fóre somewhere?

would cancel the degree of cordiality required in a question that breaks the ice; it needs an introduction, and might occur later in the conversation. To accost someone with it might invite a rebuff.

This analysis gives some idea of the possible extent of conventionalization in intonation—not grammatically or lexically (such as would be claimed by saying that a rise of X degree signifies 'question' and one of Y degree signifies 'subordinate clause,' or that a contour of a given shape is an entry in a vocabulary with a meaning such as 'contradiction') but in terms of appropriateness to discourse. The changes in nuance correspond to attitudinal and affective demands in the relationships between interlocutors. It is ordained, for instance, that in accosting a stranger one should manifest a certain degree of reserve. If we assume that the speaker retrieves from memory the intonation that fits the occasion, then we accept the conventionalization of that intonation; if on the other hand we assume that the speaker, like a Stanislavski actor, puts himself in the *mood* to be deferential, then the intonation reflects the feeling directly. A successful performer probably does both, and in either case the intonation remains expressive and a speaker who uses an intonation that he does not feel is pretending or lying.

One can agree that much of intonation has been conventionalized without expecting the sort of precise segmentation and stereotyping that is found in the lexical and grammatical side of language. Intonation remains largely freehand. What Kendon says (1980: 223) of physical gesture is true of the entire gestural complex including intonation: "the utterer has considerable freedom to create new enactments which do not then pass into any established vocabulary." If the primitive expressiveness of intonation retains its vitality, we should expect just such windows of creativity and originality. In playing with up-and-down we can, up to a point, do our own thing.

Summary of Terms Used to Describe Intonational Shapes

For the most part, the terms needed to describe the shape of intonational figures have been selected from a more or less self-evident general vocabulary: *glide, turn, trough,* etc. are familiar from everyday discussions of line and curve. As a reminder—and to pin down a few not so obvious distinctions and to add an item or two—the list is summarized here, with definitions.

dash: rapid glide, manifested as *updash* and *downdash*. (See p. 149.)

downturn: a brief turn downward; a "hook."

dropback: a lowering of pitch on one or more unaccented syllables, serving to reset a following higher pitch. (See pp. 154–55 for syntactic uses.)

glide: a more or less smooth up or down movement: specifically *upglide* or *downglide*.

peak: the highest point of a pitch movement, initial if falling, final if rising, medial if rising-falling.

resetting: the maneuver whereby a rising (or falling) profile is repeated after another rising (or falling) one, without overreaching the range of the voice; the pitch is allowed to drop back (or float up) on an unaccented syllable. See *dropback*.

skip: a more or less abrupt up or down movement: specifically *upskip* or *downskip*. (See p. 149.)

span: the compass (vertical reach) of an up or down movement: specifically *upspan* and *downspan*.

tail: the part of a profile that follows the accented syllable.

takeoff: the unaccented syllables, if any, that precede the accented syllable in a profile; medially, the takeoff of one profile may also represent the tail of a preceding one.

terminal: the pitch direction at the end of an utterance or at a major break.

tilt: gradual sustained upmotion or downmotion, the middle term between glide and monotone; specifically *uptilt* and *downtilt*.

tonal ending: a terminal that ends in the modal register (above creak), without marked sustention.

trough: the lowest point of a U-shaped curve.

upmotion and downmotion: motion up or down, whether by skip, glide, or tilt.

11. Contours in General

A CONTOUR is the shape of a *complete* intonation. Contours are to profiles more or less what sentences are to words, and have the same kind of indeterminate borders that sentences have. If linguists are still, after centuries of trying, unable to give a precise definition of a sentence, we must allow a certain imprecision where contours are concerned, provided that it is recognized and reduced as much as possible.

If a contour is made up of profiles, it follows that every contour must contain at least one profile, and therefore at least one accent. Anything less will be heard as fragmentary. There will be no definite upper bound to the number of profiles, though practically the number will be relatively small and the average will probably approach two—that is, the number of two-profile contours will be large and the number of one-profile contours will be large enough to offset those of more than two profiles. (One-word—hence one-profile—utterances are extremely common: *Yes, No, Where?, Why?, Sure, Great!, Oh, More!, Wait!, You?, Hello.*)

Certain advantages of a profile description of contours were mentioned in the last chapter (pp. 244–45). Profiles are accent-centered, and if we recognize the possibility of more than one accent per utterance, and use the utterance (the prosodic counterpart of the sentence) as the scope of a contour, then a description in terms of profiles is one way to show how a contour is articulated. It is also probably the best way if the most important points in a contour are the points that carry accents: since profiles describe how accents are realized, they set certain desirable limits to the shapes that contours may assume.

At the same time, contours have a life of their own, largely by way of what happens to unaccented syllables. The chapter on profiles described a number of alternate ways for an accent to be carried out—an A profile, for example, whose defining characteristic is a fall from the accented syllable, might have that syllable approached from above, from the same level, or from below, and might carry its fall in pitch to any depth, including creak. The result of these alternatives is that one may readily have contours that contain different profiles but display a similar overall shape, if the unaccented syllables are appropriately arranged. This is no accident; although the behavior of unaccented syllables has often been dismissed as unimportant, when they contribute to producing overall similar shapes the total impression will be similar even though the profile makeup is different. Nothing else is to be expected, if pitch movement has the significance that we have proposed it to have, in terms of tension-relaxation and the metaphorical associations of up-down. But since each profile has its own significance within this complex and the accented syllables are the weightiest, the primary description should be in terms of them. This amounts to saying that the relationship of higher and lower, which is the basis for the accents and is a relationship in which the related elements determine each other independently of any scale, takes precedence over the relationship of high and low, in which positions are relative to a more or less constant scale. Configuration comes first, regardless of how or where it is projected on the overall scale of the speaker's voice.[1]

At the same time, the two approaches overlap in their effects. We saw that Profile C, in which the accent is held down, has a "subdued" effect by comparison with A or B. This "down" is relative to other pitches in the same profile. But an A or B profile can be "held down" on the high-low scale and then has its assertive or emphatic implications similarly subdued. The upshot is that two such utterances as

^{cán't} believe that
  I
                Jóhn did it.

^{cán't} believe that
  I
               Jó_{hn} did it.

become similarly restrained, even though the first contour is B+C and the second is B+AC. The importance of the profile distinction, however, can be tested by inquiring which contour better expresses 'John rather than someone else'; for that purpose, AC is appropriate, but not C. Another such set of profile contrasts within an overall intonational sweep was that of the "contradiction contour"—actually a family of contours—described in the last chapter (pp. 245–52).

For three similar overall shapes take the following:

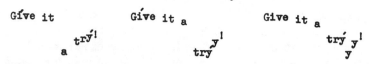

These are, respectively, B+B (with dropback on *a* necessary to achieve the upward jump to the B accent on *try*), B+C, and B+AC, yet all have roughly the same U shape and all are similarly restrained by having their terminal accent at a low pitch. The profile differences nevertheless shine through: the first, with its rising pitch on the accent, is the most keyed up; the speaker is perhaps giving a bit of rousing encouragement to his hearer. The second is the most subdued; possibly the speaker feels it necessary to coax rather than to prod. The third potentially focuses on the meaning of *try*: 'do at least that much, whatever else you do.'

Another sort of overall similar shape can be found where a tangent to a succession of A profiles has the same slope as that of a B+A contour:

$$\text{Léave} \quad \overset{\text{wín}}{\underset{\text{the} \qquad \overset{}{\text{ó}}}{}} \quad \underset{\substack{\text{dow}\\\text{pen.}}}{}$$

$$\text{Léave the window ó} \qquad \text{pen.}$$

—A+A+A and B+A, respectively. The first is more apt to be used when there has been no prior mention of 'window,' the second when 'window' is understood, but both have the same general conclusiveness.

For the constancy of profiles regardless of pitch range, take a contour consisting of a single Profile A uttered at various heights and with various distances between the accented syllable and what follows:

$$\text{Có}_{\text{me!}} \qquad \text{Có}$$
$$\underset{\text{me!}}{} \qquad \underset{\text{me!}}{\text{Có}}$$

These differ in degree of tension and degree of conclusiveness, but they show a kinship that makes the first one more similar to either of the others than to a high-pitched B,

$$\text{Có}^{\text{me!}}$$

despite the latter's similarity in terms of height and range.

Determinacy

How determinate are contours? Are there comparatively definite shapes that can be assigned more or less definite meanings or that are used under particular conditions of discourse with such frequency as to be typecast in those conditions? In a very loose sense, the answer is yes. If Profile B were not associated so often with yes-no questions, the habit of referring to an intonation "of" questions would not have arisen. A few additional instances of such comparatively tight association will be noted as the contours are enumerated—association, that is, which transcends the general one between a contour and the summed-up meanings of its ups and downs (including accents), from which the more particularized meanings are derived.

The question can be posed another way: How free is the speaker to improvise? (See Kendon 1980 on "new enactments," p. 252 above.) To the extent that profiles have determinate shapes and contours are made up of profiles, there would appear to be certain limits—one might even discover "forbidden contours." Nothing of the kind has been attested, however, and we can only conclude that any imaginable melodic shape can occur in actual speech.[2] When we consider how the accents are defined, this almost totally freehand tracing of intonational designs is understandable. Pitch accent is a matter of angular prominence, and at a change point between two successive up-to-down or down-to-up pitches there are only four corners, so to speak, that can be occupied by an accented syllable:

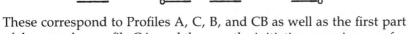

These correspond to Profiles A, C, B, and CB as well as the first part of the complex profile CA; and they are the initiating prominences for the remaining complex profiles.[3] The accent system thus exploits the possibilities about as well as they can be exploited, and there can be a great deal of "smear" without imposing an undue burden on the hearer, who has to sort out the speaker's intent.

The SMEAR is where the speaker has the greatest freedom to ad-lib. It is always open season for relative heights, for width of drops, for direction of tilts, for substitution of monotones, and for ranging into creak or falsetto, not to mention such nonintonational factors as drawling, breathy voice, and tremolo. Any of these can be used and some of them even enter certain more or less stereotyped combinations. For example, as an abrupt and imperious command to stop, one may say

$$ıt^1$$
Hóld

with a B profile contour (the initial level is missing) on which the *it* would normally be reduced in its function of mere tail to the accent on *hold*, but which here is upgraded to a full syllable and drawled at heavy volume—making use, for warning purposes, of a loud noise at high pitch. Simple B is converted to B+B.

Another instance of freedom to play with unaccented syllables can be illustrated in the following B+A contour in which the A accent is approached in different ways depending on where the syllable *I'd* goes relative to the accent and to the peak:

```
                        dó
    (1)                               (2)              I'd
              do´ it  I'd                        dó it      dó
If I could [c'd]                       If I could
                        it.                                    it.


    (3)       it                       (4)                     dó
          dó      I'd                                   dó it
If I could            dó               If I could            I'd
                        it.                                    it.
```

Version (1) is the most emphatic, with its rise through *I'd* and its A accent at the peak. Version (2) is less emphatic, and might be interpreted as pettishly final; the frank appeal or protest of (1) is missing. Version (3) is milder still; the speaker is more or less unconcerned: 'but I can't, and that's that.' Version (4) with its dropback is like (1) though more matter-of-fact: the relaxation on *I'd* suggests that the speaker is in control, not keyed up by some extraneous emotion such as annoyance but only by the sense of his words and their appeal for acceptance. That appeal would be keyed down if the second peak were lower than the first, and the contour would take on the same relative finality as can be detected in (2) and (3).

Initial position offers striking possibilities in what can be done with high pitch regardless of accent. The pronoun *it* will serve to compare unaccented elements with accented ones, because it can play either role. Take the following, which is probably best analyzed as a succession of two intimately connected contours, the second containing just a Profile A on *sure*, the first consisting either of C+B or of A+B:

```
                                        su
      It
                  difficult,
       was a bit                       but...
                  re,
```

If the first contour is C+B (with accented syllables *was* [wʌz] and *dif-*), then *it* is ground and *was* is figure. If the first contour is A+B, then *it* is accented and *was* [wəz] is ground. This is an accent of power, created for the purpose of building up the alerting effect of an initial high

pitch, just as the effect of the final high pitch was enhanced in the
Hold it! example above.[4] But an initial high does not need to be enhanced by improvising an accent there. We find a similar, but unaccented, use of mere TONE in that position, in a meditative utterance like

M-m-m-m

ye᷄s·

where the hum can be as high as falsetto, and serves as a foil to a following C accent. The lack of accent allows, but does not force, the initial high to be collapsed to the point of complete deformation of the
syllable: *It was* in the preceding example can be reduced to *'Twas* on a
rapid downglide with accent on the vowel at the lowest pitch; and an
example such as *It's nothing that can be blamed on you* can be spoken

'Sn

ǒthing that can be blamed on y͝o͝uʔ

with accent on the first vowel of *nothing*, reached by way of a virtual
downskip on the nasal—a C+B contour. The mechanics of the C profile permit this byplay: a skip down *to* needs a springboard, and the
speaker may set it at any height.

When we declare the speaker free to play with unaccented syllables, we mean freedom by comparison with the relatively tighter
constraints that the speaker observes when producing an accent.
There is no absolute freedom,[5] and much of what has been said in this
section has to be qualified by noting the constraints that keep within
certain bounds the broader configurations of up and down. Chapter 5
dealt with the hat pattern and the tendency in longer utterances to
put the major prominences in the most conspicuous positions, beginning and end. Much of what we have just noted—especially the accenting of an initial *it* or other such normally unaccented element—
amounts to an imposition of the hat pattern. We can see this also in
what happens with words that one would expect to be deaccented because they are redundant, and yet are accented at least in part for the
power effect. In the following, the speaker was talking to his son and
daughter-in-law, and was pointing to the chapel on a college campus.
The sentence starts with a conditional clause, *If you had been married
here*, and continues:

már

thát's

where you'd have been

ried.

—with an A profile at the end in spite of the fact that *married* has just been mentioned; the same content could be expressed with

```
                 whé
        thá
          t's
            re.
```

There is a slight semantic content to *married* in the 'event' component of the verb (see pp. 101–3 for the decomposition of verbs)—the speaker could have said *that's where it would have happened*, with the same accent on *happened*—but the overriding reason for the intonational shape is probably to avoid the deflation that would result from saying

```
            whére
    thá
      t's
        you'd have been married.
```

in which the speaker has not played up a logically unaccented *married*. (See p. 108 for mild interest as an excuse for power.)

The effect of playing with relative height can be illustrated by the following A+B+B contour in which the height of the first B is modified:

```
    Díd                              that!
                            thréw
                       t
        you  sée  the way he
```

With *see* at a relatively low pitch, and drawled, the speaker is probably overcome with awe—the drawling of *threw* at high pitch shows the speaker's amazement at the exploit, and we interpret the lower *see*— the recognition of the exploit—as the more hushed emotion. But *see* can be raised as much as desired, and the emotion shifts from awe to excitement.

It is tempting to object at this point that "mere emotion" does not deserve so much attention in a discussion of intonation patterns, but that is really beside the mark. Intonation is all emotion of some degree or other, and it is not difficult to find examples in which the conversational relevance of an utterance depends on whether it is keyed up or down emotionally. For example, the B+C contour with monotone is very common in utterances intended to calm or reassure, and it may be used at any pitch for that purpose. But it is more appropriate to say

```
        Thére,
            thére!
```

at high pitch to quiet a child, or to soothe someone assailed by a sudden emotion, or a "withdrawing" emotion such as grief, and on the other hand to say it at low pitch when directed toward a more aggressive emotion such as anger or impatience. In the one, the speaker implies something like 'Don't fret—I'm concerned for your sake'; in the other, 'Don't fret—it's not worth getting all that worked up about.'

The Linking of Profiles: Sandhi

The linking problem has two aspects: how and whether. The how concerns the SANDHI devices that are used to physically link one profile to another within a single contour. The whether problem concerns, for example, the contrast between two contours each consisting of one profile and a single contour consisting of two: how does one tell when a given stretch is closely enough tied together to be regarded as a single contour?

Sandhi is an especially difficult problem with intonation because one looks to some sign of 'incompletion' to cement the bond between a preceding profile and a following one, and yet the signs of incompletion are independently meaningful when they occur at the end of many utterances that we would like to regard as linguistically "complete" though they are affectively "incomplete." This dilemma was posed earlier when we looked at the close similarity between a sentence like

and a question-response pair like

We saw that in the thematic organization of a sentence the theme in a sense "posed the question" of what the sentence was about, and the rheme told what was to be told about it, that is, answered it. It is hardly an accident that the intonations are the same.

In this example the rising pitch is the sign of incompletion. From the standpoint of the tension-relaxation opposition, the speaker is not "at rest" about the matter; therefore the matter itself is not "at rest." From the perspective of the up-down metaphor, it is "up to" someone to carry on—to the speaker himself in the conditional sentence, to the hearer in the question-response pair. The incompletion is the same, whether it occurs within a B+A contour like the first example or the succession of B (contour with only a single profile) followed by A in the second. It is difficult to know, on intonational criteria alone, which extended function the incompletion has.

But if we assume that incompletion is a necessary (though not suffi- cient) condition of linkage, then we can ask in what way, intona- tionally, the incompletion is manifested. This question is more easily approached from the opposite direction: when do we have "comple- tion"? The answer, if our earlier discussion of finality (pp. 146–47, 216–17) is correct, is that a drop to very low pitch, especially creak, without a succeeding rise, signifies conclusion or finality. Any termi- nal higher pitch, whether in the form of a rise or a truncated fall, can be *used* as an indicator of contour-internal sandhi. So for example an A+A contour:

$$\text{They were} \quad \text{ful}_{\text{ly}} \quad {}^{\text{á}\text{w}} \quad {}^{\text{tí}} \quad {}^{\text{r}}\text{e}_{\text{d.}}$$

Here the pitch on -*ly* is higher than the terminal pitch. Or an AC+A or a C+A:

$$\text{They were} \quad \text{full}^{\text{y}} \quad {}^{\text{á}\text{w}} \quad {}^{\text{tí}} \quad {}^{\text{r}}\text{e}_{\text{d.}} \qquad \text{Just} \quad \text{léave it}^{\text{a}} \quad {}^{1\text{ó}} \quad {}^{\text{n}}\text{e}_{\text{.}}$$

Here the characteristic rise at the end of the AC and the C provides the link. Probably the most frequent linkup is between a B and any other following profile, since B by definition does not contain any downmotion steeper than a tilt, and generally rises. Example of B+A and of B+B+A:

$$\text{To} \, \text{mór}\text{ro}^{\text{w}} \quad \text{is} \quad \text{Thúrs} \quad \text{da}_{\text{y.}} \qquad \text{To}\text{mór}\text{ro}^{\text{w}} \, \text{I'm stáying} \quad \text{h}\text{ó}_{\text{m}}\text{e}_{\text{.}}$$

Though these higher pitches are an aid to internal linkage, they are not indispensable to it. Indeed they could not be, given the figurative extensions of 'finality,' which can mean either the less conclusive 'no need to say more' or the more conclusive 'nothing more will be said.' In the former case one gets those very categorical utterances that con- tain multiple A profiles with deep falls, e.g.

$$\text{Yés,} \quad \text{déed} \qquad \text{in} \quad \text{y!}$$

where *indeed* is expanded for the same purpose of positive speaking that motivates the two A's. The utterance can have both *in-* and -*y* at creak. Among the examples cited in Chapter 6 (pp. 84–85) were a number having multiple A profiles on single words. It would be possible for the tails of the non-final A's to drop to creak—obviously for the effect of positive speaking and not to separate the word into two halves. "Terminal" falls are perfectly normal before profiles that the speaker intends to be linked to what precedes.

Since lack of deep fall is no very safe guide to intonational sandhi, it must be that other devices are leaned on at the same time, very likely a complex of them. Among such incompletion markers are undoubtedly timing, absence of pause, gesture, syntactic or morphological cohesion, and stereotyping.

Timing is important in two ways. First, at points where speakers intend a break, their utterance—like an expended clock—"runs down." There is a pitch correlate of this as well: more successive profiles within a contour show a falling tangent to their peaks than show a rising one, and the rise on the tangent is like the terminal rise—it more often links up than not. Second, timing is the basis of rhythm, and the scope of a rhythmic pattern tends to coincide with the scope of a contour. We have already seen this in the terraced monotone utterances of Chapter 10, but it is also true of the more prosaic utterances discussed earlier (Chapter 5).

Pause is the most obvious signal of a break, but lack of pause, particularly for speakers who have a huddled manner of speaking, is not a safe indication of linkage. Nor is its presence a safe indication of separation. We even find instances of built-in, more or less stereotyped pauses within what would probably be felt as a single contour. The speaker gives strong signs of intending to continue, and is allowed to hold the floor. An example is the exclamations and hesitation sounds that are given a B profile, e.g. the following B+AC . . . that might be finished in a number of ways:

$$\text{We}^{11\cdots} \quad \text{thí}$$
$$\text{I} \quad \text{ink} \cdots$$

This would probably be overlaid with continuation gestures, e.g. the tensing of the lips that suggests readiness to go on speaking, knit eyebrows to suggest concentration and thus justify hesitating, perhaps an ingressive click right after *well*, etc.

Syntactic and morphological cohesion are probably what strike us as the clearest signs of linking. A word such as

$$\text{Tín} \quad \text{lá}$$
$$\text{áb}$$
$$\text{tin} \quad \text{u}$$
$$\text{tion.}$$

despite its three A profiles, is one word, and its intonation comprises a single contour. Similarly

$$\text{Búy}^{\text{it}} \quad \text{or I'll shóot}$$
$$\text{you.}$$

with its B+A, covered by a single contour because it is a single sentence. (The relative dependency of the "imperative" *buy it* is evident in the B profile, which makes it more or less equivalent to a conditional clause—'If you don't buy it I'll shoot you'; a genuine command is more apt to have an A profile.) But again, no noncircular definition of a sentence is any guarantee of contour unity. For example, most grammarians regard alternative questions as unitary sentences and some even prescribe intonations for them, but the same form and the same intonation can be found in clearly disjoined sentences when a following alternative occurs as an afterthought:

$$\text{Going}^{\text{nów?...}} \quad \text{or (are you) cóming along lá}$$
$$\text{ter?}$$

The uncertainty of "being expressed as a single sentence" to serve as a criterion of single-contourhood is evident in the disjunctures that speakers use to make sure of being understood when their "sentences" are heavily packed with information, for example in the following multiple wh question:

$$\text{The} \quad \text{tion}^{\text{qués}} \quad \text{how} \quad \text{would} \quad {}^{\text{how}} \quad \text{ny of us} \quad \text{to} \longrightarrow$$

$$\text{chíeve} \quad {}^{\text{bí}}$$
$$\text{a} \quad \text{our am tion.}$$

—a succession of A, AC, AC, AC, AC, A, A—however they may be organized into contours. At a faster pace the sequence could be managed in two contours, the break coming after *is*.

Stereotyping may be broad or narrow. Narrow stereotypes are those individual locutions that bring together what might otherwise be disparate profiles and—by sheer repetition in daily usage—cement them. The word *yes* as a separate response generally takes an A profile; its synonym *uh-huh* generally takes a B. But the two are commonly brought together as *Yes, uh-huh*, as a friendly affirmation—not as abrupt as *yes* alone nor as tentative as *uh-huh* alone. Such an A+B

succession is less cohesive intonationally than B+A, but the stereotyping holds the profiles together. (The reverse order, *M-hm, yes*, is
also stereotyped, but its B+A is cohesive in any case.)

Broad stereotyping is found with constructions that habitually co-
here even though separately they are in some restricted sense grammatically complete. An example of what such a thing is not would be
two sentences connected with *and* and brought under a single contour, e.g.

$$\text{I've}^{\text{tóld}\ \text{you and I've}}$$
$$^{t\acute{o}}l_d$$
$$\text{you.}$$

'I've told you repeatedly'—the speaker here is improvising the connection that makes the two sentences bear a single contour.

An example of what a broad stereotype *is* would be a sentence with
a tag, e.g.

$$\text{You}^{\text{líke}}\quad \text{it,}\quad _{\text{don't}}\,y^{\text{ou?}}$$

Both parts contain a subject and a verb, but in the second part the
subject and verb are coreferential with those of the first part, and
the intonational connection is so tight that we cannot even be sure of
having two profiles A+C—it may be a single AC, equivalent to

$$\text{You}^{\text{líke}}\quad _{\text{i}}t^{(?)}$$

in which the low pitch and following rise are taken by the unaccented
pronoun *it*, not by the tag *don't you*. For some purposes the two utterances are equivalent (in persuasion, for example)—the point will
be returned to later in this section. Furthermore, tags are often intonationally flat, without accent, and so cannot constitute a separate
profile:

$$\text{It's}\ ^{\text{quíte}}\ ^{\text{ap}}{}^{\text{pár}}{}_{\text{ent,}}\ \text{wouldn't you say?}$$

I think, as such things go, speaking confidentially, don't you know, etc. are
tags that may occupy such a terminal level, at or barely above creak.
On the other hand, a tag may be given an A or B profile of its own,
and is then a possible candidate for a separate contour, especially

(with B) if a pause intervenes and (with A) in addition to a pause there
is a change of addressee:

```
     líke            yóu?        crá
You          dón't         He's              ís
     it...                       zy...,    n't he, Gloria?
```

The question of unity or separation is not just that of how much
otherwise apparently separate material can be brought under one
contour, but also involves the splitting up of contours. A speaker who
would ordinarily say

```
            éa
     It's                    trý·
        sy once you
```

using an A+B contour, may, for dramatic effect, separate the two
halves, putting a sizable pause after *easy*. The "qualification as afterthought" may be made verbally more explicit by adding the tag *that is*:

```
                 trý, that is·
         Once you
```

The following has a similar qualification as afterthought with a B+B
contour after the A:

```
            dó
What were you                                             léft?
        ing                    áll the others had
            there,  after
```

Given the clear intention of the speaker to express the wh question
with an A profile, the only way to bring all this material into one contour would be either to treat the *after* clause as an unaccented tail, at
low level pitch after *there*, or to add low-pitched A's:

```
            dó
What were you
            ing                 áll   óth      lé
                there,  after   the   ers had  ft?
```

The original A+B+B is a sort of blend: 'What were you doing there?—
Should you have been there after all the others had left?'

It would be impossible at the present stage of our knowledge to
catalog the stereotypes, narrow and broad, that make up our stock of
structural and intonational clichés. Two more examples, to show how
varied they can be. The first is a common treatment of *at all* with separate A profiles on each word, to add great emphasis to a negative
statement:

```
                    it
             li̇ke      áa
    I don't          t ál
                          1.
```

(The separation of *at* and *all* is also manifested in the unreleased [t], unlike that of the usual *a-tall*.) The second uses an affirmative expression (*sure, naturally, yes, of course*) to confirm something immediately preceding that ends with a rising tail, e.g. the example on page 258 above. The speaker deliberately leaves *difficult* in suspense to have it resolved with *sure*, and despite the pause the utterance is felt as a unit.

Sandhi is clearly a multichannel process, something hardly amenable to precise analysis. The speaker applies not a formula but a recipe. Whether two profiles or permutations of profiles fall under one contour or more comes down ultimately to the speaker's intent, and any generalizations we can make are statistical at best.

Overlap and Ambiguity

Returning to the strictly intonational sandhi of non-fall, we need to review the ways in which it is carried out, and the consequences for distinguishing between those frequently ambiguous pitch movements that can be seen as one or as more than one contour, or—at the profile level—as a single complex profile rather than a combination of profiles.

The description of Profile A recognized two forms of the characteristic falling pitch: within the accented syllable and between that syllable and the next. When the latter choice is made, the result is necessarily a continuation into the next profile if the element taking the low pitch is syntactically unified with what follows—the two profiles are part of a single contour. Take an example like the following:

```
         knów              mèan
    I         you díᵈn't
                        that.
```

This is an A+A+A contour (or A+A if the accent on *did* is suppressed). The first A is linked to the second by the lack of any fall on *know*; the A fall occurs between *know* and *you*. The second is linked to the third in the same way—no fall within *did*, but a fall between *did* and *n't*. In both cases the accent "needs" the lower-pitched following syllable and is therefore tightly linked to what comes next.[6] This manner of treating the A's has its own bearing on the unity of the contour, but is itself a consequence of another factor that also has a bearing, namely, timing, as reflected in the completion of the pronunciation of *know* before the drop in pitch has time to occur—the result of a relatively fast pace. Further, the treatment of the unaccented syllables shows them in what Pike calls "double function": the word *you* is a foil to both the preceding *know* and the following *did*, and *n't* similarly belongs to both *did* and *mean*.

Where purely intonational sandhi fails and other factors must be relied upon is in the other kind of drop, within the accented syllable. If we hear

$$\text{knó} \qquad\qquad \text{méan}$$
$$\text{I}$$
$$\text{w you } \text{díd}_{\text{n't}} \qquad \text{that.}$$

with the drop within *know* extending to creak, the pitch cues are insufficient to distinguish this utterance from *I know. You didn't mean that.* Now it is mainly the timing that shows the utterance to be a single contour. The low drop in *know* is not for 'finality' in the disjoining sense but in the positive-speaking sense.

A foretaste of the sandhi problems affecting such distinctions as that between AC and A+C was given in Chapter 8 (pp. 182–83, 191–93). That there is a genuine ambiguity here can be shown by comparing two such utterances as

$$\text{there,} \qquad\qquad\qquad\qquad \text{want,}$$
$$\text{(1) Don't leave}^{\text{it}} \qquad\qquad \text{(2) What do you}$$
$$\text{John.} \qquad\qquad\qquad\qquad \text{John?}$$

which have identical pitch sequences and yet, without the vocative, would almost certainly differ:

$$\text{thé} \qquad\qquad\qquad\qquad \text{wá}$$
$$\text{(3) Dón't leave}^{\text{it}} \qquad\qquad \text{(4) Whát do you}$$
$$\text{re.} \qquad\qquad\qquad\qquad \text{nt?}$$

—(3) is B+AC, (4) is B+A.[7] The forms with the vocative, (1) and (2), then appear to be B+AC and B+A+C. Why the difference? It is not in the function of the vocative syllable relative to accented *there* and *want*, since in both instances the low-pitched syllable is needed to realize the drop that those accents require. The difference is that the vocative in (1) also realizes the terminal rise of the AC profile, whereas in (2), since A has no terminal rise, the fact that *John* does rise indicates a separate profile C. The word *John* is in double function, forming a profile in its own right and also providing the drop for the preceding A.[8]

It would be equally correct to express the downmotion of the A in (2) using a bare hook on *want*, or bringing *want* all the way down:

(2a) Whát do you wánt,
Jóhn?

(2b) Whát do you wá
nt, Jóhn?

In all three cases, (2), (2a), and (2b), *John* constitutes a separate profile, thus differing from

(5) Whát do you wánt,
John?

with a low and flat or low and falling vocative, where *John* is only the tail of the A profile. It reveals itself as unaccented also by lower intensity: if the *fall* on *want* in (5) is realized as in (2b), with the whole downskip occurring on that syllable, *John* can be reduced virtually to a whisper, which is not possible with (2), (2a), or (2b)—the A maneuver has already been carried out, and *John* is not needed for it.

This line of reasoning does not claim that a rise is accented as such, but that (2) has a rise over and beyond the requirements of an A as exemplified by (4). In (1), the rise is not over and beyond what is required by AC, but is part and parcel of it, and *John* in (1), despite its rise, can be viewed as unaccented. This again can be seen by realizing the AC drop in (1) and the A drop in (2) fully on the words *there* and *want*: the intensity of the vocative can be drastically reduced in (1) but not in (2).

From the standpoint of sandhi, the significance of these examples is that a profile can be completed in the next profile—this is seen in (2), where the fall of the initial A is carried out by the drop to the following C. The comma is a grammatical convention and the intonation disregards it—this is true of (1) also, where the fall and subsequent rise are simply part of the AC profile, all of which would be manifested by the one word *there*, as in (3), if no vocative were present.

Two things complicate the picture and make it sometimes impossible to tell the difference between a single complex profile and a succession of profiles. One is the fact that a C profile is *intended* to play down an accent, thus blurring the difference between an accented and an unaccented syllable (this can be alleviated by resorting to other markers of accent, but pitch too often overrides them). This is what makes the accented C on *John* in (2) so much like the unaccented ending, on *John*, of the AC in (1). The other is the fact that the low pitch of an AC (or a CAC) tends to gravitate toward the strongest syllable in the tail, and this increases the resemblance to a C. Consider the following:

dón't think we need to hire an él
(6) I   evator operator.

The AC has its lowest pitch on *op-*, the strongest syllable. The tail could also have the shapes

(7) él   (8) él

evator operator.   evator oper ator.

taking advantage of the two other full syllables -*va*- and -*a*- for the trough. Since we know from the nature of the text that there is no accented syllable after *el*-, we are free to adjust the trough and rise at will. The more syllables there are to the right, of course, the greater the tension, but there is no ambiguity between one profile and another.

The uncertainty comes when the tail is occupied by an element that potentially carries an accent, such as the vocatives we have been considering. Take a vocative such as *son of a gun*, which can be stressed *són of a gún* or *són of a gun* and thus offers two candidates, *son* and *gun*, for the trough of an AC. If *old* is added, we get a third:

there,
(9) Don't leave it   you old son of a gun!

(10) ...you old son of a gun!   (11) ...You old son of a gun!

Given other markers of accent, the vocative may be regarded as constituting a separate profile, the AC becoming AC+C or, in the case of (11), AC+B. In (11) it would be as if the speaker were not merely calling the addressee a son of a gun, but announcing the fact that he is one. That would become even more apparent if the tail were given a low-pitched AC, repeating the main contour on a smaller scale:

(12) ...you old són of a gun.

Though it was stated above that the *John* of (1) can be viewed as unaccented, as merely carrying out the last part of the AC maneuver, if as has just been claimed there may be overlapping sandhi in the case of (10) and (11), with the extra profile riding on the tail of the AC, why might not (1) represent overlapping sandhi as well, with a final C overlapping a prior AC, thus yielding not AC but AC+C—in which case *John* in (1) would be accented? Except for the subdued effect of the C accent on *John*, which makes an intended accent difficult to detect, the pitch sequences would allow either interpretation. Besides, the extra C could be separated from the AC without seeming to cause much change, as in

```
                            thé
(13) Dón't leave it
                      rᵉ, Jóhn.
```

A better example to test this ambiguity is one in which the down-up pitch turn is taken not by a vocative but by something that can more readily be accented because of its semantic content. Take the following responses to the question *Aren't you afraid that John will get violent?*

```
(14) Jóhn
                    (AC)
        wouldnᵗ.
```

```
(15) Jóhn
      Wouldn't                      (AC+C)
               húrt anybody!
```

```
(16) Jóhn
        wouldnᵗ húrt anybody!       (AC+B)
```

Whereas (14) could scarcely be thought to accent the intonational trough that is occupied by a mere auxiliary (which does little more than repeat the *will* of the question), (15) and (16) are different: *hurt* is sufficiently new to the context to be entitled to an accent, and other accent features can readily be added.

The alternative to sandhi overlap, with AC realized by the entire contour and C or B encapsulated in it, is a reduction to A+C, which would be adequate to describe the pitch movements. (As A+B could also handle AC+B.) But the difficulty with this is that the typical 'finality' of A is lacking. If (15) is reversed, we do not get C+A but C+AC:

```
                anybody? Jóhn
(17) Húrt                    wouldnᵗ.
```

—not exactly a single contour but preserving the force of the original. Assuming the overlap seems to be the better solution.[9]

To show the gradience between simple AC and AC+C we can start with an AC on a monosyllable and gradually add words to the point that a C profile is apt to develop. The following are all appropriate continuations of *Well, as for correcting these proofs it's bad enough if I have to impose on Morgenstern—I certainly wouldn't*

            yo   you

(1) force   (2) force

             u u·   to/.

           you   you

(3) force   to   (4) force   to do

                do it·   anything·

           you

(5) force   to do anything you didn't want to

                                          do/

The trough in (5) can be taken just as readily by the first *do*, by *an-*, or by *want* (and any of these, by coming after the trough, could as readily establish a B rather than a C). The likeliest possibility for AC+C rather than simple AC would be with *want* at the trough—it comes closest to being a new idea and most readily takes other markers of accent.[10]

Though the ambiguities described here are a reality within the system, it is also a reality that the problem is due in part at least to the lack of *sufficient* pitch marking, not to the absence of pitch marking altogether. That is, with sufficient contrast in pitch movement it is possible to have an unambiguous A+C or AC+C. For this purpose it is necessary that the tail of the A end at a relatively high pitch and be followed by a relatively sharp jump down to the trough of the C. The utterance

               An

             ybody but John·

with its almost negligible jump to the lowest pitch is ambiguous like the foregoing examples. It could (1) serve as a response to *Who do you want for this job?*, where *John* is actually contrastive and we would want to recognize a separate C profile. Or (2) it could be a surprised question in response to the other speaker's already having answered *Anybody but John*, to express astonishment that just *any* other person would do—*John* is now repeated and readily unaccented, and the resulting AC could be executed just as appropriately on the word *anybody* alone:

             An

              ybody?!

But now if we widen the pitch jump (most easily illustrated with a level A tail),

```
An
    ybody but
              Joh
                 n•
```

the result is appropriate to (1) but not to (2). (If attempted for the latter the astonishment would attach to *John* as much as to *any*—the speaker would be repeating what he had just heard with all its original emphases.)

It is not necessary that the utterance be a question in order to get a clear C in these circumstances. In response to *How do you feel?* one may say

```
Háp
    pier than I could have believed
                                        ible•
                                   póss
```

where the terminal rise leaves the matter open, perhaps to suggest 'ineffability.' The tail of the A may downtilt slightly, but the C is unambiguous as long as the downskip remains clear. If the tail uptilts (most likely after a deeper drop to -*pier*) the contour is better analyzed as AC+C than as A+C.

Any attempt to analyze intonation in terms of morphology—with unitary chunks that succeed one another in time, whatever the microanalysis of each chunk may be in terms of levels, features, shapes, etc.—must at some point face the problem of sandhi. The trick is not to run aground on it, in trying to navigate the essential fluidity of the pitch stream. For our system of pitch accents and profiles, the AC+C ambiguity is a sandbar, and one has to inquire whether it is real or an artifact of the analysis: could it be avoided by some other approach? As long as we admit the existence of a reverse accent, one that tries to do two opposite things at once, there is reason to believe that the problem is not self-generated but inheres in the nature of that C profile, which compels us sometimes to fall back on other markers of accent than pitch. When the time comes that we can say with certainty that the C profile is resisted by tone languages and causes similar complications there if it is found at all, the sandhi problem in English may seem small by comparison.

12. Contours in Particular

To make a full catalog of contours and their meanings would be impossible, first because there is no upper limit to the *number* of profiles a contour may embrace, second because of the intonational variation within contours which gradiently alters some aspects of their meaning, and third because of the partial stereotyping that results when a given contour reacts with a given context (whether verbal or situational) and yields apparently variable meanings attached to a single contour. The latter two problems can be illustrated by the sentence *I have an idea* with a B+A contour having different slopes (compare *They melt in your mouth*, p. 25).

$$
\text{(1) I} \quad \overset{\text{háve an i}}{} \underset{\text{a.}}{\text{dé}} \qquad \text{(2) I} \quad \overset{\text{háve an i}^{\text{dé}}}{} \underset{\text{a.}}{}
$$

The first realizes the tail of the B with a downtilt, the second with an uptilt. Imagine the following contexts:

(a) The example answers the question *What makes you think you are brighter than the others?*

(b) The example comes out of the blue—the speaker is poised to tell what the idea is.

We would probably have little difficulty in attaching (1) to (b) and (2) to (a), and we might conclude that (1) is an 'announcing' intonation and (2) is an 'explaining' one.

But suppose we force the opposite match—what would (1) suggest if it were used for (a) and (2) if for (b)? The match is not impossible, but the overtones would shift radically. As an answer to (a), (1) would sound overly assured—the speaker perhaps feels that the fact is too obvious to need stating. As for (2), if it were used to spring an announcement out of the blue it would sound as if the speaker could not wait to express the brilliant thought that has just occurred to him.

There is no change in the intonation, but the background has shifted and the impression on the hearer is radically changed. If (1) and (2) are interchangeable with relation to (a) and (b), it cannot be claimed that the basic meaning of the B+A contour in (1) is 'announcement' whereas (2) is 'explanation.' We may want to note that the (1) type is highly *frequent* in announcements and the (2) in explanations and answers to questions, but the fundamental meaning of the two shapes must be something more abstract. As we saw in earlier chapters, the overall downmoving pitch in (1) is a movement toward relaxation, conclusion, and, by extension, positiveness. The upward slope in (2) is the opposite: it shows tension, arousal, hence unexpectedness, appeal. When making an announcement a speaker initiates a conversation and takes command of the floor; it is natural then to use an intonation that shows a degree of authority. If such an intonation is used to answer a question, as it can be, the authoritativeness is the same but under the circumstances it may sound presumptuous—the hearer probably thinks that you ought instead to be deferring to his willingness to accept your answer and therefore ought to show more concern. (A different culture might have different expectations, in which case the authoritativeness of the reply might be normal. This is in fact the case with answers to questions in Spanish.) On the other hand, when (2) is used as an announcement, the high tension suggests that the speaker has been carried away.

With this difference on the tension-relaxation axis, what justification is there for saying that we are here dealing with one and the same contour? The answer should be clear from previous discussion. Both (1) and (2) start and end with the same profiles, and the A profile at the end makes the word *idea* stand out—as something important, perhaps something new—in the same way in both. The strongest basis for similarity and therefore for recognizing a single category is the treatment of the accented syllables. Furthermore, we have just seen that the two examples *can* be interchanged, though with altered overtones. With a change in the actual profiles, on the other hand, resulting in different contours, the result may approach unacceptability— for instance, if a B or a C profile were substituted in the announcement:

The first would be totally inappropriate, and the second, while not inappropriate if it occurred in the middle of a conversation, would be out of place at the start of one. And finally, examples (1) and (2) are only *gradiently* different and we can balance the difference—and neutralize the contrast—by bringing the two slopes closer together. If the tail of the B is made level and the start of the A is at the same pitch or only slightly above, the utterance is about equally suited to either (a) or (b):

```
  háve an idé
I
```

           a.

The prime importance of the profiles, over and above the differences that can be attributed to the gradient phenomena just described, can be seen by comparing two utterances as much alike as the following:

```
                  Jóhn who got ar
      Wásn't it
                            résted?
```

```
              Jóhn
      Wásn't it    who got ar
                         résted?
```

The first is B+B+C, with accents on *was-*, *John*, and *-rest-*. The second is B+A+C, with accents on the same syllables. The difference between them is crucial, for the first tells us that John has probably been spoken of already and the new fact is his arrest, while the second implies that arrest has already been spoken of and the new information is the identity of the arrestee. The meanings conveyed by the profiles with their distinctive accents take precedence.

The justification for expressing contours as combinations of profiles, then, is that it is the most practical way of clustering the patterns in terms of the meanings that count the most. Once that is accomplished, the nuancing and the situational stereotyping (announcing, question-answering, and the like) can be described. But to start with the latter is to be caught in a morass. There have been many such attempts, but they have ended in the same failure described by Gantzel (1967: 37): "subjects were asked to identify the meanings of a number of pitch patterns; their answers were so diverse that we gave up hope of classifying them."[1]

In what follows, the primary grouping of the contours will be by the profile that comes last, that being the one that weighs most heavily in the overall impression. As an illustration of the weight of the final profile, take the following in which an A changes places with a C:

```
                  hél                    could
      It                            It
          cóuldn't be                      n't be
                                              hélped.
                 ped.
```

For the most part one-profile contours will be disregarded, as their meanings have already been discussed in the chapter on profiles. Also, the question of where a contour ends is left open, because there is no precise way to determine it. Syntactic considerations enter, especially with compound or complex versus simple sentences. Is the example

<pre>
        búy   súre
I'll
        them I as   you.
</pre>

one A+A contour as a sentence, or two A contours as a succession of clauses? If we decide for the latter, then we may need to justify a different treatment for the semantically similar

<pre>
        búy   súr
I'll
        them as   edly.
</pre>

Syntactic junctures are also a factor. A succession of A's is more like a succession of separate contours regardless of the syntax, whereas a B or an AC followed by another profile is more like a single contour even when there is a clause break, because one of the functions of the terminal rise in those profiles is to suggest 'more to come,' which can be interpreted as a clausal linking under a single contour. As the effects of combining profiles are much the same within clauses and between them, the question of contour extent will be left to the indeterminate notion of what constitutes a "single utterance."

Contours Ending in A

... B+A

The multi-profile contours ending in A, especially in the simplest form B+A, are probably the most frequent set in English as well as in most if not all other Western languages. This set is even commoner in those languages than in English for some purposes where in English it has to compete with AC+A. Delattre (1965: 25) traces the curves for *The workmen from Boston were leaving* and similar sentences in German, Spanish, and French (see Fig. 1). His English contour is plainly AC+AC+A, while that of the three other languages is B+B+A. (The English could as easily, especially in a longer, noncitation context, use the same B+B+A.)

The reason for the high frequency can be found in the basic incompleteness of the B profile: it is the one that most often moves up and stays up, and that never has any steeper downmotion than a downtilt.

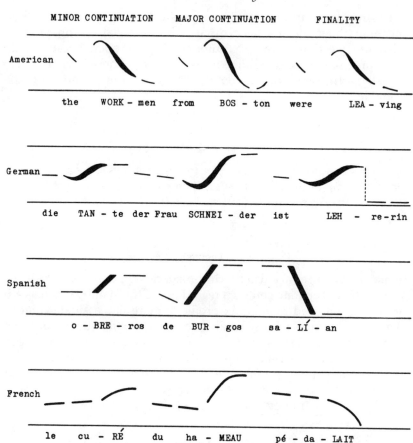

Fig. 1. Comparative contours. From Pierre Delattre, *Comparing the Phonetic Features of English, German, Spanish, and French* (Heidelberg: Julius Gross, 1965), p. 25.

So except when it is used terminally to "leave something up in the air," it is a leaner, and it most often leans on A. The leaning is evident in both form and function—the former in the sandhi between the profiles, the accented syllable of the A often forming part of the tail of the B. For example in

úse mí

Then   n_{e.}

in which the B covers only one syllable, it is marked as B by the fact that *mine* starts at the same pitch, carrying the B on just as an unaccented syllable in the same position would, e.g.

```
          úsing mí
     By           nₑ.
```

In the first example a contrasting A+A contour would require a drop within the syllable *use*, but in the second example the *-ing* would take the drop:

```
       ú   mí              ús    mí
          s                    iₙg
  Then    e          By
       nₑ.                   nₑ.
```

In function, the leaning tendency suits the B ideally for the thematic organization of sentences that are intended to relate something about something, for, as we saw earlier (pp. 46–47), the theme announces the topic of the sentence, "asks the question," which the rheme then answers. More broadly, the part of the sentence that falls under B is distinguished by not doing what the A part does, namely, bring forward the "point" of the sentence, which is often the conveying of new information. The B part tends to be predictable (see pp. 166–68). It may be no more than an annunciatory formula, as with *well* and *you know* in *Well, yes*, or *You know, I like it*; or it may quite literally repeat and tie in with what has just been mentioned, e.g. the answer to the question *If anybody asks where you've been, what'll I say?*

```
                              béen,
  If  ánybody asks where I've       just say I've been a
                                                      wáy.
```

Here the *if* clause is repeated, and is a B+B in a B+B+A contour. Physically, B is ground to A's figure (it provides the "up" from which A can come down), and semantically it is *back*ground to A's content.

It was noted in Chapter 8 (p. 169) that the height of the B relative to the A was not a defining characteristic of the B profile: it may be higher, the same, or lower than the start of the A. One may say either of the following,

```
     Démocratic                              Pár
                 Pár         Démocratic
  The                   The
              tᵧ.                         tᵧ.
```

and still have a B profile on *Democratic*. The contrast comes in a sentence like

```
     Démocratic Pár                              pár
  The                   is nót a véᵧ démₒcrátᵢc
              tᵧ                              tᵧ.
```

where the A+A segment on the second *democratic* is used contrastively rather than as part of a name.

At the same time, relative height is a factor in suiting the B profile to certain more or less stereotyped situations and contexts. Having the B higher than the start of the A produces, on top of its more or less grammaticized 'incompleteness' function, a kind of synthesizing effect. This makes it suitable for routine combinations, some of which were noted in Chapter 8 (pp. 166–78). Included are:

1. Frozen expressions (these, not being a motive for much excitement, usually have a level tail on the B):

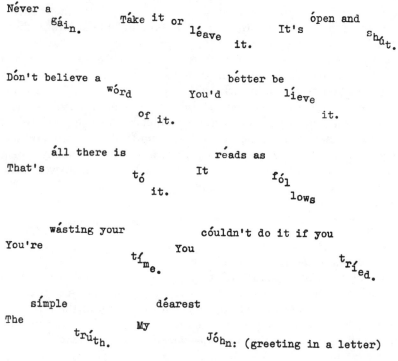

2. Compounds, including numerals, dates, titles, etc. (see Bolinger 1965: 57–66):

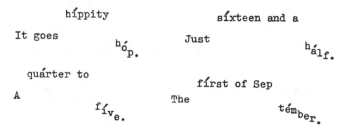

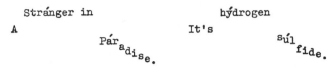

Here also belong quantifying and intensifying expressions that are attached to longer utterances, expressions such as *no end, time and again, all day long*, etc.:

$$n^{o}$$
They kidded us
(A+B+A)
$$e_{nd.}$$

In some of these the B profile interacts with the backshifting of accent noted in Chapter 5 (pp. 70–71) in relation to rhythm. The backshifting was one device for compacting a phrase by putting an accent at either end: *óbscene pláy, cómprehensive tést*. By fitting this to the B+A contour, the speaker achieves a double synthesis. The example with *sixteen* above has the B accent on *six-* despite the fact that the regular position for the stress is on *-teen*, and also despite the fact that no rhythmic clash would result in this instance if *-teen* were given the accent:

téen and a
*Just six
$$^{h}\acute{a}l_{f.}$$

—there are syllables to spare. (An A profile in this case would more readily allow either syllable of *sixteen* to be accented, e.g.

síx   téen   há
Just   teen and a ^{há} Just six   and a
$$1_{f.}$$ $$1_{f.}$$

but would be used in some sort of contrastive context, such as *How many have you got, eighteen and a quarter? — No, . . .* for the first with *síxteen*, or *How many have you got, sixteen and two-thirds? — No, . . .* for the second with *sixtéen.*) The backshifted accent and the B profile make a perfect combination for synthesizing the compound. Combinations of given name and surname behave similarly:

náme   Álexan   Smí
His   was   der
$$t_{h.}$$

(The B is established with the three level syllables *Alexan-*; *-der* could remain at the same level for higher tension.) Except in very deliberate speech (perhaps to correct someone) we would not say

```
                        án
                              Smí
           *was Alex  der      t
                                h.
```

even though no rhythmic clash would result from preserving the
regular stress of *Aléxánder*. Nor would we say

```
                       Ál
                              Smí
          *was     exander     t
                                h.
```

with A+A: the backshifting without the B is not enough.

3. Phrases with a high degree of fusion owing to nonrestriction or
redundancy—for example, noun or verb phrases with preposed nonrestrictive modifiers, or verb-plus-object phrases in which the nature
of the object makes the identity of the verb more or less predictable:

```
        bróad Pa                      Áncient Ró
    The       cíf                  In         m
              i                               e.
               c.
```

```
        slówly crept in                héartily des
    They             sí         I               pí
                       d                          se
                        e.                          them.
```

```
        bróke the                ópened the
    He           sé              lét          (B+AC+B+A)
              a                     te
               l  and                 r.
```

We observe how unnatural these would be if the predictability were
absent, e.g. in *It happened in ancient Rome, not in modern Greece*, or in
the following as an answer to *What did he do next?*:

```
             súlted Re
    ?He in           béc        rán out the
                       c
                        a  and
                                       dó
                                         or.
```

Unless the speaker intended to *present* the action from the standpoint
of feeling rather than fact, he would use here a string of A's (or of A's
with intermediate AC's, depending on sandhi overlap):

```
        súl
                   béc        rán out        dó
    He in    ted Re                  the
                      c                          o
                       a  and                     r.
```

(The apparent B on *ran out* is actually an A with delayed fall, a sort
of blend.)[2] Other verb-noun combinations that would permit fusion
follow:

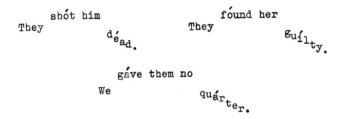

They shót him
           déad.

We
  gáve them no
              quárter.

They fóund her
              guílty.

4. Recurrent or customary actions:

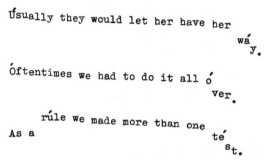

Úsually they would let her have her
                                   wáy.

Óftentimes we had to do it all ó
                                 ver.

            rúle we made more than one
As a   tést.

These tend to have downtilt. To show the contrast between recurrent action and less predictable action we can try substituting *an exception* for *a rule* in the last example. The tendency is to replace the B with A's or AC's:

          cép
As an ex
           tion we made móre than óne   (AC+A+A+A)
                                      st.
                                      té

5. Accented items that are presupposed or have been previously mentioned and therefore do not need to be singled out. Following *The house was completely blacked out* the speaker may say

        líght was left búrn
Not a   ing.

The backgrounding effect of the B in a B+A where the B is higher in pitch extends to the utterance as a whole, and we find this contour heavily represented in the background or setting of a narrative. Taking the last example and adding the further B+A

        síngle
not a
        óne.

we have a good setting for a story in which the thread of the narrative is picked up in the next sentence:

```
      súd           óut
when              of        dárk              cáme    lóud   pó
      denly,           the      ness,   there      a      re
                                                                 rt.
```
—all A's.

In all the preceding examples the A could start higher than the tail of the B, with a corresponding increase in tension. Thus

```
                        ón
            síngle
      Not a
                     e.
```

makes the fact more remarkable,

```
                  dé
         shót him
      They
                 ad.
```

is more exclamatory, or more surprised, or comes in answer to *How did they shoot him?*, or whatever. The higher A overbalances the B and may even blur the identity of the B by making the status of the unaccented vowels unclear. The difference between the last example and the same with A+A,

```
                  dé
         shót
      They      him
               ad.
```

is harder to hear than the difference between the following two, B+A and A+A respectively:

```
   shót him                    shót    dé
They                        They    him
        dé                                a
          ad.                             d.
```

More or less synthesized expressions such as the ones we have been examining are one major manifestation of utterance that does not single out individual items for attention and that aims at total effect rather than analytical significance—whose purpose, in short, is not primarily to inform. Compare the examples of B+A (or B+B+A), for ENHANCEMENT rather than information, in Chapter 8 (pp. 169–72). Another major area is where feeling, rather than fact, is uppermost. Profile B is suited for this because it maintains a relatively high pitch;

the terminal A of the B+A then comes as a marker of emphatic finality: 'That's that.' The contrast can be seen in expressions that are used
either for their logical content (A+A) or as oaths (B+A):

I'll be dám
    ⁿed if he díd
            n't.

I'll be dámned if he
                díd
                   n't.

The first may refer to true damnation,[3] the second is an oath.

When the B profile is realized on a single syllable, it automatically
picks up the extra length that is conferred when another full syllable
follows (as must happen, since the A follows immediately); but in exclamations such as the one just cited, the tendency is to exaggerate
both length and intensity, and one may readily get a separate B on an
otherwise reduced syllable, upgraded to full for the purpose (*tre-* of
tremendous, *of* of *of course*, below):

Tré
  méndous!

óf
  course!

Wéll,
   well!

dón't
You   sáy!

dámned
You're   ríght!

Gée
  whillikers!

The gestural accompaniment of raised eyebrows is as commonplace
on the B here as on B's that serve as yes-no questions. It connotes 'surprise' and all the shadings of 'remarkableness' that can be inferred,
which embrace a wide range of emotive utterance, including pleasure,

It's   wórking out
          béautifully.

They're   bétter than I ex
              pécted.

We   cán't complain at
        ál
        l.

heartfelt gratitude,

You   dón't know what this
              méans to me.

longing and pity,

                ónly I   póor old
    If   The
             cóuld.   féllow!

suspicion,

                        sómething be
            There's   hínd
                               all this.

wonderment,

    háven't seen him in   húndred to
  I   A   ón
                      yéars.   e!

       ácted   lóok at
   They   stránge   Would you   thá
               ly tonight.   t!

and imperiousness (often referred to as a "lofty" tone, which accords with the sustained high pitch of the B—the speaker is "on his high horse"),

                    éver to sée
      I don't want   You again.

             fúse to have anything to
      I re   dó with it.

             wíll if it's the last thing I
      I   dó.

             áll that it's
    And that's   wórth.

         mákes me
    It   síck.

vs. the literal

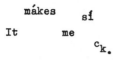

Clearly no one emotion governs these uses of B+A. Broadly, they seem to be a form of self-expression, speaker-dominant, leading not to answers that appeal for acceptance but to *comments* that the audience is expected to take at face value. Or not to take at all—B+A is the normal contour when one is talking to oneself:

```
         wónder if it's going to
   I                              rá
                                    in today.
```

—an A+A here might tempt an eavesdropper to suppose that the speaker is hallucinating, as it implies an addressee:

```
      wón
   I     der if it's going to  ráin
                                    tod
                                       ay.
```

By the same token it is the contour that is used most regularly for announcements (compare the announcing *I have an idea*, p. 274 above), commands, and wh questions where the speaker assumes the right-to-know:

```
Éverybody lis               góing to be a
              ten.  There's              méet
                                             ing tonight.

      gét yourself ó                How did they
Just              ver here.                       mán
                                                     age?
```

Also for exhortations. The following is remarkable for its suppression of long stretches of unaccented syllables after the A (that is, for the long A tails), which makes the sustained B's stand out more sharply:

```
          whó:le bús
It's the         iness of general education in the ⟶

                      Téachers should give ⟶
schools that I'm complaining about.

bóoks                                     pút the ⟶
     about historical events to their students--

means of knów
             ledge into their hands...
```

To see the difference between a comment and a straightforward answer, take a question like *What do you think of him?* If the response is A+A, nothing much is conveyed beyond the information and the speaker's confidence in its truth:

$$\text{He's a} \quad \overset{\text{bít}}{} \quad \text{too} \quad \overset{\text{sél}}{} \quad \text{f}_{\text{i}_{\text{sh}}}.$$

But if the response is B+A, there is some emotive content, perhaps disapproval:

$$\text{He's a} \quad \overset{\text{bít too sél}}{} \quad \text{f}_{\text{i}_{\text{sh}}}.$$

On the other hand, a positive emotive content is just as likely. One often hears interpositions in a discourse where the speaker uses a high-pitched B profile as an expression of approval that goes beyond logic—to use an A might suggest a doubt that needed to be rebutted, and no doubt is permitted; so with *and that's OK* in the following, where the speaker wants to clear himself of appearing to criticize. The sentence reads *From what I've observed I judge that you don't like tax accountants, and that's OK, I don't like them much myself, but . . . ,* with

$$\text{and} \quad \overset{\text{thát's oká}}{} \quad \underset{\text{y}}{}$$

at a much higher pitch than the context—and with eyebrows "up" too, and also possibly hands held up palm forward at about the level of the lower face.

An instance of B+A exploited in advertising to characterize a speaker was the radio advertisement of a Nevada casino in the 1981–82 and 1982–83 ski seasons. The speaker said

$$\underset{\text{a}}{\text{Í'm}} \quad \overset{\text{snów kind of}}{\underset{\text{gu}_{\text{y}}}{}}. \quad \overset{\text{Í}}{\underset{\text{just like to}}{}} \quad \overset{\text{fáll down in the}}{\underset{\text{sn}_{\text{ó}_{\text{w}}}}{}}.$$

—two instances of A+B+A, expressing how the speaker felt about himself. Had a desire to inform been uppermost, the B's would have been replaced with A's.

In all these examples, as in the earlier ones concerning which the same observation was made, the lower-pitched A could be raised above the B, for whatever purpose of greater tension: *He's a bit too selfish* would take on a tinge of sharper disapproval, *and that's OK* would affect a heartier concession, the education passage would become more impatient, *I refuse to have anything to do with it* would become more shrill, the commands would be more urgent, the wh questions more insistent, and so on. A person who responds to *How are you, Bill?* with *Fine, how are you?* and pitches *you* below *how are* would be heard as lacking in cordiality. If a speaker dismisses someone with

$$\text{Go\'od}\ \ _{\text{b\'y}}\ \ _{\text{e}}.$$

and the person fails to leave, the expression may be repeated with *bye* starting above *good*. Someone who asks

$$\text{Are you}\ \ ^{\text{s\'ure of your}}\ \ _{\text{gr\'o}}{}_{\text{und?}}$$

needs only a modicum of reassurance, but if *ground* starts higher than *your*, a stronger doubt has to be allayed. One who responds to the question

$$\text{Did you}\ \ ^{\text{d\'o as I}}\ \ ^{\text{t\'o}}{}_{\text{ld}}\ {}_{\text{you?}}$$

has less cause to fear a reprimand than if *told* started higher than *I*. One who says

$$\text{An}\ \ ^{\text{\'old}}\ \ _{\text{fr\'i}}{}^{\text{e}}{}_{\text{nd}}\ _{\text{came to visit me last night.}}$$

announces something of ordinary interest; but if *friend* starts higher than *old*, the interest is extraordinary. If the A is raised in

$$\text{Then}\ ^{\text{s\'o}}\ _{\text{b\'e}}{}_{\text{it}}.\quad ^{\text{N\'ot}}\ _{\text{b\'a}}{}_{\text{d.}}\quad ^{\text{W\'ell,}}\ _{\text{w\'e}}{}_{\text{ll.}}\quad ^{\text{N\'ice}}\ _{\text{d\'a}}{}_{\text{y.}}$$

the impact of the arousal is obvious. To say

$$\text{T\'op of the}\ _{\text{m\'orn}}{}_{\text{ing to you.}}$$

is less cordial than with *morn-* raised. And so on.

Relative height of the highest pitches is one source of variation within B+A, but of course there are others. Some examples have already been recorded of uptilt or downtilt in place of a level tail on the

B—the effects are predictable on the basis of gradually increasing or gradually decreasing tension. The shape of the A can be altered with the same effects as when A constitutes a contour by itself, e.g.

Dón't be so

sú
r

e.

with a slight rise-fall on the accented *sure*, makes the reproof more pointed without sacrificing the self-confidence that the lower pitch conveys—pitching the start of *sure* above *so* might sound excessively concerned. (Actually this rise-fall lies gradiently between an A and a CA profile.) Although exact intervals seldom play a crucial role in intonation, there is a special flavor to the semitone drop in something like

Óne at a tí

m
e.

where *time* starts a semitone below *a*. Whereas with a higher pitch on *time* one might be heard as encouraging the hearers to take their proper turns, and might even accompany the order with a smile, the semitone drop has a minor-mode effect and any smile would be forced; a wider drop could more readily be heard as relaxed, and the smile is again appropriate.

A further possibility is truncation of the A fall, with the expected effect of incompleteness, as in

éither John or
Jámes.
For

where *James* trails off well above creak; the hearer then expects something like *I don't care which* to follow, with a more conclusive ending. A question left up in the air in this fashion is apt to be rhetorical or to imply doubt or something beyond a desire for information, e.g.

Dóes it really mát   Whát fó

ter?   r?

—the latter example would more readily be used to suggest 'I don't think there's any use' than would the same utterance with a fall to creak. (Truncation may easily be confused with leveling off or fall-rise, which would produce AC rather than A—see pp. 182–83). The mood effects are quite different: *What for?* as B+AC would most likely be an echo question.)

Another possibility is embellishment of the B level or incline with additional non-pitch accents to produce a strongly keyed-up effect, as with the extended B tail and intensity-accented *said* in

```
Nót only what you said but what you dí
                                     dî
```

The change that makes the least difference is the simple addition of another B profile at the beginning, to give B+B+A or still more B's to the left. The multiple B's are most conspicuous in successions of coordinated elements, typically series, e.g.

```
             cárrots, péas,   tátoes,  and cául
They bought                po              iflower.
```

What makes the B's in this B+B+B+A stand out is the repetition of an identical pattern—same slopes, roughly same height, etc. In other constructions there is more variety of shape, as in

```
           sów,
As ye         so shall ye álso ré
                               a
                               P.
```

```
                                          (B+B+A)
           ínch         tákes a
Give him an      and he        mí
                                 l
                                  e.
```

To get an A on *inch* in this second example there would need to be a downturn at the end. The contrast between B and A or AC would be clear with a longer word such as *centimeter*:

```
           céntimeter...              cén
Give him a                Give him a     ti
                                           meter...
```

A succession of monosyllabic B's will tend to have intrasyllabic drop-backs because of the need to reset for height (compare pp. 153–54):

```
        ín óne éar     óut the ,
It goes            and        óth    (B+B+B+B+A)
                                 e
                                  r.
```

Though ascending monotones (see Chapter 10) are not as frequent as descending ones, we do find them, and by definition they involve B's, e.g. the B+B+A

```
                                        thá
        ányone belíeve a thing like
How could
                                        t?
```

(*How could* here is unaccented—we may assume that the question is more or less redundant. It would be just as normal, of course, for *how* to carry an A accent.)

The effect of interpolating a C is, predictably, one of imposing restraint—B+C+A, for example:

```
                                           dó
                    ,ót to de                 \
        We've    gó                            \
                       cíde what to             \
                                                 \
                                                  •
```

This bears comparison with C+C+A, for more restraint:

```
        We've                           dó
                          de               \
                 gót to                     \
                      cíde what to           \
                                              \
                                               •
```

The depths of these troughs may be reversed, though usually the second is the deeper. See below for . . . C+A.

. . . A+A

Where the B+A family represents a tight union between profiles, the A+A family represents a loose one. The drop in pitch that marks the A signifies separation of some kind when it precedes another A. It may be hard sometimes to tell whether a speaker intends a single contour or two—the latter being the case with afterthoughts, e.g.

```
            ópe        wí                        wá        drí
Then you                        I want some
            en it.    d                            te       To    n
                       e.                            r.            k.
```

The separation may be for sense or for power, as was noted in Chapter 8 (pp. 164–66). Multiple A's are the typical sequence for accents of power. Most of the instances in Chapter 6, pages 84–88, are contours of more than one A. When a speaker wants to make the usually B+A *Now take it easy!* especially forceful, he uses A+A; similarly if *He told me he would* is uttered as a protest, it is more emphatic as A+A:

```
            táke     éa                 tóld       wóu
    Now                          He
              it                        me he     1
                 sy!                              d.
```

Likewise exclamations—note the normally unaccented *it's* of the first example, here upgraded purely for power:

Ít's lú Gód míght ál mé Gré stú

   a lu! Al y! By l ans! at ff!

Stresses may be altered and more or less redundant words added to facilitate an extra accent, most potent when it results in A+A:

Í pós   Pós tíve   Whát éarth thá

m sible!   i ly!   on   is   t!

Yés déed   Dé lí   Hó díg

  in y!   e cious!   t gety!

      év   mán

How er did they age it?!

The wolf whistle is a stereotype of A+A, picked up from such exclamations when used to express appreciation, as in

sóme chick en!

(The drop from *some* here is realized by a dropback at the start of *chick-*. It could as readily—in the spoken version—be carried out on *some* alone, but that would be less effective in the whistle.)

Multiple A's—yielding medial A's—are also common in oratory for dramatic effect. (The contours generally contain B's as well, but the tightly connected B+A segments can be viewed, in effect, as single A's.) The lower the start of the A, the greater the finality and assurance—one may have A's that start so low that there is scarcely room for downmotion in the tail, as with the first and last A's (on *-cept* and *long*) in the following B+A+A+B+A:

Í just can't ac   á-a-an y   pútting up with a —→

   cépt...   one's...

   situation like that for

          lóng.

The medial A is a trick often encountered in advertising, e.g. the following 1958 radio ad for cigarets, with its A rather than B or AC on *finest*:

Máde from the Southland's fín mlld to bác

      est,   co.

The same trick in a television ad produced a ludicrous effect ('it leaves skin all over your body'). The first part is *Your very first Sardo bath is guaranteed to leave skin* and the end is

<pre>
    áll over your bó
                            frésh and yóuth
           d
            y [pause]   ful
</pre>

(Channel 2, Denver, Jan. 5, 1962.)

The same oratorical use of interior A's may be a means of playing for time without sounding weak or uncertain (as might be the case if B's or AC's were used to signal the incompleteness). The syntactic and gestural cues are relied on to imply continuation, while the intonation implies positiveness. The following occurred in an extemporized monolog at a conference (speaker, Charles N. Staubach, Oct. 23, 1964):

<pre>
            bé   í
The re súlt   and my thésis
          ing [pause] that (...)   s...
</pre>

The first part here is a B+A (tail on *-ing*) where the speaker revised the A to AC (with the rising pitch on *that*), followed by another B+A. But such mixed cues can easily cause trouble for a speaker. Great Britain's Prime Minister Margaret Thatcher intersperses many rapid falls when she speaks, and interviewers frequently misunderstand and attempt to take their turn before she is through (see Beattie, Cutler, and Pearson 1983).

Separation for sense was noted in the case of what was referred to earlier as one sentence becoming the equivalent of two (pp. 165–66). It not only makes a statement about something but introduces that something on the scene, asserts that it exists or has happened. For example,

<pre>
                      ás   Márs
           héard?   húge
Have you   A   teroid slámmed into
                                                last night!
</pre>

(This is actually B+A+B+A; the first B could be eliminated by dropping *huge*, but the example would be less effective.) Here the speaker might even pause slightly after *asteroid*—that much of the sentence, up through *asteroid*, says, in effect, 'A huge asteroid appeared.' Or a subject may be separated in this fashion not to bring it on the scene but to sharpen attention on it, to suggest 'Give careful thought to this'; for example,

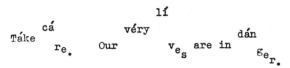

Without this justification for separate attention, the first A of the A+A would ordinarily be changed to an AC, or the sentence would be split; so, following *Have you heard the news?* one would not be apt to hear

$$\text{? The} \quad {}^{\text{i}}\text{d}_{\text{e}_{\text{n}_{\text{t}}}} \quad \text{has been im}_{\text{e}_{\text{d}_{\bullet}}}$$

Prés ... péach

but would hear instead

$$\text{The} \quad {}^{\text{i}}\text{dent has been im}_{\text{e}_{\text{d}_{\bullet}}}$$

Prés ... péach

with AC+A (*-dent* may level off or rise slightly), or

$$\text{The} \quad {}^{\text{i}}\text{d}_{\text{e}_{\text{n}_{\text{t}_{\bullet}}}} \quad \text{He's been im}_{\text{e}_{\text{d}_{\bullet}}}$$

Prés ... péach

Or the contour may be reduced to a single A (see pp. 114–15) for sacrifice of an accent to a nearby focal meaning):

$$\text{The} \quad {}^{\text{i}}\text{dent's been impeached}_{\bullet}$$

Prés

The first A of A+A is more independent of the second A than an AC or a B would be, and the question naturally arises whether the combination should be regarded as a single contour or as two, especially in cases like the asteroid one where there is a potential pause, however slight. Besides the pause, the effect of relative height is not always the same in A+A as in the other contours—the first A has more freedom, is less apt to depend on the second, than happens with B+A or AC+A. This is a relative matter and the question is probably undecidable; there is an area of indeterminacy between "one and more than one contour."[4]

One place where the second A is clearly subordinate to the first is in reverse polarity tag questions. Here we find a restriction in relative height, one that affects A+A contours but not AC+A. Whereas with AC either combination of heights is possible, e.g.

```
     knów                                        dón't
                    dón't               knów
 You                              You
            thaᵗ                           thaᵗ
                   ʸoᵤ?                               ʸoᵤ?
```

with A+A the first A must be higher:

```
     knów                                  knów      dón't
                  dón't
 You                              *You
         ᵗhₐₜ        ʸoᵤ?                  ᵗhₐₜ        ʸoᵤ?
```

This is probably not a grammatical restriction but a semantic one: there is too much quiet confidence in the main sentence with its lower-pitched A to justify the strong appeal for acceptance in the tag.

Separation for sense is also to be found in the contrast between compounds and phrases. The compound, as we saw earlier (pp. 166, 280–81), favors B+A, whereas modifier + head phrases, except when the modifier is nonrestrictive, favor A+A—restrictiveness in a modifier requires that it be given separate attention. So we get the following, where *Erie Railroad* is a compound but *eerie railroad* is not:

```
        Érie Ráil               éer   ráil
 The                                              (B+AC+A+A)
             roaᵈ is an             i
                                     e   roₐd.
```

The same relationships would be preserved if the contour were B+AC+AC+A (fall-rise on the *-ie* of *eerie*), but if B+A came at the end (A+AC+B+A or AC+AC+B+A) the mood would be drastically altered—the speaker would be making what is called a "knowing" remark, and would probably nod his head or arch his eyebrows or both when saying *eerie railroad*. As something "known," the final B+A would become appropriate.

This discussion of A+A has made free use of other contours within the A+A family. Not much more is needed by way of illustration. A B profile interposed will have predictable effects, e.g. to apply to something already present or presupposed in the context. Following *I know she remembers* one may add

```
            wísh          mémber more óf
 I just            she'd re
                                   ᵗeₙ.
```

where *remember* has already been mentioned. (A+A+A would still be normal here.) An interposed AC is little different from an interposed

A except for the incompleteness of its ending, which may be just to link up,

```
        nót    réa           qué
   It's                                  
          a                              
              sonable  re   st.
```

or, in cases of contrast, to suggest an alternative that may or may not be mentioned—in the following it is *but you are not*:

```
         yóu     réa        wóu
   If          were                      
                    sonable  I   ld.
```

An interposed C has the predictable playing-down effect. The following is a milder version of the last example:

```
         yóu                 wóu
   If          were                 I
                  réasonable         ld.
```

Here the overall effect of the A+C+A is better described in terms of the last two profiles, C+A, as set forth in the next section.

. . . C+A

In the C+A subfamily of contours the principal effect is due to the immediate succession of C and A, which represent extremes of restraint and its opposite. What precedes in the contour does not drastically modify that effect. Imagine the following introduced by *Without meaning to offend* or *Putting it as politely as possible*:

```
                         líeve
       sím    dón't                     
   (1) I    ply      be          (A+A+A)
                         you.
```

```
                         líeve
       sím                               
   (2) I    ply                  (A+C+A)
                  dón't  be
                         you.
```

```
                         líeve
       símply                            
   (3) I                         (B+C+A)
                  dón't  be
                         you.
```

(4) I   sím   dón't   ply   be   líeve   ʸouₒ   (C+C+A)

The least appropriate to the introduction is obviously (1), with its succession of unrestrained A's. The . . . C+A of (2)–(4) is a better fit, with (4) probably the best, given the built-in apology of the successive C's: the speaker restrains himself out of courtesy, without sacrificing the punch of the final A. As we have seen before, what is interpreted as restrained depends on the context. In an example such as

I   be   cóuldⁿ'ᵗ   líeᵛᵉ   iᵗ ᵂᵃˢ   pós   sibleₒ

we have restrained incredulity, and in this situation the hearer may interpret the incredulity as more intense, by *needing* to be held in check, than would be the case with successive A's:

cóuld   líeve   pós   I   ⁿ'ᵗ   be   iᵗ   ᵂᵃˢ   ˢⁱᵇˡeₒ

Along with the CB+C, CB+AC, and CB+B grouping discussed in Chapter 10 (pp. 245–52) as the "contradiction contour," the C+A family has enjoyed celebrity as the "surprise redundancy" contour in discussions by Sag and Liberman (1975) and Liberman (1979).[5] Sag and Liberman take their semantic characterization seriously enough to warrant attention here: C+A, they say, is used "where the speaker is expressing surprise" or "where the speaker is suggesting that the utterance is redundant or unnecessary" (pp. 491–92). In a note (8, p. 497) they qualify this with the possibility that "redundancy" may be secondary, inferred from surprise—that is, one is surprised to find it necessary to say something that ought to be obvious. They add "Whatever the correct account may be, it will surely treat the redundancy cases and the surprise ones as a single phenomenon."

That is undoubtedly true. But there is also a problem with "surprise," an emotion so comprehensive that it can be read into almost any sort of exercised utterance. One can be surprised and angry, surprised and hurt, surprised and frightened, surprised and incredulous, or surprised and delighted—surprise comes with the abrupt *timing* of almost any active emotion (impatience would be excluded, as it has to build up). As a consequence, high pitch in a variety of configurations can be taken as expressing surprise—the most surprised of all being a simple unwavering B profile on *Eek!* There is a similar problem with redundancy. If you ask me why I did something and I reply with C+A,

```
              félt
   Be    I
     cáuse          liₖₑ it.
```

I am saying something that is redundant (obvious) because of my protest at having to say it. But I can also express redundancy with B,

```
              félt like it.
   Because I
```

which is obviousness by way of asking why you are asking. The first could readily be followed by *That's why*, the second by *Is there any better reason?* Further, one can have redundancy as an interpretation of boredom: if something is obvious, having to say it is a bore. Ladd's description of the terraced monotone (see pp. 226–34) includes such terms as "low in information value," "routine," "predictable"—which are certainly close to "redundant."

Nevertheless the Sag-Liberman proposal is valid as a partial view, and to get a full perspective on it we need to look for utterances that use the contour but do not readily suggest either surprise or redundancy. The object is to find how "surprise-redundancy" fits the overall tension-relaxation scheme. (To save space, accent marks will be used as before, this time with a grave for the C accent and an acute for the A.)

A good place to start is with utterances that convey vehemence, which Sag and Liberman say (p. 492) is incompatible with surprise-redundancy. While it is true that the C profile "plays down," the expression may actually gain power through understatement. In the following example we can take advantage of gesture to distinguish power from redundancy (obviousness). Say your friend has gone into a fit of uncontrolled emotion and you want to restrain him. You might then use the C+A contour several times in succession:

> Tàke it éasy! I know how you must feel, but you mùst contról yourself! Hòld it dówn! Kèep your témper!

The accented verbs are lengthened. More significantly, the speaker may use a repressing gesture with the hands, which are held forward palms down but tilted up slightly, and are moved down and up slowly with the downward thrust coinciding with the accents. The emotion is being pushed down. Quite the opposite occurs with "obviousness." If you are asked *What is the best way to handle the situation?* and you reply *Tàke it éasy*, you may hold your hands palms up: 'That's the obvious way, everything is in plain view.' We see illustrated here the fault that was mentioned in Chapter 9 (pp. 204–5): the intonologist has unconsciously adopted an attitude associated with a gesture and read it into the intonation, an easy thing to do for linguists who work mostly with logical discourse and for whom 'this is an obvious answer to the question' comes readily to mind.

It is not difficult to find other instances of vehemence more or less held in check. In the following, the speaker uses the contour three times in succession:

> The pàin is térrible. It's drìving me crázy. I dòn't think I can stánd it any longer.

Consider also the insult

> I hòpe you chóke.

delivered not as an answer to a question, but volunteered after someone has eaten a morsel that you wanted. In both instances there is vehemence, but also restraint.

Next, insistence:

> Well, whàt do you sáy? Spèak úp!

This is "redundant" if we assume that it should not be necessary for one person to prod another, but the intonation is primarily a polite way of prodding. In the middle of a discourse, such prodding can be reduced to a form of mild prompting; the pitch of the A should not go too high:

> So whàt do you thínk? Shall we do it this afternoon or put the whole business off till tomorrow?

We also find a degree of insistence in forms of mildly exasperated puzzlement, as when the speaker is addressing himself as much as an audience:

> Now whère did I pút that stupid thing?

Next, defiance:

> Dòn't you dáre!

> She says you'd be afraid to leave her. — Well now màybe I just wíll—if that's going to be her attitude.

Next, enthusiasm expressed as warm greeting, response, invitation, or acceptance:

> This is my friend Jesse Maynard. — How dò you dó! I've been wanting to meet you for ages.

Hi there, Joe. — The tòp of the mórnin' to you, pal.

(Nurse to patient) Well, Mr. Smith! Hòw are we dóing today?

A lìttle ginger ále, maybe? (The guest has refused other offers, and the host insists, with restraint.)

Have some of these cherries, won't you? — You just bèt I wíll! They lòok delícious!

Have a sip? — I don't mìnd if I dó. I was hoping you'd ask.

Next, mock sympathy:

You're brèaking my héart.

Her bùrnt her wittle fínger. (With voice qualifiers. See below for lower-pitched A.)

Next, deep concern (given diagrammatically for context, C+A followed by B+A):

$$\text{I'm} \quad {}^{\text{w\'or}} \quad {}_{\text{She's}} \quad \text{n\'ever d\'one}$$
$$\text{r\'eal}^{\text{ly}} \quad \text{ri}_{\text{e}_{\text{d}_\cdot}} \quad\quad \text{this befo}_{\text{r}_{\text{e}_\cdot}}$$

The effect of context is telling. When the C+A comes as an explanation or as an answer to a real or implied question, then 'redundancy' can readily be inferred: the speaker is restraining himself, and the most likely motive for doing so is the feeling that the explanation or answer is superfluous. When the C+A comes out of the blue, the restraint is more often than not appropriate for holding in check a reaction toward something unexpected—hence surprise. But that need not be the case. If you give me an account of something, I may say one or both of the following, calmly, after you have finished:

I dòn't belíeve you.
I càn't accépt that.

This is neither surprised nor redundant (one might go on with *and it's impòrtant for me to émphasize that*), but it is suitably restrained, as something so potentially insulting has to be, if comity is to be maintained. The same utterance given in response to *Why don't you accept what I say* could be elaborated,

I dòn't belíeve you. It's as sìmple as thát.

and now 'redundancy' can easily be inferred.

There is obviously a much wider range of feelings and attitudes than surprise and redundancy involved in this contour, and to get at the underlying meaning one must look at the tension-relaxation effects of C followed by A. The C is for restraint, and in all these utterances the speaker starts by holding himself back. For a threat or a violent emotion or an expression of dislike, a bit of restraint, or the pretense of it, is socially desirable. *I hòpe you chóke* is restrained and somewhat ritualistic by comparison with an A+A on that same utterance, which would seem a little too sincere. But the ultimate effect is that of the A: the speaker starts out with restraint but his feelings get the better of him and he explodes an A. The meaning is something like 'holding back, but concern in spite of it.' To appreciate the sense of the C+A one need only contrast it with an A+A on each of these utterances: with the latter, the restraint is gone, all stops are out.

'Redundancy'—where the speaker intends it—thus does not depend on 'surprise,' but both are derived independently from the underlying meaning. In making an observation that he deems to be unnecessary, a speaker is apt to show a bit of impatience; but it is impolite to carry it very far, hence the restraint: *It's rìght there in frónt of you* is acceptable, whereas an A+A could easily be heard as rude. Similarly with surprise: *Well whàt on éarth!* curbs what might be taken as an unseemly expression of feeling such as would be the case with A+A. One can test the toning down of exclamations in general—not just those of surprise—by applying the variant of C+A that has been avoided so far, where the A starts at a pitch below the highest:

The drop in pitch to the start of the A is itself a kind of toning down. This A, not being keyed up like the higher one, may also suggest quiet confidence, as in the following, repeated from above:

It is better for rhetorical than for real questions—*I could tell the story, sure, but who would èver belíeve it?* is still open to a positive answer (*John would*), but the lower A in

virtually forecloses any answer. This is only to say that the lowered pitch is not well suited to appealing for an answer. It is normal also for nonrhetorical questions that are not very curious; e.g. the higher A in *Just one question: are you sure of your facts?* is more inquisitive than confident of what the answer will be, but the lowered A is the opposite:

Are you
súre of your fá cts?

The lowered A also lends itself to sarcasm:

Her
húrt her wittle fin ger.

But for saying the obvious, the extra restraint may seem to be over-doing things, as if the speaker felt so strongly that he had to hold back all the harder, or, as a reflection of greater confidence, were contemptuously indifferent:

It's
ríght there in frónt of you.

Gestural accompaniments could easily reverse this. For some kinds of speech acts the extra restraint would be unusual—the cases of insistence (*Well, what do you say?*) and invitation (*A little ginger ale, maybe?*) are examples; for the first, the lower A expresses too little power, and for the second, too little cordiality. And whereas *I wòuldn't give you a díme* may convey restrained indignation, the variant

I
wóuldn't give you a dí me.

verges on indifference.

The contrast between the higher and the lower A in the C+A raises a familiar problem: does it invalidate the profile-based analysis which says that both forms are C+A and are more alike than they are different? Is this analysis any better on the configurational side than Sag and Liberman's, which, judging from their diagrams, allows . . . B+A as well as . . . C+A so long as A gets the highest pitch? In other words, Sag and Liberman see unity in the relative height of A, coupling examples such as the B+A and A+B+A (pp. 496–97)

bé
It's únder the
d.

Thát's sé
the most béautiful hat I've ever
en.

along with numerous C+A's such as (p. 491)

```
                                        ór
        The                       painted
              bláckboard's                    angel
```

whereas our approach has coupled A profiles to A profiles regardless of height.

If the case is to be decided on the basis of which analysis is more efficient in separating gradient phenomena from all-or-none, the preference should probably go to the analysis in terms of profiles. That C+A is a true unitary contour seems indicated by the gradience within it. The examples of lowered A just given, which are toned down by virtue of the lowered pitch, depend, for their maximum toning-down effect, on a fairly substantial drop from the B tail to the start of the A. As that drop is narrowed, that is, in proportion as the start of the A is higher, the effect gets closer to that of an A whose pitch actually tops what goes before. In fact, if the A starts only a semitone below the preceding high, there is almost the same tension as when the A starts higher. No all-or-none barrier is breached here.

On the other hand, we do find something very much like an all-or-none difference between the sequences that Sag and Liberman lump together. It is subtle (contrasts between B and C are never so striking as those between B and A or C and A), but detectable. Take a pair that would be analyzed, on the basis of profiles, as C+A and B+A,

```
                                        éf
    (1) Would you        make an
                  nót                fort?
```

```
                                        éf
    (2) Would  y     nót make an
                 ou                 fort?
```

and try to interpret them as a request: 'Please make an effort.' Though this is not a common intonation for a request in American English, the interpretation is not difficult in the C+A: the *not* takes on the role of conducive negation and *would you not* becomes equivalent to *wouldn't you*. Contrariwise, the B+A shifts *not* to the right:[6] 'Is it a fact that you would not make an effort?' C+A allows this also, but B+A is almost unambiguous. The answer *You're right, I wouldn't* is fully appropriate. To be conducive, the B+A needs to be almost coercive. In fact, when the contrast is even greater—that is, with a wider jump down to *not* in (1) and a wider jump up to *not* in (2)—we can bring out the basic difference more clearly and, by adding *at least*, show how coercive (2) would be:

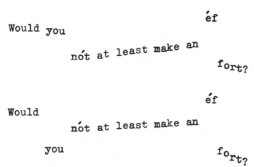

```
                                    éf
     Would you
                  nót at least make an
                                         fort?


                                    éf
     Would
                  nót at least make an
         you                          fort?
```

(As a conducive question the latter is almost rude.) The distinction is corroborated if we tag each example with *please*: it is easy with (1), and incongruous with (2) except with the unusual sense (and doubly unusual intonation) of 'Please do not make an effort.' The all-or-none distinction created by shifting the accent from the trough to the upglide (more accurately, created by changing the accentual configuration from a holding-down to a jump-up-to) is the difference between C and B. The C is restrained, which accords with 'request'; the B leans on the A, which shifts the *not* rightward syntactically.[7]

The C+A contour may be expanded leftward to any degree of complexity by adding profiles. If an extra C is added, the compression of restraint is increased and so is the explosive force of the A, for example,

```
                                    bó
        I'll
               bréak every  bóne in his
                                          dyı
```

Similarly

What àm I gònna dó?
Her bùrnt her wìttle fínger.
It's rìght thère in frónt of you.

In the last example *right* occupies both the trough and the entire upglide preceding the jump down to *there*. A downskip to the C accent makes the restraint more conspicuous, but there are other ways of disposing medial unaccented syllables. The following are all possible realizations of *I guèss it's just as wèll that he díd*:

```
                                    dí
     I
        guéss it's just as
                           wéll that he          (C+C+A)
                                       d.
```

it's just as   dí   (C+CB+A)
I
guéss   wéll that he
                                      d.

                               dí   (C+C+A)
I   it's just as
guéss   wéll that he
                                  d.

Adding a B in front of C+A produces the predictable contrast with AC+C+A. The AC is contrasty, suggests separate attention; the B is given, connected-up. In the following, the first, with B+C+A, continues talking about the already introduced *aptitude*—the contrast is in the predicate; the second, with AC+C+A, puts the contrast on the subject:

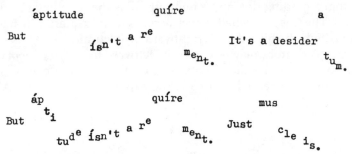

áptitude   quíre   a
But   ísn't a re   It's a desider
                      ment.   tum.

áp   quíre   mus
But   ti
     tude ísn't a re ment. Just cle is.

A B+C+A can maintain its own identity of mood in the face of syntactic change, overriding, for example, the intonational specification of an alternative question. The following can be yes-no or alternative, implying 'I've asked you before, and I am patiently asking you again':

ís it for   Já
              or
         Jóhn   mes?

Contours Ending in B

... B+B

Successions of B profiles are common (see pp. 153–55), especially on questions, and as the principal motion is in a single direction—up—some accommodation in the form of a dropback is often necessary. So in

Is there ány reason to suppóse they wíll? (B+B+B)

no additional height need be gained in the second B on *suppose*, but the third B on *will* carries the motion up. At the same time, the contour admits of overall downmotion as far as the accented syllables are concerned:

ány reason

póse   wíll?

Is there   to sup   they

(This invites comparison with terraced C's, that is, monotone, as in the following B+C+C:

ány reason to sup

póse they

wíll?

Is there

The impression this makes is distinct, both because of the difference in the accents and because of the rhythm.)

An overall downmotion may take the form of a downtilt, and an overall upmotion the form of an uptilt:

ány reason to

Is there   supPóse they wíll?

Is there ány reason to suppóse they wíll?

The relative heights of the accents appear to be free except for a higher between two lower, especially in questions, where the tension seems to favor either a steady increase or a steady decrease; something like the following would be odd:

mátter   ággravated

sáult?

? Was it a   of   as

In a statement, the lexical content of the medial item could motivate a higher B, but any succession of B's for statements expresses a mood that would not often be encountered:

mátter   précedented

pórtance.

It was a   of un   im

Downtilts and uptilts may be combined, but a final downtilt is not apt to be preceded by an uptilt:

Ísn't it   wónderful thing you ever héard of?

    the most

Ísn't it   wónderful thing you ever   héard of?
   the most

Ísn't it   wónderful thing you ever héard of?
    the most

? Ísn't it   wónderful thing   you ever héard of?
    the most

As the second example above shows, successive B's with contrary motion are possible (the reverse, up-down followed by down-up, is also normal). These successions correspond to varying impressions of tension-relaxation. An uptilt on *wonderful thing* increases enthusiasm, a downtilt may suggest ineffability.

When the tail of the B levels off at mid pitch, the result, in the case of a question, is reduced curiosity. The motive may be reticence, indifference, irony, skepticism, or whatever. It is easier to illustrate using a single B (as in the first three examples below), as added B's in themselves tend to boost the pitch, and also because motives of lessened curiosity tend to restrict themselves to single issues and therefore a single accent:

     Is thát the best they can do?

  Can't you sée what they've done to you?

  Are you ínterested in what you're doing?

  Are we stáying hóme tonight?   (B+B)

In nonquestions the level tail at mid pitch may carry two quite different implications. It may suggest a lack of arousal, which can be interpreted as wistfulness in an utterance like

    If ónly I could believe you!

but suggests power under control in

$$\text{You }^{\text{w}\acute{o}\text{n't get away with it!}}$$

Terraced levels—monotone—have the stylized effect described earlier (p. 299). The two levels (*anybody around* and *there give a*) in the following B+B+B tend to be equally timed despite the different number of syllables:

$$\text{Does }_{\text{ánybody around}}\text{ thére give a }^{\text{dámn?}}$$

The uses of B+B are the same as those of B except for implying 'more of the same.' For the most part, additional B's are a function of the length of the utterance, but, as with A, extra profiles may be added for emphasis:

$$_{\text{Dón't}}\quad_{\text{you}}\quad\text{thínk}\quad_{\text{I}}\quad_{\text{w}}\text{íll?}$$

becomes

$$_{\text{Dón't}}\ _{\text{y}}\acute{\text{o}}\text{u thínk I/ }_{\text{w}}\text{íll?}$$

(For lack of syllabic material, the B's here must incorporate their own dropback.) Emphasis can also be added by having a deeper dropback, so that a following B receives a wider upskip or upglide:

$$\text{Did they }^{\text{kn}\acute{\text{o}}\text{w that he}}\quad_{\text{re}}^{\text{r}\acute{\text{u}}\text{sed?}}$$

The basic 'left-up-in-the-air' meaning of B and B+B is, as we have seen again and again, most often interpreted as 'incompleteness.' (In B+A that had the further implication of 'attachment,' but when the B is terminal there is no profile immediately after it to attach itself to.) Following are some of the uses, which will be illustrated by examples containing a simple rise starting at the accent mark, or rises (preceded or not by dropbacks) at more than one mark. First, nonquestions:

1. Questioning answers. These suggest 'Why do you ask?'

   Are you the fellow who did that? — *I ám.*

2. Simplicity and obviousness—'Why should you ask?'

   Why can't anybody tell me what happened to her? — *Nobody knóws.*
   Did you do this? — *I díd indéed.*

3. Feedback requests—interpolations within discourse where the speaker wants assurance of the hearer's attention.

> She had on her nicest dress—you know, *the óne with the pólka dots ón it*—and came down looking like a million.

4. Hesitant assertions.

> Think we'll have a chance to see them? — *We míght.*

5. Unfinished assertions—the speaker intends to go on.

> Like it here? — *M-hm̃.* How about you?

6. Inconclusive exclamations—these suggest inability to do justice to what is being talked about.

> *It's so wónderful!*

7. Dismissal, suggesting 'I leave it with you.'

> May I take this? — *I don't mínd.*

8. Implications of 'alert'—the hearer is left in suspense and advised to take heed; implied threats, sharp commands, summonses, and introductions belong here.

> *It's nóne of your búsiness.*
> *Hóld it!* (or *Hóld ít!*)
> *Ten-shún!*
> *OḰ,* next we come to . . .

Next, questions. Questions of all types are possible with (B)+B:

1. Yes-no questions.

> *Are you plánning a tríp?*

2. Wh questions; these are less frequent, given their usual assumptions.

> *So whát do you thínk?*

3. Complementary questions.

> *His réason being?*

4. Alternative questions. These take (B)+B when they are intentionally ambiguous with yes-no or when the speaker repeats with a certain exasperation (in the latter case, the incompletion is for 'alert').

> (Stewardess offering refreshment) *Have some cándy or gúm?*
> *Were you thére or wéren't you?*

Finally, commands. When these are not for 'alert,' they represent a blend with questions. An example like *Gíve me a táste* we feel should be punctuated with a question mark, and indeed if it is to take a preamble the likely choice is *will you* rather than a word like *so, then,* or *just.*

... A + B

Because AC can almost be regarded as a sandhi variant of A when there is a link to a following profile, no attempt will be made here to distinguish A from AC, except to remark at this point that a clear A (with fall to creak) has the expected degree of assertiveness or finality, as in the example

```
             kíll
                         ,t!
 I could           tháˉ      (A+B)
           yo   for
             u
```

and to add that if the first accent represents a contrast (X rather than Y) there is a slightly stronger tendency toward AC:

```
   sóme
                              (AC+B)
 I know that                      
           of them objécted.
```

But most of the time the fall is only partial and the distinction between A and AC is indeterminate.

The uses of A+B are entirely predictable from the A and B components, and no discussion is necessary. Examples:

```
   tóld                  Jóhn
 I          wóuld.    But
     you I                    húrt anybody.
                        never
```

```
 Hów                     sór
         dó it?       It's a
     did they                ry state of afáirs.
```

```
         sá
 She had a
         d little lóok.
```

```
 Yóu
                              thát!
   don't want to have to worry about
```

```
        ón
                                      me!
                              for
   If            cáre
      ly he would


        téll

   I can't
              you what this  méans to me!
```

The last two examples clearly have an A for power.

The configuration of pitches—brief high on A and low, often extended, trough—makes the jump up to the B especially conspicuous, and this contour is therefore highly sensitive to a terminal monotone, with striking differences between higher and lower pitches. In examples like

```
   Thére's                        Dón't
               thát!                        cránky!
      no use in                        be


          Yóu
                         wórry.
             don't need to
```

the tension of the final pitch registers as a particular degree of emotion under control.

The A in this contour may readily be just for power, to fill out the hat pattern. That is true of the *there's* example above, where the normal accent on *use* is swallowed up, so to speak, in the initial crash on the existential—and normally unaccented—*there's*. In the following the A falls on an otherwise negligible pronoun:

```
       ít's
                          yóurs!
          no affair of
```

The contrast between an A for power and one (at least partially) for contrast can be seen in the following:

```
          péo
      Do                        líeve that?
         ple really be


          án
      Does                        líeve that?
         ybody really be
```

There can scarcely be a contrast intended between 'people' and 'non-people,' and the lack of such a contrast explains why the accented syllable is not amenable to any marked intensification by adding length or otherwise.[8] But such intensification is normal with the *an-* of *anybody*; the contrast with its negative *nobody* is apparent: the speaker assumes that nobody does believe it.

. . . C + B

The sandhi between C and B may be overlapping, with the tail of the C furnishing the takeoff for the B, as in

```
It's                          It's
                  wind.                          wind.
   ónly the                      ónly the
```

or the C may maintain a separate rising tail followed by a dropback for the takeoff of the B:

```
     It's
                    wind.
       ón ly the
```

In the absence of an initial unaccented syllable or syllables, the C may not be very clearly displayed, but the intended shape can be revealed by adding an unaccented word at the start:

```
   (But)
                            thát!
        thére's no use in
```

(*But* has a reduced vowel and is pronounced virtually [bt]; *there* has a full vowel.)[9]

A downtilt on the tail of the C, which was noted as somewhat exceptional when the C is final (see p. 150), occurs quite readily when the C is nonfinal:

```
   (But)
                         thát!
        thére's no use in
```

(The intended accent pattern here is *But thére's no use in thát*; the initial accent could also fall on either *no* or *use*.)

The restraining effect of the C is predictable, and may be applied to all the examples in the A+B section, converting them to C+B, as in the following:

```
  I                          (And)
               would.                        dó it?
     tóld you I                  hów did they
```

Contours Ending in C

... *C + C and ... CB + C*

The doubling of C predictably increases the impression of restraint. The clearest test is a comparison of this contour with others, applied to the same sentence, and with movements as schematic as possible:

```
                   téll        réa
      Would you        me the                        (A+A)
                                    son?


                   téll me the réa
      Would you                                       (B+A)
                                    son?


                         me        réason?
      Would you    téll       the                     (B+B)


                   téll        réason?
      Would you        me the                          (A+B)


                                    réa
      Would you                                        (C+A)
                   téll me the
                                    son?


                                    réason?
      Would you                                        (C+B)
                   téll me the


                   téll
      Would you        me the    son?                  (A+C)
                                réa


                   téll me the
      Would you                  son?                   (B+C)
                                réa


      Would you            the     son?                (C+C)
                   téll me
                                réa


                        me the
      Would you                    son?                (CB+C)
                   téll
                                réa
```

As with A+A and the up or down tangent to its peaks, with C+C it also makes a difference whether the tangent to the accented syllables is up or down. As might be expected, a rising tangent shows more tension overlaid on the general restraint, and is most commonly found in questions, especially those involving an element of surprise, e.g.

$$
\begin{array}{llll}
 & & & \text{sy?} \\
\text{But} & \text{it} & \text{that} & \\
 & & \text{éa} & \\
\text{is} & \text{-----} & &
\end{array}
$$

Otherwise the tangent is mostly falling, as it could readily be in this example as well.

The slope of the intervening unaccented syllables has predictable effects in terms of register and tension-relaxation. Someone preparing a surprise for another person, who insists on knowing what it is, might say, brightly, using C+C,

$$
\begin{array}{ll}
 & \text{you} \\
\text{Nev}^{\text{er}} & \\
 & \text{mind.}
\end{array}
$$

going into or approaching falsetto, which makes the admonition playful. A more serious admonition might use CB+C:

$$
\begin{array}{ll}
 & \text{er you} \\
\text{Nev} & \\
 & \text{mind.}
\end{array}
$$

This falling slope is relatively confident, as in

$$
\begin{array}{l}
\quad\quad \text{n't it be better to} \\
\text{Would} \\
\quad\quad\quad\quad\quad\quad \text{wait?}
\end{array}
$$

The rising slope of C+C here would be more keyed up, more uncertain, more curious. A stronger plea is contained in the C+C

$$
\begin{array}{l}
\quad\quad\quad \text{please} \\
\text{Could you} \\
\quad\quad\quad\quad\quad\quad \text{me?} \\
\quad\quad\quad\quad \text{help}
\end{array}
$$

than in the same with the falling slope of CB+C.

. . . A + C and . . . CA + C

Contours . . . A+C and . . . CA+C are considered together because of the status of CA as an emphatic variant of A.

Following A or CA, the C profile—in an utterance whose first accent is one of interest rather than power—tends to represent known information: the pitch is held down because the material is of secondary importance. Thus in either of the following

```
           some
But                                   them.
           body must have  told                    (A+C)
```

```
           bod
But                                   them.
   some       y must have  told                    (CA+C)
```

the question of telling has already come up. Similarly in

```
                 ger
     I'm not          to
                         ap
          ea              por it.                   (CA+C)
                     ply
```

the question of applying has already come up. As the material occupying the C is redundant, the question arises whether it is accented at all. The amount of material that can intervene—plus the fact that the trough is taken by the element that *would* normally be accented if an accent were there—argues for the separate accent. But the fact that the entire pitch movement can be condensed on a single syllable favors regarding the fall-rise as merely the last part of a profile that starts with A or with CA, that is, to regard it as AC or as CAC. To illustrate the latter, more complex, possibility, take an utterance that could be the conversational equivalent of the *eager to* example above:

```
           júst    só    ó
     I'd        as    on n
                             ot.
```

—the rise-fall-rise of the CAC is carried out on *not*, and the discourse effect is the same as when it is expanded to cover several syllables. As was noted in Chapter 8 (pp. 191–92) there is a zone of uncertainty here. This is accentuated by the fact that a C profile (or the tail of an AC or a CAC) is the usual intonation for a variety of more or less redundant tags. The last example could be expanded slightly to keep *not* at a high pitch and provide a low-pitched foil:

```
           júst    só    ót,
     I'd        as    on n
                           you
                               know.
```

And so for the usual question tags:

You   lí^ke it,

               don't y^{ou?}

If the material on the C in the position we are discussing were always redundant, we might wonder whether to allow for an independent C at all after an A or a CA. But the restriction seems to apply only to accents of interest. If the first A or CA is an accent of power, the C may introduce new material into the discourse (see pp. 179–80). In a command, the initial high may be just for impact:

               gét

Then   (A+C)

          the he_{ll}   o^f he^{re!}

              óut

Since phrasal verbs have the main accent on the particle, we suspect that *out* here is accented; and it is the "point" of the utterance. Similarly with a powerful word such as *sure*:

             that

I'm   (CA+C)

    súre   they   re   it.

                     sént

Here, *resent* can be new to the discourse. And similarly with a question that approaches a command:

            téll

Would you   me the   s^{on?}   (A+C)

                 réa

The C of the A+C may develop an extra B profile on the upglide, a case of sandhi overlap. Along with

      Thére's

            an óld^{ie!}   (A+C)

made as a casual remark out of the blue, as speaker and hearer pass an old house (the syllable *old* is drawled), there is the matching

      Thére's

            an   óld hó^{use!}

(with *old* similarly drawled). Rather than A+C, this is A+C+B. *House* is accented by length and intensity as well as by configuration—and also by implication: it has not been mentioned before.

... B+C

The "leaning" tendencies of the B are almost as evident in B+C as
in B+A. In fact, virtually all the examples in the discussion of B+A
are easily transformed to B+C, with the predictable overlay of restraint that C contributes, as in the veiled warning of the example on
page 179:

```
                     yóu trying to
          Are
                           thréaten me?
```

Occasionally a more dramatic difference emerges at a point where
some question of grammar hinges on the presence or absence of restraint. For example, a reclamatory question (calling for a repetition)
does not sort well with B+A; a question like

```
               gót there whé
          They
                          n?
```

involves no repetition. But the corresponding B+C,

```
               gót there
          They
                     whén?
```

is normal as a reclamatory question and also (though less likely) as an
original question. In the latter case it serves the same grammatical
function as the B+A, but sounds flaccid by comparison perhaps because there is so little need to tone down a B+A in an original question. But we note that B+B is also normal for a reclamatory question
and is a lot more demanding:

```
                           whén?
               gót there
          They
```

which suggests that the B+C in the reclamatory question represents
pragmatically the toning down of a B+B. There is more need to curb
that near-shriek.

A discourse contrast shows up in certain courtesy situations, e.g.
apology. A B+A is more apt to convey a fact (though it can be used to
apologize), a B+C to apologize (though it can convey a fact):

```
          trúly                    bég your
     I'm                      I
          sórry.                        párdon.
```

(The latter example is also stereotyped as an apologetic reclamatory question, 'What did you say?', and becomes almost certainly that when the tail of the B takes an uptilt.)

Miscellaneous examples of B+C (in the examples that are not diagrammed, the grave accent marks the C):

Whatéver you sày.
Then you tóok him at his wòrd?
Cóuldn't they tèll who it was?
Táke them alòng with us?!
Your óccupàtion?
She cáught the mèasles you say?
For Hénry and mè is it?
Wóuld it be wròng to?
Whát did they sày?

These are optional as to the slopes after the first accent, which makes CB+C a normal alternative. Although the slope is generally in a uniform direction, it appears possible, as in the following, to have a slight rise-fall or fall-rise:

The sag in the first of these seems to be something that might occur more or less automatically (the highest pitch may occur at any point, and the contour already involves rise + fall). In the second, we may have a weak extra B on *make* (the location of the trough is less free, and the overall movement is more complex).[10]

Another place where contrariwise motion may make a difference is in the cases of possible sandhi overlap, where by one interpretation an additional accent develops on the tail of the C. In a shape like with the C tail on a downtilt, the reversed direction of *friend* is a fairly clear sign of an intended B profile, yielding a B+C+B contour. But a level or rising tail without much (additional) rise on *friend* is more apt to be intended as B+C (*friend* has probably already been mentioned). A monotone B+C is pretty obviously that and not B+C+B:

Îsn't it

wróng to injure a friend?

Monotone gives the same "no news" stylization noted earlier. Whereas

Dón't

wór^rʸ·

plays things down for the sake of reassurance, the unflappable or bored

Dón't

wórry.

adds 'it isn't worth it' to the reassurance. This B+C downskip with monotone suggests 'indifference,' and is encountered typically on utterances like *Thát's àll, ÓǨ, Whý bòther, Nó mòre, Néver mìnd, Whát's the màtter?* (long-suffering boredom), and also on utterances where the speaker assumes imperturbability, such as *Nó you dòn't, Ás you wère, Óne sìde please, Whát nòw, Góod Gòd, Whát fòr for goodness' sake!*

Contours Ending in AC

The "unfinished" implication of the terminal upmotion in the AC profile is usually innocuous when AC occurs medially—unfinishedness normally has to do with the fact that something more is to be added in the utterance: the speaker is not through *speaking*. But with AC in terminal position, the speaker is usually not through *implying*—he could add more if he would, but chooses to leave matters up in the air, for whatever reason. And since AC embodies the same contrastivity as A, the implications are apt to be powerful. We do find a medial use where something more than mere incompleteness is implied when a speaker slows down and carefully produces the upglide characteristic of AC, making it clear that AC and not a truncated A is intended. The AC is more emphatic than A under these conditions (i.e., medially), with predictable effects on both power and interest. The former shows up in exclamations; compare the A with the AC in the following:

$$\text{Wé}_{1_1,} \quad \text{wé}_{1_{1_!}} \qquad \text{Wé}_{1^1,} \quad \text{wé}_{1_{1_!}} \qquad \text{You}^{\text{dó}}{}_{\text{n'}_{\text{t}}}\text{sá}_{\text{y!}} \qquad \text{You}^{\text{dó}}{}_{\text{n't}}\text{sá}_{\text{y!}}$$

If sarcasm is intended, the AC+A examples are heavier with it. And so with contrastivity; in fact, AC becomes a pretty good theme-marker regardless of position. Note the reversal of profiles in the following:

$$\text{Cýn}^{\text{dór}} \qquad \qquad \text{(AC+A)}$$
$$\text{thi}^{\text{a}}\text{ they a}\;{}_{\text{e}_{\text{d}_.}}$$

$$\overset{\text{dór}}{\underset{}{}}\;\overset{\text{Cýn}}{}$$
$$\text{They a}\quad\;\;\text{thi}^{\text{a}_\bullet} \qquad \qquad \text{(A+AC)}$$
$$\quad\quad{}_{\text{e}_{\text{d}}}$$

The likeliest interpretation either way is 'As for Cynthia (theme) they adored her (rheme).'

... B + AC

The affinity of B to a following AC is as close as to a following A. The amalgam is so tight that here almost more than anywhere else one gets the impression of a holistic contour, especially when the B is rising, the AC starts higher than the end of the B, and the tail remains high in pitch—the trough is high and shallow and may flatten to a high terminal level. The tune is associated with a number of stereotypes including the vocal segregates *m* (hum) and *ah*. When hummed in answer to a question,

$$\text{M-}^{\text{m-}}{}^{\text{m-}}{}^{\text{m!}}$$

we have (for at least some speakers) a response equivalent to 'I don't know'; and *Ah-ah-ah!* on the same tune, with glottal stops at the hyphens, is a warning. The same intonation is heard on ordinary locutions with the same two meanings: *You tell me, I wish I knew,* etc., and *Don't do that, Better watch out,* etc.

The implication, in keeping with the pitch movement, is something like 'arousal plus suspense,' and from that broad emotive stance the speaker is able to produce a wide variety of special effects. If he says to a companion,

$$\text{Háve}^{\text{e}}{}^{\text{f}}{}_{\text{ún!}}$$

he may be licking his lips in vicarious pleasure or warning his hearer of consequences but disclaiming responsibility (suspense, 'It's up to you to finish this'). These completely different interpretations of the same basic meaning can be seen separately in *Déelíciöus* versus *It's yóur fúnèrál* or *I háte to say I tóld you sö.* (The marks on the nondiagrammed examples here show direction of pitch: ´ up, ` down, ˇ down-up, ˜ up-down-up.) As was noted in Chapter 8 (p. 183), warnings and cautionary statements are common. One who hears *Ánything you sãy* knows that the speaker is washing his hands of responsibility. Similarly *He hád it cómĭng—I could sée it all alŏng—he should have héeded my wárnĭng*, or *Bétter stúdÿ or you'll flúnk your exam*, where the speaker repeats the same intonation.

Other circumstantial interpretations:

Urging to prompt action (again it's "up to" someone, usually the hearer): *Cóme ŏn; Tén minutes to gŏ; Pút that dŏwn.*

Enthusiastic acquiescence, willingness to join in prompt action: *Indéed you mãy; You bét I dŏ; Ríght-ŏ; I'm behínd you every inch of the wãy.*

Anticipation of impending results: *Ín they cŏme; Hére we ãre; Awáy they wĕnt; Dówn he fĕll; It's abóut to pŏp; Whát do we do nĕxt?* Presentative adverbs (*here, down, there, over*, etc.) are common here.

Salutation or leave-taking that expects a quick response: *Sée you tomórrŏw; Péekabŏo; Góod-bÿe.* The simple AC *Hellŏ* belongs here (used also on the telephone to prompt a response, after an original *Helló* has failed), as do other informal courtesy exchanges like *Thánks very mŭch, Níce to have mét yŏu.*

Demanding question: *Háve you the mónĕy?; They dó mean to hélp ŭs?; Whó wás ït?* As the shallow trough deepens, such questions tend more and more to be echo in American English, though British English readily uses them as original questions: *Does it máke any dìffèrénce?* (The problem remains even when the AC starts lower than the end of the B tail, so long as that tail is rising.) The depth of the trough has no such relatively sharp effect in nonquestions: *It mákes no dìffèrénce.* The reason for the special status of echo questions is probably the need to tone down, out of courtesy, the parroting of what someone else has just said.

Explanation that demands acceptance; the speaker puts it "up to" the hearer: *He hád it to dŏ; They díd what they cŏuld; I wíll if I cãn; It was bóund to háppĕn; I'm sórrier than I can sãy* (and you have no right to expect more); *He tried áwfully hãrd; What móre do they wãnt?*

Alerting of the hearer that there is more to come: *That's áll I need to knów abòut ít* (and now I can proceed); *Dón't worry about mẽ* (I can take care of myself); *It's nót for either of ŭs* (so it must be for someone else).

Concession—the matter is now "up to" the speaker himself: *I've nó compláint, it's mý fáult; It cóuld bĕ, you máy be ríght; It's áll trŭe, éverything they sáid abòut mé; I wísh I hăd.*

Compliment that demands acceptance—a sort of figurative warning, as if to tell all and sundry that this had better be agreed to: *A fíne wómăn; Wónderful sálad you sèrved ús; That was a gréat dáy we hăd.*

A lowering at any position has predictable effects of relaxation, as can be seen in the following, all B+AC but with different slopes and accent heights:

The contrast is more striking when the initial B is eliminated and everything rides on a simple AC contour. In the following,

the raised trough in the second makes that utterance suitable for preening oneself on being right ('You had your warning, I wash my hands of the matter'), whereas the first is equally suitable for expressing a contrast on *told*: 'I told you but I guess you weren't paying attention.'

The "brightness" of the higher-pitched accent makes a difference in the likely interpretations of the following, in answer to *Did you take the chairmanship?*

The first may readily suggest 'Yes' and is easily tagged,

—implying 'Why shouldn't I?' The second is more apt to suggest 'No' and to be followed by an explanation for the refusal.

Replacing the uptilted tail of the B with a downtilt makes questions on this contour more normal, at least for American English. They are less tense, less demanding. Take the rhetorical question *Do you think I'm crázÿ?!* in response to another's outlandish suggestion. With uptilt it is almost out of bounds, but with downtilt it is quite normal:

```
                  thínk I'm crá
          Do you
                             zÿ?!
```

The relative height of the AC is also involved here, and is quite evident even when the B profile remains the same. Both of the following have downtilted B tails,

```
                          whý?
        tóld you the rea   ⌒⌣        tóld you the rea   whý?
They                             They                      ⌣
              son                                    son
```

The first, with its high tension, can hardly occur elsewhere than in great surprise or heavy dispute, perhaps implying 'How could you be so stupid as to suppose they were just thoughtless?' It makes no difference whether we interpret it as a question (and even add *didn't they?*) or a statement. The second might easily be a normal question-for-confirmation, to which the other person answers *Yes* and the first speaker goes on with *I was afraid they might have neglected to.*

Monotone gives the usual stylization, and is especially effective with the AC part of B+AC at high pitch, since the musical intervals stand out sharply. In the following passage the reference is to children:

> I gave their threats little credence, because I realized that often this was their way of saying, "You'll be s-o-r-r-y." (*Atlantic Monthly*, May 1943, p. 49.)

The quotation is to be interpreted as the jeering chant

```
                          s-ó-r-
                   be          r-y!
        Yóu'll
```

... A +AC and ... CA +AC

As noted in Chapter 8 (p. 183), A+AC is more amenable to "logical" interpretations than is B+AC with its lack of a pitch drop in the middle and resulting higher tension. So in the following, with two successive A+AC's, we have a double contrast in accents of interest:

```
                   gé t,        cán
      cán't              e                           gí
   I       expect you to for    but I   expect you to for  veͦ·
```

The inconclusiveness of the AC in the first clause can be taken in the syntactic sense—'more coming'—but that of the second clause leaves it up to the hearer to draw his own conclusions. Similarly with

```
         gót      dó
It's         to be   nᵉ•
```

with either peak the higher (if the second is lower, there is less urgency: 'sooner or later' rather than 'the sooner the better'). In a question, the inconclusiveness of course is the expectation of an answer:

```
        dó
You        be lieve
                  me?
```

—here *don't you?* would be a natural sequel.

A+AC can take accents of power, and this puts the contour in competition with B+AC. The difference is that A+AC is more controlled, less immediate, more thoughtful, less excited. While that quality makes it less obviously offensive, it may invite deeper offense by seeming to be more serious. Thus a person who hears the B+AC *Yóu'll be sórrÿ* may take it as an overwrought and hence idle threat, and feel actually more endangered by

```
Yóu'll
            sór
      be
            rÿ•
```

Relative height of the accents may make a striking difference here, just as in B+AC. Thus in an apology such as

```
                                                sór
      áw                            áw              rÿ•
I'm       sór                 I'm
      fully   rÿ•                   fully
```

the first could be a sincere apology, with inconclusiveness suggesting that more could be added by way of showing contrition; but the second has a take-it-or-leave-it ring: like many of the B+AC examples, the speaker 'leaves it up to' the hearer.

There is no need for special exemplification of CA+AC, since CA can replace A with little change except greater emphasis. In place of the last example, first version, we could have

```
             ful
                  sór
      I'm
          áw
             ly    rÿ•
```

with CA on *awfully*. A similar shift could be made in the terminal profile, AC to CAC, with *sor-* incorporating the upskip. Offering such an apology would probably seem to be protesting too much.

. . . AC+AC

A non-final AC may or may not mark a clause break. If it does, part of the function of the terminal rise is to link up with the following clause. (The *if* clause in the sentence you have just read is an example, with a likely AC on *does*.) Though not by strict grammatical rule, this function is best observed when a subordinate clause precedes a main clause, as in the following instances of AC+A:

```
                    fínd
    When you                         knó
                          t,  let me
                        i               w.
```

```
                    líeve                 lóo
    If you don't be
                             e,  just
                           m              k.
```

The association is tight enough to be preserved when the clauses are reversed, so that the AC to some degree marks the subordinate clause regardless of position (compare previous instances of "theme-rheme reversal"):

```
        lóok
                            líeve
    Just                                      (A+AC)
            if you don't be
                                m   e•
```

```
                    Jó              scré
    Listening to                              (AC+A)
                    hn,  I could        a
                                         m.
```

```
        scré
                            Jó
    I could                                   (A+AC)
            am, listening to      hn•
```

On the other hand, an AC ending a main clause tends to take on other nuances of incompletion, depending on context. This is especially true when the main clause comes last:

                jóg   cáre
If you go   (AC+AC)
            g^{in}g' just be   fu^{l.}

The admonition in this context hinges mainly on the last AC but is supported by the first one, despite the latter's mainly linking function. The same is true if the clauses are reversed.

This is to say that the inconclusiveness of a medial AC even at a point where it is expected syntactically may have other implications than mere connectedness. A speaker who says

                éa   gé
It will be   s_{i}
                    ^{e}r if you just for   t.

with two clear A's is making a stronger and more confident injunction than if he ended the first clause with the fall-rise of an AC. And if the last profile is changed to AC, the A on *easier* becomes incongruous in the intended sense 'It will be easier for you just to forget'[11]—an AC at that point becomes necessary not just for linkup but as an anticipation of the final AC.[12] The same matching of profiles can be seen in the B+AC+AC

        Hére he có   bró
                    mes, with his   ther.

A medial A would be incongruous here, just as in the last example. Sandhi overlap in this case would yield

        Hére he cómes   bró
                    with his   the^{r.}

On the other hand, it may be that the problem is not the matching of profiles but rather the matching of KEY. That is, if a final AC upglide is apt to range too high (and the nature of a given utterance would determine that), then a medial A will be a poor choice to precede it—perhaps on the principle that it is not good for the middle of an utterance to be "more final" than the end. But if the utterance is such—say from a high degree of positiveness—that a final AC may engage the creak range, then the sequence is normal. That is the case with the A+A+AC

            wás   bést   cáp
    It
        n't the   that he's   ab_{le}   o^{f.}

—said as a good-humored understatement of someone's failure.

The nonlinking functions of the AC are more readily detected when the utterance is a single clause and the intonation is not called upon to cement two otherwise separate elements. If the CA of the last example in the preceding section is changed to AC,

$$\text{áw} \qquad \text{sór}$$
$$\text{I'm} \qquad\qquad\qquad\qquad \text{(AC+AC)}$$
$$\text{full}^{\text{y}} \qquad \text{r}^{\text{y}\bullet}$$

the hearer might be led to expect the speaker to add something, perhaps *but what can I say?* or some other form of excuse. If we compare the A+AC (with fall to creak) and the AC+AC in the following,

$$\text{súre} \qquad\qquad\qquad\qquad\qquad \text{súre}$$
$$\qquad\qquad \text{knó} \qquad\qquad\qquad\qquad\qquad\qquad \text{knó}$$
$$\text{He} \qquad\qquad\qquad\qquad \text{w}^{\text{w}\bullet} \quad \text{He} \qquad 1^{\text{y}} \text{ would} \qquad \text{w}^{\text{w}\bullet}$$
$$\qquad 1 \qquad\qquad\qquad\qquad$$
$$\qquad\quad {}_{\text{y}} \text{ would}$$

we find that the AC+AC inspires less confidence—the uncertainty already present in the A+AC is compounded. And when AC rather than A accompanies the *will* in

$$\text{wí} \qquad \text{fé} \qquad\qquad\qquad \text{wí} \qquad \text{fé}$$
$$\text{You} \quad 1 \qquad {}_{\text{s}}\text{s}^! \qquad \text{You} \quad 1 \qquad {}_{\text{s}}\text{s}^!$$
$$\qquad\quad 1 \text{ con} \qquad\qquad\qquad\qquad 1 \text{ con}$$

a possible 'eventually' gives way to 'now!'—the hearer imagines consequences if he fails to comply.[13] A request tag such as *won't you?* is unlikely with AC+AC here unless the incompletion is taken as an urgent request for a reply rather than an urgent demand to act. The facial gestures of course differ.

. . . C+AC

The C+AC bears the same relation to B+AC that C+A bears to B+A: there is initial restraint and then release (see above, p. 302). The final AC with its suspensive ending can be made to stand out more by the sharper contrast between the two profiles than is the case with B+AC, but whether the livelier B+AC or the restrained C+AC is more emphatic depends on other factors. The two are so much alike that all the examples cited above (pp. 321–23) can be uttered with C+AC, to much the same effect. The only exceptions are a couple of the courtesy expressions in which "need to restrain" would seem to be overdoing it, e.g. *Nìce to have mét yŏu, I'm sòrrier than I can săy.* In *Wònderful sálad you sèrved ús!* the speaker might seem to be overstating the compliment by implying that his feelings were such that he had to restrain himself; the more perfunctory B would probably go over better.

Ambiguity in AC Contours

We review here—for the benefit of AC contours, the ones most affected—the discussion of sandhi overlap presented in the last chapter. As we saw there (pp. 268–73) and in Chapter 8 (pp. 191–92), it is sometimes hard to tell the difference between an AC profile and one that develops an extra accent on what would otherwise be the tail of the AC. This means a zone of uncertainty between AC and A+C or AC+C. All contours ending in AC are affected. Take the simple AC contour, for example. In both of the following there is the same shape and the same warning to escape:

$$\text{Po}\quad {}^{\text{li}}\text{ce!}\qquad\qquad \text{Po}\quad \text{lice}_{\text{man}}\ _{\text{coming!}}$$

and since in a corresponding statement, *A policeman is coming*, the word *coming* is deaccented (see p. 114) we can assume that the fall-rise on *coming* is only the tail of the AC profile. The same would be true of utterances using unaccented tags on the tail, e.g. *Don't tattle, now!*; *Come along, my friend; Step aside, please; He's working, you know.* But what of

$$\text{A po}\quad {}^{\text{man}}\text{ patrols this}\ _{\text{beat!}}\quad {}^{\text{lice}}$$

—a similar warning, but carrying what could be a second, much lower, prominence if the contour were A+A:

$$\text{A po}\quad {}^{\text{man}}\text{ patrols this}\ {}^{\text{bé}}{}_{\text{at.}}\quad {}^{\text{líce}}$$

—hence at least potentially carrying a C accent on what would otherwise be the tail of the AC. Since the initial profile can carry the full movement of an AC,

$$\text{A po}\quad {}_{\text{m}}{}^{\text{an}}\text{ patrols this}\ _{\text{béat.}}\quad {}^{\text{líce}}$$

the collapsed contour can be seen as a case of sandhi overlap, that is, AC+C. The same would be true of an accented tag, as in the matched pair

$$\text{Not for}\ {}^{\text{me,}}\text{ you}\ _{\text{don't!}}\qquad\qquad \text{Not for}\ {}^{\text{mé,}}\smile\text{you}\ _{\text{dón't!}}$$

And also of an utterance containing potentially accented repeated material, e.g.

told

I   You not to go _{through} t^{he}^{re}[!]

—a type of utterance that, given only A's, might well develop a subordinate A (as in *beat* above):

tóld

thróugh

I   you not to go   t_{her}_{e.}

In fact, some of the examples of B+AC cited above could as well be regarded as B+AC+C: *That was a gréat dáy we hăd, Wónderful sálad you sèrved ús* (p. 323)—this last example showing the potential full AC on *salad*:

Wonderful ^{sal}

a^d you _{served} u^s[!]

The close similarity if not identity between the two forms can be seen in their use together, e.g. AC followed by (probably) A+C or AC+C:

me   I didn't

Not   ^ee[!]   _{say} an^{ything.}

or even in a sequence involving material new to the discourse; for example, in answer to the question *How are you going to stand up against an enemy as formidable as that?* one might say

I'm   I

^{no}t a   r^{d.}   ^{wo}uldn't   n.

cow^a   ru

Similarly in comparing

you see my ta   that ta

i   i

Can   l   l li^{ght}   i^{ng?}

li^{gh}t? Is   burn

the first with B+AC and the second with the same or with B+AC+C, we find little difference in overall impression—either could be used in the same conversation. *Burning* is an apparently new-to-context item. Does that entitle it to a C of its own on the tail of the AC? Not necessarily, in view of something like

cu   tail

tell

Ex   could you   is my

^se,   ^me,   light burning?

where *burning* is an unaccented item on the tail of the A—an instance in question form of the familiar kind of deaccenting discussed in Chapter 7 (pp. 114–15). To someone who pretends not to be worrying one might say either of the following,

```
                     ams
      aren't your ex
But                                          (B+A)
                    coming up in a week or two?


      aren't your exₐ
                    m
But                  ˢ                             ?      (B+AC)
                      coming up in a  week  or  tʷᵒ
```

without intending an accent on *week* in either case.

As the last pair of examples shows, in a putative B+AC contour it does not matter that the AC starts lower than the B, as far as the resulting ambiguity is concerned. We noted earlier (p. 322) that American English has difficulty with B+AC for original questions when the tail of the B rises. There is no such difficulty when it tilts down. So

```
            wéren't you afrá
But                        ᵢᵈ?
```

is perfectly normal—and obviously B+AC. The following, in response to *I hope my wife has fond memories of London*, would be normal American English and it illustrates the development of a possible C on the tail of the AC, this time with an old-to-context item:

```
       Didn't you me
                   et her in
                           Londᵒⁿ?
```

Though ambiguity is rampant, a clear enough pitch marking can obviate it, as we saw in the last chapter (pp. 272–73).

The uncertainty surrounding terminal fall-rises is probably inherent in the system and not a defect of analysis. Human beings created anatomical problems for themselves when they decided to unbend themselves and walk upright. Intonation created problems for itself when it turned to deemphasis as a form of emphasis, using a drop in pitch both to mark an accent and at the same time to play it down. Low-pitched accents are not always satisfactorily marked by pitch, and interpretation depends on contextual and other factors that might otherwise be redundant.

Productivity

There is no limit, in theory, to the length of contours or to the number of profiles that can be included in a single contour. The relatively simple, mostly two-profile, contours described in this chapter barely scratch the surface, though they do show the main combinatorial effects, such as the tight linkage of B, C, or AC to a following A or AC and the relative independence of a medial A. The speaker is free to combine and to iterate, and to make the combinations loose or tight in such a way that one can never be absolutely sure, even with a change of speakers, that a given contour has wrapped itself up and another is about to begin. In the five-profile contour on page 180, *So just as I'm about to doze off to sleep the thing starts popping,* one might choose to divide after *sleep,* creating two contours—a division that would appeal to a syntactician. And when is something merely tagged on, instead of forming an integral part of a contour? Take a desultory conversation in which someone mentions Manchester. After a bit of silence another speaker says,

kíd bró

My

ᵗʰer lived in   chester••• ,

Mán   come to ᵗʰink of it•

—B+A+C with a tagged B.[14] The syntax is loose and one is tempted to regard this as a separate contour; but exactly the same succession of profiles—minus the pause—would be equally appropriate if the last five words were replaced by the more tightly linked *for a time.* Junctural closeness is gradient from zero (no separation at all) upward, indefinitely, regardless of the grammar.

The speaker is also free to manipulate unaccented syllables to produce varied effects of tension and its opposite. We saw (p. 187) the effect of relaxing just one syllable in the sentence *Elizabeth was sick.* In the following A+C+C examples, the first, which allows the tail of the first C to go higher and gains an abrupt drop to the second C, has a more condescending effect than the second—it is almost as if one were speaking to a child who had to be admonished and yet dealt with tenderly, tension followed by quick restraint:

trý

Just   to be cóurteous when yoᵘ

spéaᵏ•

The same buildup can be achieved by lengthening syllables, upgrading them to full for the purpose if they are normally reduced. In the following, the syllable *im-* is accented to produce a B profile, and also lengthened (we often do the same with *Ex-actly!*, *Cor-rect!*), and *Now!* is stretched as if to make it a cross between B and A, with extra volume on the downglide:

Correspondingly, the drop of an A may be delayed slightly so as to involve part of a following syllable at the high pitch, again in order to sustain that pitch—it is as if the speaker were saying 'I'm too tensed up about this to let go.' In the example, the vowel of *it* becomes a curious compromise between the full vowel of the truly accented allomorph [ɪt] and the shwa of the usual unaccented allomorph [ət]:

Similarly in an emphatic answer to *What are you doing?*, involving the syllable *-ing*:

The speaker also has wide freedom to introduce accents of power at advantageous positions to increase the force of the utterance or to provide—at the beginning of an utterance—a bit of thunder to demand attention. An example of the first is the double accenting of *It's óutrágeous!* and the shift of accent in *It's quíte cómplex* (rather than *quíte compléx*) to get the advantage of juxtaposed A's. An example of the second is the expression *as I was saying*, which is normally accented on *I* and *say-*, but to an inattentive audience a speaker may shift the first accent to the normally unaccented *as*:

Similarly with the following treatment of *it*, for emphasis on the utterance as a whole:

```
ĭt
     doesn't make any difference!
```

And again with *it*, an emphatic two-A-profile replacement for what normally has only one A (meaning 'It's worthless,' in response to *What do you think of it?*):

```
ĭt's    bú
                 s
          a      t
                   !
```

Such cases are of a piece with emphatic A's on exclamations, e.g. *Óh, yés!*, *Í knów!*, *Whó-ée!*, and the like.

Other features of tempo, loudness, register, and movement (abruptness, glide, etc.) are also available. Of these the one most clearly intonational is the monotone. The steady pitch calls attention to the degree of tension that must be maintained to keep it up, and yet the weariness of doing so, suggesting boredom or redundancy. Compare the following example from Goldsmith (1981):

```
Wĭll you stóp                    Cóke bottles on my desk!
          putting those empty
```

The monotone can be applied to any contour. An example of B+A with monotone tail on the A:

```
Lóok out beló
              ow!
```

A monotone C on a B+C contour ("plain" intonation would have a rising tail on the C):

```
Lĕt's
     gó-o-o.
```

Examples of monotone B on an A+B contour (the level can be at any height, with varying degrees of surprise, wistfulness, etc.):

```
Dó              Név           Dŏ
     réally?          mĭnd!          tóld you please!
  you            er            as  I
```

Finally, successive monotones that are isochronous, e.g. this B+C+A:

```
         térnally
    E             péstering me to
                                 có
                                   m
                                    e.
```

To paraphrase Kendon (1980: 223) again, every contour that is uttered is a "new enactment," with certain relatively constant configurations in the shape of accent profiles, but with slopes, intervals, intensities, lengths, and successions that answer to each moment's fluctuation of mood.

Conclusion

What is the least that can be said from which the most can be inferred? That is the question this book has looked to answer.

One risk is saying too little. For all its attractiveness, the simple binarity of up and down or high and low is not enough, as we saw in Chapter 10. With a bit of finagling it will account for monotones if plus and minus signs are used: a monotone is minus-up, minus-down. A little more finagling will take care of ups and downs *within* ups and downs, a redoubling that occurs when tangents to peaks and troughs rise or fall. But when *amounts* of rise or fall become critical, as they do in the contrasts among the profiles, with resulting ambiguity when there is not enough of one or the other, then a gestalt approach is called for: we have to consider figure and ground in determining, for example, the difference between Profile A and Profile B—a "down" that is figure in the skip that delineates an A profile is ground in the gradual descent that is sometimes found in the tail of a B. The two-way contrast of up and down does much of the work in defining affect and emotion, but only partly describes the configurations of the accents. And it tells us nothing about register, beyond the fact that if the voice goes high enough or low enough it will "break" into falsetto or creak. (One could argue that this is irrelevant: it is only a "quality" of the voice, and since we are not considering other qualities, such as gruffness, tearfulness, huskiness, or stridency, we should not consider register either. But falsetto and creak *are* an aspect of up and down, and are coupled too closely with the up and down in modal register to be excluded.) The fact that intonational configurations are matched by configurations of facial expressions and bodily gestures, that the two operate much of the time in parallel, and that their similarities betoken similarities of function, points to the configurational approach as the most likely to succeed.

The opposite risk is saying too much. The most obvious thing about

intonation to the amateur's ear is what it contributes toward interpreting an utterance as a question, a command, etc.; and the amateur
tends to feel that there are intonations *of* these various kinds of speech
acts. But we have found that intonation is too free-wheeling to be confined in such a way. The rising pitch associated with many questions
is also associated with clause breaks within utterances. And we find
on looking more closely that the formal similarity is related to a functional one: it marks something as incomplete. This more abstract
value of intonation would have gone unrecognized if our search had
been limited to a level no more refined than those larger chunks of
discourse.

Avoiding excess at this stage does not mean ignoring the manifold
and complex interactions of intonation with all the other antics that
communicators engage in. Intonation is important for who is speaking, for who will be taking the next turn, for how the act is to be
understood (explanation, apology, challenge), for how the speaker
will be evaluated (as an individual, as a native speaker, as a member of
a given social class)—to mention only a few of the things that affect
our roles as speakers and listeners. It is important for distinctions in
grammar—for marking quotations, parentheses, and compounds; for
identifying presuppositions, themes and rhemes, coordinations, parts
and wholes, and the scope of negation. It is indispensable in all this,
and yet it remains itself, and our vision is blurred if we start with categories that are too inclusive and too ill-defined. Our search here has
been for the FORMS of intonation, making unsystematic use of functions mainly to corroborate the forms. How involved and inward-
turning this can be we discovered with Profile C and its "politeness"
function. Within a formal setting one is expected to act with a certain
degree of reserve. That reserve, and the intonational restraint that
marks it, often becomes a mask for a hostility that is betrayed by other
parts of the speaker's behavior, with the result that "being polite" becomes a telling way of "being impolite." We damn not only by restraining our enthusiasm in

$$\text{She's}$$
$$\text{nic}^{\text{e}\cdot}$$

but also by restraining our temper in

$$\text{I}$$
$$\text{know}$$
$$\text{tha}^{\text{t}!}$$

Beyond the minimal use of functions for identification, there are
many intricate questions of grammar and discourse that have not
been treated in this volume.

Between a diet that is too lean and a diet too abundant for the constitution, how can one be sure of having found the minimum with maximum benefit? There are no certainties with a medium as fluid as intonation. Something like the configurations here dubbed profiles must approach a kind of reality. Experiments are too consistent in showing that certain angular prominences (see p. 257) are reacted to as figures in an intonational gestalt. But the profiles as they have been identified in this book are not the only possible ways of carving up the rather continuous territory over which the accents are spread. Appendix B discusses arguments in favor of combining certain forms of Profile B with Profile C. Our own analysis showed some hesitation in separating CB from C (p. 161) and CA from A (pp. 155–56). It would be reasonable to view modalities of A as sharing characteristics of B and C. An A that is jumped up to as well as down from resembles B+A— compare the following:

```
        A                    B        A
      prom               give you my prom
  I                   I
        ise.                          ise.
```

—peaks and plateaus have much in common. An A that is jumped down to as well as down from has somewhat the restraint of a C, though the similarity here is less marked. All we can do to decide whether to reclassify or perhaps to add subclasses is to make the best physical description we can in view of the functions that a given shape performs. With Profile A the downward jump comes as close to being unmistakable as any physical break can be, and on the functional side it marks an all-or-none split when compared with a gradually downmoving B tail. That sudden drop and trail-off is an icon of 'separation,' and is what signals the contrastivity and finality of the A profile. Whether the downskip is approached from below, as in

```
                    Jo
          It was
                 hn.
```

or from above, as in

```
          It was  Jo
                 hn.
```

the result serves equally well in an utterance like *It was John, not Mary*; a B on John would not serve in most contexts, even though it shares with the first A above all but the terminal downmotion:

```
                 John.
          It was
```

One could also argue for lumping A and C together in opposition to B, on the grounds that C, like A, can show contrastivity, whereas B cannot—A and C would be associated as mirror images, with a factor of 'reversal' attached to C. Though our choice here was to make the very conspicuous characteristic of 'restraint' the basis for regarding C as independent, that characteristic could be assigned to a different level. In short, there are various alternatives both in defining and in formalizing the basic A, B, and C profiles. The configurations that cause certain elements to stand out over others are more or less given, but which are "same" and which are "different" in a phonological sense is not an easy question to answer.

As for the more complex profiles, they add the further problem of segmentation. When a rising terminal is attached to what would otherwise be an A profile, is it now an A profile plus a rising tail or is it an independent AC profile? We could recognize (as some have) the rising terminal as a more or less independent formative, attachable to B and C as well as to A—in fact, for B it would almost be diagnostic, since most B's have rising tails. But then we would have to consider whether a tonal ending in an A, or a level or slightly falling tail in a B, constitutes a "rising" terminal—both remain at a relatively high pitch and share with rising terminals quite similar implications of incompleteness. If we decide that it does, then the supposedly affixal terminal becomes a necessary part of Profile C, which is required to end at a pitch appreciably higher than the lowest in the range, usually a rising one. The more practical solution seemed to be to count AC as a separate profile on a par with C. And as long as 'restraint' was allowed as the notional correlate of C, the same restraint of the initially held-down pitch would justify recognizing CA (and of course CAC and CB).

Whether or not a terminal is regarded as a modification of an independently defined profile, there are other modifications that function in a different dimension. The most important of all is the ornamentation of rising and falling with its implications of upness and downness, tension and relaxation, manifested more than anywhere else in the unaccented syllables that provide the approaches to and the tails following the accented syllables. To some degree this feature determines the profiles themselves: upness in B and downness in A, but the downness of C, more than a downness of relaxation, is a downness of being held down. The ground of C is relatively high, betokening tension; the push away from the ground is forceful in a sense even though it is in a downward direction, and other accentual cues—length and intensity—may add to the force. All the same, when C is used to calm someone—calming and reassuring being among its chief uses—C is, in a sense, relaxing. As an accent, C is "strong"; as an affective signal it is the opposite. If this seems paradoxical, consider the common injunction "*Try* to be relaxed."

This separation of functions—accentual and modal—explains why, in the treatment of accentual prosody, it was possible to put off a detailed discussion of the profiles. It made little difference in Part II what particular shape the accent had: any profile could be used for power or for interest (though Profile A was favored in the examples). Even with revisions of the sort suggested above, the structure of accentual prosody would remain pretty much the same. Though we find ambiguities in both performance and perception, a speaker either intends or does not intend a syllable to be accented, and gradience is less of a problem than with the rest of intonation. The fact of the accent outweighs the form of it.

But the forms—or profiles—are the core of melodic prosody. They are the domain of ups and downs that are significant as ups and downs and not merely as obtrusions from a reference line. The primary profiles, A, B, and C, have abstract meanings that ultimately derive (whether historically or ontogenetically or both) from metaphors associated with rising and falling, which are shared with facial expressions and bodily gestures. Profile A with its terminal fall is a coming-to-rest. The fall conveys notions related to termination. The most important is the cutoff: I'm through with speaking, now it's your turn, that's the end of the conversation. But being 'finished' can be transferred in two additional directions. One is demarcation for separate importance: we saw how A, in contrast with B, can be used in the middle of an utterance to assert an independent fact. The other is 'finality' in a modal sense: I'm sure of myself, that's that, end of argument; a string of A's is the most assertive kind of utterance. It is significant that the words we use to describe the mood effects represent the same metaphorical extensions that are cued by the intonational figures: *finality, downright* (a *down*right person is a positive one), *finished* (a finished piece of work), the issue is *closed*, I *rest* my case, etc.

The essential feature of B is a going up, and the meaning is the opposite of A on the 'finality' axis: it is 'upness' carried through various metaphorical transformations, two especially: 'up-in-the-airness' or 'incompletion,' and 'keyed-upness' or high emotivity, which may be excitement, anger, surprise, or merely the curiosity that goes with having a question to ask. On the incompleteness side, B is the typical leaner, with numerous syntactic and morphological applications, from marking compounds to serving as the main cue to interrogation in complementary questions. The most common gestural analog and concomitant of B is raised eyebrows.

Unlike both A and B, C is typified by a holding down of the accented syllable but with no downward jump *from* that syllable. The ground is typically higher than the figure, always (unless truncated) before and usually after. Whereas the fall in A demarcates the relatively high pitch of the accent, which ranges upward at will, and the rise of B allows the same, C is opposed to both in that it checks any rise on the point of the accent (a TERMINAL rise is optional and customary). Again there are metaphorical associations related to reining in, checking, restraint, with many discourse applications (but few grammatical ones that are not at least as frequent with A or B). These include restraint for courtesy (as in asking an accosting question or making an apology or gently contradicting someone), restraint projected on the hearer (as to reassure an adult or comfort a child), restraint to minimize the importance of something. The most common gestural accompaniment of C is with the head, a bowing movement that matches the intonational "bow" of the C.

Along with the characteristic up or down marking the accent, which is an invariant feature of the configuration, any profile can be modified by more or less independent ups and downs, a raising or lowering of part or all of the profile affecting the accented syllable alone, the unaccented syllables alone, or both together. An AC, for example, can be entirely located high in the speaker's overall range, and this is fairly regular in many warnings (it would sharpen a warning like *Look out!*, but applied to an innocuous phrase such as *I guess* it would be no more than a flip way of dismissing responsibility). The complexity of these modifications can be illustrated by the effect of giving a C profile a low or high terminal rise to see how either modification will suit an utterance that ends a conversation. Ordinarily we expect a terminal fall—hence an A profile—at the end of a conversational exchange. But a C is normal enough in that position especially if the trough is low and the tail either remains level or has only a slight rise. So in a leave-taking where the speaker wants to caution a friend about to venture on the freeways, the last utterance can comfortably be

$$\text{Just }^{\text{be}}$$
$$\text{care}^{\text{ful.}}$$

at a fairly low pitch. Without adding more, the speaker may turn his back. But if the terminal goes up more, and particularly with a higher pitch throughout, the appropriateness to ending a conversation with such an utterance diminishes: one expects something more to be added, say *I wouldn't want you to get hurt*. The higher pitch implies the up-in-the-airness of incompleteness and concern. That is, it does when the speaker wears a sober expression. If he smiles, then the utterance may again comfortably end the exchange. Now the upness is partly one of being upbeat—the higher pitch is an intonational smile matching the facial one.

We observed a similar gradience in the modifications of all the profiles. Though an A must have a terminal fall, and the terminal fall is associated with finality, the fall itself can be graded. If it ends well above creak, some degree of incompleteness may be implied. A speaker asked why he does not drink wine who answers

```
                    like
        I don't
```

```
                    it.
```

with *it* at creak, is not obliged to continue, though he may. But with *it* well above creak, the hearer will be surprised if something more is not added, say *It doesn't agree with me*, now with *me* at creak—or, if it is not at creak, the hearer is invited to develop the thought in his own mind—something is unfinished about the utterance. Here again a characteristic that defines a profile—the terminal high of B—is found in diluted form attached to a different profile. Up and down are what they are no matter where they are encountered.

This ubiquity of the primary metaphor brings us back to the proposal embodied in the Preface, to test every observation about intonational meaning against the hypothesis that that meaning is somehow expressed in the forms of the profiles and their modifications—a reductionist hypothesis, but one that the author felt had to come first in any program of research. Many examples have been offered in which grammatical and discourse distinctions become more understandable—and are more efficiently generalized—when referred to the up-down metaphor and to the inferences that can be drawn from it. There are no holistic contours in the sense that they have meanings divorced from the meanings of the parts—unlike what happens in verbal locutions, where holistic words are assigned meanings that are typically unrelated to the meanings of the parts; in fact, the parts in this case are typically arbitrary and meaningless. Nor are there configurations with particular grammatical meanings, as there are again with verbal locutions, where things like *John saw Jane* and *Jane saw John* define a relationship of actor and patient; questions do not "have" intonations except as they are *felt* to be incomplete and are uttered accordingly.

All the same, it would be foolish to deny that intonation is in many ways conventionalized. We do not hesitate to classify people as grouchy, waspish, obsequious, domineering, complaisant, gloomy, enthusiastic, down-in-the-mouth, while agreeing that they may not "really" be that way: the classification reflects the way people act when they are in the corresponding mood, but it has somehow become fixed upon certain individuals. So an intonation that reflects a feeling may be fixed upon expressions used when that feeling is to be expected. We end up here in a psychological bind. The question of free will pursues us. How much of what human beings do do they do because they are driven to, and how much do they do from conscious choice? And, in between, how much do they do because a choice has become a habit? We begin by dropping our pitch because we are finished speaking and the energy is shut off; later we fake the sensation and insert falls when we are not finished, to get the desired effect in our hearer. Eventually "fall" becomes a sort of conventional marker of certain kinds of utterances. But the convention never becomes so stereotyped that the feeling is not readily reattached to it—affective intonation is probably reprogrammed from below with every new generation. Much of what we do in intonation is what we are expected to do and what we accordingly choose to do, but there is no clear line between conscious choice and unconscious reaction. At least part of the significance of anything we say is due to the fact that it *might* have been said that way under the influence of some attitudinal or emotive push.

As we get more thorough and detailed descriptions of the intonation of other languages—in all the richness of its contribution to grammatical, interpersonal, and situational relationships—and particularly as we learn more about how children shape their native predispositions into communicative skills, we may be able to determine how far the harnessing of intonation's expressiveness has gone, how conventional it has become. Till then it is best to keep the investigation of intonational meaning as close as possible to its native base. There *is* a syntax of intonation: utterances have a canonical shape with accents normally fore and aft; tune-text associations are loosely predictable in terms of themes and rhemes; profiles may be bent one way or another but are not wrenched out of shape unless by some form of shock. Yet under these more or less conventionalized materializations there is always the expressive metaphor. If, as Bickerton (1981) claims, our predisposition to be speaking creatures enables us to quickly build a new language from the wreckage of old ones— pidgins to creoles in one generation—it is easy to suppose that the first stable feature of that new language will be its intonation.

Appendixes

Appendix A. Vowel Reduction, Derivation, and Stress

The reduced vowels have been classed by most analysts as special versions of the full vowels, and there are undeniably correspondences between the two sets; yet there are good reasons for keeping them apart.

The best evidence is probably the phonetic character of the sounds. The full vowels are distinguished from one another on three dimensions: tongue height (high versus low), tongue fronting and backing (front versus back), and lip rounding and spreading (round versus spread). The reduced vowels are indifferent to the first and third of these dimensions—practically speaking, they are distinguished from one another only by fronting and backing. In *Willie* the vowel [ɨ] is fronted (that is, the tongue is thrust forward); in *willow* the vowel [ɵ] is backed; and in *Willa* the vowel [ə] lies midway between—it is CENTRAL.

Indifference to tongue height means that the reduced vowels are slack-jawed; indifference to rounding means that they are slack-lipped. The [ɨ] of *Willie* can be pronounced with a tongue height anywhere in the range of [i], [ɪ], [e], or [ɛ] and it will make no difference, though with the full vowels these differing heights are exactly what tells us whether we are saying *keyed, kid, cade,* or *Ked.* In words spelled with *-ia* (*Lydia, mania, pneumonia, sepia*) one can observe two of the reduced vowels in contrast, and the wide range of tongue heights that they allow: the [ɨ] segment can have any height from that of [i] to that of [e], and the [ə] segment any from that of [æ] to that of [a] (including that of [ʌ])—the difference will not be noticed unless attention is directed to it. The only essential is that the [ɨ] segment be front and the [ə] segment be central. Words like *folio, cameo, radio,* and *Antonio* exhibit a similar contrast, front-to-back: [ɨ] followed by [ɵ]. In *Genoa* the contrast is back-to-central, [ɵ] followed by [ə].

As with the full vowels, there are dialectal preferences in pronunciation, especially where [ɨ] is concerned: the Northeast of the United States, with some notable exceptions (e.g. eastern New England and New York City), favors a higher tongue position, close to that of [i]; the South favors a lower position (see Bronstein 1960: 147).

Figure 2 shows the reduced vowels set against the background of the full vowels, displayed in terms of tongue position, front versus back and high versus low. The reduced vowels are sometimes referred to as CENTRALIZED (they are pulled toward the center of the large triangle), sometimes as OBSCURE (no one of them corresponds to any particular one of the full vowels).

If the phonetic dissimilarities we have noted are to count in justifying the reduced vowels as independent phonemes, they must "make a difference" in distinguishing one word from another. Not all dissimilarities do make a difference. The [p] of *rope* may be "released" or not (that is, we may pronounce *rope* with or without opening the mouth right after the [p] to let the air out), but we hear both kinds of [p] as "the same"—no words in English are distinguished by that contrast. On the other hand, in spite of their resemblance to each other (both are nasal), we do use the dissimilarity between [n] and [m] to distinguish words: *noose–moose, dinner–dimmer, rune–room*. Reduced vowels will have to pass this word-distinguishing test, and indeed they do. First, as we have seen with *Willie–Willa–willow*, their distinctness from one another is put to use. Further, they are distinct from the full vowels, including the ones that they resemble most. Not many pairs of words are distinguished solely by the contrast between a reduced vowel and a similar-sounding full one, but there are a few (not all speakers will agree on all items):

Reduced Vowel	Full Vowel
chicor*y*	chickar*ee*
And*y*'s	And*es*
troch*e*	troch*ee*
boot*y*	boot*ee*
farr*ow*	Phara*oh*

On the other hand, pairs in which the vowels are just one of the contrasting features are more common:

Reduced Vowel	Full Vowel
vom*i*t [ə]	womb*a*t [æ]
org*a*n [ə]	Shog*u*n [ʌ]
mark*e*t [ə] or [ɨ]	Márc*o*tte [a]
lass*o* [ɵ]	Es*au* [ɔ]
gall*ows* [ɵ]	al*oes* [o]
cours*er* [ər]	cors*air* [ɛr]

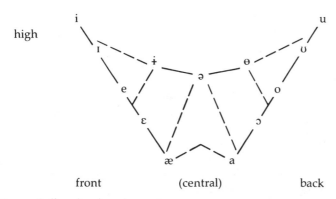

front   (central)   back

Fig. 2. Full and reduced vowels

The facts are clear enough to dispel the notion that the reduced vowels are merely full vowels that got phonetically shortchanged. At the same time, we need to understand the basis for that idea, because it contains a truth that has simply been misapplied. Historically, the reduced vowels came from the full ones, and the process continues. When a new word is adopted, speakers tend to treat it in a gingerly fashion, pronouncing it precisely. As they get used to it, they grow more careless, speed up, and shift some of the vowels to a speedier set, often moving the position of the stress as well. When the word *silicon* was adopted in the second decade of the nineteenth century, the vowel of *-con* was full; it is now recorded with shwa [ə] in both British and American dictionaries. When *levee* was first borrowed from French, it had a stressed [i] in the last syllable. Then the stress moved to the first syllable, but the vowel remained [i]. Now, for most speakers, the vowel is [ɨ] and *levee* is homophonous with *levy*. (This has not yet happened to *shivaree*, which is still distinct from *shivery* even when stressed on its first syllable.) The process is rapid enough for both pronunciations, [lɛvi] and [lɛvɨ], to be present to the mind of many speakers—some will be unsure of which one they use—and this cements the notion of one being derived from the other, historically true but descriptively false if we realize that these are *rival* forms and one is almost certain to disappear.[1]

The picture is further blurred by the cognate forms in which an alternation between full and reduced vowels has become firmly established. Whereas the verb *confront* has the full vowel [ʌ] as in *cud*, the noun *confrontation* normally has shwa. *Allege* has [ɛ] as in *Ked*, but *allegation* has either shwa or [ɨ]. *Infanticide* has [æ] as in *cad*, but *infant* has shwa. Similarly *sentential–sentence*, *instantiate–instance*, *moron–moronic*. Examples can be multiplied from all the vast lexicon of

Latin- and Greek-based words that English has inherited or adopted. There are enough regularities to make it possible to relate the corresponding forms by "derivational" rules, and a great deal of effort has gone into describing English morphology in these terms (distinguished more by its success in accounting for similarities among the highbrow words than for contrasts among the lowbrow ones). One of the goals has been to fit the reduced vowels into predictable relationships with full ones.

For our purposes, the derivation of a reduced vowel makes no difference. We take it as part of the given, as a prime in the system, in order to say something about the rhythm of phrases in which it occurs. (See Bolinger 1981 for discussion.)

One last confusion—in terminology—needs to be cleared up. True to their conception of reduced vowels as merely full vowels in disguise, most analysts have classed them by the feature that supposedly accounts for the difference. Instead of recognizing their status as three individual and unique phonemes, this view lumps them together as an undifferentiated set labeled "unstressed." A word such as *attaché* [ætæ'še] is said to contain not three full vowels but three stressed vowels, and one such as *camisole* two stressed vowels and one (the middle) unstressed. This obviously conflicts with the use of *stress* defined at the beginning of Chapter 2 as the potential for accent. By that account—which is adhered to in this book—*attaché* is stressed only on its last syllable (though it contains three full vowels, hence three full syllables), and *camisole* is stressed only on its first, though both that syllable and the last one are full. As has been emphasized previously, all stressed syllables are full (*-ché, cam-*), but not all full syllables are stressed (*at-ta-, -sole*). It is on this last point that the two descriptions differ.[2]

The advantage of marking just one stress per word is that it affords a clearer statement about accent. By definition, the stressed syllable is the one that carries an accent if the speaker decides to highlight the word. Normally no other syllable in the word is accented. But there is one exception: sometimes an accent is allowed to go on a full syllable to the *left* of the stressed syllable. This is not permitted on a full syllable to the right; thus even though the last syllable of *cóntraband* is full, it cannot bear an accent—we are allowed to use the first but not the second of the following pronunciations:

```
con                    *con    ba
   traband                 tra   nd
```

The contrary case is a word such as *overséas*, stressed on its last syllable: the preceding full syllable *ov-* qualifies for an accent if the speaker elects to put one there. This is usually done to give an extra lift to the word, as for instance in its "citation" form (the form we use when naming the word or telling how it is pronounced) or in order to be emphatic. In such cases it is normal to accent both syllables, for example

Ov se
er as.

in answer to *What was the word you said?* It is also done to avoid having accents come too close together (see pp. 61–62). In this case an accent on the preceding full syllable may replace the accent on the stressed syllable: *óverseas vóyage* (to be emphatic we might say *óvérséas vóyage*, pulling out all the stops, but not **overséas vóyage*). There is no problem with *a vóyage overséas* because the stressed syllables are well separated. On the other hand, a word like *cóntraband* offers no remedy to the crowding of accents. If the speaker wants to accent both *good* and *contraband* in *góod cóntraband*, the two accents will be side by side—it is not normal to say **góod contrabánd*. (Again, there is no problem with *cóntraband góods*.) Some more examples of words with an early stress and only one possibility of accent: *ácrobat, ágitate, réprimand, cóntroversy, álimony, Cánterbury.* Some examples of words with late stress and more than one possibility of accent: *shívarée, íntermédiate, Méditerránean, óutsíde, rámpáge.*[3]

The dual possibilities for accent reflect the history of English, which is a battleground of early accent versus late accent in words. The language by and large favors the early position of the stress. This is truer of adjectives and nouns than it is of verbs, which more readily preserve a terminal stress—as we can see in such pairs as *cómbine* noun, *combíne* verb; *réject* noun, *rejéct* verb; *cóme-on* noun, *come ón* verb. (Even when not stressed on the end, the verb, if it has more than two syllables, is apt to retain a full vowel in the last syllable: people who say *a graduate* with [ə] in the final syllable will say *to graduate* with [e].) The differing treatment of nouns and adjectives on the one hand and verbs on the other is probably the result of the favored accent pattern for sentences discussed in Chapter 5—the verb is more apt to be toward the end of the sentence and the noun or adjective toward the beginning, with rightward and leftward accents respectively. The effect of this favoritism—especially with nouns—is as with *levee*, and has been especially marked with loanwords from French, which regularly enter with terminal stress and almost as regularly end up by backshifting it. In the last century we had *sabotáge*; now we have *sábotage*—but for most speakers still with a full vowel in the last syllable. Other examples: *intrígue* → *íntrigue* (but the verb remains *intrígue*), *allý* → *álly, rondéau* → *róndeau*. The word *platéau*, from French military usage, was naturalized in the nineteenth century and has still not shifted. There are cases of reborrowing, with the older loan now back-shifted but the newer one still retaining the French stress: *Látin, latéen; dívers, divérse.* (French origin is not essential—the wholly made-up word *ampersand* has gone from *ampersánd* to *ámpersand*, and the British pronunciation *Waterlóo* has been imported as *Wáterloo*, in Iowa.) There are so many of these cases that the shift has—for some speakers and some words—become a two-way street, with a certain piquancy assigned to a terminal accent (this is related to climax—see Chapter 6). Adjectives especially are affected, because they are the words that typically signify "qualities." So although *gallant* was a loanword from French and is regularly pronounced *gállant*, to call someone *gallánt* is to add a flair. Colorful adjectives such as *abjéct, obtúse, concíse, ornáte, avérse, absúrd, obscéne, picturésque, verbóse, inténse, repléte, robúst, divíne,* and many more acquire a special intensity by virtue of the terminal accent, and they resist backshifting the stress. Nouns too are affected, though less markedly: *prestíge* [prɛstiʒ] is more prestigious than *préstige* [prɛstidʒ]; a person who refers to the *Crúsades* as a prosaic historical fact may revert to *crusáde* in referring to a campaign that serves a passionate cause; *revénge* is more potent than *véngeance.* Sometimes it is the relative infrequency of a word that preserves its unshifted form. The noun *assígn* (as in *heirs and assigns*) is comparatively rare. The *-cord* nouns are clearly keyed to frequency: *accórd* is the least frequent and keeps the terminal stress; *díscord* is next, and has shifted but preserves the full vowel in the second syllable; the commonest is *récord,* which has both backshifted the stress and reduced the last vowel, at least in American English. (There is currently a reverse tendency, as many Americans resort to a "spelling pronunciation" in such forms as *actor, juror, defendant.*)

These examples suffice to show the lingering effect of stress on vowel quality: a stressed vowel must be a full vowel and a once-stressed vowel on losing its stress does not immediately reduce. So there is a temptation to say that it is "still stressed" and to analyze the syllable structure of words in terms of stress rather than of vowel quality—this despite the fact that experiments have shown stress to be relied on far less than vowel quality in word recognition.[4]

Up to this point we have been discussing the reduced vowels as if their separate existence were a fully established fact, and we have cited examples where it clearly is. But given their origin in the deaccenting of full vowels and given also the continuing presence of full vowels that in rapid speech are deaccented, it would be strange if there were not areas of uncertainty, full vowels that sometimes tend toward reduction without yet having reached it completely.

This is but one more manifestation of indeterminacy in fast speech,

itself one of the main causes of phonological change. A good example
is what happens when one says the word *cordial* slowly and carefully,
and what happens when one speeds up. The slow pronunciation is
(or can be) [kɔrdiəl]; the fast pronunciation is [kɔrdʒəl]. Is one to say
that the [dʒ] sound in English is only a byproduct of palatalizing a [d]
in fast speech? Clearly that won't do, because in *cudgel* no amount of
slowing down or speeding up makes any difference: [dʒ] is an established part of the system. If this ambiguity can affect a consonant, it
can equally affect a vowel, and we should not be surprised that in
some positions and at some speeds a given vowel sound may waver.

Where reduced-versus-full is concerned, this uncertainty is most
vivid in relation to the position of stress. In word-final position, the
reduced vowels are stable and well contrasted, both among themselves and against full vowels as a class. (This applies also to the comparatively rare cases in which the vowel is in the final syllable though
not in absolute final position: thus *epic* is distinct from *epoch*.)[5] But
elsewhere in the word there is a difference between what happens
next to the stress and what happens at a distance from it, and also
between what happens before the stress and what happens after. The
second of these two factors influences the first. If we have an immediately posttonic syllable (that is, a syllable right after the stress) that
is also final in the word, normally (as was noted above) its being next
to the stress does not interfere with the clarity of the vowel. Here belong the paradigm cases of *Willie–Willa–willow* etc., where all three
reduced vowels are clearly distinguishable; and instances of full
vowels in that position are also fairly common—*Hindu, Camay, Curlee,
argon*. The clarity of this position—regardless of the proximity of the
stress—probably has to do with accent: as is noted in Chapter 5, it is
important for the development of a pitch turn to have the material following the accented syllable laid out clearly, and if there is only one
syllable following, that syllable will not be slighted. But if another syllable follows *that* one, then the position next to the stress may affect
the quality of the vowel rather drastically—the additional material farther from the stress supplies what is needed for the pitch turn, and
the accented syllable more readily overpowers the vowel directly after
it (often to the point of blanking it out altogether, as has happened
with *Wednesday*). So in *cánopy* the second vowel may vary on a scale of
indifference between [ɵ] and [ə], and in *índigo* it may vary between [ə]
and [ɨ]. The syllables following the deafened one are again more readily distinguishable (there is a tendency, even when all the vowels are
reduced, to alternate a higher and a lower degree of clarity, so that in
a word like *fórmidableness* the syllables -*da*- and -*ness* stand out more
than -*mi*- and -*ble*-), and we find—besides the clear reduced -*py* of

canopy and the clear unreduced *-go* of *indigo*—cases like *enema* and *enemy* where the words are distinguished by their reduced vowels, *sýnonym* and *Sýnanon* distinguished (in part) by their full vowels, and *íntimate* (adjective) and *intimáte* (verb) distinguished by a reduced versus a full. Or like *récipe*, where the position protects the full [i] which may or may not go to [ɨ].

There are even a few pairs distinguished by reduced vowels in the threatened position right after the stress. The Webster *Ninth New Collegiate Dictionary* marks *oracle* with [ə] in the second syllable and *auricle* with [ɨ]. Whether generally accepted or not, speakers can resort to such a contrast when necessary to distinguish an unusual word, as when *allegator* is pronounced with [ɨ] so that it will not be heard as *alligator* with its shwa.

The effect of position next to the stress can be observed more easily *before* the stress because of the heavily prefixing nature of English morphology—there are countless words with elements added just before the stress. The most drastic effect is the complete submergence of the syllable, for example *police* reduced to *pleece*. But we are more interested in what happens to the vowel short of complete loss. In a syllable immediately before the stress, the vowel undergoes a certain amount of reduction even when it remains unmistakably a full vowel, and there is a strong tendency in rapid speech to reduce it completely. So it is not uncommon to find syllables where speakers waver. In the words *affectátion* and *incantátion* the second syllables have [ɛ] and [æ] respectively in careful speech but may go all the way to [ə] in rapid speech—and at intermediate speeds, intermediate values may be found. The verb *digést* has a first vowel that varies along a scale from the diphthong [aɨ] to shwa [ə]. The variation is confirmed by the latitude speakers have to change the value if the utterance requires it. So in a sentence like *That is impossible to digest*, a shwa in *di-* following the shwa in *to* creates a tongue-twister, and we tend to resort to the diphthong; but that is unnecessary in *What are you doing? — Digesting what you said*. Similarly the relatively uncommon *abjéct* would easily be confused with the common verb *objéct* if both words were permitted to use shwa, and we accordingly keep a fairly clear *æb-* in the first one. The same is true of the relatively uncommon *proscríbe* and the common *prescríbe*, and of the relatively uncommon *eménd* and the relatively common *aménd*. Speakers are apt to resort to a spelling pronunciation when they are conscious of the possibility of confusion, and the rarer and more studied the word, the greater the tendency is: compare *exercise–exorcise*, *manner–manor*, *edition–addition* (the latter influenced by *add*). *Absúrd* and *obscéne*, on the other hand, have no troublesome near-homonym and may more readily use shwa, though in emphatic speech [æb] and [ab] can still be heard.

Words with distinctive, separately meaningful prefixes tend to keep the full vowel: *biséct, defróst, co-cháirman, amóral, untíe, evért*. Speakers may give careful attention to learnèd words and often overcompensate in pronouncing these prefixes—as with the diphthong [ai] sometimes heard in the first syllable of *disséct* and *diménsion*. One finds here and there a similar careful treatment of a suffix; the *-iz(e)* of *civilization, centralization*, etc. may keep its full [ai] diphthong in careful speech. And this care is exercised not only with prefixes and suffixes. The speaker who fears that the connection with *creátive* may be lost will pronounce *creatívity* with full [e] rather than shwa in the second syllable. Similarly with the [ɛ] of *condémn* and the [ɛ] rather than shwa in *condemnátion*, and with the unreduced [a] of *mobócracy*—to keep the tie with *mob*—by contrast with the potentially reduced first syllable of *autócracy*. The overcautious pronunciation of almost any learnèd word will lead to a full vowel directly before the stress: *fidélity* and *diréct* with [ai], *traumátic* with [ae], *tabóo* and *anfráctuous* with [æ], *poltróon* with [a], *mystíque* with [ɪ], etc. Alongside these analogic and precisian influences there is an equally powerful one in the emotional loading of the word or of its base. The word *fix* has no such loading and *fixátion* easily reduces its first vowel; not so with *vex* and *vexátion*. *Detést* is more loaded than *protést*, and *detestátion* keeps its second syllable intact, unlike *protestátion*. *Pompósity* is less apt to be affected by reduction than *verbósity*.

With highly colloquial expressions the opposite occurs, even when the element affected is an independent word. So *come ón, go báck, sit dówn*, and *get úp* (to a horse) are sometimes spelled as heard: *c'mon, g'back, siddown*, and *giddap*. The verbs here are relatively colorless—the adverbs carry most of the information; one would not expect the same to happen to a phrasal verb such as *run báck* or *head ín*.

(What strikes the analyst in this extremely complex situation is the item-by-item solution of pragmatic difficulties. Words may have formal idiosyncrasies just as they have semantic ones. Ordinarily our choice of meanings leads to a choice of words that impose, by their structure, certain fairly automatic and predictable relationships among the sounds. But often the choice of words does not suffice to carry the message clearly, and we must go a step lower and choose among alternative forms of the word, to fit the context and avoid ambiguity. To handle all this our store of information about each word resembles what one finds in an encyclopedia rather than the meager and schematic entry in a dictionary. The latter could never tell us, for example, that in saying *Wait till he gets there* we are allowed to say *wait'll*, but in saying *Fight till you drop* we cannot say **fight'll*.)

Since it is position directly before the stress that leads to the obscuring of the vowel, if the syllable in question is at a remove from the stressed syllable we may expect a different treatment. The vowel of the prefix *in-* of *infér* may waver between [ɨ] and [ə], but the same prefix in *innováton* retains its full vowel [ɪ]: here the *in-* is separated from the stressed syllable *-va-*. And since the vowel is full and precedes the stress, that syllable may receive an accent, as we noted earlier. For convenience, we may call it a secondary accent to distinguish it from the primary, which occurs on the stressed syllable. The secondary accent defines much the same relations to the syllables adjoining it that the primary does to its adjoining syllables. The nouns based on verbs in *-fy* make good illustrations: *rámificátion, códificátion, ámplificátion, réctificátion, solídificátion.* Here the *-fi-* syllable is overpowered by the primary following it, and the syllable immediately before that is overpowered by the secondary (*ram-, cod-*, etc.). One can appeal of course to the etymology of these words to explain the behavior of the secondary—it falls on the same syllable that is stressed in the underlying verb: *rámify, códify, ámplify, réctify, solídify.* Similarly with other verbs having underlying cognates: *témperaméntal, ágoraphóbia.* But the rule does not depend on any such connections; it applies equally in words like *Cássiopéia, ánacolúthon, ónomatopoétic, Córiolánus, coátimúndi, gállimáufry, kángaróo, lálapalóoza.*

(We account for the secondary accent by appealing to a higher level. These longer words—in their citation forms—simply assume the accent pattern of full utterances. There is no accentual difference between *gástroenterítis* and *gástric enterítis.* It is as if a citation form were an answer to the question *What word do you use here?* or *How do you pronounce this word?*, and took the same question-answering intonation that one finds in the answer to *Where did you go?*,

```
                                  ca
                     went
             I            to Chi
                                go.
```

with one prominence, on *went*, toward the beginning, and another, on *-ca-*, toward the end. Accordingly, if one asks *What do you call an irritation of the digestive tract?*, the answer is

```
                          i
             Gas
                 troenter
                          tis.
```

with the same two prominences. This intonational shape is discussed in Chapter 5.)

Though the reductions we have been discussing are less clearly targeted, there still appears to be a tendency toward the three-vowel system that is so much clearer after the stress. Though shwa is also possible, [ɨ] is commonly heard in such words as *detéct, declíne, dený, deménted, discérn, replý, requést, repáir, sedúce, sevére, Kefáuver, guitár, ce- mént, mystérious,* and it distinguishes *prepóse* from *propóse* (the latter with [ə]), *depóse* from *oppóse, depréss* from *oppréss,* and (in part) *epístle* from *a pístol.* It is the regular vowel in the *de-* privative prefix, as in *denáture, devítalize, decáffeinate,* and it preserves the hiatus (that is, the vowel contrast) in *teleólogy,* which would be lost if the second vowel of *tele-* went to shwa as it does in *telephónic.* (This is the same phenome- non that we observe with the definite article in *the man* with shwa but *the otter* with [ɨ], and in words like *meánder, Leánder, Minneápolis, theól- ogy, geógraphy.*) The back reduced [ɵ] is less common but is heard in *mortálity, obése, donátion, procéed* (versus *precéde,* with shwa or [ɨ]). It too alternates with shwa in certain words, e.g. *Indonésia, allophónic, compositíon.* And instances of unvarying shwa are legion: *commánd, famíliar, avért, alóne, suppórt, finágle, gelátinous, seléction.* Though there is still a good deal of wavering, speakers appear to favor a definite choice: in pronouncing the noun *incantátion,* one usually says either [kæn] or [kən], not something in between.

The numerous instances of [ə] alternating with [ɨ] and with [ɵ], and the high frequency of [ə], point to shwa as a sort of last stage of reduc- tion before the vowel is lost completely. The forms of *police* alluded to above can be used as illustration:

$$[\text{pə'lis}] \rightarrow [\text{pə'lis}] \rightarrow [\text{plis}]$$

The drift toward shwa is simply a further step in the "centralization" of the reduced vowels, as shwa is the most central vowel (see Fig. 2). (The drift, as we might expect, is manifested mostly elsewhere than at the end of words, though a few exceptions are found such as *fella* for *fellow* and *tomorra* for *tomorrow*—but not **morra* for *morrow.*) The fact that shwa is the evolutionary terminus of reduction, so to speak, is one more reason why many analysts see reduction as a process rather than a state and tend to regard the reduced vowels as an undifferenti- ated set. But so long as the three-way contrast remains distinctive— spelling the difference between *folly* and *follow, Calley* and *calla, min- now* and *mini,* etc.—the reduced vowels must be recognized as vowels in their own right. Not only are the words distinguished by them nu- merous but a large proportion are among the most frequent in the language.

To repeat: those who prefer to see vowel reduction as a process rather than an accomplished fact in the description of a given period of English (no one denies that it is a process in the *history* of English) will argue that the reductions we see in syllables next to an accent prove that the reduced vowels are not a determinate set but are reflexes of stages of the full vowels. But the fact that fast speech distorts full vowels in the direction of reduced ones does not mean the dependence of all instances of reduced vowels on full ones any more than the fact that fast speech distorts *got you* toward *gotcha* threatens the independence of the consonant shared by *choose, rich,* and *hatchet.* The shwa in *obscene,* when indeed there is one, may be the same as the shwa in *gallon,* but the latter will remain the same no matter how much we slow our speech down. It is established—an instance of STABLE reduction. Reduction that comes and goes is UNSTABLE. (Technically PHONOLOGICAL reduction and PHONETIC reduction, respectively—the terms used by Pettersson and Wood 1983 for reduced vowels in Bulgarian.)[6]

The question remains why the scheme of reduced versus full vowels has not been more widely recognized. Although the way it is reflected in syllabic and accentual rhythm is its chief interest for our purposes, it has other reflexes in the sound system of English. One is the effect of reduced versus full vowels on an immediately preceding voiceless stop consonant. A full vowel is accompanied by a delayed release of the consonant—often called "aspiration"—whereas a reduced vowel, especially in the interior of a word, allows the voicing to start earlier and overlap the consonant to some degree, with the result that the distinction between voiced and voiceless is blurred: [p t k] come to sound like [b d g]. This is true even in unaccented syllables, as the following pairs show:

Súnapee	cánopy
mánatee	humánity
Mánichee	fínicky

The result is that the last part of *reciprocity* may sound identical to *prosody,* and if one says *repliga* in a context that calls for *replica,* the difference may pass undetected. Unless this phenomenon is assigned to the full-reduced opposition, one is compelled to attribute it to "stressed" syllables that are not really stressed, which results in some bizarre methods of indicating pronunciation in English dictionaries. Take the current Merriam Webster series, including the 1983 *Ninth New Collegiate* (a fine dictionary in nearly every respect). First, it falls back on stress marks to indicate the distinction between full and reduced syllables: *Manichee* is transcribed 'man-i-,kē, *finicky* is transcribed 'fin-i-kē, using the same vowel symbol for both [i] and [ɨ] in the final syllable. Next, it looks for a way of indicating the voicing overlap mentioned above, but takes note of only one of the consonants, [t] and its shift toward [d], no doubt because that is where the difference can be heard most distinctly. To accommodate this, the syllables are divided in a way that is not consistent with the division in the case of [p k] and [b g]. Whereas with *Manichee* and *finicky*, as we saw above, the syllables are divided identically, with *manatee* and *humanity* they are 'man-ə-ˌtē and hyü-'man-ət-ē, with the *t* in different syllables. The idea is to take advantage of the fact that when a [t] is at the end of a syllable it is not released—we don't hear the aspiration. (The classic pair to illustrate this is *night rate* and *nitrate*, with [t] in different syllables, where the spelling helps—in *night* the *t* is at the end of the word.) There are disadvantages to this procedure in addition to its inconsistency: first, slowing down the pronunciation makes it clear that speakers do not feel that syllabication to be the correct one—*humanity* in an emphatic context (*This is for the good of HUMANITY!*) divides *hu-man-i-ty*.[7] Second, not all dialects of English have unreleased [t]'s in cases like *night rate*. These complications are avoided when reduced vowels are recognized in the transcription. *Manatee* becomes ['mænəti] and the last three syllables of *humanity* become ['mænəti]; the grammar contains a rule to the effect that [t] will not be aspirated before the reduced vowel. A related rule will explain the fact that in *shogun* the [g] before the full vowel is a fully closed stop, while in *Hogan* the [g] before the reduced vowel is half-continuant. (See Bolinger 1967 for these and other advantages of the two-tiered vowel scheme.)

Other dictionaries have other problems traceable to the failure to recognize the reduced vowels as an independent set. One is how to represent a reduced vowel when you are committed to transcribing it as a full vowel. The vowel [i̇] is written as [ɪ] in Kenyon and Knott (1953) and the *American College Dictionary*, but as [i] in most other American dictionaries; [ɪ] is recorded for British usage by the recent Longman dictionaries (*Longman New Universal*, 1982; *Longman Dictionary of Contemporary English*, 1978). As far as reduced [ə] is concerned, the Longman dictionaries simply identify it with [o]. But the Merriam dictionaries show in their transcriptions an awareness of the problem, identifying [ə] with a range rather than with a single full vowel. Thus *billow* is transcribed 'bil-(ˌ)ō, -ə(-w), and this contrasts with *bimbo* 'bim-(ˌ)bō for the full vowel. The secondary accent mark, too, is significant, in showing the uncertainty of that criterion. Kenyon and Knott (1953) also indicate a range. These complications and uncertainties could be reduced by the simple expedient of recognizing the reduced vowels as vowels in their own right and noting the optional ranges diagrammed in Figure 2.

There is an object lesson in the way another dictionary, the *Oxford English Dictionary* (and its supplements), writes the various sounds. One can infer without too much difficulty when a vowel is reduced, since the OED scheme, a product of nineteenth-century phonetic overprecision, has distinctive signs for all three reduced vowels (compare *fancy* with *banshee*, *mellow* with *limbo*, etc.; no secondary "stresses" are marked on unaccented syllables). The problem began when such highly detailed systems of phonetic signs were "phonemicized" in the early decades of this century. (The heavy use of "stress" dates from the same period; it was even given the task of differentiating such items as *light housekeeper* and *lighthouse keeper*—see Bolinger and Gerstman in Bolinger 1965: 85–93.) That was a necessary step, in order to identify the truly distinctive sounds and get rid of predictable differences due to dialect, environment, etc. But the phonemicizers did not phonemicize the reduced vowels, perhaps not realizing at the time how widespread the phenomenon of two-tiered vowel systems is (pointed out by C. A. Ferguson, personal communication)—it was hard enough at first to identify the clearly recognizable vowels in the languages that were being analyzed.

Recognition came slowly for English too (and is still not part of prevailing doctrine). Hubbell (1950) and Hultzén (1961) proposed that the reduced vowels be given independent status. Householder (1957) anticipated the three-point scheme of [ɨ ə ɵ] though with some uncertainty where [ɵ] was concerned (perhaps justifiably, as [ɵ] is the least secure of the three—not all speakers seem to have it, though a few may actually have more than three). Especially noteworthy is Stockwell and Bowen (1965: 90, 92) who independently singled out the identical system that is used here. Apparently it was elaborated by Stockwell and C. A. Ferguson, as a sort of best compromise that would fit the largest number of speakers. Catford (1985) identifies the same three for British English, though instead of keeping them as a category of reduced vowels he regards them as "transitions." He gives the minimal set *We don't like emissions, We don't like a mission,* and *We don't like omissions* for [ɨ ə ɵ], respectively.

Layered schemes have been suggested for Bengali (Ferguson 1977) and for Germanic (Haugen 1970). And now we have the three-point system for Bulgarian proposed by Pettersson and Wood (1983).

Appendix B.
The Supposed Equivalence of
Certain Forms of B and C

The critique of Profiles B and C in Ladd (1980: 61–64) calls for a justification of the treatment I have used in Chapter 8. Ladd puts his finger on a weakness in the description of Profile B in Bolinger (1965: 50).
In that study, B was given two alternative shapes, a jump up *from* as
well as the jump up *to* identified in Chapter 8. I agree that that was
inconsistent, and I now associate the jump up from with Profile C: the
accent is HELD DOWN, and that is the gestural significance of C. In the
text of this book I retain the description of C as a jump down to,
which embraces the major variants. I suspect that a C accent strictly
level with the preceding unaccented syllables is comparatively infre-
quent, and is apt to involve the loss of some preceding higher-pitched
unaccented syllables that would otherwise provide the springboard
for the jump-down-to:

(Are you) _{al}ways so careful?

Ladd's attempt to incorporate the profiles in a British-style definition
of "head" is another matter, and I think is incorrect. The profiles as I
conceive them are intonational gestures; this is explained at length in
Chapter 9. The accented syllable is the most telling one, in a contour,
in determining the attitudinal effects of upward and downward motion. As I see it, to equate Profile B and Profile C because they may
alternate at a certain point is to attach too much importance to grammar and too little to the difference between a lifting up and a pushing
down, which remains constant regardless of where the profiles occur
in the utterance as a whole. "Accents [= profiles] simply index positions of particular relevance *sui generis*, without specifying which
positions or what levels are relevant" (Gibbon 1981: 89). That both
profiles may be used in a given location suggests some interesting

shared functions, but both may be used elsewhere as well, with quite different effects.

Ladd borrows from the British tradition the terms *tonic* and *head*, where *head* is everything preceding the tonic. The tonic (often also called the *nucleus*) is roughly what we have called the rhematic accent. His critique concerns the relationship between the tonic and one or more pretonic accents, i.e., accents in the head. It is in the latter function that he argues for combining certain variants of B and C.

The argument runs like this: Profiles B and C with level tail (labeled B1 and C1 to distinguish them from the otherwise same profiles with rising tail, B2 and C2) are essentially the same when they occur in the head, that is, in combination with a following tonic profile: "B1 and C1 must be lumped together as 'pretonic accent,' a jump up or down to a prominent syllable in . . . the head" (1980: 64). The examples in Ladd (1980) are difficult to work with because they have too few flanking unaccented syllables. Ladd has kindly supplied (personal correspondence) a more practical pair. The following sentences are intended, then, to show the equivalence between B1 and C1 that he has in mind; they are to be imagined as replies to *Where did you hear something like that?*

```
          ría O'
                 Súllivan's
   (1) Ma
                          bróther told me.
```

```
                 Súllivan's
          ría O'
   (2) Ma
                          bróther told me.
```

The question comes down to a point of comparative resemblances. If we are required to match (1) and (2) with (3) and (4),

```
            ría O'
   (3) Ma           Súllivan's
                          bróther told me.
```

```
            ría
   (4) Ma      O'Súllivan's
                          bróther told me.
```

does (1) resemble (2) more than it resembles (3), and does (2) resemble (1) more than it resembles (4)? Consider what the pairs have in common: (1) and (2) share the monotones, and whatever it is of lackadaisicalness, expectedness, or routine that a monotone conveys, but they differ in terms of profiles (B+C+C, B+B+C); (1) and (3) share the C profiles (B+C+C), but (1) contains monotones, (3) does not; and similarly (2) and (4) share the B's (B+B+C) but differ in monotone and lack of it. If we are willing to grant that both the monotone and the profile make a difference, then which makes the *greater* difference, such that it can be taken as basic with the other a modification of it? For Ladd it is the direction of the tail; for the position adopted in this book, it is the profile.

There are two main drawbacks to Ladd's sentences: they are in statement form, which does not give the best contrasts for C versus B, and they mix profiles, making it difficult to observe the full effect of B versus C—all of them end in C. It would be better if we could contrast a series of B's with a series of C's. Suppose we match (1)–(4) above with (1)'–(4)', using a command, *Just tell me which one is for me,* in response to some such question as *How can I satisfy your need to know?*

```
(1)' Just
          téll me which                                    (C+C+C)
                       óne is for  ,
                                 mé.


                                       mé.
                        óne is for                         (B+B+B)
          téll me which
(2)' Just


(3)' Just
          téll me which
                        óne is  for                        (C+C+C)
                               me.


                                      mé.
          téll  me which óne is for                        (B+B+B)
(4)' Just
```

Here (1)' and (3)' share the playing down and reassuring effect of the three C's, and are equally acceptable, whereas (2)' and (4)' are rather flip—as if to imply that the question is superfluous: one could appropriately add *How else?* In addition, the monotone of (2)' carries an indifference that is a bit unusual.[1] The best match is in terms of profiles, not in terms of level versus rising tail.

We can also test with questions, and now the attitudinal contrast yields a potential grammatical contrast, that between original and echo question:

```
(1)" What
         sórt of a                                         (C+C+C)
                   réason is
                        thát?
```

that?
réason is

(2)" What sórt of a   (B+B+B)

(3)" What
sórt of a
réason is   (C+C+C)
that?

that?
(4)" What sórt of a réason is   (B+B+B)

Here (1)" and (3)" have in common the fact that they are typically original wh questions; they quite normally come out of the blue. They differ, of course, in the stylization of (1)" and the nonstylization of (3)", but if grammatical significance is given top billing, they are more alike than they are different. (The grammar, I would argue, is incidental to the attitude, but I emphasize the point to show that even from the grammatical standpoint the matchings hold up.) There is nothing "impossibly subtle" about this similarity, and the same goes for the comparable similarity of (2)" and (4)", which would tend to be echo questions. A normal continuation for either (2)" or (4)" would be *Well, it's just the sort of reason that makes the most sense.*

Ladd's case for lumping B1 and C1 together rests not only on the association with "heads" but also on the semantic effects of changing B1 to B2 and C1 to C2—B1 and C1 "share the semantic function of deemphasizing the prominent syllable to which they apply" (1980: 63). Ladd draws a parallel between this deemphasis and the supposedly same deemphasis that a B1 has by contrast with an A in a pair such as the following (1980: 61):

B1   A   A   A
really go   real   go
(5a) It's   (5b) It's   ly
       od.   od.

There is no denying the extra emphasis that comes from changing the B on *really* in (5a) to the A in (5b). The contrast is so striking that—as we saw in Chapter 12—a number of grammatical distinctions partially hang on it: B is "connected to" a following A, whereas a preceding A, as in (5b), is "separated from" a following A—and 'separately important' is one interpretation of the separation. But Ladd sees in the B1 of (5a) a matter of level versus nonlevel tail, and holds that the opposite way of achieving nonlevelness, having the tail rise instead of fall as in (5b), will have the same effect as the fall—a tail that does something other than remain level produces the (5a)–(5b) contrast, not specifically level tail versus falling tail.

If that were the case, then giving *really* a rising tail should contrast with (5a) just as effectively as giving it a falling one:

<pre>
                        gó
                  réallʸ
(6) It's
                            od.
</pre>

But this does not occur. The rising tail does not contrast effectively with (5a) but it does with (5b). Level and rise are both B's, and if we apply the same commutation to the examples in Chapter 12 we can see the essential sameness (that is, the merely gradient difference) between level and rise. What extra punch (6) has comes mainly from the higher-pitched A on *good*, and that can be achieved just as easily with a level-tailed B:

<pre>
                         gó
                  réally
(7) It's
                            od.
</pre>

The pair that Ladd cites (1980: 62) to show the equal contrastivity of level-versus-fall and level-versus-rise is the following:

<pre>
                  góod?   góod?
            réally   réallʸ
(8a) Is it   (8b) Is it
</pre>

—(8b) supposedly has the same "extra punch" on *really*, conferred by the rising tail, that *really* has in (5b) with its falling tail. But there is a misunderstanding here. Ladd regards both (8a) and (8b) as having terminal B2's, whereas (8b) actually has a terminal C: the accent on *good* is skipped down to. For a proper test of the rising-tail theory there must be no changes in the profiles of the contour: we must compare B+B, not B+C. To do so, we can contrast (8a) with

<pre>
                           góod?
                  réallʸ
(8c) Is it
</pre>

—B+B, both with rising tails. Here the rising tail makes little difference beyond what is caused by the increased height that results from the double rise, and that can be achieved in (8a) by merely raising the pitch of *good*. The "extra punch" in (8b) was due to the switch from B to C, not to the rising tail, except to the extent that a rising tail increases the width of the downward jump in the following C. And we can test this latter gradience by simply lowering the C step by step— the lower it goes, the greater the punch:

(9a) Is it réally góod?   (9b) Is it réally góod?   etc.

This additional lowering also accounts for the supposed C1 and C2 differences cited by Ladd (1980: 62):

(10a) Is it C1   C2   (10b) Is it   C2   C2
            really good?   real ly go od?

A fair comparison requires that the relative depths of the accented syllables remain the same:

(11a) Is it C1   C2   (11b) Is it   C2   C2
            really good?   really good?

Now there is very little difference—the emphatic plunge to a very low C on *really* is gone, and the only difference remaining comes from the general boredom of the monotone in the C1 of (11a).

Altogether, from both directions—grammatical and semantic—it seems to me that the better match is B1 = B2 and C1 = C2, not B1 = C1. Looking again at examples (1)–(4), we sense the difference between (1)' and (3)' to be purely gradient—a little more rise in the tails will change (3)' in the same direction that (3)' differs from (1)'. Furthermore, the primary relevance of the profiles, and not the general direction of pitch, can be seen in the fact that the tangent to the troughs in (3)' can be made rising rather than falling, and the resemblance to (1)' remains greater than the resemblance to (4)':

(3)' bis Just me which   is   for mé.
          téll   óne

—a command that combines the restrained politeness of the C with the greater arousal of the rising tangent. If we try to give (4)' a comparable treatment with a *falling* tangent, the result is odd:

                       me
                 téll   is
(4)' bis Just   óne
                 which   mé.
                        for

Similarly with (1)"–(4)". It does not matter what we do to the tangents of the accents in (3)" and (4)"; (3)" remains more likely as original than as echo question whether the tangent rises, falls, or stays level. And (4)" is only slightly less likely to be echo if it has a level or falling tangent (and this minor shift can be outweighed by the height of the rising terminal).

It might be argued that what "really" makes the difference is the terminal profile, and that if the differences between B and C are as important as I hold them to be, it should not be necessary to contrast contours embodying straight B's or straight C's—the differences should shine through comparisons in which the terminal profile is one and the other profiles the other. We should be able to keep them as Ladd has them, all ending in C. To test this, substitute a C with rising tail at the end of (1)", (2)", and (4)"—no change in (3)" is necessary since it already ends in a C with rising tail. Though slightly weakened, the contrasts remain: (1)''' and (3)''' are more apt to be original questions, (2)''' and (4)''' are apt to be echo, though they can be rather exercised original questions. Here are the new shapes:

(1)''' What
     sórt of a
          réason is
               thát?

                  réason is
        sórt of a
(2)''' What
               thát?

(3)''' What
     sórt of a
         réason is
            thát?

(4)''' What sórt of a réason is
              thát?

Ladd comes at the question of B1 and C1 equivalence from a further direction: the degree to which they share the function of deaccenting with terminal levels (1980: 64–67). If the word *butcher* is used as an epithet (see pp. 169–70) for 'surgeon' it may take either a B (or C) before the rhematic accent or no accent at all if it comes after the rhematic accent:

        bútcher almost
   The   kíll
                e
                 d
             me.

```
        álmost kíl
                   l
I was               ed
                by the butcher.
```

There is no denying that both of these differ from the 'separately important' implications of the A profile. But that does not make them equivalent on other dimensions. A better comparison can be drawn using an item that is not an epithet but is presupposed for some other reason, say because it has been mentioned already. In answer to *Tell me more about the alligator* one might have any one of the following:

```
         álligator      cáught       húnt
(1) The            got                          (B+A+A) (B=B1)
                           by the
                                    ers.
```

```
        álligator          cáught      húnt      (B+A+A) (B=B2)
(2) The            got            by the
                                         ers.
```

```
(3) The                    cáught      húnt
        álligator got             by the         (C+A+A)
                                        ers.
```

```
         húnt    cáught
(4) The      ers
                    the alligator.
```

It would not be appropriate to say

```
        húnt    cáught    ál
(5) The     ers          the
                            ligator.
```

and this accords with Ladd's deaccenting hypothesis. On the other hand, (1), (2), and (3) put a degree of attention on *alligator* that is lacking in (4). It would be equally appropriate to say

```
                        cáught       húnt
(6) The alligator was          by the
                                        ers.
```

in which *alligator* receives the same deaccenting before the rhematic accent (here two accents) as it receives at the end in (4), and for the same reason: it has already been mentioned. (It is certainly relevant that in both [4] and [6] we would be more likely to use *it* than *the al-*

ligator, and that in both cases *it* is unaccented.) Are we now to claim that (6), being "the same" as (4), is also the same as (1), (2), and (3)? Surely the accentual prominence in the B and C profiles of those three utterances counts for something. Without going into further details, it is at least fair to claim that those profiles ANNOUNCE, rather than take for granted, the theme of the sentence. As we saw in Chapter 5 (p. 46), the theme resembles a question—it is "what" the sentence is about. So (2)—and also (1) in a less curious way—resembles

```
       ᵃₗₗⁱᵍᵃᵗᵒʳ?
                        cáught        húnt
    The              He got       by the

                                    ers.
```

There is no such implication in (4) or in (6).

We can conclude from this that if comparisons of accents or nonaccents are to be made, they should be made not across positions necessarily but in the same position, both of them before the rhematic accent, or both after. And this brings us to what the "after" possibilities are. If we can have deaccenting as well as accenting before the rhematic accent, can we have accenting as well as deaccenting after? In other words, is it possible to have significant bumps on that otherwise flat terminal landscape?

Ladd apparently rejects this possibility. Thus he would regard the example on page 166, labeled "presentative,"

```
    suddenly
                    nói
                          bróke        nⁱ
    Then        a     se       the       ght.
```

as being identical to the same utterance without the low-pitched accents on *broke* and *night.* It is true that 'broke' and 'night' with these accents are subordinated to the notions of 'suddenness' and 'noise,' but the accents are nevertheless significant. They point up the event of breaking the night as something noteworthy for whatever reason— perhaps for dramatic effect, perhaps because the speaker feels that that aspect of the event is unknown to the hearer. On the other hand, if the hearer responds with

```
                        flásh
        whát if    blínd
    But         a       ing

                had broken the night?
```

then the sheer repetition is conducive to a flat level at the end.

As for the British-style analysis, I believe that it confuses two concepts of relative height. By assigning "low rise" (= C) to only those pitches that are low in the overall range, it misses the significance of patterns in which a low in the configuration is actually fairly high in the range. The *gesture* of bringing a pitch down from its surroundings does not depend on how high or how low the configuration is on the range. But the mood effects of the C profile naturally become easier to detect the more the trough is pushed down, and the two "lows" thus interact.[2]

For a critique of the British notions of *head* and *nucleus* (= tonic), see Gibbon (1984), especially page 187.

Reference Matter

Notes

Chapter 2

1. The preeminence of pitch cues for accent, as against duration and loudness (intensity), has been confirmed in a long series of experiments starting with those of Dennis Fry in 1955. (See Bolinger 1965: 17–36 for Fry's and other experiments up to that date. See also Brown and McGlone 1974, who conclude that "vocal intensity was not a significantly used parameter by the speakers to denote stress," whereas "Fundamental frequency was most significantly related to stress.") English is not unique in this respect. Shetler and Fetzer (1964), describing Balangao, a Philippine language, find that accents cannot be distinguished when pitch and duration cues are obscured, even when loudness cues are retained.

Chapter 3

1. Unless it is possible, without begging the question, to define intonation in such a way as to exclude whatever difference is due to the slide; see references to "ideophonic" below. For those who believe that intonation is primarily grammatical, this alternative is apt to be attractive.

Chapter 4

1. Most English vowels are typically diphthongized even when the diphthongization is not significant; this is what gives the drawling impression that a speaker of French detects in English. Some dialects of English diphthongize more than others—for example, pronouncing *this* as [ðɪəs], as if spelled *thius*. Diphthongization is especially marked in words with [e]: *cade* has a vowel that could more accurately be transcribed as [ɛɨ]. When we say that these diphthongal elements are not significant we mean simply that they do not serve to distinguish words: [ked] without a diphthongal element is the same, to a speaker of English, as [kɛɨd] with such an element; so it is safe to use the simple transcription [ked] without worrying about the diphthongization. The diphthongs listed in the text do distinguish words. *Sighed* with [aɨ] is distinct

from *sod* with simple [a]. No more will be said about these finer discriminations, as they play no pertinent role in the prosody.

See Appendix A, n. 7, for the reduced vowels as semiconsonants.

2. The division into metrical feet, and especially the fact that one syllable can constitute a foot in itself (when "strong") or combine into higher-order feet (when followed by "weak"), is recognized in a number of recent studies influenced by Liberman and Prince (1977)—a particularly relevant one is that of Selkirk (1980), which takes the step, adopted here, of eliminating "stress" as a factor in the strong-weak contrast. But Selkirk does not break with the custom of "deriving" vowel reduction from other aspects of the morphology (specifically, word prosody), and as a result has to supply a rhythmic superstructure in the shape of metrical feet and superfeet. In the approach adopted here, the priorities are reversed. If the two-level system of vowels is recognized, the metrical feet follow as a natural consequence, and there is no need for superfeet or any other form of metrical hierarchy. The approach agrees with Thompson (1980) that rhythm is linear and purely a question of string-adjacency.

We can illustrate the problems that beset the rhythm-first approach by a word such as *canopy*. If it is transcribed as [kænəpi], the foot structure is predictable—the first syllable is full and the two following ones are reduced, and therefore the word constitutes a single foot (or superfoot, as Selkirk would call it to preserve the binarity of her scheme). The metrical information is built in. But if we start by merely designating the word *canopy*—in its conventional spelling—as constituting a foot, strong-weak-weak (or a superfoot, strong-weak plus weak), there is no way to determine the pronunciation beyond the fact that the first syllable contains a full vowel and the second and third contain reduced ones. Of course no one would stop with this: the likely procedure would be to transcribe the word as /kænopi/ and trust to certain rules of vowel reduction to yield the pronunciations [ə] and [i] for the second and third syllables. But the choice of /kænopi/ is arbitrary, just as the spelling *canopy* is. The shwa in the middle syllable could "come from" /i/ as in *competition* based on *compete*, or from /e/ as in *palace–palatial*, or from /ʌ/ as in *welcome–come*. *Canopy* has no convenient cognate from which it can be "derived," and this is true of countless other words containing stable reduced vowels (do the two identical shwas in the homonyms *bizarre* and *bazaar* come from different "sources" just because of the spelling?). As long as the rhythm-first scheme is coupled with the one-level system of vowels, it is unable to decide among /kænopi/, /kænipi/, /kænepi/, and /kænʌpi/, to say nothing of how the final [i] would be derived. To avoid this, it has to be enriched, and the obvious enrichment is with a two-tiered vowel system, which renders the rest of the apparatus superfluous.

3. The indifference to the location of the foot separation affects a line of argument that was popular at one time, namely that the rhythmic structure of words like *foolscap, steamboat, carport, inchworm, clambake, stockpot, storefront, seashore, has-been, lighthouse,* and a host of other compounds was due to their composite makeup: *steam* and *boat, car* and *port, sea* and *shore,* etc. are words in their own right. By our account the monobeat rhythm is simply a reflex of

the vowel quality and has nothing to do with the composite nature of the word. The compound *fruit bat* has the same syllable timing as the unit words *cómbat*, *dingbat*, and *wombat*. It is unquestionably true that more words with this structure are composite than not—compounding is the most prolific source of new words in the language, and a fresh compound tends to keep intact all the sounds of its separate parts. In fact, the monobeat is so frequent in two-syllable compounds that it is virtually characteristic of them. But it is neither necessary nor sufficient as a condition of compound status. It is not necessary because certain older compounds are no longer monobeat—their second syllable has been reduced. The compounds in *-man* are the best examples: while *trash man* and (for some speakers) *mail man* are monobeat, *chairman*, *footman*, *workman*, *postman*, *doorman*, etc. are trochaic—*man* has become a virtual suffix. And while most noun compounds made of a combination of adverb + verb consist of two monobeats, e.g., *íntake*, *óutflow*, *úpset*, *dównturn*, a few older ones are simple trochees: *inlet*, *outlet*. Similarly the older *Newport* has a reduced *-port*, but in the newer *Shreveport* the *-port* is full. The older compound *selvage* now has the same structure as *salvage*, with reduced *-age*, in spite of having been originally *selfedge*. As to whether monobeat is a *sufficient* characterization of compounds, that too fails: it is easy to find noncompounds that have the same monobeat structure, as we saw with *wombat* etc. above. *Crow-bait* can be matched with *probate*, *come-on* with *moron*, *bow-saw* with *Warsaw*, *rosebush* with *ambush*, *mudpie* with *magpie*, *oarlock* with *warlock*, *cóarse hair* with *corsair*, etc. The word *rampage* is as deliberate as if it were *ram-page*. The rhythm of our words is only a dim reflection of their origins.

4. The same prolongation of emphasized adjectives is found in Japanese. See Kôno (1957).

Chapter 5

1. For the term *rhematic* here, compare Keijsper (1983: 271): "a word which carries the last accent belongs to what we call Rheme." The impression that the rhematic accent is the most prominent one is drawn from various languages: "In dialects of Japanese that have word accent, the sentence accent is often powerful enough to perturb it. In dialects that have no word accent, sentence accent has command" (Yamaguchi 1961). "Each phrase [in Aguatec Maya] has a strong stress, stronger than the word stress, usually but not always occurring on the stressed syllable of the last word in the phrase" (McArthur and McArthur 1956: 76). At least in part, the impact of the rhematic accent is due to its position—"last heard best remembered"—since, as we see later in this chapter (pp. 58–60), a thematic accent may be more prominent, given a change in the intonation. As far as measurable prominence is concerned, any accented syllable can be as prominent as any other, and Culicover and Rochemont (1983: 127) are partly right in their objection when they say, "We do not share the view of Schmerling 1976 and Bing 1979 [= Bing 1980] that, in sentences like our ex. 1 [*John told Bíll about Súsan, and Sám about Géorge*], the rightmost stressed element is perceived to have relatively greater

prominence than the other stressed elements in the sentence. In our view, all the nuclear stressed elements have equal relative prominence." This is correct if *have equal* is changed to *may have equal*. There is still a tendency, within an intonational phrase, to give greater prominence to the first and last accents. In the example cited, this means that in the first phrase, *John told Bill about Susan, John* and *Susan* will be more prominent than *Bill*, assuming that the utterance comes as a response to the question *What happened?* (That is, nothing is presupposed.) The *and Sam about George* part does not affect this, as it comes after a pause—the speaker "starts over." (And the sentence as a whole is unlikely anyway in response to *What happened?*; it would be a better fit for *Who told whom about whom?*, where each name is a separate answer to *who(m)*.)

2. The contrast would be even clearer if the wording were

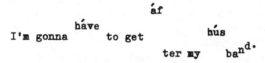

using the same intonation as in (1). Not only is 'husband' now part of the background: the implication is probably that you have asked about him, he has already been mentioned: 'As for my husband. . . .' The difference in implication between *my husband*, here presupposed to the extent of actually having been mentioned in the context, and *that husband of mine* (or *that husband I keep around the house*, or *that husband I feed every day*), as in (1), treated as something familiar but not necessarily mentioned in the context, resides in the wording, not in the prosody. *That* plus noun plus modifier presents the noun as something requiring identification, and the thematic accent with its terminal rise overlays a suggestion of 'familiarity.' The speaker treats the husband "as if" previously mentioned. One gets the sensation in example (1) that the wife is almost talking to herself, telling herself what to do rather than informing the hearer; and she does not have to inform herself about her husband: he can be "old stuff" without actually having been mentioned.

3. J. R. R. Tolkien, *The Return of the King* (London: Unwin Paperbacks, 1979), p. 253.

4. The submergence of a secondary can be illustrated in fuller utterances as well as within the word. In answer to *Why didn't you do it?* one may say *No need*, and though both *no* and *need* here are "content" words and are essential to the meaning, *no* loses some of its prominence in the intonation

```
                     né
            No
                        ed.
```

though not in the intonation

```
            Nó
               néed.
```

The former is the more frequent intonation on unit words, and accounts for the obscuring of the secondary in

```
        bú
     ro
            st.
```

Compare *need* in the above with *requirement* in

```
         quíre
   Nó
      re
            ment.
```

in which *no* is not directly before the accent on the primary stress.

5. This shows up best in words that are emphatic by nature. Take *outrageous*, for example. Its secondary, like that of the word *outside*, is immediately followed by the primary; but in *outside* the deafening effect is such that *out* has little or no prominence:

```
                 sí
     It's out
                de.
```

(We are still permitted, though, in exaggeratedly insistent speech, to give *out* a pitch turn:

```
                  sí
            óu
     It's     t
                de!
```

—perhaps implying 'If you'll just unstop your ears you'll get it.') But with *outrageous* it is quite natural to say

```
                rá
           óu
     It's  t
                geous!
```

with an unmistakable secondary accent; we can even say

```
           óu
               rá
     It's   t
                geous!
```

with the first peak the higher of the two.

6. Historically there *is* a shift as speakers simplify matters by turning the secondary into the primary and thus eliminating one accent. As we saw in Chapter 4, this occurs especially in the naturalization of many foreign words that on first entering the language are stressed on the last syllable. But it also happens with many native words, especially compounds, as the separate meanings of the parts are forgotten or disregarded and the word is semantically fused. The word *oatmeal* was originally stressed *óat méal*—actually a noun-noun phrase like *brán másh* or *chícken gíblets*—and some speakers still

say *óatméal;* but for others it is *óatmeal,* an unanalyzed term for a breakfast dish. Other examples in which the secondary has taken over from the primary, for many speakers: *Thánksgiving, ápple pie, Róbin Hood, páper doll, Gráham crackers.* For those who have only the single stress in these words, the clash of successive accents may be unavoidable: the *óatméal* speaker can say *góod oatméal*—as well as *an óatmeal púdding*—but the *óatmeal* speaker will have successive accents in *góod óatmeal.*

7. Avoiding a rhythmic jingle is of a piece with avoiding poetic devices generally when one is using language for the sake of the message rather than the vehicle—the jingling *-ings,* for example, in *That's what I was regretting getting.* See Bolinger (1979).

8. We saw the workings of a cognate form in *acádemícian* based on *acádemy.* This is a common phenomenon especially with people who encounter an unfamiliar derivative for the first time and take a guess. A newscaster refers to the *Chúrch of the Apóstolic Fáith,* drawing on *apóstle.* Another newscaster speaks of a *párental role,* drawing on *párent.* The only pronunciation for *agentive* recorded by the *Century Dictionary* (1914) is *agéntive;* the only one recorded by the Merriam *Third* (1961) is *ágentive*—obviously influenced by *ágent.*

There is probably a further analogical influence at work here, noted earlier with the word *reconstitution* (p. 57), that of certain prefixes that seem to lead a more or less independent existence. They are found in full as well as reduced forms, and apparently we recognize them as "the same" prefix regardless of the nature of the vowel, and feel free to choose the full form for rhythmic advantage. The word *extreme,* for example, always has a reduced vowel in its first syllable when the primary is accented, that is, *éxtréme* is not a normal pronunciation; and yet we are allowed to say *éxtreme únction, éxtreme vérge.* The fact that *ex-* with its [ks] is a heavy syllable helps, of course, but the main reason is probably morphological: *ex-* appears with a full vowel in many words. Similarly with *com-* and *ab-.*

9. *Abstract* seems to be an instance of an adjective whose first vowel is on the way to reduction but has not fully arrived. (The point is worth noting as an instance of how our memories must keep track of the idiosyncrasies of individual words.) In a sentence like *One thing I don't want to worry about is obscene allegations,* the first vowel of *obscene* may be fully reduced; but this is less likely of *abstract* in the same position. A better place to observe the phenomenon is in terminal position with the word being intonationally intensified: *Why don't you like it? — It's obscene! (abstract!).* In *obscene* the reduction can reach the point of partial devoicing of the vowel and of [b]; with *abstract,* though the vowel attains shwa, it remains voiced and so does the [b]. Something similar happens when the two words are contrasted with their antonyms—*obscene* may reduce the first vowel, *abstract* tends to keep it full: *Is it moral or obscene? Is it concrete or abstract?*

10. This is to say that the accent on *out-* has the effect of singling out the separate meaning of that element. As we see in Chapter 6, an accent for that purpose is an "accent of interest." In the context of this example, it is hard to put any other interpretation on the accent, and even if we use a verb such as *lambáste,* in which the syllable *lam-* is meaningless, the hearer is tempted to

wonder if perhaps it does have some sort of meaning when it occurs as *lám-baste* with that intonation. But the point is that whether *óutdo* or *lámbaste* here is intended as an "accent of interest" or an "accent of power," the reason for accenting the first syllable is not to separate the accents on *lambaste* and *John*. (An accent of power is easier to infer if the intonation is altered to include a steady initial rise,

$$\text{I'm } \text{gónn}^{\text{a}} \quad \begin{array}{c} \text{lám} \\ \\ \text{baste} \\ \text{hn·} \end{array} \quad \begin{array}{c} \text{Jó} \end{array}$$

perhaps coming right after *You'd better warn him!*)

Chapter 6

1. The speaker was the character Murray on the Mary Tyler Moore television program aired February 26, 1977. The error here is not purely a matter of failure to deaccent the last word, but also one of "key," that is, of reaching too high a pitch following the accent on *future*. For key, see pp. 241–44. Although the usual thing is to deaccent the word completely, it may also carry a low-pitched accent. See p. 127 for these small bumps on the terminal accent.

2. Reported by Dr. Edwin Ardener, July 1977.

3. In some cases we would avoid a climactic accent because it does suggest a literal focus on a particular word that is incompatible with the idiomatic meaning of the phrase. Thus while we can say either *Not by a héll of a lot* or *Not by a hell of a lót* (even if we do allow for focus on *lot*, it is appropriate to the meaning of the whole), it is more difficult to shift from *Not by a lóng shot* or *Not by a dámn sight* to *Not by a long shót* or *Not by a damn síght*, since *shot* and *sight* are irrelevant to the meaning of the phrase, which is 'not at all.'

4. J. C. Masterman, *An Oxford Tragedy* (London: Penguin, 1954), p. 76.

5. *Saturday Evening Post*, Feb. 13, 1960, p. 88.

6. The routineness of this is allied to the shifts of stress that occur in compounds, e.g. *ice cream*, *Boy Scout*, *apple pie*. See Chapter 5, n. 6.

7. The various works of several linguists of the Prague school on "Functional Sentence Perspective," especially those of Jan Firbas, are recommended on this point.

Chapter 7

1. Repetition may be a matter of information, though, as with the anguished young lady who reported after a visit to a restaurant,

I asked the waiter where I could wash my hands and he showed me where I could wásh my hánds!

Here *wash my hands* has two different meanings, in contrast in the environment: 'toilet' and literally washing one's hands.

2. The same labeling problem turns up in Dutch. Noteboom, Kruit, and Terken (1981: 21) speak of the difficulty of determining "the precise distribution of NEW and GIVEN information" when more than one of the constituents are new to the discourse. Later (p. 26) they allude to a referent that may be, "for whatever reason, . . . particularly salient"; and this suggests that the problem lies in the way the theoretical question is posed. It is easy enough, when only one item is new to a discourse, to identify it as the one that will pretty definitely carry the major accent; here, the objective facts accord with what we observe. But if two items are new, the objective criterion vanishes: how is one to determine which will be more salient? The answer is a subjective one in both cases (or intersubjective: speakers tend to agree): in the first, the one new, surprising, unexpected item will also be the most interesting one; in the second, we yield to nature's customary imbalance, fixing on one as more interesting than the other; equal newness does not usually mean equal interest.

3. As will be apparent from discussion later in the chapter, contrast is apt to be more a matter of deaccenting than of accenting. Thus in the *red shirt* example, if *shirt* is not accented it is still expected. We have already been talking about shirts. And that leads to taking 'shirt' as representing the class-of-things, the set, within which the red shirt is singled out. If there is some other clear reason for not accenting the noun, then we do not take it as referring to a set. For example,

I noted a wéary look about her.

This could just as well be expressed by *I noted a weariness about her*—*look* belongs to a class of "empty words" that are regularly deaccented (like the *problem* example in the text), and does not define a set within which one is thinking of weary looks versus perky looks, impassioned looks, etc.

4. For the same reason, time and place adverbials are the ones most often deaccented when they occur at the end of the sentence:

Anything happen while I was gone? — Well, Henry got a new jób a couple of days ago, but nothing much élse has happened around here since you left.

This simply reflects the ubiquity of the here and now or the there and then, and the relative superfluity of emphasizing either.

5. How an accent of interest can also function as an accent of power is shown in the stereotyping of *just that* as a way of being emphatic and pointing sharply at the referent of *that* at the same time. In the second sentence, if *just* were omitted, the sentence would be deflated, because the accent would then have to disappear from *that* as well: *It will show you how to dó that*. To say *It will show you how to dó thát* would probably be taken as contrastive—do that rather than do something else.

6. The same idea is implied in Fuchs (1980: 450). Her SṔ—a sentence with deaccented subject—is judged impossible in all-new utterances.

7. A similar criticism can be made of Sharp (1958: 137), who notes that

I've peeled the po^{tá}
$_{to}$e^{s}.

as readily implies 'but I've not made the beds' as 'but I've not peeled the apples.' To be fully appropriate to the first of these two interpretations, *peeled* would not be deaccented unless peeling potatoes were a routine activity, since the act of peeling has not previously been referred to in this context. Lindsey (1981: 8) makes essentially the same claim as Ladd: "Thus sentences with neutral tonicity [having the nuclear accent on the last 'lexical item'] are vague between maximally [broad focus] and minimally [narrow focus] contrastive interpretations."

8. Sweet (1898: §1887) notes this accent as equivalent to *even*.

9. This could easily be contrastive—John is nice, not unpleasant as his enemies claim—but it could also represent an emotive backshift (see pp. 83–84), and is quite readily accompanied by an appreciative shake of the head.

10. See note 4 above for lack of interest in locatives. But it is possible for power to override lack of interest:

mé$\setminus$ thé

       to fool e!   you're in re!
Don't try $_{\text{I}}$ know

There of course could be more informative if it were in contrast with 'somewhere else': *I knów you're in thére, nót in the wóodshed.*

11. The wavering is such that one may legitimately wonder how it is possible to draw a line between compounds and open phrases. *Hilltop* and *treetop* are compounds—we "know" because we write them solid. But what about *car top*? The stress is the same, and in both cases it answers to some sort of relationship between the component nouns. Take the sentences

What happened? — He accidentally broke the cár window.
What happened? — He accidentally broke the cóttage window.

In the first, apparently 'window' is such an integral and predictable part of a car that breaking it is seen as, in a sense, breaking the car. In the second, the window is a less predictable part. The predictability of 'window' in *car window* is manifest in the fact that one can look at such a window (in a stockroom, for example) and identify it as a car window, one made for a car; the same is not true of *cottage window*. Compounds are institutionalized names and their tightness reflects the degree of institutionalization. *It looks like a car window* is normal; *It looks like a cottage window* is strange unless accompanied by an explanatory context.

12. Though compound *nouns* are used for exemplification in this section, a full treatment of compounds, such as that of Marchand (1969), must recognize compounding as characteristic of all classes of words. The principles, as far as accentuation is concerned, are the same. Take the adjective compounds *oóval-shaped* and *yéllowish-looking*. As Jones (1956: §948) points out, *-shaped* and

-looking add virtually nothing to the meaning of the whole, since *oval* is already a shape and *yellowish* is already a look.

13. A grammatical rule proposed by Liberman and Prince (1977) has it that when the second member of a compound is itself compounded, the stress is on that second element, e.g. *college bóokstore*. This is doubtless true as a statistical tendency, but in reality it only reflects the fact that if the right-hand member is already compounded, it is likely to be more informative, more interesting. Otherwise, the accent will fall on the first element, as in the following attested example:

> It looks like a cinder from a locomótive firebox.

The speaker was more interested in introducing the idea of 'locomotive' than that of 'firebox.' See Bolinger (1981: Appendix A).

14. See Bolinger (1957: 299): 'There are Baptists there' or 'There's a seminary there.' But *Methodist mínister*.

15. One reason for this is the tendency for prominences directly before a main accent to be obscured. The effect is more drastic sometimes than the mere loss of accent: in that position full vowels are often centralized toward a corresponding reduced vowel. See Appendix A, pp. 354–56.

16. We have the formal *indeed*, as in

> Did he go? — He indéed went.

but *yes* is not allowed as a modifier, as happens with the Spanish equivalent *sí* in *Yo sí voy* 'I yés am going.' But other affirmatives are possible, some—as Sweet (1898: §1898) observed—cliticizing *not* in much the same way that it is cliticized with *do*, e.g. *The vóyage is cértainly not a lóng one.* Sweet calls *certainly not* a "sort of compound."

17. On the equivalence of emphasis and affirmation, Joos (1964) "makes the interesting observation that *do*, which many grammars call emphatic, actually is used to add insistence on the truth-value of the whole clause." (From review in *Modern Language Journal* 49 [1965]: 329.)

18. Not quite always. *Do* may be combined with other affirmation-carriers and then may lose the accent to them or share it with them—such words as *certainly, surely, seem, indeed, too, so*:

> It cértainly (súrely) does séem that way, doesn't it!
>
> You don't believe me? — I do indéed believe you! It's just that it took me a long time to be convinced!
>
> John didn't do it. — He did tóo (só) do it! I saw him!

The freedom of the affirmation accent to fall on any of these elements can be seen in the equivalence of the following, based on the second example above:

> I do indéed believe you = Indeed I dó believe you.

—as well as in the extra boost that can be given the content verb with other accents suppressed:

You surely do belíeve me, don't you?

and in the fact that all the affirmation-carriers can be accented at once:

You súrely dó belíeve me, don't you?

19. This identical phenomenon has been observed in Spanish. A Mexican speaker says

Tengo QUE levantarme mañana 'I plain háve to get up tomorrow.'

An Argentinian speaker, expecting a room to be dirty, finds it clean and says

Che. Este cuarto ESTÁ limpio 'Hey, this room ís clean.'

20. W. V. Quine, "On what there is," in Leonard Linsky, ed., *Semantics and the Philosophy of Language* (Urbana: University of Illinois Press, 1952). The word *for* is italicized in the original.

21. Similarly in the negative, when the 'to-ness' is denied to someone:

I didn't do it because I was forbidden tó do it.
. . . because I wasn't allowed tó do it.

But restraint applied to the person, holding the person back, calls for *from*:

I didn't do it because I was prevented fróm doing it.

The verb of course can be the carrier in any of these.

Though it approaches the relative independence of *to* from the formal side rather than the semantic, there is a restriction on the accenting of *to* that points to a need for it to be independent:

I won't buy it unless I'm forced (obliged) tó buy it.
I won't buy it unless I really need tó buy it.
*I won't buy it unless I have (I've got) tó buy it.

Have to and *got to* have been fused into the new quasi-auxiliaries *hafta* and *gotta*, to the point that *to* is no longer felt to be a word in its own right, even when the full *have to* and *got to* are used. We can accent the new auxiliaries as a unit (*háfta*, *gótta*), but with them it is a requirement, whereas with *forced to* etc. it is an option.

The need for some kind of inherent contrastivity in *to* can also be seen in our preference not to accent it when it is repeated. Of the two following, the first is better because *have*, unlike *get*, does not require *to* with the infinitive, and the *to* of the answer is new to the context:

Looks like a tough job. Why don't you have somebody help you? — There's nobody here tó.
?. . . Why don't you get somebody to help you? — There's nobody here tó.

22. Ellery Queen, *The Virgin Heiresses* (New York: Pocket Books, 1954), p. 24.

Chapter 8

1. Normally accents occur no more than one per syllable. But see p. 191 for successive accents on the single word *No!*

2. To get the fall within the syllable, the syllable has to be stretched, and this can be accomplished in two ways: either by using a more or less smooth glide, or by splitting the syllable in two, so to speak, with half at one level and half at another. If the voiced portion of the syllable contains a shift in quality, e.g. between a vocalic nucleus and an offglide or a sonorant, the split tends to be made at the point of the shift. For example, to put the question *How?* on an A profile we do not divide it in the middle of the vowel nucleus [a] but between the [a] and the [ə]:

Ho
w?

Similarly with *bo-y, mai-l, chas-m*. The aim seems to be to get the best contrast between one level and the other that can be managed with the vowel and vowel-like sounds available. (See Pike 1945: 71 for *ta-ll*.) In the intonational diagrams in this book, there is no attempt to make any precise representation of such a division. A diagram like

ba
d

merely signifies that the syllable *bad* contains a fall. The phonetic division here, of course, would have to be *ba-ad*.

3. This is perhaps better analyzed as AC—see below. But the problem is the same.

4. The downtilting tail of the C is thus "allophonic" with a sustention or a rise, whereas the equal downtilt of the A tail is equivalent to a fall. The ability to categorize the same thing in two different ways is aptly described by Siertsema (1961: 147) in reference to Akpea, a West African tone language. Nonnative speakers attempting to reproduce what was clearly heard as a fall were judged incorrect by native speakers. It turned out that the fall was arrested by a slight sustention, which the native speakers interpreted as a rise, and, in fact, could be correctly replaced with an obvious rise. For the C interpretation in the English example the drop in pitch from *satch-* on must be gradual in order to be regarded as equivalent to a rise. On the other hand, if there is an abrupt drop not after *satch-* but right after *-el*, we have either a delayed A-type drop (as might happen in very rapid or otherwise pressured speech), or we have a CA profile, which in turn would permit an upskip to *-el* rather than a mere sustention on *-el*—here again, the sustained *-el* is equivalent to a rising *-el*. As the A and CA profiles are already very close in meaning, being distinguished mainly by the fact that CA is more emphatic, and as at these relatively low terminal pitches a distinction in emphasis does not come through very clearly, the difference between A and CA is virtually nil.

5. The same difficulty arises with successions of B profiles. If a preceding B tail ends on a syllable that can be interpreted as accented (that is, a full syllable), there may seem to be an A profile there:

```
           always that        siderate?
Is she                  incon
```

The word *that*, depending on whether it has less or more intensity or length, may be the end of the B tail or the accent of an A. The safest choice is to end the B tail with *-ways* and include *that* as part of the dropback:

```
           álways                síderate?
Is she             that incon
```

6. And is skillfully imitated by the actor Robert Hardy in the 1982 PBS television series "Winston Churchill: The Wilderness Years."

7. But does not necessarily subordinate them, as claimed by Ladd (1980: 64–67), referring to Bolinger's B profile with level tail preceding a main accent. For Ladd, this kind of B is "somehow the same phenomenon" (p. 64) as terminal deaccenting. Thus the B on *butcher* in

```
      bútcher charged me a thóusand bú
The
                                       cks.
```

has the same motivation (*butcher* as an epithet for 'surgeon') as the deaccent in

```
      chárged a thousand búcks
I was
                      by that butcher.
```

in which *butcher* is deaccented.

There is a kinship here, but it is not an identity, and it is not due to the configuration, as Ladd supposes, but rather to the "key" (see pp. 241–44) of the B. The lower the pitch of the B profile, whether with level tail or rising one, the more it suggests something already known, assumed, or familiar. The point of identity is reached only when the B profile disappears altogether, and (in the example here) *butcher* is deaccented at the beginning as well as at the end. As the B rises higher, it becomes more suitable for the introduction of "new" material. Thus in

```
      dámage it suffered     médiable?
Was the                  irre
```

where the first B is as high as the second, even though the tail is level the 'damage it suffered' may be new to the context. If a rising tail makes a difference, it is not because of the configuration but because a rise may tend to attain a higher overall pitch. See Appendix B for discussion of Ladd's B1 (level) versus B2 (rising) B.

8. A similar example of mishearing comes from a literary anecdote, involving the "flattened A" described on pp. 147–48:

"I was startled recently when my little granddaughter demanded insolently 'Whose bookisthis?' The child is not an insolent baggage, and I stared at her in amazement. Then it came to me that what she really wanted to say was 'Whose *book* is this?' or perhaps 'Whose book *is* this?'"

"The style of asking a question with the accent entirely on the first word of a sentence seems to be growing. To an old-fashioned person like myself it is strangely offensive to have a question fired point-blank: '*What* isyourname? *Where* doyoulive? *What* areyoudoing?' And one would shudder to think that Juliet, leaning on the balcony, might have murmured, '*What's* inaname?'" (*The Reader's Digest Reader*, New York: Doubleday, Doran, 1940, p. 401.)

It is a safe bet that the child was correctly accenting *book*, but on a C profile:

Whose

bóok is tʰⁱˢ?

—and the grandparent interpreted it as an AC.

9. *Bats Fly at Dust* (New York: Dell, 1960), p. 7.

10. A distinction is necessary here between the C profile and a low-pitched CAC profile, the latter commoner in British than in American English:

A

gá
gⁱⁿ?!

—the syllable *-gain* is divided into a rise and a fall before the final rise. A better display of syllables shows the contrast more clearly:

E   E

rádⁱcᵃᵗᵉ?   rádⁱ   ᵉ?
                                cᵃᵗ

The latter is more likely as an exclamatory question; it is not so pure a playing-down as the former.

11. See Bolinger (1965: 38–40) for this same ambiguity with the phrase *go on*.

12. Whether to treat such cases as a single profile or as a combination is a problem that has baffled a number of intonologists. Schubiger (1958: 109), Kingdon (1958: 79–80), Hultzén (1959: 115), and Esser (1983: 126) recognize it. Sharp (1958) looks to other cues (e.g. rhythm) to make the distinction. Pike (1945) does not avow the difficulty but a number of his scorings show that it must have troubled him; for example, p. 57 has what appears to be the contour

That can't be

truᵉ˙

marked with main accent on *that*, but the syntax requires that it be on *true*, which makes this an instance of B+C, with a played-down main accent. The confusion is with

That

cᵃⁿ'ᵗ bᵉ
truᵉ˙

an AC with accent only on *that*, or an A+C with accents on *that* and *true*. See pp. 268–73 for further discussion.

13. These authors refer to "peaks" rather than to accents; but the substitution is justified by the fact that, true to the tradition of most studies of stress and accent, virtually the only accents tested are those manifested as peaks.

Chapter 9

1. According to Scherer (1974: 252), "one may be justified in speculating about the existence of unlearned neural programs for the vocal expression and recognition of emotion, especially given the strong correspondences between respiratory phenomena and physiological correlates of affective state." For the complex interactions of fundamental pitch and voice quality see Scherer, Ladd, and Silverman (forthcoming).

2. A good deal of strictly phonological learning of course has to accompany the process. To name just one factor: words are "exciting" as wholes, but as a rule pitch accent affects only the stressed syllable within a word. The process is aided by the frequency of monosyllables at the early stages and by the liberties that children can take with unstressed syllables, often simply omitting them.

3. I owe this reference to Anne Cutler (private communication).

4. See, for example, Dascălu (1974, 1979).

5. This is a concept fundamental to the linguistic philosophy of Roman Jakobson. See Sangster (1982: 897).

6. See Bolinger (1946: 93) for an early mention of parallel motion. Birdwhistell (1970) refers to it, according to Kendon (1980: 221).

7. The two most important controls of voice pitch are the intrinsic muscles of the larynx and the abdominal and chest muscles responsible for subglottal air pressure. How relaxation and 'down' are associated in the latter system is manifest in the vocalized sigh by which we signal that we are coming to rest after an effort. Air pressure during effort must be kept up to supply oxygen, but when effort is terminated the system relaxes and the elastic recoil of the lungs causes them to empty. As pressure falls, so does the pitch of the voiced sigh—automatically, without any necessary readjustment of the vocal cords. It was to this "expiratory fall" phenomenon that Lieberman (1967: 27) attributed what he called the "archetypal normal breath group," the span of utterance that is delimited at the end by falling pressure and falling pitch and coincides with normal unemphatic statements.

The intrinsic muscles of the larynx control pitch by changing the tension of the vocal cords. Here again tension = 'high.' Given a constant subglottal air pressure, pitch will rise and fall as laryngeal tension increases and decreases. At lower pitches effort again increases as an extrinsic muscle, the sternohyoid, becomes active, drawing the larynx down and thereby lowering the pitch. But this latter effort is not sufficient to override the association of tension = 'high' in the main part of the system. Furthermore the lowest pitches are not fully exploited: lower modal pitches tend to give way to creak, which is itself a marker of relaxation and termination (see Chapter 10, pp. 216–17). To the extent that the high-low metaphor is conventionalized, it does not matter how the pitches are achieved; their meaning will be maintained.

8. What happens with smiling has already been noted. Fónagy (1981: 138) calls attention to the distortion of the vowels by the kissing gesture, in mothers' speech to young children.

9. Ekman and Friesen (1975: 12–13) regard this questioning "emblem" as a modification of eye-widening for surprise. It may well be a universal gesture. See also Meo-Zilio and Mejía (1980: 18) and Ekman (1979: 185).

10. Some such term as *receiver* is needed to replace *hearer* to signify the person receiving the entire message, not just the audible or visible part. Ekman and others have used *percipient*, but that ignores sending and receiving as intentional acts.

11. Of course one can claim that all imperatives are underlyingly *will* sentences. But to claim that is also to claim that the similarity between the *Tell me how you did it* (rising version) and *Will you tell me how you did it?* portrayed in the text is no closer than that between (1) and (3) or between (2) and (3) in the following:

(1) Will you ^{téll} me how you did it? *(displayed as an intonation contour)*

(2) Will you ^{téll} me how you did it? *(displayed as an intonation contour)*

(3) Téll me how you did it. *(displayed as an intonation contour)*

I doubt that any native speaker of English would agree that there is any such close similarity here—as close as the sensation, in the other case, that the speaker has simply deleted that low-pitched *will you*, much as he may delete other instances of auxiliary plus subject: *Go there alone (did he)?, Buy herself a car (will she)?* To avoid the idea of a shift of syntax under the weight of those intonational and gestural cues, one would have to adopt the radical position of Bolinger (1977: 152–82) and deny the imperative as a category. The bare infinitive then remains just what it is, a pure hypothetical, and imperativeness is inferred pragmatically.

12. See Bolinger (1977: 37–65, especially pp. 56–57), and compare:

I'm bored with this place. — Aren't there any books you can read? I can think of lots of things to do!

I'm bored with this place. — Are there no books you can read?

In the second conversation the addition of *I can think of lots of things to do* would be a virtual non sequitur; the possibilities for action have been foreclosed. One can test with tags. *It has no purpose, has it?* is odd as a conducive question; it is more apt to be a sarcastic response to someone who has said *It has no purpose,* and is equivalent to *So it has no purpose, eh?* On the other hand, *It doesn't have any purpose, does it?* is a normal conducive question, appealing for confirmation. It is "open," and the gestures match.

13. With allowances made for possible phonesthematic effects. We may find, for example, that a given tone language has an unusually large proportion of high-toned words suggesting 'smallness.'

Chapter 10

1. Numerous studies bear on this point, for example Abramson (1959), Meyer-Eppler (1957), Lehiste (1982).

2. A stereotyped example was the catch line used by the character Digger O'Dell in the "Life of Riley" radio program in the 1940's: *She's so gay!* said with vibrato on a lugubrious uptilt without terminal upglide: the near-monotone upmotion plus trembling voice suggested 'smiling through one's tears.'

3. Hollien (1972) adopts the term *modal* and retains the more or less traditional *vocal fry* and *falsetto,* though he prefers, for scientific description, *pulse, modal,* and *loft.* See also Hollien, Gould, and Johnson (1975).

4. One such speaker overheard in 1982 was a supervisor of Alameda County, California, Mr. Fred Cooper, who managed the usual intonational contrasts entirely within the creak range.

5. Part of the difficulty of the smile with *no* is that [o] is a rounded vowel whereas the smile requires spreading. What we do is compromise, giving the center of the lips the task of rounding while smiling with the cheeks and slightly with the corners of the mouth. An easier example would be with some such negative as *hardly.*

6. The dependency is not absolute. A further qualifier frees it. The speaker may use modal register with *no* and be seen as smiling if the utterance is accompanied by a chuckle.

7. Young children may note this association and use low pitch in place of grammatical negation. The author's daughter at age three did this, saying, for example,

It

hùrt me, Bruce.

'It didn't hurt me, Bruce.' Weeks (1982: 164) records a similar instance. Speakers generally will use a higher pitch for *Yes, I do,* and a lower one for *No, I don't,* perhaps partly out of courtesy—it might seem rude to be insistent when rejecting someone else's proposition, whereas affirming it might seem too half-hearted if pitched low. There is no fixed rule here, of course, but the infants' use of it shows how an intonation can become grammaticized without actually departing from the up-down metaphor. If asked to associate *yes* and *no* with *up* and *down,* few would hesitate to do so in that order.

8. This prolongation is probably unrelated to the sort that is used for intensification, e.g. on *long* and *big* in *a long: way, a big: ship.*

9. Most of the time if one desires to exaggerate the effects of the monotone it is not necessary to distort, because there is the recourse of simply treating additional full vowels within a word as if they were stressed, and allowing the corresponding syllables to start separate levels. So a speaker who wishes to imply that something called an investigation is not worthy of the name may say

In
vésti
    gátion?

The author of this book caught himself saying

Gíve me the
    rúta
       bága.

10. This must be qualified slightly to recognize the effect of glottalizing a final consonant. When that happens, creak is effectively raised in pitch, and a speaker then can give the impression of producing a lower fall. But the compensation is only partial.

11. The discussion in this section lays a proper groundwork for a point of theory and of terminology that otherwise might better have preceded the identification of the profiles in Chapter 8. Ladd adopts a description that has been traditional among British intonologists: in place of *Profile B, high rise* is used; in place of *Profile C, low rise*. (Profile A has its matching unit among the falls, but that need not concern us here.) The parallel is obvious: a B is marked by an accent that is risen to, and a C by one which, if there is any rise at all (as there generally is), is risen from; relative highness and lowness are therefore implied.

The problem with the British approach is twofold. First, we have seen in this section that monotone and rise in a C profile are best viewed as only gradiently different, so that "rise" is irrelevant (unless monotone is defined as a variety of rise). Second, we have also seen, here and earlier, that the treatment of the accented syllable is responsible for the most striking contrasts, and that in turn depends on the configuration, especially as it affects Profile C: it is not the rise from the accented syllable that counts primarily in this profile, but the fact that the accent is HELD DOWN, contrary to the tendency of all emphasized elements, which is to go up. A Profile C accent may be at a relatively high pitch and the rise after it will be correspondingly high, so that "low rise" is a misnomer (unless duly qualified to refer to configuration only). For example, in response to *Do you think Rowley would ever do anything like that?* one could readily say

He
    míght·

with a C profile in high key (plus other "up" elements—smile and arched eyebrows), to alert the receiver to the lively possibility or to counter in a spirited way what the speaker feels may be the contrary opinion. This hardly qualifies as a low rise, but it does qualify as having a pushed-down accent with precisely the implications that that pattern has. Similarly one may go through the motions of asking a question with little or no interest in the answer, in which case it is normal to have a low-key Profile B—for example, in responding to *I think I'd rather vote for Jeffers* one might say

$$\text{You } \overset{\prime}{\text{w}}\text{ould?}$$

as a polite gesture of affected interest, with *would* relatively low and barely rising. The meaning of Profile B resides in the pattern, and the fact that the overall pitch is low—and overlays the meaning of the profile with its own (in some ways contradictory) meaning—does not destroy that meaning, despite the lack of a "high rise." It is important to keep configuration and range distinct, if we are to understand the contribution of each and how each reacts in the presence of the other.

12. According to Dr. Dina Dahbany-Miraglia, personal communication.

13. It is likely that downdrift is also manifested in microcosm in the form taken by most reduplicative words, e.g. *flimflam, seesaw, hee-haw, flip-flop, mishmash, dingdong, rickrack, ticktock.* The vowel with the lower second formant comes last. We saw earlier in this chapter how the second formant is used as a stopgap for intonation in whispering.

14. There are other versions. The pioneering work on this system is Palmer (1922).

15. The original proposal is by Liberman and Sag (1974). See also Cutler (1977) and Bolinger (1982).

Chapter 11

1. The same has been observed for Swedish intonation: "The overall Fo course of an utterance is essentially formed by the relations between successive, local excursions for accentuation" (Bruce 1982: 51).

2. Certain shapes are inappropriate for certain uses, of course, but that does not bar the physical shape itself. An instance of the stronger claim—that a given physical shape is excluded—is found in Pierrehumbert (1980: 90, 301), e.g. her Fig. 36D, which in effect says that the contour diagrammed on p. 157 of this volume, *Contaminated is what it was,* is impossible. Pierrehumbert takes the ideal shape of CA—with no more than one high-pitched syllable standing between the low-pitched accent and the subsequent drop—as the necessary shape, whereas with a higher degree of tension the drop can be delayed. There is a similar claim in Ladd (1983a: 749) regarding a shape that is supposedly found in Dutch but not in English:

$$\text{al niet gega}_{\text{an}}?$$
$$\text{Ben je helema}$$

'Didn't you go at *all?*' But if I have interpreted this correctly (Ladd uses a line drawing), a normal English counterpart would be

Why would án ybody wánt to?

—a CB+A with truncated fall and extra intensity on the syllable *an-*.

In an informal experiment at Haskins Laboratories a recorded sentence was modified by removing the original intonation and imposing a sine wave randomly on the text. Listeners judged this purely mechanical variation of the pitch to sound more natural than a monotone.

3. On the analogy of tone language systems one might also predict a dynamic prominence associated with pitch glide rather than pitch jump, so that one could have an accent cued by a downglide, for example. If none such are attested, it might be because, given the inertia of the vocal organs and the fact that there are glides in any case, such a prominence would tend to be ambiguous between a fall from and a fall to.

4. Compare also the accent on *he* in *He not only swore*, p. 49. See also p. 111 for *it* as normally unaccented.

5. Whether what freedom there is comes as conscious choice or as automatic response to transient emotive states is a question for psycholinguists and philosophers. From a descriptive standpoint, a zone of freedom is a zone of unpredictability within the descriptive apparatus.

6. The alternative would be to hear a B on *I know* and to make a separate utterance (with independent contour) of *You didn't mean that*. As far as the sequence of pitches is concerned this is possible, but the timing would virtually rule it out.

7. The B status of the accents on *don't* and *want* can be seen by prefixing the word *just* at initial level. It could, however, be construed as initial C, with a jump down to the accent. Such incomplete profiles can be ambiguous, though within a discourse the speaker's average levels usually clear up the ambiguity. A relatively high pitch on *don't* and *want* would probably mark the profile as B.

8. For speakers who admit an original—non-echo—question like

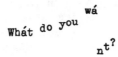

example (2) potentially becomes like (1), a case of B+AC. This contour used for an original wh question may not be unusual in British English, but is distinctly so in American English.

9. Autosegmental analysts may see in this wrestling with ambiguity a confirmation of their preference for first laying down an intonational shape and then adjusting the accents to it. That procedure would rely on other markers of accent and would leave the speaker free to put accents at various points on the curve without the analyst's having to worry about overlapping profiles. There would simply be a contour, with one accent on it in one case, two in another, or possibly more. But this would lead to our having to ignore the configurational distinctions that have been noted many times in previous

chapters. For example, if (15) is taken as basically a falling-rising contour, the way the accent is realized at the trough is still crucial. In (15) there is a C accent, but the same overall shape could be maintained with an AC:

Jóhn

Wouldn't ^{húrt} anybody. (AC+AC)

and this AC has its typical contrastivity in comparison with C. This is the same situation as the one discussed above, p. 256, with the example *Give it a try.*

10. The discussion in the text concentrates on the uncertain line between AC and AC+C, but the same applies to CAC versus CAC+C.

Chapter 12

1. Gantzel (pp. 48–50) correctly insists on the need to distinguish abstract and general meanings, and criticizes Pike for reading in contextual meanings after proclaiming the same need for abstraction.

2. The blending is with a full double-accenting on both components of *ran out*:

rán óut the dó
and
or.

There is a conflict between making *ran* more prominent by the backshift and at the same time preserving the accentual marking of the normal stress on *out.* To ensure a B on *ran out*, we need the syllable *the* at that same pitch, as in the preceding example.

3. Since an A can nearly always substitute for a B to make the emphasis seem 'sincere,' the first example here could also be used as an oath; but the second could not be used to inform, except under conditions already described—where foreknowledge is involved, for example.

4. The point has some theoretical importance for the problem of "accents after focus." It is often assumed that within a given contour the focus is the final position at which pitch will mark an accent. According to Gårding (1981: 152), "One . . . rule which is fairly general across languages is that there are no pitch movements in connection with accents after focus." Or—if we can assume that the "tonic accent" is always the focus—then the statement will read "no pitch accents after the tonic." But the *asteroid* and *very lives* examples seem to show that with A+A there may indeed be a pitch accent after the tonic. One way out of this is to allow more than one tonic within the contour, but that begs the question of what a tonic is. Another is to define contours on tonics, but that begs the question of what a contour is. See Ladd (1982) for some related discussion. The solution adopted in our approach is to view focus as a relative matter, dependent on other factors in addition to intonation. See pp. 126–27, for earlier discussion.

5. B+A is also involved. See pp. 303–4.

6. Compare the similar shift from indirect to direct discourse in the C+A *Tell me which is the better* versus the B+A *Tell me, which is the better?*

7. The contrast is more difficult to bring out when the B+A and the C+A have a lowered A, probably because a request calls for the appeal embodied in the high pitch; but it can be managed if the request is such as might be toned down by the lowered A. It might be one that comes as a final plea in a series of requests:

$$\text{Thén}_{\cdots}\ \text{at}\ {}^{\text{lé}}_{\text{a}}{}_{\text{s}}{}_{\text{t}\cdots}\qquad\text{cóuld}\qquad\text{yo}_{\text{u}}\ \text{nót}\ \text{try}\ \text{to}\ {}^{\text{be}}\ \text{kí}_{\text{n}}{}_{\text{d?!}}$$

This C+A is a normal instance of conducive negation. Moving the *not* onto the upglide, to get a B+A, is either anomalous or, if interpreted as conducive, compels the impression of something like indignation—there is the same coercive overtone that was noted for the B+A with higher A, when interpreted as a request.

8. A further contrast needs to be pointed out in the second example. In place of A+B, a fairly close approximation can be made with B+B in which the first B has a downtilt plus a dropback:

$$\text{Do}\quad {}^{\text{péople}\ \text{really}}\ \text{be}^{\text{líeve that?}}$$

The difference is that the B+B questions only the fact, whereas the A+B is more complex. As in some earlier cases (p. 294) the A implies an existential: 'Are there actually people who believe that?'

9. Care must be taken in an example like this to interpret the two words correctly. It is not that a function word such as *but* cannot carry an accent of power in this position, only that that is not the intention here, as the vowel shapes would show. The *It's only the wind* example could, in fact, be an instance of A+B, and in that case *it's*, instead of being reducible to *'ts* (*'Ts only the wind*, with a downdash on *'Ts on-*), would receive extra length and intensity—an accent of power that has nothing to do with the meaning of *it*.

10. Insufficiently marked accents at a high pitch are difficult to categorize. Another instance is with wh questions, which, being questions, are apt to maintain a high pitch. In a case like

$$(1)\ \text{Hów did they}\ \text{dó it?}$$

we obvously have a B+C. But in

$$(2)\ \text{How}\ ^{\text{did}}\ \text{they}\ \text{do it?}$$

(in which *did* is reduced to a double alveolar tap—i.e., *did* is not accented) the configuration looks to be that of either CA+C or CAC—pretty definitely the latter if *how* is contrastive, that is, if the question means 'You're asking me *how* they did it (rather than, e.g., why or when)?'—an echo question in which *do* is repeated and is therefore potentially unaccented, thus favoring CAC over CA+C. Example (1) can also be echo, but does not select *how* for contrast— the whole original question is duplicated and *do* is accented as much as *how* is.

As expected, given the closeness of CA to A and CAC to AC, (2) is synonymous with (3)—the latter again potentially an echo question selecting *how* for contrast and repeating *do* from previous mention:

(3) How
did they
do
it?

So, viewing the three examples as echo questions, we find a fairly clear contrast between (1) and either (2) or (3): (1) remains B+C, simply imitating the original question; (2) and (3) highlight *how* at the expense of everything else, and probably are to be regarded as CAC and AC rather than as CA+C and A+C.

On the other hand, when viewed as original questions the distinction between (1) and (2) is less clear. The word *do* is new to context, which makes for a two-profile analysis of (2) as well as of (1), and the upmotion in (2) can be heard as a B with an uptilt—two cases, therefore, of B+C. Only with a more striking CA configuration could we be confident in comparing (2) to (3), with *how* a CA or an A not as an accent of interest (contrast on its meaning) but as an accent of power.

11. The *if* clause is virtually an extraposed subject, with *it* standing in lieu of it. There is no problem with this intonation if the conditional clause is syntactically more independent, as would happen if the clause were repeated, e.g. in answer to *What would happen if we just forgot?*, or if the clause were offered as a suggestion, equivalent to 'if you will just forget.' In the latter case, the *if* clause might come as an afterthought: 'It will be easier—if you'll just forget, you know.' In both cases the main clause then becomes a logical conclusion and may more readily take a conclusive intonation.

12. A possible solution to the A versus AC problem is to regard medial AC as the unmarked form.

13. If a monosyllable—such as *will* in the second example—is given an AC, the sheer effort of producing the turn of pitch in so short a space may make that word stand out more than if it carried an A. An example from the previous section is

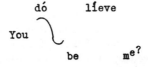

This is not owing to any emphatic property of AC by comparison with A, but merely to the forced slowing down. The speaker could achieve even more emphasis by slowing down an A so as to let the word *do* incorporate its own downmotion instead of depending on the low pitch of *be-*:

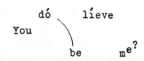

—with no upmotion before the upskip to *-lieve*.

14. B+A+C rather than B+AC+C (with overlap), on the strength of regarding *kid brother* as presentative, as in the *asteroid* example. This would be equivalent to *My kid brother—he lived in Manchester, come to think of it*. It would be most reliably signaled by having *-ther lived in Man-* at creak.

Appendix A

1. For the spread of [ɨ] versus the relative narrowness of [ɪ] in *Polly* and *Betty* versus *cigaret* and *it's* see Hewitt and Lehmann (1965).

2. Putting it another way, unstressed syllables may be either full or reduced, since the only stressed syllables are the ones carrying the potential for accent, and not all full syllables have that potential. In *commíserate*, *-mis-* is stressed and all the other syllables are unstressed, but *-ate* is still full, as, of course, is *-mis-*. The opposing description, for which only the reduced vowels are "unstressed," has to recognize two levels of stress, one higher (*-mis-*) and one lower (*-ate*). The advantage of the scheme advocated here in eliminating one of those levels was noted by Stockwell and Bowen (1965: 92, n. 4).

3. The practice in most dictionaries is to place a "secondary stress" mark beside the syllable that may get the extra accent (when it precedes the primary): ˌshiv-a-ˈree (or the equivalent ˈˈshiv-a-ˈree). The Merriam Webster *Third New International Dictionary* is an example, and illustrates the confusion over stress and accent discussed here and in Chapter 4. A word such as *population* is marked ˌpop-u-ˈla-tion, one such as *Seminole* is marked ˈSem-i-ˌnole. In the latter case all that the lower mark tells us is that *-nole* is a full syllable (which can be inferred if we know the nature of the vowel—the mark is unnecessary)—no accent normally occurs there. But in *population* the lower mark tells us that an accent *can* occur on the syllable, and may outrank the accent on the stressed syllable itself in a phrase such as *pópulation dénsity*.

Normally, syllables after the stress behave intonationally the same regardless of whether they are full or reduced. The pitch contour is the same in both of the following:

```
máy              má
    pole              ple
```

—with the purely phonetic and nondistinctive difference that the full vowel may lead the speaker to maintain a higher pitch at the end.

4. See Cutler and Clifton (1983). See also Cutler (1983: 91): "Lexical stress . . . seems to be perceived by speakers as inessential for communication; maintenance of the word's canonical pattern of full and reduced vowels is what is important for word recognition." Of course if the labels *reduced vowel* and *unstressed vowel* designate the same entities, and those entities are recognized as functioning in their own right, then it makes no difference. But this

solution has the terminological problem of precluding us from saying that in the word *houseboat* "the stressed element is the first," since both are "stressed." And it has the more serious difficulty of making no distinction between stable reduced vowels, which no longer alternate with full vowels in native words in English, and unstable ones, which do alternate and where reference does need to be made to stress as a potential for accent.

5. The two are of course distinct regardless of the final vowels for those who pronounce the first syllables differently: British speakers generally say [ipǝk]. Many if not most American speakers make the distinction on the basis of the second syllable. Apparently for some the two words are homophones, though they are not so marked in recent American dictionaries. The contrast as recorded there is between [ɛpɨk] and either [ɛpǝk] or [ɛpǝk].

6. Vowel reduction in Bulgarian shows remarkable similarities to that in English, not only in the distinction between stable and unstable reduction but also in its three-point system of reduced vowels as against a more complex system of full vowels, and in what has been referred to here as the "slack-jawed" trait of reduced vowels. See Pettersson and Wood (1983, esp. pp. 151, 152, 162).

7. This is not to claim that syllable division is a waste of exercise in dictionaries. In fact, since they use it anyway they could take advantage of it to condense the whole scheme of diphthongs, semiconsonants, and reduced vowels to a single set of contrasts. If a recording of *yacht* is played backward, it yields *tie*, and the two can be symbolized as [yat] and [tay], where [y] is the same as [ɨ]. Similarly *wad* and *Dow* as [wad] and [daw], with [w] the same as [ǝ]. The syllable divisions enable us to dispense with any special symbols for the reduced vowels. The contrast between *Hillyer* where [y] is a consonant and *hillier* where it is a vowel (and where we would have written [ɨ] rather than [y]) is shown by the syllable divisions: [hɪl-yǝr], [hɪl-y-ǝr]. *Bulwer* versus *Bullower* becomes [bul-wǝr], [bul-w-ǝr]. We could then write (omitting the syllable divisions where they are not necessary) [mɛny] for *many* and [mɪnw] for *minnow*.

Appendix B

1. But it is not correct to say that the final monotone here—a B1 in final position—is something that does not occur at all, as conjectured by Ladd (1980: 64). The example *Does anybody around there give a damn?* with a level-tailed B on *damn* was cited (Chapter 12, p. 309): it is a "knowing" question, by contrast to the same B carrying a rising tail.

2. See Chapter 12, p. 309, for a succession of monosyllabic B's (*Dón't yóu think Í wíll?*) in which the only way to get an assured B is to aim for a rise well up in the range. Since each syllable takes an accent, it must incorporate its own dropback and resetting, and that makes the configuration virtually equivalent to a C. Another case of MONOSYLLABIC AMBIGUITY.

References

Abramson, A. S. 1959. Vocoder output and whispered speech in a tone language: Thai. *Journal of the Acoustical Society of America* 31: 1568.

Aizawa, Keiko. 1981. Lengthening of sounds for emphasis of intensity. *Bulletin of the Phonetic Society of Japan* 167: 5–8.

Allen, George D., and Sarah Hawkins. 1980. Phonological rhythm: definition and development. In Grace H. Yeni-Komshian et al., eds., *Child Phonology*, vol. 1, *Production*, pp. 227–56. New York: Academic Press.

Allsopp, S. R. R. 1972. Some suprasegmental features of Caribbean English and their relevance in the classroom. Unpublished paper.

Ayers, Lucille, Hazel McLaughlin, Mrs. Roy Mobley, and Foster Olroyd. 1950. Expressions from rural Florida. *Publications of the American Dialect Society*, no. 14: 74–80.

Bearth, Thomas. 1980. Is there a universal correlation between pitch and information value? In Brettschneider and Lehmann 1980, pp. 124–30.

Beattie, Geoffrey, Anne Cutler, and Mark Pearson. 1983. Why is Mrs. Thatcher interrupted so often? *Nature* 300: 744–47.

Bickerton, Derek. 1981. *Roots of Language*. Ann Arbor: Karoma.

Bing, Janet M. 1980. *Aspects of English Prosody*. Bloomington: Indiana University Linguistics Club.

Birdwhistell, Ray L. 1970. *Kinesics and Context*. Pittsburgh: University of Pennsylvania Press.

Bolinger, Dwight. 1945. Inhibited and uninhibited stress. *Quarterly Journal of Speech* 31: 202–7.

———. 1946. Thoughts on *yep* and *nope*. *American Speech* 21: 90–95.

———. 1955. Intersections of stress and intonation. *Word* 11: 195–203.

———. 1957. English stress: the interpenetration of strata. In *Study of Sounds*, pp. 295–315. Tokyo: Phonetic Society of Japan.

———. 1961. Three analogies. *Hispania* 44: 134–37.

———. 1965. *Forms of English*. Edited by Isamu Abe and Tetsuya Kanekiyo. Cambridge, Mass.: Harvard University Press; Tokyo: Hokuou.

———. 1967. A grammar for grammars: the contrastive structures of English and Spanish. *Romance Philology* 21: 186–212. (Review of Stockwell and Bowen 1965.)

————, ed. 1972. *Intonation: Selected Readings.* Harmondsworth, England: Penguin.

————. 1977. *Meaning and Form.* London: Longman.

————. 1978. Intonation across languages. In Greenberg 1978, 2: 471–524.

————. 1979. The jingle theory of double -ing. In D. J. Allerton, Edward Carney, and David Holdcroft, eds., *Function and Context in Linguistic Analysis: A Festschrift for William Haas*, pp. 41–56. Cambridge: Cambridge University Press.

————. 1980. A not impartial review of a not unimpeachable theory. In Roger W. Shuy and Anna Shnukal, eds., *Language Use and the Uses of Language*, pp. 53–67. Washington, D.C.: Georgetown University Press.

————. 1981. *Two Kinds of Vowels, Two Kinds of Rhythm.* Bloomington: Indiana University Linguistics Club.

————. 1982. Intonation and its parts. *Language* 58: 505–33.

————. 1983. Affirmation and default. *Folia Linguistica* 17: 99–116.

————. 1985. Two views of accent. *Journal of Linguistics* 21: 79–123.

Bosshardt, H.-G., and H. Hörmann. 1982. Der Einfluss suprasegmentaler Information auf die Sprachwahrnehmung bei 4- bis 6jährigen Kindern. *Archiv für Psychologie* 134: 81–104.

Brettschneider, Gunter, and Christian Lehmann, eds. 1980. *Wege zur universalien Forschung.* Tübingen: Gunter Narr Verlag.

Bronstein, Arthur J. 1960. *The Pronunciation of American English.* Englewood Cliffs, N.J.: Prentice-Hall.

Brown, W. S., and Robert E. McGlone. 1974. Aerodynamic and acoustic study of stress in sentence productions. *Journal of the Acoustical Society of America* 56: 971–74.

Bruce, Gosta. 1982. Developing the Swedish intonation model. *Phonetics Working Papers* (University of Lund) 22: 51–116.

Catford, J. C. 1985. "Rest" and "open transition" in a systematic phonology of English. In W. Greaves and J. Benson, eds., *Systemic Perspectives in Discourse*, pp. 333–48. Norwood, N.J.: Ablex.

Classe, André. 1939. *The Rhythm of English Prose.* Oxford: Blackwell.

Cohen, A., and J. 't Hart. 1967. On the anatomy of intonation. *Lingua* 19: 177–92.

Coleman, H. O. 1914. Intonation and emphasis. *Miscellanea Phonetica* (University College London: International Phonetic Association), pp. 6–26.

Condon, William S. 1982. Cultural microrhythms. In Martha Davis, ed., *Interaction Rhythms: Periodicity in Communicative Behavior.* New York: Human Sciences Press.

————, and William D. Ogston. 1971. Speech and body motion synchrony of the speaker-hearer. In Horton and Jenkins 1971, pp. 150–73.

Cooper, William E., and John M. Sorensen. 1981. *Fundamental Frequency in Sentence Production.* Berlin: Springer-Verlag.

Coulthard, Malcolm, and David Brazil. 1982. The place of intonation in the description of interaction. In Deborah Tannen, ed., *Analyzing Discourse: Text and Talk*, pp. 94–112. Washington, D.C.: Georgetown University Press.

Coustenoble, Hélène N., and Lilias E. Armstrong. 1934. *Studies in French Intonation.* Cambridge, Eng.: Heffer.

Cowan, George M. 1972. Segmental features of Tepehua whistle speech. In Rigault and Charbonneau 1972, pp. 695–98.

Cruttenden, Alan. 1981. Falls and rises: meanings and universals. *Journal of Linguistics* 17: 77–92.

Crystal, David. 1969. *Prosodic Systems and Intonation in English.* Cambridge: Cambridge University Press.

Culicover, Peter W., and Michael Rochemont. 1983. Stress and focus in English. *Language* 59: 123–65.

Cutler, Anne. 1977. The context-dependence of "intonational meanings." *Papers from the Thirteenth Regional Meeting of the Chicago Linguistic Society,* pp. 104–15.

———. 1980. Syllable omission errors and isochrony. In Hans W. Dechert and Manfred Raupach, eds., *Temporal Variables in Speech: Studies in Honour of Frieda Goldman-Eisler,* pp. 183–90. The Hague: Mouton.

———. 1983. Speakers' conceptions of the functions of prosody. In Cutler and Ladd 1983, pp. 79–91.

———, and Charles E. Clifton, Jr. 1983. The use of prosodic information in word recognition. In H. Bouma and D. G. Bouwhis, eds., *Attention and Performance,* Hillsdale, N.J.: Erlbaum.

———, and D. R. Ladd. 1983. *Prosody: Models and Measurements.* Berlin: Springer-Verlag.

———, and David Swinney. 1980. Development of the comprehension of semantic focus in young children. Unpublished paper.

Daneš, František. 1960. Sentence intonation from a functional point of view. *Word* 16: 34–54.

Dascălu, Laurenţia. 1974. On the "parenthetical" intonation in Romanian. *Revue Roumaine de Linguistique* 19: 321–48.

———. 1979. On the intonation of questions in Romanian: the rising pattern. *Revue Roumaine de Linguistique* 24: 35–44.

Deakin, G. T. A. 1981a. Indirect speech acts and intonation. Master's thesis, Australian National University, Canberra.

———. 1981b. Overlap and gradient relationships in English intonation. In David Bradley, ed., *Working Papers in Linguistics* (University of Melbourne) 7: 39–77.

Delattre, Pierre. 1965. *Comparing the Phonetic Features of English, German, Spanish, and French.* Heidelberg: Julius Gross.

———, Carroll Olsen, and Elmer Poenack. 1962. A comparative study of declarative intonation in American English and Spanish. *Hispania* 45: 233–41.

Dressler, Wolfgang U., et al., eds. 1981. *Phonologica 1980.* Innsbruck: Innsbrücker Beiträge zur Sprachwissenschaft.

Efron, David. 1941, 1972. *Gesture and Environment.* New York: King's Crown Press. Reprinted as *Gesture, Race, and Culture: Approaches to Semiotics,* no. 9. The Hague: Mouton.

Ekman, Paul. 1979. About brows: emotional and conversational signals. In M. von Cranach et al., eds., *Human Ethology,* pp. 169–249. Cambridge: Cambridge University Press.

———, ed. 1982. *Emotion in the Human Face.* 2d ed. Cambridge: Cambridge University Press.

————, and Wallace V. Friesen. 1975. *Unmasking the Face.* Englewood Cliffs, N.J.: Prentice-Hall.

————, and Wallace V. Friesen. 1982. Felt, false, and miserable smiles. *Journal of Nonverbal Behavior* 6: 238–52.

————, Wallace V. Friesen, and Phoebe Ellsworth. 1982. Conceptual ambiguities. In Ekman 1982, pp. 7–21.

————, and Harriet Oster. 1982. Review of research, 1970–1980. In Ekman 1982, pp. 147–73.

Esser, Jürgen. 1983. Tone units in functional sentence perspective. *Journal of Semantics* 2: 121–39.

Ferguson, Charles A. 1977. New directions in phonological theory: language acquisition and universals research. In R. W. Cole, ed., *Current Issues in Linguistic Theory*, pp. 247–99. Bloomington: Indiana University Press.

Fernald, Anne. 1984. The perceptual and affective salience of mothers' speech to infants. In L. Feagans et al., eds., *The Origins and Growth of Communication*, pp. 5–29. Norwood, N.J.: Ablex.

————, and Thomas Simon. 1984. Expanded intonation contours in mothers' speech to newborns. *Developmental Psychology* 20: 104–14.

Fónagy, Ivan. 1980. Interprétation des attitudes a partir d'informations prosodiques. In Wolfgang U. Dressler et al., eds., *Comprendre le langage: actes du colloque 1980*, pp. 38–42. Paris: Didier.

————. 1981. A semiotic approach to the study of prosodic irregularities. In Dressler et al. 1981, pp. 137–52.

————, and Pierre Léon. 1979. *L'Accent en français contemporain.* Ottawa: Didier.

Fretheim, Thorstein, ed. 1981. *Nordic Prosody II: Papers from a Symposium.* Lund: Tapir.

Fridman, Ruth. 1980. Proto-rhythms from nonverbal to language and musical acquisition. In Key 1980, pp. 77–92.

Fuchs, Anna. 1980. Accented subjects in "all new" utterances. In Brettschneider and Lehmann 1980, pp. 449–61.

Gage, William Whitney. 1958. Grammatical structures in American intonation. Ph.D. dissertation, Cornell University, Ithaca, N.Y.

Gantzel, Lars. 1967. The meaning of terminal pitch pattern. Ph.D. dissertation, Stanford University, Stanford, Calif.

Gardiner, Duncan B. 1980. *Intonation and Music: The Semantics of Czech Prosody.* Bloomington, Ind.: Physsardt Publications.

Gårding, Eva. 1981. Contrastive prosody: a model and its application. *Studia Linguistica* 35: 146–65.

Gibbon, Dafydd. 1981. A new look at intonation syntax and semantics. In Allan James and Paul Westney, eds., *New Linguistic Impulses in Foreign Language Teaching*, pp. 71–98. Tübingen: Gunter Narr Verlag.

————. 1984. Intonation as an adaptive process. In D. Gibbon and H. Richter, eds., *Intonation, Accent, and Rhythm: Studies in Discourse Phonology*, pp. 165–92. Berlin: De Gruyter.

Givón, Talmy. 1983. Topic continuity in discourse: an introduction. In T. Givón, ed., *Topic Continuity in Discourse: A Quantitative Cross-Language Study*, vol. 3, *Typological Studies in Language*. Amsterdam: Benjamins.

————. 1985. Iconicity, isomorphism, and non-arbitrary coding in syntax. In John Haiman, ed., *Iconicity in Syntax*. Amsterdam: Benjamins.

Goldsmith, John. 1981. English as a tone language. In D. L. Goyvaerts, ed., *Phonology in the 80's*, pp. 287–308. Ghent: Story-Scientia.

Greenberg, Joseph. 1978. *Universals of Human Language*. Vol. 2, *Phonology*; vol. 4, *Syntax*. Stanford, Calif.: Stanford University Press.

Greenberg, Steven, and Eric Zee. 1979. On the perception of contour tones. *Working Papers in Phonetics* (University of California, Los Angeles) 45: 150–64.

Gussenhoven, Carlos. 1983. Focus, mode and the nucleus. *Journal of Linguistics* 19: 377–417.

Halliday, M. A. K. 1967. *Intonation and Grammar in British English*. The Hague: Mouton.

Harries-Delisle, Helga. 1978. Contrastive emphasis and cleft sentences. In Greenberg 1978, 4: 419–86.

't Hart, J. 1981. Differential sensitivity to pitch distance, particularly in speech. *Journal of the Acoustical Society of America* 69, no. 3: 811–21.

Haugen, Einar. 1970. Phonemic indeterminacy and Scandinavian umlaut. *Folia Linguistica* 3: 107–19.

Hewitt, Helen Jo, and Winfred P. Lehmann. 1965. *Selected Vowel Measurements of American English Speech*. Austin: University of Texas Press.

Hill, A. A. 1982. Intonation pattern and syntactic ambiguity. In Horst Geckeler et al., eds., *Logos semantikos: studia linguistica in honorem Eugenio Coseriu, 1921–1981*, 4: 13–16. Berlin and New York: De Gruyter; Madrid: Gredos.

Hirst, D. J. 1981. Phonological implications of a production model of intonation. In Dressler et al. 1981, pp. 195–202.

Hollien, Harry. 1972. Three major vocal registers: a proposal. In Rigault and Charbonneau 1972, pp. 320–31.

————, W. J. Gould, and Beverly Johnson. 1975. A two-level concept of vocal registers. *Communication Sciences Laboratory Quarterly Report* (Department of Speech, University of Florida) 13, no. 2: 2–8.

Horton, David L., and James J. Jenkins, eds. 1971. *Perception of Language*. Columbus, Ohio: Merrill.

Householder, Fred W., Jr. 1957. Accent, juncture, intonation, and my grandfather's reader. *Word* 13: 234–45.

Hubbell, Allan F. 1950. The phonemic analysis of unstressed vowels. *American Speech* 25: 105–11.

Hultzén, Lee S. 1957. Communication in intonation: General American. In *Study of Sounds*, pp. 317–33. Tokyo: Phonetic Society of Japan.

————. 1959. Information points in intonation. *Phonetica* 4: 107–20.

————. 1961. System status of obscured vowels in English. *Language* 37: 565–69.

————. 1962. Significant and nonsignificant in intonation. In *Proceedings of the Fourth International Congress of Phonetic Sciences*, Helsinki 1961, pp. 658–61. The Hague: Mouton.

Jassem, Wiktor (with Dafydd Gibbon). 1980. Re-defining English accent and stress. *Journal of the International Phonetic Association* 10, no. 1–2: 2–16.

Jones, Daniel. 1956. *An Outline of English Phonetics.* New York: Dutton.

Joos, Martin. 1964. *The English Verb: Form and Meanings.* Madison: University of Wisconsin Press.

Keijsper, C. E. 1983. On themes and rhemes. In A. G. F. van Holk, ed., *Dutch Contributions to the Ninth International Congress of Slavists* (Kiev, Sept. 6–14, 1983), vol. 3, *Studies in Slavic and General Linguistics,* pp. 265–309. Amsterdam: Rodopi.

Kelso, J. A. Scott, and Betty Tuller. 1982. Exploring the information support for speech. *Status Report in Speech Research,* no. 69: 43–54. New Haven, Conn.: Haskins Laboratories.

Kendon, Adam. 1980. Gesticulation and speech: two aspects of the process of utterance. In Key 1980, pp. 207–27.

Kent, R. D. 1984. Brain mechanisms of speech and language with special reference to emotional interactions. In Rita C. Naremore, ed., *Language Science: Recent Advances,* pp. 281–384. San Diego: College-Hill Press.

Kenyon, John S., and Thomas A. Knott. 1953. *A Pronouncing Dictionary of American English.* Springfield, Mass.: Merriam.

Key, Mary Ritchie, ed. 1980. *The Relationship of Verbal and Nonverbal Communication.* The Hague: Mouton.

———, ed. 1982. *Nonverbal Communication Today: Current Research.* Berlin: Mouton.

Kingdon, Roger. 1958. *The Groundwork of English Intonation.* London: Longmans, Green.

Kôno, Akira. 1957. Long sounds in the Hiroshima dialect. In *Study of Sounds,* pp. 475–76. Tokyo: Phonetic Society of Japan.

Krasheninnikova, E. A. 1976. Accent and prominence in "Blockung-type" formations. Paper presented at Third World Congress of Phoneticians, Tokyo. (Abstract appears in Guidebook, p. 62.)

Kvavik, Karen H. 1982. Spanish multiaccent intonations and discourse functions. In James P. Lantolf and Gregory B. Stone, eds., *Current Research in Romance Languages,* pp. 46–62. Bloomington: Indiana University Linguistics Club.

Ladd, D. Robert. 1978. Stylized intonation. *Language* 54: 517–40.

———. 1980. *The Structure of Intonational Meaning.* Bloomington and London: Indiana University Press.

———. 1982. Review of *Questions of Intonation,* by Gillian Brown, Karen L. Currie, and Joanne Kenworthy. *Language* 58: 204–8.

———. 1983a. Phonological features of intonational peaks. *Language* 59: 721–59.

———. 1983b. Levels vs. configurations, revisited. In Frederick B. Agard and Gerald B. Kelley, eds., *Essays in Honor of Charles F. Hockett,* pp. 49–59. Leiden: Brill.

Lakoff, George, and Mark Johnson. 1980. *Metaphors We Live By.* Chicago: University of Chicago Press.

Lehiste, Ilse. 1972. The timing of utterances and linguistic boundaries. *Journal of the Acoustical Society of America* 51: 2018–24.

————. 1982. Signaling of syntactic structure in whispered speech. *Journal of the Acoustical Society of America* 72: S17.

Lenneberg, Eric. 1971. The importance of temporal factors in behavior. In Horton and Jenkins 1971, pp. 174–84.

Liberman, Mark. 1979. *The Intonational System of English.* New York: Garland.

————, and Alan Prince. 1977. On stress and linguistic rhythm. *Linguistic Inquiry* 8: 249–336.

————, and Ivan Sag. 1974. Prosodic form and discourse function. *Papers from the Tenth Regional Meeting of the Chicago Linguistic Society,* pp. 416–27.

Lieberman, Philip. 1967. *Intonation, Perception, and Language.* Cambridge, Mass.: MIT Press.

Lindsey, Geoffrey. 1981. Intonation and pragmatics. *Journal of the International Phonetic Association* 11, no. 1: 2–21.

Lock, Andrew. 1980. *The Guided Reinvention of Language.* New York: Academic Press.

Marchand, Hans. 1969. *The Categories and Types of Present-Day English Word-Formation.* Munich: C. H. Beck.

Mathews, Mitford W. 1963. *The Beginnings of American English: Essays and Comments.* Chicago: University of Chicago Press.

McArthur, Harry, and Lucille McArthur. 1956. Aguacatec (Mayan) phonemes within the stress group. *International Journal of American Linguistics* 22: 72–76.

McCarthy, John J. 1982. Prosodic structure and expletive infixation. *Language* 58: 574–90.

McMillan, James. 1980. Infixing and interposing in English. *American Speech* 55: 163–83.

Meo-Zilio, Giovanni, and Silvia Mejía. 1980. *Diccionario de gestos.* Bogotá: Instituto Caro y Cuervo.

Meyer-Eppler, Werner. 1957. Realization of prosodic features in whispered speech. *Journal of the Acoustical Society of America* 28: 760.

Noteboom, Sieb, Truus Kruit, and Jacques Terken. 1981. What speakers and listeners do with pitch accents: some explorations. In Fretheim 1981, pp. 9–32.

Ohala, John J. 1983. Cross-language use of pitch: an ethological view. *Phonetica* 40: 1–18.

Onishi, Masao. 1957. Nature of prominence in Japanese. *Bulletin of the Phonetic Society of Japan* 94: 8–10.

Palmer, Harold E. 1922. *English Intonation.* Cambridge: Heffer.

Pettersson, Thore, and Sidney Wood. 1983. Vowel reduction in Bulgarian. *Phonetics Working Papers* (Lund University) 25: 151–78.

Pierrehumbert, Janet B. 1980. The phonology and phonetics of English intonation. Ph.D. dissertation, Massachusetts Institute of Technology.

Pike, Kenneth L. 1945. *The Intonation of American English.* Ann Arbor: University of Michigan Press.

Putnam, George N., and Edna M. O'Hern. 1955. The status significance of an isolated urban dialect. Language Dissertation no. 53. *Language* 31: 4 (Part 2).

Pye, Clifton. 1983. Mayan telegraphese: intonational determinants of inflectional development in Quiché Mayan. *Language* 59: 583–604.

Redican, W. V. 1982. An evolutionary perspective on human facial displays. In Ekman 1982, pp. 212–80.

Rigault, André, and René Charbonneau, eds. 1972. *Proceedings of the Seventh International Congress of Phonetic Sciences*, Montreal, 1971.

Robins, R. H. 1951. *Ancient and Medieval Grammatical Theory in Europe*. London: G. Bell and Sons.

Sag, Ivan, and Mark Liberman. 1975. The intonational disambiguation of indirect speech acts. In Robin E. Grossman et al., eds., *Papers from the Eleventh Regional Meeting of the Chicago Linguistic Society*, pp. 487–97.

Sangster, Rodney B. 1982. Review of *Roman Jakobson's Approach to Language: Phenomenological Structuralism*, by Elmar Holenstein. *Language* 58: 897–99.

Schane, Sanford A. 1979. The rhythmic nature of English word accentuation. *Language* 55: 559–602.

Scherer, Klaus R. 1974. Acoustic concomitants of emotional dimensions: judging affect from synthesized tone sequences. In S. Weitz, ed., *Nonverbal Communication*, pp. 105–11. New York: Oxford.

———. 1984. Componential patterning of vocal affect expression. Unpublished paper.

———, D. Robert Ladd, and Kim E. A. Silverman. Forthcoming. Vocal cues to speaker affect: testing two models. *Journal of the Acoustical Society of America*.

Schmerling, Susan. 1976. *Aspects of English Sentence Stress*. Austin: University of Texas Press.

Schubiger, Maria. 1958. *English Intonation, Its Form and Function*. Tübingen: Niemeyer.

———. 1961. The interplay and cooperation of word order and intonation in English. In David Abercrombie et al., eds., *In Honour of Daniel Jones*, pp. 255–65. London: Longman.

———. 1979. English intonation and German modal particles II: a comparative study. In Linda R. Waugh and C. H. van Schooneveld, eds., *The Melody of Language*. Baltimore: University Park Press.

Selkirk, Elisabeth O. 1980. The role of prosodic categories in English word stress. *Linguistic Inquiry* 11: 563–606.

Sharp, Alan E. 1958. Falling-rising intonation patterns in English. *Phonetica* 2: 127–52.

Shetler, Jo, and Anne Fetzer. 1964. The obscuring of word accent in Balangao. *Oceanic Linguistics* 3: 101–7.

Siertsema, Berthe. 1961. Language learning and language analysis. *Lingua* 10: 128–47.

Sinclair, Aileen. 1944. Speech melody: an analysis. Master's thesis, Stanford University.

Stockwell, Robert P., and J. Donald Bowen. 1965. *The Sounds of English and Spanish*. Chicago: University of Chicago Press.

Sweet, Henry. 1898. *A New English Grammar, Logical and Historical. Part II— Syntax*. Oxford: Clarendon Press.

't Hart. *See under* Hart.

Thompson, Henry S. 1980. *Stress and Salience in English: Theory and Practice*. Palo Alto, Calif.: Xerox Corporation.

Thorsen, Nina. 1981. Intonation contours and stress group patterns in declarative sentences of varying length in ASC Danish. In Fretheim 1981, pp. 75–89.

———. 1983. Standard Danish sentence intonation—phonetic data and their representation. *Folia Linguistica* 17: 187–220.

Tronick, Edward C., Heidelise Als, and T. Berry Brazelton. 1980. The infant's communicative competencies and the achievement of intersubjectivity. In Key 1980, pp. 261–73.

Van Hooff, J. A. R. A. M. 1962. Facial expressions in higher primates. *Evolutionary Aspects of Animal Communication* (Symposia of the Zoological Society of London) 8: 97–125.

Vanvik, Arne J. 1961. *On Stress in Present-Day English.* Bergen and Oslo: Norwegian Universities Press.

von Raffler-Engel, Walburga. 1983. On the synchronous development of gesticulation and vocalization in man's early communicative behavior. In E. de Grolier, ed., *Glossogenetics: Proceedings of the International Symposium on Glossogenetics* (UNESCO), Paris, 1981, pp. 295–311.

Weeks, Thelma. 1982. Intonation as an early marker of meaning. In Key 1982: 157–68.

Yamaguchi, Yukihiro. 1961. An inquiry into mono-pattern accent in the Japanese language, from a standpoint of sentence accent. *Bulletin of the Phonetic Society of Japan* 106: 13–14.

Additional Works by the Author

Works by Dwight Bolinger that are related to prosody but are not cited in this volume are listed below. Items marked by an asterisk are reprinted, with slight revisions, in Bolinger 1965 (see above), which contains one essay, "Pitch accent and sentence rhythm," not previously published.

1945. The minimizing downskip. *American Speech* 20: 40–45.

Spanish intonation. Review of *Manual de entonación española*, by Tomás Navarro. *American Speech* 20: 128–30.

1946. The intonation of quoted questions. *Quarterly Journal of Speech* 32: 197–202.

1947. American English intonation. Review of Pike 1945. *American Speech* 22: 134–36.

Comments on Pike's American English intonation. *Studies in Linguistics* 5: 69–78.

1948. The intonation of accosting questions. *English Studies* 29: 109–14.

1949. The what and the way. *Language Learning* 2: 86–88.

Intonation and analysis. *Word* 5: 248–54.

1951. *Intonation: levels versus configurations. *Word* 7: 199–210.

1954. English prosodic stress and Spanish sentence order. *Hispania* 37: 152–56.

1955. The melody of language. *Modern Language Forum* 40: 19–30.
Intonation as stress-carrier. *Litera* 2: 35–40.
1956. Stress on normally unstressed elements. *Hispania* 39: 105–6.
1957. *Maneuvering for stress and intonation. *College Composition and Communication* 8: 234–38.
*On certain functions of Accents A and B. *Litera* 4: 80–89.
Interrogative structures of American English. *Publications of the American Dialect Society*, no. 28.
*Disjuncture as a cue to constructs. *Word* 13: 246–55. With Louis J. Gerstman.
1958. *Stress and information. *American Speech* 33: 5–20.
On intensity as a qualitative improvement of pitch accent. *Lingua* 7: 175–82.
Intonation and grammar. *Language Learning* 8 (1957–58), no. 1–2: 31–38.
*A theory of pitch accent in English. *Word* 14: 109–49.
1959. The intonation of "received pronunciation." Review of *English Intonation: Its Form and Function*, by Maria Schubiger. *American Speech* 34: 197–201.
1961. Acento melódico, acento de intensidad. *Boletín de Filología* (Universidad de Chile) 13: 33–48. With Marion Hodapp.
*Contrastive accent and contrastive stress. *Language* 37: 83–96.
Review of *A Practice Book on English Stress and Intonation*, by Kenneth Croft. *Language Learning* 11: 189–95.
*Ambiguities in pitch accent. *Word* 17: 309–17.
1962. Review of *The Sentence Intonation of Contemporary Standard Russian as a Linguistic Structure*, by J. E. Jurgens Buning and C. H. van Schooneveld. *Language* 38: 79–84.
Secondary stress in Spanish. *Romance Philology* 15: 273–79.
*Binomials and pitch accent. *Lingua* 11: 33–44.
1963. Length, vowel, juncture. *Linguistics* 1: 5–29. Revised, *Bilingual Review* 3 (1976): 43–61.
1964. Around the edge of language: intonation. *Harvard Educational Review* 34: 282–96. Reprinted in Bolinger, *Intonation: Selected Readings* (1972).
Intonation as a universal. In Horace G. Lunt, ed., *Proceedings of the Ninth International Congress of Linguists* (Cambridge, Mass., 1962), pp. 833–48. The Hague: Mouton.
1966. Review of *Recherches sur les caractères et le rôle des éléments musicaux dans la prononciation anglaise*, by Georges Faure. *Language* 42: 670–90.
1970. Relative height. In Pierre Léon, ed., *Prosodic Feature Analysis*, pp. 109–27. Montreal: Didier. Reprinted in Bolinger, *Intonation: Selected Readings* (1972).
1972. Review of *On the Intonation and Position of the So-called Sentence Modifiers in Present-Day English*, by Hans H. Hartvigson. *Language* 48: 454–63.
Accent is predictable (if you're a mind-reader). *Language* 48: 633–44.
1978. Yes-no questions are not alternative questions. In Henry Hiż, ed., *Questions*, pp. 87–105. Dordrecht: Reidel.

1980. Intonation and nature. In Mary LeCron Foster and Stanley H. Brandes, eds., *Symbol as Sense*, pp. 9–23. New York: Academic Press.

Accents that determine stress. In Key 1980, pp. 37–47.

1981. Some intonation stereotypes in English. In Pierre Léon and Mario Rossi, eds., *Problèmes de prosodie*, vol. 2, *Expérimentations, modèles et fonctions*, pp. 97–101. Ottawa: Didier.

1982. The network tone of voice. *Journal of Broadcasting* 26: 725–28.

Nondeclaratives from an intonational standpoint. In Robinson Schneider, Kevin Tuite, and Robert Chametzky, eds., *Papers from the Parasession on Nondeclaratives*, pp. 1–22. Chicago: Chicago Linguistics Society.

On preaccentual lengthening. *Journal of the International Phonetic Association* 12: 58–71. With Richard Dasher.

1983. Intonation and gesture. *American Speech* 58: 156–74.

Where does intonation belong? *Journal of Semantics* 2: 101–20.

1985. The inherent iconism of intonation. In John Haiman, ed., *Iconicity in Syntax*, pp. 97–108. Amsterdam: Benjamins.

Index